NUCLEAR ARMS CONTROL

Julie Dahlitz has a Master of Laws degree from Melbourne University and a Ph.D. in international law from the Australian National University. She has travelled widely, speaks several languages, and has been a representative at many major international conferences, including both of the Special Sessions of the General Assembly on Disarmament, held by the United Nations in 1978 and 1982. During 1978–80, Dr Dahlitz worked in a professional capacity at United Nations Headquarters in New York. In the latter part of that period she was a Political Affairs Officer in the Centre for Disarmament, Department of Political and Security Council Affairs. Dr Dahlitz has published several shorter papers concerning arms control, as well as many related articles on a range of international issues. In her early postgraduate days, and while her children were young, she engaged in private law practice as a barrister and solicitor of the Supreme Court of Victoria.

NUCLEAR ARMS CONTROL

with effective international agreements

Foreword by Rikhi Jaipal

JULIE DAHLITZ

London
GEORGE ALLEN & UNWIN
Boston

First published in 1983 by
George Allen & Unwin (Publishers) Ltd,
40 Museum Street, London WC1A 1LU, UK

George Allen & Unwin (Publishers) Ltd,
Park Lane, Hemel Hempstead, Herts HP2 4TE, UK

Allen & Unwin, Inc.,
9 Winchester Terrace, Winchester, Mass. 01890, USA

ISBN 0 04 341023 5
ISBN 0 04 341024 3 (pbk)

First published in Australasia in 1983
by McPhee Gribble Publishers, Melbourne

Printed in Great Britain by
Butler & Tanner Ltd, Frome and London

CONTENTS

Acknowledgements

Due to the interdisciplinary nature of the study, it could not have been undertaken without co-operation from many quarters. At the Australian National University, as well as the usual privileges extended by my Faculty, being the Faculty of Law, I was also made welcome in the Research School of Pacific Studies, at the Department of International Relations and at the Strategic and Defence Studies Centre. Participation at the school in a course of seminars, attended by colleagues from both the Department and the Centre, was especially helpful.

I am most grateful to the Professor of International Law in my Faculty, Professor D.W. Greig, for his many incisive comments on the manuscript. He also helped to make it possible for me to attend the first Special Session of the General Assembly devoted to disarmament, held in New York in 1978, shortly after I commenced this study. My consequent inclusion as an Observer with the Australian Delegation was invaluable because it gave me an insight into the practical problems faced by decision-makers when confronting issues of nuclear arms proliferation.

During five weeks spent in the United States on that occasion I took the opportunity to visit Washington. There I had the privilege of a number of interviews with Members of the United States Congress and with specialists in the field of nuclear arms control in the Department of Energy, as well as in the Department of State, notably in the Arms Control and Disarmament Agency. Those discussions with many legal and technical specialists, and some political representatives, impressed on me the awesome burden of responsibility that rests with the persons who formulate and who carry out the nuclear weapons policies of a Superpower. To a limited extent, I was able to balance those experiences with impressions gained during a few interviews granted to me by Delegates of the Soviet Union attending the Special Session.

Subsequently, on my return journey via Geneva, I was in a position to acquaint myself with the work at the International Law Commission. From there I travelled to Austria and the Federal Republic of Germany, where I had interviews with Departmental experts, as well as discussions with interested executive members of the Parties in Government. In Austria I also had extensive interviews with legal and technical experts in the International Atomic Energy Agency.

Towards the end of 1978 I accepted a position with the Department of International Economic and Social Affairs as a member of the United Nations Secretariat, in which capacity I was able to observe and to participate in the methods of work of the United Nations. Later I was

1

transferred to a temporary post as a Political Affairs Officer in the Centre for Disarmament, where I spent the first half of 1980. It was a position that proved to be conducive to a many-sided study of the issues involved in nuclear arms control.

Valuable indications of world opinion on matters relevant to my study were also gained as a result of my membership and attendance at meetings held by organisations like the World Federation United Nations Associations, the Australian Institute of International Affairs and the United States Political Science Association. Participation at formal meetings of these associations, as well as informal discussions with other members and guest speakers have been enlightening.

I am indebted to several Librarians in various parts of the world for their kind co-operation. In particular, this applies to the Librarians at the Australian National University – especially those attached to the Law Library. Similar assistance was given by Librarians in other Canberra libraries, notably the libraries of the Australian Government Department of Foreign Affairs and the National Library. I also received further valuable assistance from the Librarians in the library and in the reading room of the United Nations, and from research assistants attached to the Library of Congress in Washington.

Several other persons have also helped with materials and comments. Professor A. Grahl-Madsen of Sweden kindly sent me copies of Papers delivered at a Seminar, held in June 1981, that had been organised by him in conjunction with the University of Uppsala and UNITAR. The proceedings of that Seminar will be published by Walter de Gruyter, Berlin and New York, under the title 'The Spirit of Uppsala: The Proceedings of the Joint UNITAR-Uppsala University Seminar on International Law and Organization for a New World Order'. Towards the end of my research Professor J.L. Richardson, Dean of the Department of Political Science, read part of the manuscript and was good enough to draw my attention to several oversights. My sincere gratitude also goes to the Chief of the Geneva Unit of the Centre for Disarmament, Mrs L. Waldheim-Natural, for sending me some of the reports required for this work between 1978 and 1982, and for her generous encouragement.

Foreword

At the second special session on disarmament of the UN General Assembly held in New York in June 1982, the Heads of Government and others who addressed it were all agreed that there was no question more important and urgent and indeed more complex than disarmament, because any discussion of it was necessarily related to the survival of mankind.

Unfortunately, they were unable to establish an agreed global disarmament policy for ensuring the future of mankind in conditions of enduring peace and safety in a world free of the menace of nuclear war, the consequences of which, however, were acknowledged to be unlimited, indiscriminate and irreparable.

The main reason for the failure to reach agreement was the continued conviction of those States that possessed nuclear weapons that such weapons were vital for the preservation of their security, and that peace could be maintained only through the strategy of nuclear deterrence. But of course if this strategy should fail, nuclear war could follow with all its devastating consequences both to the warring nations as well as to the non-belligerent ones.

One hopes therefore that the fact that the resulting destruction could be global in nature would act as a deterrent upon the nuclear-weapon States. However, it is not altogether apparent that these States take this fact into their policy calculations. If they do so, it is presumably in the context of their own survival, with which is inextricably and inexorably bound the survival of all.

When nuclear-weapon States speak of their security, they mean in fact their survival, and it is against perceived threats to their survival that they build their nuclear arsenals, conduct research, increase their quantity and improve their quality. The threat to their survival emanates from their assumption that a foreign ideology is bent on dominating their own, and this sets in motion the race for natural resources, raw materials and spheres of influence as well as the arms race itself. Like all races, the primary objective in the arms race also is to remain ahead, for the credibility of the doctrine of deterrence, and through it the assurance of security and survival, is based on winning the arms race.

This race so far has been a never-ending process, dependent for its momentum on scientific and technological advances. Arms control negotiations have resulted in limiting and regulating certain types of weapons for specific periods of time. They have not yet halted the arms race itself, or placed legal restraints on the research and further development of weapons of mass destruction. One hopes that the current series of

3

negotiations will lead to a substantial reduction in the number of weapons and forces, and in their destructiveness.

Where a particular State perceives that its adversary has acquired a critical military advantage, it invariably insists that the balance should first be restored either by proportionate reductions in the arsenals of its enemy, or by increasing its own. If the adversary also perceives that its military strength is at a disadvantage, its reactions are the same and the arms race receives a further impetus from which it seldom recovers. The quest for relative parity is seldom sought through reductions but rather through increases. Negotiations on nuclear arms control have therefore remained far behind the technological race for more effective weapons, greater precision in guidance, better accuracy in delivery and total invulnerability.

Despite the certain knowledge today that nuclear war would wipe out civilization, the Superpowers persist in the nuclear arms race, apparently prepared to incur the awesome risks to themselves and the rest. In the circumstances the view that nuclear arms control 'institutionalises' the arms race is not entirely unjustified.

If the USA had unilaterally given up the A-bomb after August 1945 and proposed an international Convention banning the military use of nuclear power, rather like the Geneva Protocol of 1925 prohibiting the use of chemical weapons, the course of history might have been different. It is a pity that even today pledges of non-first-use of nuclear weapons are discounted, because of the unwarranted implication in them that the use of other types of weapons is somehow permissible.

Mutual distrust among nations underlies such reactions, and the demand for stringent verification techniques consequently assumes disproportionate importance in negotiations. The aim should rather be for adequacy of verification, supplemented by appropriate procedures for investigation of alleged violations and for punitive or deterrent action against proved violations.

Another matter that could contribute to the successful pursuit of the disarmament process is the dissociation of arms control negotiations from domestic partisan politics. Surely the future of human survival calls for agreed results of negotiations to be consolidated and for the negotiations to be pursued further, regardless of the vagaries of local elections.

It is interesting that at the second special session of the UN on disarmament the following views should have been expressed by more than one delegation: (a) that parties to disputes often have the feeling that they have no other course except resort to the use of force, (b) that East-West rivalries should not be exported to other regions, (c) that scrupulous respect for non-alignment by the major military alliances as well as by the non-aligned themselves is an essential element in a global policy for peace, and (d) that inter-dependence among States should not be allowed to become another form of dependence, since it breeds more insecurity. There is no valid reason why as an integral part of the disarmament negotiations greater attention should not be given on a sustained basis to the peaceful resolution of all outstanding international disputes during the next five years, for without such political groundwork, disarmament efforts will have little chance of success.

Although the process of disarmament will ordinarily thrive and yield results in conditions of international security, nevertheless it has to be independent to the extent necessary in order to start the process and sustain it, so that in turn it may make a positive impact on security. Disarmament negotiations have become so important today for the human race's future that once begun they should not be suspended even in times of tension. Also the gains of negotiations should be quickly consolidated, and it goes without saying that this will not be possible unless all concerned display maximum restraint and do nothing that may jeopardise them.

World public opinion has increasingly become aware of the probability of nuclear war in our time, because of over-armament, destabilization of new technologies, and the danger of first strikes through accident or fear. The safeguarding of the future of mankind is no longer the exclusive concern of governments, whose policies are now being required by public opinion to conform to their peoples' demand for the avoidance of nuclear war.

In this book, Julie Dahlitz presents the issues of nuclear arms control with great clarity and objectivity, and raises the very important matter of the applicability of international law and custom in the changing nuclear world. This question clearly ought to be the subject of detailed examination by the legal organs of the UN system. For nuclear weapons are here to stay for some time and we must evolve rules of law to ensure that their use can be avoided.

For my part, I take the view that the existing legal distinction between combatant and non-combatant, the present prohibition against causing unnecessary and aggravated suffering, and the validity of the principles of humanity to the law of war would make an express prohibition of the use of nuclear weapons almost redundant. Nevertheless, the General Assembly of the United Nations on several occasions has explicitly resolved that nuclear weapons should not be used and that their use would constitute a crime against humanity.

The facile argument that the use of a weapon is legal as long as there is no express legal prohibition against its use cannot lightly be extended to the nuclear weapon. The NPT is in fact such a prohibition applicable to the vast majority of States. And the Partial Test-Ban Treaty is a further such prohibition of nuclear explosions in the atmosphere. The intent is obviously to save the world from the scourge of nuclear war, rather than to make nuclear weapon States the trustees of humanity. Is it necessary to pose a threat to the survival of mankind at large in order to guarantee the security of the trustees?

Arms control negotiations are clearly necessary and should be pursued with faith and tenacity, even though the results may be limited at present to regulating competition, banning certain weapons, stabilising the arms equilibrium and building confidence. At the same time, it is essential that a political dialogue should be started between the Superpowers designed to exorcise their terrifying fears of one another, to clarify their ideological misunderstandings, to moderate their social and political aims and to evolve a code of mutual self-restraint.

The next spiral in the nuclear arms race, according to Julie Dahlitz, involves the development of weapons for use in extreme cases requiring self-defense, or in an almost totally disarming first strike. The probability of nuclear war is increasing in porportion to the growth of the nuclear arms race, the depth of mutual fears and suspicions, the inertia of most governments and the appalling apathy of the vast majority of the potential victims.

An essential matter that has so far not been given the attention it merits is the prevention of nuclear war. There are certain well-established procedures for dealing with accidents, failures of communication etc., and they should be improved. But there is at present no political means for the prevention of nuclear war through the collective control and management of crises. I believe that it is urgently necessary to evolve new procedures designed for the purpose of coping with critical or confrontational situations between Superpowers, which unless checked could lead to nuclear war. This is clearly a shared responsibility and the wit and wisdom of all nations and peoples should be harnessed to that end.

Rikhi Jaipal   *Geneva, 27 July 1982*

Ambassador for India to the United Nations
Secretary of the Committee on Disarmament and
Personal Representative of the Secretary-General

Introduction

Confronted by the spectre of annihilation in a nuclear war, the overwhelming portion of mankind, including the vast majority of those who are most influential in their societies, have failed so far to take the necessary measures for their own self-preservation, for the protection of their loved ones, and for the perpetuation of all they hold dear. Failure to respond appropriately to much lesser threats of a traditional kind, like a flood or attack by wild animals, would be regarded as the extreme of cowardice or foolishness.

Reluctance to respond purposefully to the threat of nuclear war is due to a lack of understanding, which tends to lead people to accept one of three fallacies. Two of these fallacies paralyse response altogether. These are –

1. *That nuclear war is not* really *going to happen* or, if so, then only to other people.
2. *That nothing can be done to prevent nuclear war* except, perhaps by someone else.

The third fallacy consists of the belief that it is possible to prevent or to win a nuclear war with the same type of response that has been used to prevent or fight other wars. Hence, the third fallacy is –

3. *That nuclear war can be averted by further armament,* unyielding threats etc. This is in the nature of an inappropriate response, something like mistaking a threatened flood for a fire, and pouring more water into a swollen river in the vain hope of preventing it from bursting its banks by those means.

The fundamental misconception that gives rise to the three fallacies is that the danger of nuclear war, as well as the methods to avert it, can be understood without substantial effort. No one would think it possible to become a builder without spending considerable time over it, or to learn how to grow crops, educate children or cure the sick, without sustained endeavour. Yet none of those worthy and life-promoting enterprises can have further meaning unless time and hard work are devoted by large numbers of people to acquiring some understanding of nuclear war and by what means it could be averted. There can be no doubt that everyone who is able to do so should at least take the trouble to be informed about the major problems involved, to learn what has already been done, and to enquire what measures are being proposed in order to solve the problems.

This book is published for the people who have decided to make such an effort, and there are many levels at which the material presented is intended to be useful to them. People largely unfamiliar with nuclear arms control may wish merely to skim over the contents. Even that would convey an indispensable overview of the subject that would help the reader to marshal

7

information acquired through the mass media into a more realistic perspective. Others may decide to read the book quite thoroughly, yet be content to overlook some portions that they find particularly detailed or unfamiliar. Such readers, who have some background knowledge of the material, could broaden their understanding significantly without necessarily absorbing every paragraph.

Those with previous expertise in the field will, hopefully, gain new insights to complement their previous understanding, perhaps leading to further concrete initiatives on their part or by those Governments, corporate bodies or individuals whom they are in a position to advise. Both fact and opinion are presented here, but great care has been taken to make it evident at all times when an opinion is being advanced. Such opinions do not purport to be the last word but rather a stimulus for further thought and greater effort to find solutions.

A detailed study of nuclear arms control methods is not the only appropriate response to the universal peril presented by nuclear weapons. An emotional response giving expression to fear and determined opposition to the potential disaster can help to galvanize the demonstrators, together with spectators, ultimately to pursue the objective by more direct means. The beneficial end result of demonstrations can only be to spur officials and public alike to become more thoroughly informed, in order to ensure that all resources are utilised so that effective nuclear arms control measures may be adopted by States.

The next few pages of the Introduction have been written primarily for the benefit of experts in international law, international relations, strategic studies and arms control, with a view to defining, as precisely as possible, what the book sets out to accomplish.

Scope and Specific Objectives

This is essentially a feasibility study on nuclear arms control from a predominantly legal point of view. Central to the theme is the examination of international systems for the creation and observance of nuclear arms control agreements. Consideration is given to possible advances in the relevant methodologies, based on a review of current initiatives regarding the negotiation, implementation, verification and enforcement of international agreements.

Subject matter selected for examination is focused on short term variables in preference to an enumeration of all pertinent factors, including those that are not foreseeably amenable to change. Control of nuclear weapons is interpreted as denoting both their regulation and elimination, with the emphasis on stability as the criterion of success.

Assessment of what constitutes stability is an underlying theme throughout. The basic assumptions are that stability increases with the discouragement of attempts to gain political or economic advantage by the acquisition, deployment, threat or use of nuclear weapons as a deliberate policy; by maximization of the time available for making anti-nuclear-weapon choices; adoption of procedures to mitigate the consequences of nuclear accident; avoidance of action-reaction compulsion; simplification of deterrence, whenever possible, as well as strengthening the survivability

8

of some deterrent systems; provision of opportunities for compromise; and ongoing machinery facilitating universally acceptable resolution of every kind of international dispute. All of these measures are seen to have legal or quasi-legal connotations.

In the interests of cohesion and brevity, several subject areas have been examined only in a limited context. For example, the historical background is restricted to the observation of trends with direct relevance to current issues and institutions. Several nuclear strategies are noted only cursorily, in order to demonstrate the nature of the complexities entailed and the unpredictability of outcomes. Likewise, the imprecision of the distinctive terminology applied to the various strategies is mentioned merely to illustrate the nature of the problems faced by policy-makers and negotiators. The examination of general conflict resolution principles and techniques is also confined to those aspects that have a bearing on the negotiation and compliance enforcement phases of nuclear arms control agreements.

Not all relevant variables are examined but only those that can be embodied in international agreements for the control of nuclear arms and matters directly related to such existing or putative agreements. This demarcation requires the omission from detailed consideration of many issues that have a vital bearing on the efficacy of nuclear arms control agreements, including the management of national bureaucracies and the international politics of States; and the local, regional and global interplay of ideological divisions and sectional interests.

The issues enumerated in the above paragraph are adverted to only in general terms as part of the genus of 'primary' conflicts. The lack of distinctive treatment is felt to be permissible on the ground that the menace of nuclear devastation is indiscriminate, and because precepts for the peaceful settlement of international disputes have a similarly universal application. Therefore, it is felt that the line of demarcation should not be excessively distorting. Controversies about nuclear arms parity, and the equities of the competing security interests of States and groups of States, are regarded as 'consequential' international disputes. The control of weapons of mass destruction other than nuclear weapons is excluded from consideration, except to illustrate homogeneous features where other examples are lacking.

Despite the simplifications invoked, the topic is an unwieldy one due to the many facets of nuclear arms control. In particular, it is overshadowed by Socialist-Free Enterprise enmity which, like other primary conflicts, is treated as a given fact. No attempt is made to adjudicate on its merits or even to probe the rationality of its motivation and pursuit. The geopolitical background and the correlations between various aspects of the topic have been more fully examined in three published papers written during the course of the study, entitled *Proliferation and Confrontation*,[1] *Co-existence, Reciprocity and the Principle of Marginal Restraint*,[2] and *Arms Control in Outer Space*.[3]

---

1 *Australian Outlook*, April 1979, Vol.33 No.1 p.27.
2 *Australian Outlook*, April 1981, Vol.35 No.1 p.78.
3 *The World Today*, April 1982, Vol.38 No.4 p.154.

Nuclear Arms Control

The feasibility of avoiding, by means of nuclear arms control agreements, the untoward consequences of the nuclear arms race, including the disaster of nuclear devastation, would not warrant study if it took the form of a probability calculation. Clearly, if it were found that there is only a modest chance of escaping the direct or indirect deleterious consequences of the nuclear arms race with nuclear arms control agreements, the recommendation would have to be that the chance be taken. The sole contra-indication would be if a higher probability were found to favour the avoidance of nuclear war with the attainment of a disarming first strike capability by stealth. A conclusive evaluation of that possibility is beyond the scope of this study, which rests on the assumption that the probability of avoiding nuclear war by that means is negligible.

Thus, the question is not whether agreements should be sought in the pursuit of nuclear arms control, but what measures are likely to produce the best results in the light of experience and informed conjecture. That, in turn, entails the selection of priority issues and the designation of collateral measures to be taken. In addition, it becomes necessary to assess existing principles, forms and institutions facilitating international concurrence, with a view to identifying such changes as may be prerequisite to the attainment of the objective.

CHAPTER 1

The Feasibility of International Agreement to Control Nuclear Arms

First Initiatives

Among the many onerous and pressing concerns of the international community since World War II, none has been more demanding than the problem of nuclear arms control (NAC). The devastation caused by the two nuclear bombs detonated over Hiroshima and Nagasaki, on 6 and 9 August 1945, left no doubt that nuclear weapons heralded unprecedented dangers for mankind.

When the Treaty setting up the United Nations came into force on 24 October 1945, only the United States had a nuclear capability, nuclear weapons were small by current standards, no missile systems existed for their delivery, and relatively little was known about the dangers of radioactive fallout. Nevertheless, from then onward the eradication, or at least the control of nuclear weapons became a major, if not the prime international preoccupation. Accordingly, the first Resolution of the United Nations General Assembly was directed towards the solution of that issue. Resolution 1(1) was adopted unanimously on 24 January 1946, establishing an Atomic Energy Commission.[1] The Commission was to report to the Security Council and to make specific proposals –

(a) for extending between all nations the exchange of basic scientific information for peaceful ends
(b) for control of atomic energy to the extent necessary to ensure its use only for peaceful purposes
(c) for the elimination from national armaments of atomic weapons and of all other major weapons adaptable to mass destruction
(d) for effective safeguards by way of inspection and other means to protect complying States against the hazards of violations and evasions.

The fate of the Atomic Energy Commission was typical of many later attempts to control nuclear arms, even to the present day. Despite its high status and unanimous mandate, the Commission eventually lapsed into a two year stalemate and had to be dissolved on 11 January 1952,[2] without achieving any of its objectives.

Like many of its successor negotiating bodies for NAC, the Commission was hamstrung by the overriding rivalry between the United States and the Soviet Union and paralysed by obstinate efforts to devise international institutions modelled on national law enforcement prototypes. The attempt by some members of the Commission to set up an International Atomic Development Authority,[3] to be in charge of all nuclear activities in the world, was the first of many over-ambitious attempts, in the interests of

11

disarmament, to wrest a greater abrogation of sovereignty from States than they have been prepared to concede.

The first manifestation of Superpower rivalry and distrust in the field of NAC was the move by the United States to forestall the development of nuclear weapons by the Soviet Union. It began with the proposed imposition of strict inspection and control procedures concerning the utilisation of nuclear materials for weapons, for peaceful uses and for research.[4]

Understandably, the United States was not ready to give up its nuclear advantage until a system of verification and sanctions was in place. The proposal was advanced by the United States delegate to the Atomic Energy Commission, Mr Bernard Baruch, and it became known as the Baruch Plan. For its part, the Soviet Union was evidently concerned about its position and sought to eliminate the American nuclear advantage. It demanded that the destruction of all atomic weapons should occur prior to the imposition of a system of international controls for prohibiting their ongoing manufacture.

The impasse continued until 23 September 1949, when the Soviet Union exploded its first atomic bomb. A few months later the Soviet Union withdrew from the Commission in protest against the failure to seat the representative of the newly formed *de facto* Government of the People's Republic of China.[5]

The next attempt to attain international agreement regarding NAC, and to create effective institutions and procedures for doing so, was prejudiced at its inception by growing antagonism between Socialist and Western States and by the outbreak of the Korean War. In 1950 the General Assembly established a Committee of Twelve,[6] composed of the same nations as the membership of the Security Council at that time, together with representation from Canada, to report on the feasibility of merging the Atomic Energy Commission and another existing Commission dealing with the control of conventional armaments. On the basis of the Committee's report, a Disarmament Commission was set up, consolidating the two previous Commissions. The Soviet Union voted against the General Assembly Resolution which established the Disarmament Commission, on 11 January 1952.[7] Within the year of the new Commission's inauspicious beginnings, the United Kingdom exploded its first atomic bomb, on 3 October, and the United States exploded its first hydrogen bomb, on 1 November.

The mandate of the Disarmament Commission required it to prepare proposals, *inter alia,* 'for the effective international control of atomic energy to ensure the prohibition of atomic weapons and the use of atomic energy for peaceful purposes only'.[8] As with previous and subsequent initiatives, the recommendations put forward by Western States emphasised the need for disclosure, verification, inspection and international control of both nuclear and conventional arms. The Soviet Union, on the other hand, stressed the preliminary requirement to eliminate and prohibit all atomic weapons, justifying its stance by drawing attention to the alleged great preponderance of combined Western military might in relation to that of the Soviet Union and its allies.

The year 1953 marked the beginning of a more conciliatory and businesslike attitude to NAC. The change can be attributed to accumulated negotiating experience concerning the subject and to several significant international events affecting the two emerging Superpowers, including the election of General Eisenhower to the Presidency of the United States, and the death of the Soviet leader, Marshal Stalin. The year also witnessed the end of the Korean War and the first explosion of a hydrogen bomb by the Soviet Union, on 12 August. For the first time there arose the worldwide recognition that war would not only continue to be 'the scourge' of mankind, as stated in the United Nations Charter, but that it could destroy civilisation altogether. The preamble of a unanimous General Assembly Resolution of 28 November 1953, expressed the prevailing attitude in the following terms–

Believing that the continued development of weapons of mass destruction such as atomic and hydrogen bombs has given additional urgency to efforts to bring about effectively controlled disarmament throughout the world as the existence of civilisation itself may be at stake . . .[9]

It was in this atmosphere, eleven days later, that President Eisenhower made his famous 'atoms for peace' proposal in the General Assembly, recommending the establishment of the International Atomic Energy Agency (IAEA).[10] Another four years passed before the Agency came into being, as the first breakthrough in the international regulation of the utilisation and disposal of radioactive materials.

During the intervening period, the Disarmament Commission formed a Sub–Committee,[11] composed of Canada, France, the Soviet Union, the United Kingdom and the United States, which held 157 meetings. In 1954 a French and British plan was discussed for verified nuclear disarmament in stages. The Soviet Union countered with amendments to the disarmament schedule and with a proposal for an international Control Commission under the auspices of the Security Council, to ensure that the veto would be available to the Council's permanent members.[12]

In 1955, in the course of negotiations on compromise solutions, both the Western Powers and the Soviet Union put forward additional, far-reaching amendments to the plan. The issues were again raised at a Summit Conference convened in Geneva, in July 1955, between France, the Soviet Union, the United Kingdom and the United States. Again the main issue was that of precedence between nuclear disarmament and international inspection. Stressing the latter, the United States suggested an agreement among the nuclear Powers to permit reciprocal aerial photography as a means of verifying NAC agreements.[13] The Soviet Union preferred ground control posts. At this time the Soviet Union also advanced a proposal for undertakings by the nuclear Powers not to be the first to use nuclear weapons.[14]

Gradually international opinion was swinging to the view that halting the nuclear arms race among the existing nuclear-weapon States, and preventing the use of nuclear technology for military purposes by additional States, would have to be sought through step by step agreements with limited goals. At no time was the concept abandoned of 'general and complete disarmament under effective international control',[15] as the ultimate objective. The above, and similar wording, has been used on innumerable occasions in the preamble of NAC treaties and in UN resolutions. Nevertheless, ten years of total failure in NAC, served as an irrefutable argument for the adoption of new tactics to reach that objective. In 1956, despite a rise in international tension due to unrest in Eastern Europe and the Suez crisis, negotiations were successfully concluded for the establishment of the IAEA. The Statute of the Agency came into force on 29 July 1957, just a couple of months after the United Kingdom exploded its first hydrogen bomb on 15 May.

The establishment of the Agency in Vienna, with a large expert bureaucracy, has remained the most tangible NAC achievement. Over the years, the Agency's influence continued to increase. It has acted as the executive agency for subsequent NAC agreements, most notably, the Non-Proliferation Treaty[16] and the Treaty of Tlatelolco.[17] In addition the IAEA became a catalyst for the emergence of more NAC agreements, including the Partial Test-Ban Treaty[18] and the moratoriums that preceded it.

For example, the Agency, which was also given the responsibility for establishing health and safety standards relating to the use of nuclear energy, helped to focus attention on the dangers of radioactive contamination of the environment. When moves to ban all nuclear testing had failed, concerted efforts were made to prohibit the testing of nuclear weapons at least in environments where fallout was thought to be most dangerous.

Simultaneously, the obligation, through the IAEA, to promote nuclear technology for industrial uses, raised the spectre of more rapid horizontal proliferation[19] than had been anticipated previously. The expected inhibiting effect of a nuclear test-ban on the spread of nuclear weapons capability, added a further strong impetus to test-ban efforts. From 1958 onward, a series of conferences and unilateral moratoriums on testing were undertaken by the three nuclear-weapon States. The first explosion of an atomic bomb by France, on 13 February 1960, threatened to undermine that initiative but the pressure of world public opinion intervened, culminating in the signing of the Partial Test-Ban Treaty, on 5 August 1963, by the Soviet Union, the United Kingdom and the United States.[20]

At the time of the establishment of the IAEA in 1957, the Soviet Union proposed the transformation of the Disarmament Commission into a permanent body of the United Nations with the participation of all Member States. After the defeat of that proposal on 6 November 1957,[21] the Soviet Union withdrew from the Commission, despite the addition of fourteen States to that body by the General Assembly.[22] With the refusal of the Soviet Union and its allies to participate in the work of the Disarmament Commission, it became unsuited to remain a negotiating forum for disarmament, and it consequently failed to reconvene in 1958.

The issue of representation at multilateral disarmament negotiations was soon to be resolved by other developments. Acceleration of the decolonisation process led to the emergence, in the early sixties, of a Third World political force. In acknowledgement of the new distribution of power, the General Assembly, on 13 December 1961, created the Eighteen Nation Disarmament Committee (ENDC) comprising eight Non-aligned States, five Western States and five Socialist States. It was the direct predecessor of the present Committee on Disarmament (CD).

The ENDC changed its name in 1969, when its membership was enlarged to twenty-six. It became known as the Conference of the Committee on Disarmament (CCD), and its representation was further increased to thirty-one in 1974, so as to keep pace with the growing membership of the United Nations. After the first Special Session of the General Assembly devoted to disarmament (SSD I) in 1978, it was renamed the Committee on Disarmament and its membership increased to forty including, for the first time, all five permanent members of the Security Council.[23] By that time both France and China had become thermonuclear Powers, China exploding its first atomic bomb on 16 October 1964, and its first hydrogen bomb on 17 June 1967. France exploded its first hydrogen bomb on 24 August 1968. It is significant that since China became a nuclear Power, no additional State has admitted testing a nuclear weapon. In 1974 India exploded a nuclear device stated to be for peaceful purposes,[24] and in 1979 there was some evidence that a nuclear explosion had occurred in the atmosphere off the coast of South Africa.[25]

Two prominent theoretical issues hindered NAC negotiations during the early postwar years.[26] One involved questions of national security, such as whether total disarmament was possible or desirable in the short term. The other contentious issue had a more legal and administrative orientation and concerned the institutional management of disarmament, notably NAC. The most vexed question that arose in that context was whether any type of veto power should be retained, especially by nations also members of the Security Council. The Western States, which had a majority in the United Nations at the time, were adamant that no exercise of the veto should be permitted with respect to the functions of any of the proposed supranational disarmament or arms control bodies.

In addition to those contentious issues, from the earliest agreements to the present, including debates about the unratified SALT II Treaty, NAC has been the subject of criticism especially from within the United States. Some critics have contended that the agreements merely handicap a too honest and trusting United States in an inevitable nuclear arms contest which it could otherwise win. This contention relies on the argument that inadequate verification and compliance enforcement provisions enable other States, notably the Soviet Union, to breach NAC agreements to America's detriment.[27]

A more belligerent version of the theory advocates deliberate confrontation, described in the following terms by the first head of the policy planning staff of the United States Arms Control and Disarmament Agency, Barry M. Blechman –

> To many Americans these postures are wrong, both morally and in terms of U.S. security interest. They believe that the United States must seek to change Soviet society and, that to do so, it must remain in a state of tension with the Soviet government. They argue that if it is isolated, the Soviet State eventually will crack of its own internal contradictions – nationalities problems, economic failures, corruption, the natural yearnings of individuals for freedom, and so forth. This means that the United States should seek to construct a wall of implacable hostility around the U.S.S.R., a political-cum-military alliance among the nations of Western Europe, Japan, China

15

and others in the Third World. Only America can galvanize such an alliance, it is argued, and to do so the United States must avoid bilateral agreements or even bilateral negotiations, as these imply permanent acceptance of the Soviet regime and accord legitimacy to it. The ABM treaty, the SALT II treaty, and the SALT process itself – to say nothing of other arms negotiations – are thus seen to undermine the long-run objective of causing fundamental change in Soviet society.[28]

Other critics have maintained that NAC agreements only restrain armaments production in growth areas thought to be useless or of marginal military value. This objection to NAC agreements encompasses the notion that they merely 'institutionalise' the nuclear arms race. For example, in the case of the IAEA and the Treaty on the Non-Proliferation of Nuclear Weapons (NPT), acquiescence in the existence of nuclear Powers and the sharp dichotomy between the rights and duties of nuclear-weapon and non-nuclear-weapon States, has been characterised as an entrenchment of the spurious principle that might is right. With respect to the Partial Test-Ban Treaty, it has been claimed that the agreement gives tacit approval to the underground detonation of nuclear weapons. As recently as the signing of the SALT II Treaty in 1979, a similar genre of criticism has been levelled, contending that the Treaty gives a certain legitimacy to the nuclear arms race by sanctioning the retention and further production of most nuclear weapons.

Another objection to NAC agreements has been less a criticism of the nature of the agreements than of the whole process of attempting to reach agreement in view of sharply conflicting national interests.[29] These critics believe that, whether desirable or not, and even if adequately verified, NAC is not going to be effective because technological advances will soon outstrip all conceivable formulas for control. The emphasis here is on the expectation of the circumvention and eventual repudiation of the agreements rather than of their breach.[30]

By contrast, the list of NAC agreements bears witness to the views of those, both within and beyond the United States, who have favoured NAC agreements. Their position has been that half a loaf is better than none. Chastened by the long initial period of arduous but fruitless negotiations, they seek to utilise to the best advantage the maximum degree of co-operation that States may be prepared to contribute to NAC at any given time. Apart from coming to terms with the limits of co-operation, supporters of less than ideal NAC agreements have tended to adopt a more optimistic view of the willingness of States to abide by their undertakings. They also tend to place greater reliance on the feasibility of holding States to their NAC agreements, even in the absence of ironclad verification, adjudication and enforcement provisions.

Supporters of NAC cover a wide ideological spectrum. For instance, some advocates dismiss the likelihood of circumvention with the argument that additional agreements can be devised to accommodate technological advances as they arise. European disarmament specialists frequently stress the importance of confidence building measures and often adopt the position that consensus acted upon begets further consensus. There are those who go so far as to expect that in time, with increasing manifestations of global interdependence, military rivalry itself will decline. Others, at the lower levels of confidence in NAC, regard it as a holding operation aimed only at decreasing the pace of nuclear armament and the chances of inadvertent conflagration.[31]

Renewed concern about the issues involved in NAC has been expressed, by both Governments and professionally involved individuals, apropos to SSD I held at United Nations Headquarters in New York, during May–June 1978. Preparations for the second Special Session of the General Assembly devoted to disarmament (SSD II), held in June–July 1982, at the same venue, also generated worldwide interest in NAC agreements already concluded, as well as in nuclear-weapon issues proposed to form the subject of future agreements.

Existing Multilateral NAC Agreements

The NAC treaties referred to in Table 1, (see page 24) were no doubt negotiated with a variety of expectations as to their future effectiveness. While those original assessments cannot be established with any certainty, it is evident from the terms of the treaties that they were formulated so as to achieve a universal consensus, even at the expense of restricted goals and range of application. Of the NAC related agreements concluded during approximately the past two decades, eight were substantive multilateral treaties that are still in force today. Without exception, they were the subject of intensive and prolonged negotiation before agreement was reached.

The main thrust of the treaties is to prevent the spread of nuclear weapons and to preserve the status quo, but no attempt is made to dismantle existing nuclear arms and facilities. The objectives of the treaties are modest in other respects also, when compared with the ambitious goals espoused during the first fifteen years of unsuccessful NAC negotiations. For example, repudiation of the treaties is usually available on three months' notice. Those provisions can be attributed to a realistic appraisal of the difficulties involved in attempting to coerce a State to adhere to a treaty after a decision has been made by it to withdraw. It is also a device for maintaining the status of treaties, by permitting States to assert their sovereignty without having to transgress obligations solemnly entered into under international law.

In a similarly pragmatic vein, the treaties have avoided setting up any institutions, except in the case of the IAEA and the Agency for the Prohibition of Nuclear Weapons in Latin America (OPANAL).[32] Apart from the operation of those Agencies, administrative functions are restricted to measures required for accession, review, consultation, amendment and repudiation, to be performed by the depositary States. In practice, whenever necessary, especially in the organisation of review conferences, the administrative facilities of the United Nations have been successfully invoked.[33]

While it is clearly intended that the treaties should be endowed with the full force of international law, punitive provisions for breach are either minimal or omitted altogether.[34] Such punitive provisions as there are, largely consist of notifying the other Parties and the United Nations of the facts constituting the breach. The provisions also require the non-complying Party, and any aggrieved or particularly interested Parties, to engage in consultations or to refer the matter to arbitration by consent. Failing those methods the treaties, either explicitly or implicitly, refer the Parties to the International Court of Justice, again by consent only.

None of the treaties requires acceptance of compulsory jurisdiction by the Court with respect to the observance of its terms. Specific references to the Court do not appear to alter whatever general rights the Parties may have to invoke the Court's jurisdiction, but treaty provisions regarding the obligation to engage in consultations and other conciliatory measures would no doubt have to be discharged as conditions precedent. This would be necessary so as to fulfil the agreed undertakings and in order to demonstrate that all alternative avenues of redress have been exhausted.

Having largely refrained from imposing sanctions with teeth, the treaties appear to rely on fear of discovery as the main inducement for compliance by reluctant States.[35] To this end, emphasis is given to verification methods, and also adjudication procedures to the extent necessary to establish the acts and circumstances of non-compliance. Verification relies to some extent on notification by each Party of its own records and planned activities relevant to the terms of the treaty. Thus, the IAEA, and the treaties that rely on its safeguards methods for verification, utilise the records of national systems of accounting. The Antarctic Treaty and the Outer Space Treaty require notification of intention to proceed with certain designated activities.

No treaty could exclude verification by national technical means (NTM) which are, by definition, within the ambit of a State's sovereign rights.[36] In addition to remote observance, most multilateral NAC treaties specifically authorise on site inspection by the Parties, by their designated observers, by experts or, as in the case of the IAEA, by inspectors who are not under the guidance of any individual Party in the performance of their tasks.

Provision for consultations is also an integral part of the verification and assessment process, devised for the supervision of compliance. Consultations avoid misunderstandings and can, on occasion, facilitate face–saving explanations and adjustments. They also provide opportunities for last minute avoidance or rectification of outright breaches, when discovery becomes imminent. Such eleventh hour reprieves are permitted because the emphasis is not on the exposure of non-complying acts but on their avoidance.

Despite the dearth of coercive provisions and institutional support, the record of implementation of the multilateral NAC treaties has been remarkably good. For the time being, at least, the objectives set out by the treaties have been largely attained. The record can be summarised as follows:

– Since the Statute of the IAEA came into force, no State receiving assistance in the use of nuclear power for peaceful purposes has utilised that assistance so as to become a nuclear-weapon State.

– Since the Antarctic Treaty came into force, no establishment of nuclear bases, detonation of nuclear explosions, or disposal of nuclear wastes has taken place on that Continent.

– Since the Partial Test-Ban Treaty came into force, the three major nuclear Powers have confined their testing of nuclear weapons to underground detonations, as prescribed. They have refrained from conducting any nuclear explosions, in any of the environments forbidden for testing. The other two nuclear-weapon States, France and China, are not parties to the Partial Test-Ban Treaty. France, which for a period persisted with atmospheric testing, has ceased to do so since 1975, and now only China continues to conduct nuclear tests in the atmosphere, at the rate of about one a year.[37]

– Since the Outer Space Treaty came into force, no evidence has become publicly available to suggest that any weapons have been installed on celestial bodies or that any nuclear weapons have been placed in orbit around the earth.

– While the extent to which the Treaty of Tlatelolco is presently in force could become a matter of contention,[38] Latin America is apparently totally free of nuclear weapons and all peaceful nuclear facilities there are subject to IAEA safeguards inspections.

– Since the Non-Proliferation Treaty came into force, there has been no addition to the number of declared and/or demonstrated nuclear-weapon States beyond the then existing five, being all of the permanent Members of the Security Council.

– Since the Sea-Bed Treaty came into force, no nuclear weapons or related facilities have been deployed at the bottom of the seas and oceans.

– Since the Convention on the Prohibition of Military or Any Other Hostile Use of Environmental Modification Techniques (ENMOD Convention) came into force, no hostile modification of the environment has occurred with the aid of nuclear forces or otherwise.

The level of participation in the treaties has also been encouraging. In assessing the significance of the number of ratifications, it should be borne in mind that the subject matter of the treaties has scant relevance to States that are not technologically advanced. In many cases these States apparently regard accession to the treaties to be superfluous. Two of the treaties, the Antarctic Treaty and the Treaty of Tlatelolco, contain geographical limitations on participation.

Significantly, the United States, the Soviet Union and the United Kingdom have ratified all of the multilateral treaties enumerated in Table 1 (see page 24). France has ratified the Antarctic Treaty and the Outer Space Treaty, as well as undertaking to abide by the prohibitions of the Non-Proliferation Treaty and, in fact, observing the substantive terms of the Partial Test-Ban Treaty. China has only ratified Protocol II of the Treaty of Tlatelolco.

Although the hope of attaining universal accession to the treaties by all eligible States has not been realised, it is noteworthy that State Parties are not withdrawing from the treaties. In round figures, the treaties are in force for the following number of States: IAEA – *c* 100; Antarctic Treaty – *c* 20; Partial Test-Ban Treaty – *c* 110; Outer Space Treaty – *c* 80; Treaty of Tlatelolco – *c* 25; Non–Proliferation Treaty – *c* 110; Sea–Bed Treaty – *c* 70; ENMOD Convention – *c* 30.

Existing Bilateral NAC Agreements

The bilateral NAC agreements in Table II (see page 28) are, in some aspects, complementary to the multilateral agreements in Table I. The multilateral agreements, for the most part, aim to prevent the spread of nuclear weapons to non-nuclear-weapon States, zones and environments. This process is referred to as the prevention of 'horizontal proliferation'. On the other hand, the bilateral agreements chiefly seek to curtail quantitative and qualitative improvements of nuclear weapons systems between existing nuclear powers, notably the two Superpowers. This process is referred to as the prevention of 'vertical proliferation'.[39]

The Non-Proliferation Treaty goes so far as to require 'negotiations in good faith' on measures to halt the nuclear arms race, which has been interpreted as a direct plea to the Superpowers to cease vertical proliferation as a *quid pro quo* to non-nuclear-weapon States for their renunciation of nuclear weapons. This interpretation is incorporated into the preamble of the SALT II Treaty. It is perhaps the most obvious juxtaposition of the two kinds of nuclear proliferation, one pursued via multilateral agreements and the other by way of bilateral agreements.

The nuclear Powers, especially the Superpowers, are clearly the most influential Parties in all of the multilateral NAC agreements, so much so, that without the concurrence of the 'Big Three', most of them could not have been seriously contemplated. At present, at least two of the multilateral NAC treaties, the Outer Space Treaty and the ENMOD Treaty only have relevance for the Superpowers. Non-nuclear-weapon States, and nuclear-weapon States not Parties, have no formal role whatever in the bilateral NAC treaties between the superpowers.

Unlike the multilateral NAC agreements, not all of the bilateral NAC agreements are registered with the United Nations as formal, current treaties. For instance, the most concrete NAC measures between the Superpowers, contained in the two Strategic Arms Limitation Treaties, SALT I and II,[40] do not exist in the most binding form available in international law. SALT I which had been ratified by both Parties expired, according to its terms, on 3 October 1977, although the Parties had indicated some weeks before that date that they did not intend to contravene its terms for a further unspecified period of time. The SALT II Treaty was duly signed on 18 June 1979, after a seven year negotiation, but has still not been ratified by an exchange of documents of ratification.

Likewise, the Threshold Test-Ban Treaty and the Peaceful Nuclear Explosions Treaty, signed by the Superpowers on 3 July 1974 and 28 May 1976 respectively, have not been ratified, yet both Parties have abided by their substantive terms. The Agreement on Basic Principles of Relations between the Soviet Union and the United States, signed on 29 May 1972, and the Vladivostok Accord, signed on 24 November 1974, have also remained unratified. However, the two last named agreements are of lesser significance, as they are predominantly general statements of intention and guidelines for further negotiations that have already taken place in other contexts. Similarly, the simultaneous Statement by the Soviet Union and the United States on the Reduction of Fissionable Materials Production, made on 20 April 1964, which has not been given the form of a treaty, has now been superseded and would have to be entirely renegotiated to become currently relevant.

All of the bilateral, formally correct NAC treaties in force between the Superpowers, relate to the immediate, day to day prevention of nuclear war. These are the 'Hot Line' communications agreements; the Nuclear Accidents Agreement; the Agreement on the Prevention of Incidents on and over the High Seas; the SALT ABM Treaty; the Standing Consultative Commission Agreement; and the Agreement on the Prevention of Nuclear War.

Verification of the agreements is almost entirely by NTM. None of the agreements contains any provisions for verification, adjudication or administration of sanctions by any third party neither State, individual nor international entity. Only bilateral consultations are held out as the means of resolving disputes. Consequently, the operation of the treaties is largely unknown by non-Parties. Not only are they excluded from any formal participation, but the Superpowers have kept the details of disputes confidential. Published records of queries regarding performance indicate mutually thorough verification of the agreements and an excellent record of compliance by both Parties.[41]

At present, assessment of compliance by non-Parties by means of NTM are mostly out of the question because they lack the necessary sophisticated satellite observation systems. However, this situation could change in time with the establishment of an International Satellite Monitoring Agency[42] or with improved NTM by additional States.

Notes*

1 *Official Records of the General Assembly*, First Session.
2 Res. 502 (VI).
3 *Official Records of the Atomic Energy Commission*, First Year, No. 1.
4 Id. p. 7.
5 The Soviet Union withdrew from the negotiations on 19 January 1950, see A/1253 and A/1254.
6 Res. 496 (V).
7 Res. 502 (VI).
8 Ibid.
9 Res. 715 (VIII).
10 Treaty establishing the International Atomic Energy Agency came into force on 29 July 1957.
11 On 19 April 1954; See *Official Records of the Disarmament Commission*, 35th meeting and Supplement for April, May and June 1954.
12 In the General Assembly on 30 September 1954.
13 *Official Records of the Disarmament Commission*, Supplement for April to December 1955, Annex 20 (DC/SC.1/31).
14 Id. Annex 18 (DC/SC.1/29/Rev.1).
15 E.g. *Final Document* of SSD I, A/RES/S–10/2 'Declaration' para. 19,

---

* Unless otherwise specified all document references relate to the United Nations, the Specialised Agencies or records of the IAEA.

'Programme of Action' para. 43; For an early approach see the *Draft Treaty on General and Complete Disarmament Under Strict International Control*, submitted to the ENDC at its first Session in 1962 by the USSR, Official Records of the Disarmament Commission, Supp. for January 1961 – December 1962, DC/203, Annex 1, Section C (ENDC/2); First Official recognition of the objective was in G.A. Res. 1378 (XIV) of 1959, expressing the hope that 'measures leading to the goal of general and complete disarmament under effective international control will be worked out in detail and agreed upon in the shortest possible time'.

16 Table I (see page 00).

17 Ibid.

18 Ibid.

19 The acquisition of nuclear weapons capability by additional States.

20 A/35/257 pp. 10–14.

21 At the 893rd meeting of the First Committee.

22 On 19 November 1957, by Res. 1150 (XII).

23 For a procedural account of the evolution of the CD, see *The United Nations and Disarmament: 1945–1970* (UN Publication, Sales No. 70. IX.1); *The United Nations and Disarmament: 1970–1975* (UN Publication, Sales No. E. 76 IX.1); *Final Document* op.cit., para. 120.

24 See Fischer, D.A.V. *Nuclear Issues: International Control and International Co-operation* (The Australian National University, Canberra 1981) p. 22.

25 Known as the 'September Event' on 22 September 1979, Report of the Secretary-General, A/35/402 and Corr. 1.; Involvement of South Africa has been suggested in A/RES/35/146, also by SIPRI in *The Second NPT Review Conference* (Reprinted from SIPRI Yearbook, 1981) p. 301.

26 The issues were a recurring theme, as recounted in the *resume* published by the Dept. of Political and Security Council Affairs of the United Nations in *The United Nations and Disarmament 1945-1970*, op.cit.

27 Shortly after the election of President Reagan an opinion poll conducted by Louis Harris & Associates (The Harris Poll) found that while 90% favoured NAC negotiations with the Soviet Union, 50% of those opposed signing any agreement 'because the chances are that we will keep our end of the bargain and the Russians will not . . .'.

28 Blechman, Barry M., 'Do Negotiated Arms Limitations Have a Future?', *Foreign Affairs*, Fall 1980, Vol. 59 No. 1 p. 110.

29 Conclusions of the *Panel on the Strategic Arms Limitation Talks and the Comprehensive Test Ban Treaty*, Committee on Armed Services, House of Representatives (U.S. Govt. Printing Office, Washington, December 1978) p. 23 – 'The hope has also been expressed that arms control agreements such as SALT could prevent a nation from acquiring a technological capability that would be destabilizing to the strategic balance. Unfortunately, most such technological developments are not verifiable and thus not amenable to arms control, if monitoring of compliance is considered critical and denying the emergence of a breakout threat is the objective. The ABM treaty illustrates this point. Despite the 1972 treaty to limit ABM deployment, the Soviet Union continues to devote a significant amount of resources to ABM development and, in fact, according to the Under Secretary of Defence for Research and Engineering, Dr. William J. Perry, the Soviets are acquiring the capability to develop a rapidly deployable ABM system'.

30 Andrews, Walter, 'Soviet Military Space Threat Bared', *Army Times*, 8 March 1982, p. 7. – claims that U.S. Defence Department's 'top scientists' expect the U.S.S.R. to instal weapons in space circumventing the Outer Space Treaty.

Provided the weapons were not weapons of mass destruction, or stationed on celestial bodies, they would not be in *breach* of the Treaty as presently interpreted, infra Chapter 9.

31 Blechman, Barry M., op.cit. pp. 108-9.

32 For concise accounts of the operation of the IAEA and OPANAL see *Disarmament: A Periodic Review by the United Nations,* July 1980, Vol. III No. 2 p. 35 and p. 43 respectively.

33 Review Conferences of the Non-Proliferation Treaty, the Sea-Bed Treaty and the ENMOD Convention.

34 See Table I (page 24).

35 Ibid.

36 Infra Chapter 10.

37 NPT/CONF. II/PC. III/11 Annex: also *World Armaments and Disarmament:* SIPRI Yearbook 1980 (Taylor & Francis, London 1980) pp. 361 and 364.

Data on Nuclear Explosions

Year	USA a	u	USSR a	u	UK a	u	FRANCE a	u	CHINA a	u	INDIA a	u	Total
1963	0	14	0	0	0	0	0	1					15
1964	0	28	0	6	0	1	0	3	1	0			39
1965	0	29	0	9	0	1	0	4	1	0			44
1966	0	40	0	15	0	0	5	1	3	0			64
1967	0	29	0	15	0	0	3	0	2	0			49
1968	0	39	0	13	0	0	5	0	1	0			58
1969	0	28	0	15	0	0	0	0	1	1			45
1970	0	33	0	12	0	0	8	0	1	0			54
1971	0	15	0	19	0	0	5	0	1	0			40
1972	0	15	0	22	0	0	3	0	2	0			42
1973	0	11	0	14	0	0	5	0	1	0			31
1974	0	9	0	19	0	1	7	0	1	0	0	1	38
1975	0	16	0	15	0	0	0	2	0	1	0	0	34
1976	0	15	0	17	0	1	0	4	3	1	0	0	41
1977	0	12	0	16	0	0	0	6	1	0	0	0	35
1978	0	12	0	27	0	2	0	7	2	1	0	0	51
1979	0	15	0	28	0	1	0	9	0	0	0	0	53

a = atmospheric, u = underground

38 Due to required additional ratification of Protocols, as well as extensive reservations by some Parties.

39 For a more detailed analysis of the relationship between horizontal proliferation and vertical proliferation see Dahlitz, J., 'Proliferation and Confrontation', *Australian Outlook,* April 1979, Vol. 33 No. 1 p. 27.

40 Infra Chapter 9.

41 E.g. see United States Administration Report on 'Compliance With the SALT I Agreements', *Department of State Bulletin,* April 1978, Vol. 78 No. 2013 pp. 10-14.

42 Infra Chapter 10.

Name of Treaty and Abbreviated Name	Opened for Signature	Entered into Force	Major NAC Provisions	Review	Verification Provisions
Statute of the International Atomic Energy Agency (IAEA)	26 October 1956	29 July 1957	Prohibition of the use for military purposes of nuclear 'materials, services, equipment, facilities and information', either made available to Parties by the Agency or designated for exclusively peaceful use under contract with the Agency. Safeguards agreements with the Agency may be entered into by States pursuant to other treaty obligations, independent contractual obligations or voluntarily.	After 5 years as determined by simple majority of the General Conference for implementation the following year. Thereafter by similar procedure.	Agency designated inspectors to have 'acce at all times to all places and data and persons' relevant to the detection diverted nuclear materi in a recipient State. Inspectors also to appre nuclear facilities and processes to ensure feasibility of effective safeguards; to supervise operating records and national systems of accounting; and to requ temporary deposit with Agency of any excess nuclear material.
The Antarctic Treaty	1 December 1959	23 June 1961	Prohibition of nuclear bases, nuclear explosions or disposal of radioactive waste in Antarctica.	After 30 years if Parties so request.	Parties entitled to designate observers wh have access to whole Continent and air space including access to ship and aircraft. Observers be under the jurisdictio appointing Party. Parti to be advised of all expeditions to Antarcti
Treaty Banning Nuclear Weapon Tests in the Atmosphere, in Outer Space and Under Water Partial Test-Ban Treaty	5 August 1963	10 October 1963	Prohibition of all nuclear explosions in the atmosphere, in outer space or under water. Prohibition of nuclear explosions in any environment if radioactive debris would escape beyond territorial limits of the Party.	No provision.	No provision.
Treaty on Principles Governing the Activities of States in the Exploration and Use of Outer Space, including the Moon, and Other Celestial Bodies Outer Space Treaty	27 January 1967	10 October 1967	Prohibition on testing or placement of nuclear weapons in orbit around the earth, installing on celestial bodies, or stationing them in outer space in any other manner. Interpreted as permitting ballistic missiles and perhaps Fractional Orbital Bombardment Systems (FOBS) with nuclear warheads.	No provision.	Potentially harmful activities to be notified Party's own initiative c request. On receipt of reasonable notice, all installations and equipment on celestial bodies to be available fi inspection provided interference with norm operations is avoided.
Treaty for the Prohibition of Nuclear Weapons in Latin America Treaty of Tlatelolco	14 February 1967	For each Government Individually	Prohibition of any form of possession, manufacture or testing of nuclear weapons by Parties, in their territories and/or under their jurisdiction. Nuclear material used for propulsion excluded from the definition of 'nuclear weapon'. Query whether article purporting to authorise nuclear explosions for peaceful purposes is compatible with other provisions.	Through OPANAL or at special meeting of all Parties at request of any Party.	Control system implemented by Agenc for the Prohibition of Nuclear Weapons in L America (OPANAL), including special inspections. Full scope safeguards agreements with the IAEA are mandatory.

24

Adjudication of Disputes	Sanctions Provisions (UN sanctions are available under the Charter)	Amendment	Repudiation
Non-compliance to be reported to Dir-Gen., then transmitted to Board of Governors for referral to all Parties and the UN Security Council and General Assembly. Disputes *re* interpretation or application to be referred to ICJ unless Parties concerned agree otherwise. General Assembly may authorise Board of Governors to seek ICJ advisory opinion.	Agency to take corrective action forthwith if a non-complying recipient State fails to take 'fully corrective action within a reasonable time'. The Board of Governors may curtail or suspend assistance and recall material and equipment given. Persistent violators may be suspended from privileges of membership by Board of Governors on two-thirds majority vote.	Having considered observations by the Board of Governors on each proposed amendment, by two-thirds majority of the General Conference and accepted by two-thirds of all Members.	Promptly by notification or whenever a Party is unwilling to accept an amendment to the Statute. Withdrawal does not affect contractual obligations entered into with the Agency, whether as recipient of Agency assistance or *re* safeguards obligations.
Immediate consultations *re* jurisdictional disputes. *Re* Treaty interpretation, Parties to choose form of negotiation. In case of stalemate referral to ICJ by consensus of all Parties.	No provision.	At any time by unanimous agreement of Parties. At Review Conference by simple majority including a majority of States listed in the preamble.	If amendment remains unratified for two years, the defaulting Party is deemed to have withdrawn.
No provision.	No provision.	At Conference convened by one third of the Parties, by simple majority including all of the original parties.	After 3 months notice, due to extraordinary events jeopardising the supreme interests of Party.
No provision as among Parties. Practical questions regarding activities in space of intergovernmental organisations to be resolved by the Parties with the organisation or with the States members of the organisation.	Party liable for damages to other Parties and their nationals caused by any space object it has launched.	At any time by simple majority.	After twelve months notice.
Report of special inspections to be transmitted to all Parties, the UN Sec.-Gen., Security Council and General Assembly and to the Organisation of American States. In the case of stalemate referral to ICJ, with prior consent of Parties to the dispute.	On recommendation of General Conference of OPANAL.	At special session of the General Conference by a two-thirds majority present.	After 3 months notice, due to circumstances arising under the Treaty or its Protocols, affecting the supreme interests of the Party or the peace and security of Party.

Name of Treaty and Abbreviated Name	Opened for Signature	Entered into Force	Major NAC Provisions	Review	Verification Provisions
Treaty on the Non-Proliferation of Nuclear Weapons Non-Proliferation Treaty (NPT)	1 July 1968	5 March 1970	Prohibition on nuclear-weapon States to transfer, impart control over, or assist in acquisition or manufacture of nuclear weapons or other nuclear devices. Prohibition on non-nuclear-weapon States to manufacture or acquire such devices etc. correspondingly.	After 5 years. Thereafter at 5 yearly intervals as determined by simple majority of Parties.	For all non-nuclear-weapon State Parties ful scope safeguards agreements with the IA are mandatory.
Treaty on the Prohibition of the Emplacement of Nuclear Weapons and Other Weapons of Mass Destruction on the Sea-Bed and the Ocean Floor and in the Sub-Soil Thereof Sea-Bed Treaty	11 February 1971	18 May 1972	Prohibition on deployment of nuclear weapons or related facilities on the bottom of the sea for any purpose.	After 5 years. Thereafter at time and place determined by simple majority.	Right of observation without interference of a relevant activities. After consultation between disputants, notification other Parties and co-operation in further verification procedures agreement of all interest Parties. Report by initiating Party to other Parties.
Convention on the Prohibition of Military or Any Other Hostile Use of Environmental Modification Techniques (ENMOD Convention)	18 May 1977	5 October 1978	Only marginal NAC application. Prohibition of hostile modification of the environment. The use of nuclear material for such a purpose is forbidden.	After 5 years. Thereafter at time and place determined by simple majority. After any 10 year interval, Depositary to initiate with consent of one third or ten Parties.	Convening of a Consultative Committee Experts within one mon of request by a Party, in order to prepare a factua report for information of all Parties.

Adjudication of Disputes	Sanctions Provisions (UN sanctions are available under the Charter)	Amendment	Repudiation
For non-nuclear-weapon States, in compliance with their agreements with the IAEA and in accordance with the Agency's Statute.	For non-nuclear-weapon States, in compliance with their agreements with the IAEA and in accordance with the Agency's Statute.	At Conference convened by one third of Parties, by simple majority, including all nuclear-weapon States Parties and all Parties members of the Board of Governors of the IAEA at the time.	After 3 months notice, due to extraordinary events jeopardising the supreme interests of Party.
Unresolved serious breach may be reported by aggrieved Party to UN Security Council for action in accordance with Charter.	No provision.	At any time by simple majority.	After 3 months notice, due to extraordinary events jeopardising the supreme interests of Party.
Evidence of breach may be reported to UN Security Council by any Party. All Parties to co-operate with consequent Security Council investigations.	None, but assistance is to be given by all other Parties to a Party found by the Security Council to have been disadvantaged on account of breach of the Treaty.	At any time by simple majority.	No provision.

27

TABLE II – *MAJOR BILATERAL AGREEMENTS BETWEEN THE SUPERPOWERS CONTAINING PROVISIONS RELEVANT TO NUCLEAR ARMS CONTROL*

Name of Agreement and Abbreviated Name	Signed	Entered into Force	Major NAC Provisions
US-USSR Memorandum of Understanding Regarding the Establishment of a Direct Communications Link 'Hot Line' Agreement	20 June 1963	20 June 1963	Treaty establishes telegraph, radio-telegraph and teleprinter communications between the Superpowers, especially useful for emergency communications in times of crisis.
Agreement on Measures to improve the US-USSR Direct Communications Link 'Hot Line' Modernisation Agreement	30 September 1971	30 September 1971 (Amended 29 April 1975)	Treaty adds satellite communications to earlier communications links between the Parties.
Statements by the US and USSR on the Reduction of Fissionable Materials Production	(Made on 20 April 1964)		Simultaneous formal Statements undertaking to limit the production of fissionable materials for weapons purposes by substantial, specific amounts.
Agreement on Measures to Reduce the Risk of Outbreak of Nuclear War Between the US and the USSR Nuclear Accidents Agreement	30 September 1971	30 September 1971	Treaty requires each Party to give – 1. Immediate notification and to take preventive action *re* any unauthorised incident involving possible detonation of a nuclear weapon. 2. Immediate notification of the detection of an unidentified object by their respective missile warning systems, or of interference with the warning systems. Advance notification of planned missile launches beyond borders in the direction of the other Party.
US-USSR Agreement on the Prevention of Incidents On and Over the High Seas	25 May 1972	25 May 1972	Treaty establishes rules of conduct between the Parties with respect to military ships and aircraft in international waters and airspace. Requires notification of situations of danger and the exchange of factual information *re* incidents or damage suffered by ships and aircraft involving the other Party.
Protocol (As above)	22 May 1973	22 May 1973	Treaty forbids simulated attacks on non-military ships of other Party so as to constitute a hazard.
US-USSR Treaty on the Limitation of Anti-Ballistic Missile Systems SALT ABM Treaty	26 May 1972	3 October 1972	Treaty limits permissible ABM systems to the defence of the capital of each Party and one other site housing ICBM. Also limits numbers of launchers, interceptor missiles and ABM radars, as well as radar performance.
Protocol (As above)	3 July 1974	25 May 1976	Treaty reduces the two permissible sites for deployment of ABM systems to one site for each Party and provides for possible choice of alternative site.

Name of Agreement and Abbreviated Name	Signed	Entered into Force	Major NAC Provisions
US-USSR Interim Agreement on Certain Measures with Respect to the Limitation of Strategic Offensive Arms SALT I Interim Agreement	26 May 1972	3 October 1972	Treaty and Protocol, which is an integral part of the Agreement, fix the permissible numbers of ICBM and SLBM launchers and restrict their conversion for a period of 5 years.
Statement regarding conduct of Parties on expiration of the Treaty (as above)	September 1977		Formal reciprocal Statements by the US and USSR that they would refrain from actions incompatible the SALT I Interim Agreement and the goals of ongoing SALT negotiations.
Agreement on Basic Principles of Relations Between the US and USSR	29 May 1972		Agreement establishes principles for the conduct of the Parties towards each other, including: avoidance of military confrontation and nuclear war; coexistence on the basis of equality; limitation of strategic arms, preferably in the form of concrete agreements; the ultimate objective of general and complete disarmament.
US-USSR Memorandum of Understanding Regarding the Establishment of a Standing Consultative Commission SCC Agreement	21 December 1972	21 December 1972	Treaty establishes a Standing Consultative Commission composed of a Commissioner, Deputy Commissioner and additional staff representing each Party, to promote the implementation of the Nuclear Accidents Agreement, the SALT ABM Treaty and the SALT I Interim Agreement.
Protocol (As above)	30 May 1973	30 May 1973	Treaty lays down procedural rules for the Standing Consultative Commission.
US-USSR Agreement on Basic Principles of Negotiations on the Further Limitation of Strategic Offensive Arms	21 June 1973		Agreement recognises that attempts by either Party, directly or indirectly, to gain unilateral advantage over the other would prejudice their peaceful relations. Envisages further SALT negotiations and acknowledges the need for verification of strategic arms limitation measures by NTM.
US-USSR Agreement on the Prevention of Nuclear War	22 June 1973	22 June 1973	Treaty enjoins each Party to refrain from the threat or use of force against the other party or its allies in circumstances endangering international peace, and to hold urgent consultations in situations involving risk of nuclear war.

Name of Agreement and Abbreviated Name	Signed	Entered into Force	Major NAC Provisions
US-USSR Treaty on the Limitation of Underground Nuclear Weapon Tests Threshold Test-Ban Treaty (TTBT)	3 July 1974		Treaty prohibits underground nuclear weapon tests producing yield in excess of 150 kt and Parties pledge to keep number of underground tests to a minimum. Provides for exchange of data to assist verification by NTM. Tests for peaceful purposes excluded from consideration.
Joint US-USSR Statement on the Question of Further Limitations of Strategic Offensive Arms Vladivostok Accord	24 November 1974		Agreement outlines the elements of proposed further SALT Treaty.
US-USSR Treaty on Underground Nuclear Explosions for Peaceful Purposes Peaceful Nuclear Explosions Treaty (PNET)	28 May 1976		Treaty limits permissible energy yields of underground nuclear explosions for peaceful purposes. It also provides for exchange of information and on-site inspection in certain cases, to supplement verification by NTM. A Protocol proscribes given military benefits that might otherwise accrue from the explosions.
US-USSR Treaty on the Limitation of Strategic Offensive Arms (With Protocol; Memorandum of Understanding; and Joint Statement) SALT II Treaty	18 June 1979		Treaty sets ceilings on ten categories of strategic offensive weapons including: launchers of ICBM, SLBM and ASBM, with sublimits for relevant MIRV. Restrictions also *re* ALCM, missile launch weight, throw weight, testing and deployment of ballistic missiles and FOBS. Interference with verification by NTM is prohibited. A data base is declared on the numbers of strategic offensive arms of each Party. Guidelines are provided for subsequent negotiations.

31

CHAPTER 2

The Changing Scope of Nuclear Arms Control

The Subject Matter of the Agreements

Negotiation and supervision of the implementation of NAC agreements have become substantially more difficult in the 1980s than in the sixties and seventies, when most of the agreements in Tables I and II (see pages 24 and 28) were concluded. The change is the outcome of vast technological advances in the field of nuclear weapons. As the result of better techniques and simplified methods, non-nuclear-weapon States have become more susceptible to horizontal proliferation. At the same time, NAC among nuclear-weapon States has vastly increased in complexity, as designs and performance of weapons have undergone successive refinements. The trend continues while a substantial portion of the world's most able physical scientists is constantly engaged in further extending and perfecting the weapons.[1]

Nuclear weapons today can release four thousand times the energy released by the atomic bomb that was detonated over Hiroshima.[2] Today there is no limit to the attainable levels of energy released by a single weapon. The explosive yield of present nuclear arsenals is about 13000 million tons of TNT, which has been estimated to be equivalent of about one million Hiroshima bombs.[3]

Since SSD I in 1978, it has been universally acknowledged that a full scale exchange of nuclear weapons between the Superpowers could put an end to all human life, and would, at the least, threaten the survival of civilisation.[4] However, it is not the destructive power of nuclear weapons that makes them a technologically difficult subject for international agreement, but rather the diversity of the systems involved and the rate of change to which they are subject.

Delivery systems are acquiring greater range, speed, accuracy, and mobility. Intercontinental ballistic missiles (ICBM) now have a range of about 13000 km and can reach their target within 30 minutes over that distance.[5] Intermediate range missiles can deliver their nuclear payload within 5-7 minutes.[6] Over the 13000 km range, targeting accuracy has increased about a hundred-fold during the past 25 years, bringing ICBM to an approximate accuracy of 50 metres using terminal guidance systems.[7] No sooner were the necessarily large missiles fitted with intricate guidance mechanisms than it became possible to use satellite navigation systems to guide smaller missiles with the aid of computer links, which are now being installed.[8] Technology is believed to exist for manoeuvring re-entry vehicles (MARV), designed to evade missile defences such as anti-ballistic missiles (ABM).[9] Both Superpowers have already deployed multiple independently targetable re-entry vehicles (MIRV), which can be released and targeted one by one, over an area of approximately 150 km by 500 km.[10]

There are submarine launched ballistic missiles (SLBM) and air to surface ballistic missiles (ASBM). The aircraft can be based on land as well as on aircraft carriers. One of the most recent systems of weapons are cruise missiles, which, after launching from land, ship or aeroplane, are internally guided winged or wingless craft, using stellar automatic data link, or terrestrial mapping systems. They can take the form of missiles or of low flying miniature aircraft.[11]

In some cases the destructiveness, range and blast, of nuclear weapons has been deliberately curtailed. Arsenals of nuclear weapons exist that have been miniaturised to the point where their destructiveness is similar to that of powerful conventional weapons. Another favoured modification is a low blast weapon with enhanced radiation (ER), in which residual radiation is increased by the use of special casings around the warhead.[12]

Some of the most far reaching innovations are being made with respect to the command, control and communications (C^3) networks of the Superpowers. These networks, *inter alia,* form the nerve centre of nuclear weapons systems, by positioning potential targets, transmitting military commands, and performing weapons guidance functions. As these systems are greatly dependent on satellite transmissions, the vulnerability of military satellites and their status in international law are directly involved.[13]

The variety of functions to be performed by the present generation of nuclear weapons, makes calculation of equivalence possible only as a rough approximation, or not at all. Demarcation between the various systems of weapons is also difficult due to interlocking, overlapping and backup systems. As demonstrated at the United States Senate hearings concerning the operation of the SALT II Treaty, substantial differences of opinion about equivalence can arise, not merely between adversary States, but also among leading experts within a State.[14] While policy differences have always existed, uncertainties on technical grounds are a growing problem.[15]

New time scales are also presenting difficulties. As noted above, the delivery speed of ICBM is down to about 30 minutes, with medium and short range strikes commensurately faster, while launch times are down to a few seconds. Such speeds have made reaction times to false alarms, miscalculations and technical faults so brief that, increasingly, only automatic and pre-programmed responses could be utilised. For instance, it has been said that –

> Soviet defence specialists viewed the ground-hugging Cruise missiles and Pershing II, with its short delivery time, as so threatening that their deployment would cause the Soviets to set their SS-20 medium-range missile force for a hair-trigger response to an attack . . .[16]

Under these circumstances, the usefulness of the various Hot Line Agreements is greatly reduced or, in the worst case, entirely eliminated.

By contrast, the lead time for research and development, manufacture and deployment of improved nuclear arms systems has increased to several years, and is estimated as more than a decade regarding some foreseeable developments. This means that NAC agreements have to be made in anticipation of those possible additions to arsenals, so as to forestall them or, at least, to take them into account when striking a bargain.

Changing Nuclear Strategies

A growing body of world opinion holds that nuclear weapons have no utility whatever. The view was cogently stated by the delegate of Sri Lanka to the Committee on Disarmament, Mr H.M.G.S. Palihakkara, when he said –

> We are up against an absolute weapon, the unleashing of which, however limited that may appear to those who advocate it, will leave neither the victor nor the vanquished and therefore does not serve any realistic political or military purpose.[17]

If this were a universally held opinion, then all nuclear weapons would be dismantled. Although there is an overwhelming convergence of expert opinion about the destructiveness of nuclear weapons, it does not follow that all share the view that nuclear preparedness 'does not serve any realistic political or military purpose'. It is necessary, therefore, to take note of the military strategies in accordance with which it has been envisaged that nuclear weapons may be employed, as well as the political objectives that might be served by the use, or merely the threatening presence, of nuclear weapons.

The only time when the strategy for the use of nuclear weapons was clear-cut, was when the United States had a monopoly of the weapon. With the growing threat of retaliation to any use of nuclear weapons, the possibility of translating their destructive potential into political advantage has become increasingly obscure. As Ambassador B.A. Nzengeya of Zaire has said –

> Twenty years ago, the desire of the nuclear Powers following the cold war, to acquire a deterrent or striking force, was understandable to the peoples of the world as being aimed at the maintenance of international peace and security. Now, however, the capacity of the new nuclear weapons to destroy all life on earth several times over no longer makes them a deterrent force and consequently no longer corresponds to the original aims of these States. [18]

It compounds the difficulty of assessing acceptable terms in NAC agreements when the usefulness of the various weapons systems, in policy terms, is not at all clear.[19]

The confusion is exacerbated by the adoption of imprecise, interchangeable, and often deliberately euphemistic terminology. For example, a *strategic attack* has been defined as one aiming to eliminate the adversary as a war fighting unit.[20] At the same time, long range, high yield nuclear weapons are usually referred to as *strategic weapons*. There is no clear distinction between these and *intermediate-range weapons*, also known as *medium-range* or *theatre weapons*, for use over a more limited range, as well as *long-range theatre nuclear forces*.

Another meaning of the terms is to refer to strategic weapons in relation to a possible exchange between the Superpowers, and theatre weapons in the context of a regional, such as a European, conflict. Miniaturised, namely *tactical* nuclear weapons are also regarded as relevant to a European war, or they are envisaged in a Third World setting. Nuclear weapons suited for both strategic and theatre purposes are referred to as *grey area weapons*.[21] And yet, all of these weapons could be used in various military situations.

However, nuclear strategies can be categorised not only with respect to the location of military conflict but also regarding the targets to be sought out and the sequence of strikes to be made. Whether over intercontinental distances or within a region, nuclear weapons could be used for *counter-value* strikes against troops, industrial centres and/or population centres. This could be a *first strike* or in retaliation. *Counterforce* targeting, meaning a strike against the nuclear missile launching and communications systems of an adversary nuclear power, is another contemplated utilisation of nuclear weapons. Despite the misleading terminology, *counter*force, like *counter*-value, could be used in a first strike, as well as in retaliation. If counterforce were used to cripple an adversary only partially then, like any of the other aforementioned uses of the weapons, it would invite further incalculable retaliation.

The efficacy of a counterforce strike as a manoeuvre to disarm the enemy depends on the timing of the retaliatory strike. If the other side were to *launch on warning,* namely before the counterforce missiles reached their targets, then only a third strike could be prevented, while the second strike aimed at the instigator State could be a counter-value strike. In the view of Henry Trofimenko, head of the Institute of United States and Canada Studies, Moscow, it would be immaterial whether the first strike were targeted as a counterforce or a counter-value strike because, in either event, it would elicit a retaliatory counter-value launch. He describes the situation in the form of a question –

> The Pentagon has estimated that such a disarming strike would require the launch of more than 2000 warheads against the enemy targets. Tell me, who, with the exception of God himself, in the few minutes available could determine that this vast number of warheads already in mid-flight is a 'limited' counterforce rather than an all-out countervalue attack and, accordingly, give the command for an appropriate limited retaliation?[22]

The variety of ways in which nuclear weapons may be employed is said to facilitate a *flexible* response to threats. Public approval of the policy was sought pursuant to United States Directive 59 of 1980, issued by President Carter. In accordance with this policy, the development of many new types of nuclear weapons is justified on the ground that, otherwise, the only option would be an all out strike, which would not be a credible deterrent because of the corresponding full scale retaliation it would predictably elicit. This strategy contains two ambiguities. First, it is not predictable that a relatively low level nuclear exchange could be prevented from escalating to total nuclear war. Second, it has not been adequately explained why many varieties of nuclear weapons are essential to nuclear flexibility. It would seem that flexibility could be achieved, if this were desired, by curtailing the number of weapons launched and restricting the targets chosen.

Estimation of the outcome of the abovementioned nuclear strategies is largely guesswork. The only use of nuclear weapons with reasonable predictability of outcome, other than total disaster, would be their use in a counterforce operation, provided the enemy could be reliably disarmed at one strike and prevented from effecting a launch on warning. This is referred to as a *first strike capability,* when a State has acquired the capacity to deliver a nuclear strike against the other without risking an intolerable reprisal. Although no nuclear Power has attained this capability at present, improved positioning techniques of enemy mobile craft, combined with the present speed of launching and accuracy of targeting, the growing ability to disrupt C^3 systems, together with the theoretical feasibility of effective ballistic missile defence, could perhaps make a disarming first strike capability a technical possibility for the Superpowers in the foreseeable future.[23]

Again, the terminology is misleading, because a nuclear *disarming* capability could be exercised either at a first strike or in retaliation to a lesser nuclear attack. Further confusion results from the concept of a *pre-emptive* strike, which would consist of launching nuclear weapons in anticipation of nuclear attack, before the enemy weapons have been launched. To speak of such a pre-emptive first strike does not necessarily denote the capability of a disarming strike. It could refer to a desperate measure, despite the anticipation of crippling retaliation.

A further obstruction in NAC dialogue has been the confusion between the concept of *nuclear parity* and that of the *strategic balance.* As the result of geographical differences, the diverse performance of nuclear weapons, and other variables, the concept of *asymmetrical parity* or *essential equivalence* in strategic arsenals has been accepted. However, this is not the same as the balance of terror, which continues to exist between nuclear Powers, especially the Superpowers, irrespective of parity, so long as neither side acquires a first strike capability.

Imprecise Motives

The difficulty of achieving agreement on limiting the proliferation and perfection of nuclear weapons does not only lie in the novelty of those weapons, nor the complexity of the strategies relating to their use. The primary problem is the perceived advantage to be derived from the possession of nuclear weapons or, stated another way, the disadvantage that could flow from abjuring, abandoning or curtailing nuclear weapons preparedness. Neither the uncertain nature of the advantage, nor its altered applicability in a new technological environment has, so far, led to a unilateral renunciation by any of the five nuclear Powers. Even if the precise utility of the weapons cannot be demonstrated, the image of military might they are thought to project has been sufficient to justify their retention and rapid build-up.

The offensive use of nuclear weapons would be contrary to the provisions of the United Nations Charter,[24] as is the offensive use of any weapon. While this provision of the Charter is often flouted by thinly disguised aggression with conventional weapons, the provision has been observed in the case of nuclear weapons. In some Third World conflict situations it has not been clear that the only inhibition to the use of nuclear force was fear of retaliation in kind. It would seem that the use of nuclear weapons for attack has been deemed to be inadvisable, at least in part, because of the probable reaction of world public opinion, which could lead to a broad international alliance against the aggressor. For the last-mentioned reason, nuclear weapons are not only impractical as offensive weapons, but also as threatening offensive weapons, which makes them unsatisfactory instruments for aggressive political leverage.[25]

There could be some exceptions to the above considerations. One would be the offensive use of nuclear weapons against a State held in universal disfavour by the world community, such as South Africa might become if deprived of all Western support. Aggressive use of nuclear weapons could also occur in a disarming first strike by one Superpower against the other, after which world public opinion would have diminished relevance. In that case, the problems arising within the aggressor State itself could be the more significant.[26]

The attainment of a disarming first strike capability would require overcoming political obstacles as well as technological ones. The mere striving for a first strike capability would undoubtedly be perceived as an aggressive act, which is the reason why both Superpowers periodically reiterate that their objective is the retention of strategic parity.[27] If, nevertheless, one Superpower were to approach outright prominence,[28] this could result either in the universal acceptance of the dominant Superpower as omnipotent, or it could invite a pre-emptive strike from the other Superpower.[29] The type of response by the other Superpower, as well as the political realignments that would occur in the world as a consequence of the changed threats and expectations, are quite unpredictable.

It is widely acknowledged that the extreme stress on decision-makers in charge of conducting a nuclear war would be likely to result in inefficient and erratic behaviour. The contention was advanced in its most unequivocal form by Ambassador A. Salah-Rey of Algeria, during nuclear arms control negotiations in the Committee on Disarmament. He said –

> The idea entertained in certain quarters that a new nuclear war, whether limited or not, can be waged and won is not only extraordinarily dangerous because of the risks it imposes on mankind but also logically unacceptable because it is based on the assumption that the adversary's response will remain within rational limits. There is no need to be a great theoretician to foresee that, when that stage has been reached, the behaviour of the opposing camps will defy all the laws of rationality that we are today in a position to identify.[30]

By contrast, the literature still does not acknowledge the probability of similarly erratic behaviour under conditions when the exercise of a first strike capability may become imminent. More specific international attitudes can be expected to emerge in opposition to strivings for nuclear-weapons pre-eminence, as soon as technical obstacles cease to be effective barriers to the option.

The threat of use of nuclear weapons for genuinely defensive purposes may be another matter. Such threats could be effective even if the State making the threat were not an overtly nuclear Power but only suspected of possessing a few nuclear weapons. Perhaps it might be argued, for example, that India has discouraged Chinese incursions across its borders and that Israel has kept its Arab antagonists at bay by having acquired the reputation of possessing nuclear weapons.[31]

Threat of defence with nuclear weapons against attack by conventional weapons is less acceptable when it is an overt threat by nuclear-weapon States. Increasingly during the past few years, non-nuclear-weapon States have been insisting on assurances by nuclear-weapon States that the weapons would not be used against them, even in defence. The unstated theoretical basis of the demand is, that the only legitimate use of nuclear weapons would be in retaliation against another State that has used them or, perhaps, in retaliation against a nuclear-weapon State that had launched an attack with conventional weapons with the threat of escalating to nuclear weapons.

When giving the requested assurances of non-use of nuclear weapons,[32] the nuclear-weapon States, with the exception of France, described in some detail the circumstances under which they would be prepared to use the weapons. While China has always ruled out the first use of nuclear weapons under any circumstances, the United States and the United Kingdom did not reject their possible first use in support of an ally on foreign soil, even against a non-nuclear-weapon State, if it were acting in collusion with a nuclear-weapon State. In accordance with this doctrine, the use of nuclear weapons against North Korea and North Vietnam during the recent wars there could have been justified. The policy statement of the United States is consistent with the view that the non-use of the weapons on those occasions was in deference to world opinion, and not because such an act would have been categorically ruled out against non-nuclear-weapon States.

The heavily qualified negative security assurances given by nuclear-weapon States, which could be read as threats to use nuclear weapons in given circumstances, have been justified by the respective Governments with the argument that they are designed to forestall aggression, not only by nuclear forces, but also by superior conventional forces.[33]

In a statement to the United States Foreign Relations Committee, in November 1981, the Secretary of State, Alexander Haig, listed the enduring functions of nuclear weapons as assisting 'deterrence, crisis management, and day to day diplomacy'. Although he claimed it to be common ground between the Superpowers that strategic nuclear forces are 'central instruments of foreign policy', he failed to show how these functions are performed by the weapons. Illustrations to support his argument referred only to supposed perceptions of the weapons' efficacy. For example –

The nuclear balance inevitably affects the political and psychological environment within which deep international crises must be managed.

Similarly –

. . . the strategic nuclear balance casts a shadow which affects every geopolitical decision of significance. The image of U.S. strength and the perception of U.S. commitment permiates into every region of the world.[34]

It is not intended here to explore in depth what advantages may be derived from the possession of nuclear weapons and their delivery systems, at the various levels of sophistication of those systems, and in the diverse situations applying to the particular States. The intention is merely to demonstrate that in the eyes of influential world leaders there are persuasive incentives for both horizontal and vertical proliferation.[35] It is also sought to show that the indeterminate character of those advantages[36] prevents the formulation of clear-cut priorities. This makes it unavoidable to introduce subjective criteria into the evaluation of the relative benefits and disadvantages of provisions in relevant NAC agreements.

The aims ascribed to NAC are the prevention of nuclear war; the halting of the vertical and horizontal nuclear arms race; the reversal of the nuclear arms race; and eventually, the total elimination of nuclear weapons and their delivery systems.[37] The first priority is well nigh universally shared, although the subsequent priorities appear to enjoy less wholehearted adherence. The strongest support for NAC relates to the prevention of the imminent outbreak of nuclear war by regulating events that could lead to miscalculation, error, or any confrontation liable to rapid escalation.

By contrast, the assessment as to what levels of armaments are likely to lead to nuclear war in the longer term is highly subjective, so that while some see a vigorous programme of NAC as the best protection, others hold the view that additional armaments are necessary. Both Superpowers claim that they seek no more than parity with each other, yet both maintain that they are obliged to continue the extension of their nuclear armaments in order to maintain that parity.

A committed lobby of support for NAC comes from States which believe that they would benefit economically from any curtailment of the nuclear arms race. Those are mainly the developing countries, most belonging to the so-called *Group of 77*,[38] and advocating the establishment of a New International Economic Order. The annual financial cost of the nuclear arms race being approximately one thousand million US dollars, it is estimated by the States concerned that a rich source of economic aid would become available if the material and human resources used in the nuclear arms race were to be diverted to assist in economic development.[39]

The possibilities for NAC are predicated on the attainment of a number of objectives external to the content of NAC agreements. Some of these have been repeatedly identified at international forums. They include the availability of means for the peaceful settlement of international disputes and the adoption of a number of confidence building measures designed to reassure States regarding their security which, in combination, would result in the relaxation of international tension.

Prevention of horizontal proliferation is believed to require an adequate assurance by nuclear-weapon States, to non-nuclear-weapon States, that nuclear weapons, or the threat of their use, will not be turned against them. Likewise, adequate safeguards on all nuclear activities of non-nuclear-weapon States have been widely accepted as essential for the prevention of horizontal proliferation. Developing nations tend to stress the importance of the non-discriminate application of safeguards, while the developed nations place emphasis on the need for full scope safeguards to be universally adopted by all non-nuclear-weapon States.[40]

Various principles of international conduct have also been noted as prerequisites for arms control, in particular NAC. These include the principle of the inviolability of international frontiers; the recognition of the sovereign equality of States; the prevention of the use of force or the threat of force against the sovereignty, territorial integrity or political independence of any State; the right to exercise self-determination and independence from foreign domination; and non-interference in the internal affairs of other States.[41]

Guidelines for the conduct of NAC negotiations pinpoint the need for mutual responsibilities between nuclear-weapon and non-nuclear-weapon States; the requirement of undiminished security for all States at each stage of the disarmament process, to be achieved at the lowest possible level of military forces; and the requirement for verification measures satisfactory to all parties to the proposed agreement. The desirability of universal participation in appropriate NAC agreements has also been stressed at international forums from time to time.

It may be more appropriate to regard NAC not as a series of separate objectives, in turn dependent on the attainment of certain prerequisites, but as part of an integrated process. The aim of that process is to prevent a chain of events that could one day lead to wholesale nuclear devastation, either in the course of limited wars or in a universal holocaust.

Examined in this light, the objective of NAC has not changed over the years. As stated by Ambassador Yoshio Okawa, the Japanese delegate to the Committee on Disarmament, during a press conference in November 1981, the danger of nuclear war has not abated. Japan, at present 'the only country' to have experienced bombardment with nuclear weapons could become, he said, 'the first of many'.[42]

Variable Standards of Success

If the objective of NAC is seen as the prevention, rather than the postponement of nuclear war, then it is not sufficient merely to persevere with the process leading towards the elimination of nuclear weapons. Eventual nuclear war could only be prevented with the maintenance of the required momentum of the NAC process, whereby the forces promoting nuclear weapons build-up would be outweighed by the forces inhibiting such steps.

It is inevitable that at any given time, some facets of the NAC process are more successful than other facets. A purported comprehensive balance sheet of progress and regression towards effective NAC would be inconclusive, because weighting the various indicators of success and failure would have to rely on a large measure of subjective assessment. For example, the same technological developments that give rise to new systems of nuclear weapons, can also produce techniques to improve the verification of performance of NAC agreements. Similarly, sectional alliances motivated by the desire of protection by the 'umbrella' of a nuclear-weapon State, thus dividing the world, may simplify methods of international accommodation, by reducing the diversity of policy alternatives under consideration during negotiations. Attempts to evaluate the positive and negative features of these developments would be futile.

Nevertheless, it is possible to identify some clear-cut indicators of current tendencies. One way to measure the progress being achieved, is to examine the NAC process with respect to the initiatives believed to be most urgent, as well as those issues that appear to be the most amenable to short term resolution. The proposed Comprehensive Test-Ban Treaty (CTB), satisfies both the criteria of urgency and relative ease of implementation.

All relevant United Nations bodies have currently designated a CTB Treaty to be the first priority in NAC efforts.[43] The matter has been given precedence for several reasons. One reason is that it would be a relatively simple, straightforward step. The view that explosions above a yield of 5 kilotons can be reliably detected is virtually unanimous, while much eminent expert opinion suggests that today there are no genuine problems of verification at all with respect to a CTB.[44]

The Treaty would not affect the balance of power between the Superpowers and it would be a move towards equalizing the sacrifices demanded of the nuclear-weapon and non-nuclear-weapon States. It is not disputed from any quarter that a CTB would have a strong inhibiting influence on both vertical and horizontal proliferation. A less readily acknowledged, but nevertheless foreseeable consequence of CTB is the pressure it would exert on China and France to acquiesce in an NAC regime and to relinquish their efforts to maintain a relativity with the major nuclear Powers. Another cogent reason for supporting a CTB at the present time is that it could help to build confidence in NAC and, therefore, that it could act as a prelude to other urgent agreements, such as a SALT III Treaty and an Outer Space II Treaty.

Attempts to reach a CTB are not new, nor have the long negotiations been without success. The whole process has been an excellent example of the persistence and determination required to achieve agreement on NAC issues. It also illustrates that, although the anticipated result may not be achieved exactly as planned, negotiating efforts are usually rewarded with some measure of progress.

The desirability of concluding a CTB was first raised in the General Assembly in 1957. After six years of effort the attempt to conclude a comprehensive treaty was abandoned in favour of the Partial Test-Ban Treaty of 1963.[45] Nevertheless, negotiations continued for the conclusion of a Treaty to ban underground nuclear tests in the Eighteen Nation Disarmament Committee (ENDC), and later in the Conference of the Committee on Disarmament (CCD), until the Special Session in 1978. Sweden took an important initiative in 1965, when it proposed verification of a CTB by an international exchange of seismic data, to be supplemented by on-site inspections in order to resolve the occasional uncertainties that may arise.

Despite the Swedish and other initiatives, the Superpowers still failed to agree on a CTB verification formula when the Non-Proliferation Treaty was concluded in 1968.[46] The preamble to that Treaty expressed disappointment that a CTB had not been concluded, inferring that such a Treaty was expected to be concluded in the near future, in fulfilment of the obligation of the nuclear Powers *vis-à-vis* the renunciation of nuclear weapons by the non-nuclear-weapon States. The ENDC, and its successor the CCD, continued to make no appreciable headway, but in 1974 the two

41

Superpowers agreed on a Threshold Test-Ban Treaty.[47]The Treaty prohibited underground nuclear tests with a yield of more than 150 kilotons and prescribed specific testing sites for the permitted explosions. In 1976 the Superpowers reached agreement on the Peaceful Nuclear Explosions Treaty,[48] to supplement the Threshold Test-Ban Treaty.

In that year, also, the CCD established an *ad hoc* Group of Scientific Experts to consider international co-operative measures to detect and identify seismic events. After SSD I, the Group of Scientific Experts continued to meet under the aegis of the Committee on Disarmament. By 1980, the Group had collated a programme for a seismological verification system, to consist of about 50 teleseismic stations situated around the globe and exchanging data by way of the telecommunication system of the World Meteorological Organisation. Methods for the collection, analysis and distribution of the data were largely agreed upon by the scientists during 1980, and they proposed a practical test of the seismic network. This would have required the co-operation of the relevant States, and at that point the programme lost momentum. In the meantime, during 1977, bilateral negotiations on a CTB were commenced by the Superpowers, with the United Kingdom joining later in the year. The trilateral negotiations continued until July 1982 when they were terminated by the United States. In the same year the Committee on Disarmament set up a multilateral Working Group with a limited mandate to discuss the topic.[49]

With the entry into force of the Partial Test-Ban Treaty, the Treaty of Tlatelolco[50] and the Non-Proliferation Treaty, as well as the Superpower agreements on the Threshold Test-Ban Treaty and the Peaceful Nuclear Explosions Treaty, many objectives of a CTB, as originally envisaged, have already been realised. The Partial Test-Ban Treaty forbids all nuclear tests with the exception of those conducted underground; the Treaty of Tlatelolco and the Non-Proliferation Treaty, *inter alia,* debar all non-nuclear-weapon States from the right to conduct nuclear tests; the Threshold Test-Ban Treaty prohibits the two Superpowers from testing nuclear weapons with a yield exceeding 150 kilotons, while the Peaceful Nuclear Explosions Treaty, in effect, extends the Threshold Test-Ban Treaty to include purportedly 'peaceful' nuclear explosions. While the aforementioned Treaties have not attracted accession by all eligible States, and the two last-mentioned Treaties remain unratified, in essence the terms of all the Treaties are being universally observed.

Thus, although there has been a failure to secure the outlawing of all nuclear explosions with military potential, a large measure of success has been attained towards that end.[51] Had the technological environment remained static, the *rate* of progress towards a CTB would also be very satisfactory, when compared with previous international efforts to put legal curbs on military competition.

Yet, in present circumstances, a different yardstick of success may be appropriate. Since a CTB was first mooted, NAC-related problems have snowballed. The avoidance of accidental nuclear war, in a world saturated with complex, high speed nuclear weapons, is more perilous; maintenance of an increasingly intricate nuclear· balance between the Superpowers is more tenuous; prevention of the spread of nuclear confrontation into space and the emergence of new weapons of mass destruction are more pressing;

and it is increasingly difficult to restrain horizontal proliferation at a time when the manufacture of nuclear weapons and delivery systems is within the technological and financial reach of a growing number of States. In this overall situation, with an ever increasing number of more and more complicated treaties to be concluded, the failure to negotiate a simple CTB could be regarded as a sign that the NAC process is faltering because the requisite momentum of progress is not being maintained.

Notes

1 E.g. see *Soviet Military Power* (US Govt. Printing Office, Washington undated, approx. Dec. 1981–Jan. 1982.

2 *Comprehensive Study on Nuclear Weapons*, Report of the Secretary-General, A/35/392, p. 10.

3 Ibid.

4 Final Document SSD I, A/RES/S-10/2, pp. 4-5 — 'Existing arsenals of nuclear weapons alone are more than sufficient to destroy all life on earth.'

5 A/35/392, p. 12.

6 Id. p. 43; Also, *Whence the Threat to Peace*, USSR Ministry of Defense (Military Publishing House, Moscow) 1982, p. 60 – 'In Pentagon thinking, surprise attacks with high-accuracy Pershing-II missiles (flight time of 5-6 minutes) on the Soviet Union's strategic weapons would reduce the impact of a retaliatory blow against the USA in the event of aggression against the USSR.'

7 A/35/392, p. 43; For imminent developments, *Whence the Threat to Peace*, op.cit. p. 29 – 'The program launched in 1979 for rearming 300 Minuteman III ICBM with the highly accurate new Mkl2A 350-kiloton warheads (circular error probable (CEP) – 180 meters) is in the stage of completion.'

8 Karas, Thomas H., *Implications of Space Technology for Strategic Nuclear Competition*, July 1981, Occasional Paper 25 (The Stanley Foundation, Iowa, USA) esp. pp. 10-11; Also A/35/392 p. 47.

9 A/35/392 p. 46 para. 106.

10 Id. p. 14.

11 Huisken, Ron, *The Cruise Missile and Arms Control* (The Strategic and Defence Studies Centre, Australian National University, Canberra 1980).

12 A/35/392, p. 36.

13 Dahlitz, J., 'Arms Control in Outer Space', *The World Today*, April 1982, Vol 38 No. 4 p. 154.

14 See *SALT II: An Interim Assessment* – Report of the Panel of the Committee on Armed Services, House of Representatives (US Govt. Printing Office, Washington 1978); *The SALT II Treaty*, Hearings Before the Committee on Foreign Relations, US Senate (US Govt. Printing Office, Washington 1979.)

15 Metcalf, A.G.B., 'Editorial', *Strategic Review*, US Strategic Institute, Summer 1981, Vol. IX No. 3 esp. p. 7; Torrey, Lee, 'America's New Missiles Fail to Impress', *New Scientist*, 4 June 1981, p. 603.

16 *The Age*, newspaper, Melbourne, 14 January 1982, p. 7. quoting Randell Forsberg, Director of the Institute for Defence and Disarmament Studies, Boston, United States, following her discussions with Soviet arms control specialists.

17 CD/PV.107 of 17 February 1981, p. 7.

18 CD/PV.145 of 11 August 1981, p. 9.

19 See Carver, Field Marshal Lord Michael, 'The Case for Conventional Defence', *The Guardian Weekly*, 27 December 1981, p. 9.

20 A further complication is that in the Soviet literature, military plans are referred to as *tactics* to distinguish them from overall political *strategies*, in accordance with Leninist terminology, e.g. see Trofimenko, Henry, 'The "Theology" of Strategy', *Arms and Control and Security: Current Issues* (Westview Press, Boulder, Colorado 1979) esp. p. 109.

21 The performances of two of the most controversial grey area weapons, the Pershing-II missile and the Tomahawk cruise missile have been described in the following terms by – Mazing, Valery, 'Dialogue, Not Missile Build-up', *New Times*, 1981, Vol. 18 p. 10 – 'The Pershing-II has a radius of about 2000 kilometres, nearly three times that of the Pershings now deployed. Consequently, it can be used for entirely different purposes since it is able to hit targets deep in the Soviet Union. The Pershing-II can reach its target within 4-5 minutes, which increases the US first-strike armoury. The cruise missiles are a fundamentally new weapon. By flying at low altitudes (50-60 metres) they can avoid enemy air defences and hit targets, with great accuracy, at a distance of 2600 kilometres.' C.f. SS-20 missiles which are claimed to have a range of 5000 km. *Soviet Military Power* (US Govt. Printing Office, Washington) p. 26. However, these weapons are deployed in areas from which they could not reach the other Superpower, ibid.

22 Trofimenko, Henry, 'The "Theology" of Strategy', *Arms and Control and Security: Current Issues*, op.cit. p. 110; Also see infra Chapter 9.

23 There is an important distinction between a first strike capability, and the attainment of such a capability by stealth. Concealment of weapons systems developed towards that goal does not seem possible – infra Chapter 9; see also *Comprehensive Study on Nuclear Weapons*, A/35/392 p. 14 para. 20 – 'With increasing missile accuracy and many RVs per missile, MIRV has raised the spectre that a fraction of one side's ICBM forces may in a "first strike" destroy the opponent's ICBMs still housed in their hardened silos. This would be possible with sufficient accuracy and reliability of the attacking RVs, and if the ICBMs to be attacked were not launched before they were destroyed. This situation is therefore considered to be potentially unstable, since in time of crisis each side may consider launching its missiles rather than risk their destruction.' For estimate of timing, *Whence the Threat to Peace*, op.cit. p. 36 – 'The agreed schedule of the Pentagon plans for building up strategic offensive armaments and deploying anti-missile and space defense systems is timed to complete the development of a so-called first-strike potential in the 1980s.'

24 Art. 2(4) 'All Members shall refrain in their international relations from the threat or use of force against the territorial integrity or political independence of any state, or in any other manner inconsistent with the Purposes of the United Nations.'

25 An indication can be gleaned from the international furore following a remark by US President Reagan, which fell far short of a deliberate threat – 'I don't know. I could see where you could have an exchange of tactical weapons against troops in the field without it bringing either one of the major powers into pushing the button.'

26 C.f. problems with disaffection of youth in the US and other Western States resulting from the Vietnam war.

27 E.g. President Reagan's statement in October 1981 – 'Our strategy remains, as it has been one of flexible response: maintaining an assured military capability to deter the use of force – conventional or nuclear – by the Warsaw Pact at the

lowest possible level . . . As all presidents have acknowledged any use of nuclear weapons would have the most profound consequences. In a nuclear war, all mankind would lose. Indeed, the awful and incalculable risk associated with any use of nuclear weapons themselves serve to deter their use.'

Also Leonid Brezhnev's statement during the exchange between the two leaders – 'Only he who has decided to commit suicide can start a nuclear war in the hope of emerging a victor from it.'

Both statements quoted in the *International Herald Tribune* newspaper, 22 October 1981, p. 1 col. 8. Referring to the US publication *Soviet Military Power*, a further Soviet denial as follows – 'Soviet military doctrine, too, is presented in a distorted light. Referring to non-existent 'Soviet publications' and 'statements of Soviet leaders', the authors of the pamphlet and, for that matter, also certain officials of the US Administration, allege that Soviet military doctrine is of an aggressively offensive nature, and that the Soviet Union counts on winning a nuclear war by means of a pre-emptive strike. These allegations are entirely groundless, as are the references to the Soviet leadership. None of the Soviet Party leaders or statesmen has ever stated, nor could have stated, anything of the sort. The very opposite is true.' *Whence the Threat to Peace* (Military Publishing House, Moscow 1982) p. 11.

28 An unanswered question is, what amounts to 'outright prominence'? Even the early monopoly of nuclear weapons and later supremacy in delivery systems only gave the US marginal political leverage. See n. 36.

29 Karas, Thomas H., 'Implications of Space Technology for Strategic Nuclear Competition', *Occasional Paper 25*, publication of The Stanley Foundation (Iowa July 1981) p. 10 – Referring to the proposed installation of bhangmeters *viz* nuclear explosion detectors on GPS satellites as part of an Integrated Operational Nuclear Detection System to establish instantly where US nuclear weapons have detonated, the author observes that – 'The new systems may also arouse Soviet suspicions of US intent to acquire a strategic first-strike capability. Such suspicions may in turn increase Soviet incentives to consider preemptive strikes more seriously.'

30 CD/PV.107 of 17 February 1981, p. 15.

31 Infra Chapter 8.

32 Infra Chapter 3.

33 'The American doctrine governing use of nuclear weapons has always had a central core of ambiguity, and properly so . . . The first line requires Washington to communicate a deadly intent and the second a sense of restraint. This is the heart of the nuclear paradox. It is unavoidable, and it lends itself to confusion in the best of times.' *The Washington Post*, reproduced in the *International Herald Tribune* newspaper, October 24–25 1981, p. 4 col. 2.

34 US Department of State, *Current Policy* No. 339 of 4 November 1981 (Bureau of Public Affairs, Washington).

35 E.g. '. . . on the strategic side, there are two dangers. One is the danger to our land-based missiles. I do not believe that the Soviets will exercise that capability against our land-based missiles, except that it will give them greater confidence in the handling of regional crises, some sought by them, some developing out of revolutionary situations.

So, even if a strategic equivalence were achieved, we would still have the serious problem of how to remedy the various regional balances around the world that have arisen.' Testimony of Henry Kissinger, then Secretary of State, *The SALT II Treaty*, Hearings Before the Senate Foreign Relations Committee, July–August 1979 (US Govt. Printing Office, Washington 1979) p. 196.

36 E.g. 'We had a huge advantage in strategic weaponry for a long time, and we found ourselves unable to discover any kind of doctrinal foundation for using it to advance American national goals. It turned out to be a posture that gave us superiority but did not really give us the basis for dealing with threats to our interest that we perceived around the world.' Id. September 1979, testimony of Prof. Richard A. Falk, p. 228.

37 See 'Elements of a Comprehensive Programme of Disarmament', *Disarmament: A Periodic Review by the United Nations*, May 1980, Vol. III No. 1 p. 40 esp. 'Objectives, principles and priorities' p. 41; For the origins of a Comprehensive Programme of Disarmament, specifying aims and priorities, see Jack, Homer A., 'Progress Towards a Comprehensive Program of Disarmament', *WCRP Report*, 1982, SSD II/7.

38 A caucus of more than a hundred developing nations in the UN with a varying membership, largely overlapping with the Group of 21.

39 Study on the *Relationship Between Disarmament and Development*, A/36/356 of 5 October 1981.

40 Infra Chapter 8.

41 Infra Chapter 7 esp. G.A. Resolutions 2131 (XX) of 1965; 2625 (XXV) of 1970; 2734 (XXV) of 1970; 2936 (XXVII) of 1972; 3314 (XXIX) of 1974; 31/9 of 1976; 32/155 of 1977; and 34/103 of 1979.

42 Statement at U.N. Headquarters on 20 November 1981, quoted in *Disarmament Times* (New York) Vol. 4 No. 6, p. 2.

43 See the study on a *Comprehensive Nuclear Test Ban*, A/35/257 of 23 May 1980.

44 Ibid. p. 40 para. 154; Also infra Chapter 3.

45 Table I (see page 24).

46 Ibid.; At about the same time a Latin American regional non-proliferation treaty was also concluded, the Treaty of Tlatelolco.

47 Table II (see page 28).

48 Ibid.

49 See also Infra Chapter 3.

50 Table I (see page 24).

51 The number of nuclear tests conducted underground remains high. Supra Chapter 1, n. 37.

CHAPTER 3

Norm Creation by Negotiation for the Control of Nuclear Arms

Methods of Multilateral Norm Creation for NAC

The creation of authoritative standards for NAC is in the forefront of international endeavour. Its aim is to devise, and to oversee the implementation of specific arms control measures, which is a deliberate and painstaking process. The method used, based on initially achieving widespread consensus regarding the principles involved, has a bearing on the effectiveness of the agreements ultimately reached. Similar negotiating methods have been used at other times and in relation to other issues, but with less collective persistence.[1]

Generally the process involves three successive phases, although the second phase is often regarded as an end in itself. In the first phase, initiatives for major new NAC measures are usually proposed by Governments to their allies in NATO, The Warsaw Pact, or the Non-aligned Movement, before presentation to the appropriate United Nations body. Proposals for the elaboration of international norms relating to NAC are also made by a variety of non-governmental organisations and peace research institutes. Often these are Government supported at the national level and at the international level they have consultative status with the United Nations. In addition, emerging NAC proposals are sometimes considered at *ad hoc* international conferences on topics having a bearing on the subject; NAC treaty review conferences; expert study groups commissioned by the United Nations; and through an exchange of initiatives devised at the academic, scientific or other professional level.

During the second phase, debates are conducted at the United Nations with a view to reaching consensus on the basic elements of the subject matter. The chief organisational vehicles for the establishment of NAC norms in the United Nations are: the Committee on Disarmament, with its formal and informal Working Groups; the Disarmament Commission; the First Committee; and the General Assembly. Within the United Nations Secretariat there is the Centre for Disarmament; the United Nations Institute for Training and Research and its offshoot, the newly constituted United Nations Institute for Disarmament Research. Legal problems may be referred to the International Law Commission[2] or to the Sixth Committee.

Upon reaching general consensus, the third phase consists of a plenipotentiary conference where the final text of the treaty is drafted by intending State Parties, for adoption by signature and subsequent ratification in conformity with traditional diplomatic practice. In the past, bilateral NAC treaties were almost exclusively negotiated between the Parties themselves at all stages. However, the current trend is to involve the whole international community in a few chiefly bilateral issues, on the ground that all States are affected by the outcome.

Since the commencement of the first NAC negotiations, some negotiators have spent most of their working lives engaged in this task. Irrespective of the particular forum, they continue to confront each other in a global village atmosphere. The personal element ensures a thorough understanding of negotiating positions adopted by the various States, as well as the negotiating style of colleagues. It also enhances considerations of national honour, credibility and a degree of personal trust. Hence the diversity of subjects considered and the varied locations of meetings give a misleading impression of fragmentation. Existing NAC agreements, ongoing negotiations and emerging initiatives are unified, not only by the interrelationship of the subject matter, but also by the continuing participation of a number of outstanding national representatives.[3]

The State most involved in the process of NAC, the United States, is the one that has tended to be denied the benefits of continuity. Due to wholesale changes of both delegates and senior policy makers with each new Administration, there has been a repeated loss of expertise and adjustment. This is not only a periodic disadvantage for the United States. It is a continuous and cumulative global impediment to the evolution of an international arms control ethos. The problem was squarely faced by the United States delegate to the Committee on Disarmament, Ambassador C.C. Flowerree. Himself a mid-term appointee under the Carter Administration, he admitted during his address in August 1981 –

> It will not have escaped the notice of members of the Committee that the United States delegation has been relatively silent during our 1981 session. Apart from my April 7 intervention and a recent brief discussion of chemical weapons last month, my delegation has spoken only when spoken to – that is, when it has been necessary to put our position on an issue on the record. We have thought this to be an appropriate posture, given the fact that the review of United States arms control policy is still continuing.[4]

Existing processes of norm creation for NAC employed by United Nations organs are indicative of prevailing opportunities and limitations. An examination of the issues that are under consideration, and the working procedures of the various bodies, reveals the discrepancy between the concerns of legal theorists and those of international lawyers directly engaged in NAC negotiations. The Under-Secretary-General for Legal Affairs of the United Nations, Professor Erik Suy, has urged that, 'Contemporary international law must deal with these new "prescriptive norms".' He advanced the view that it has become necessary to decide 'to what extent' the decisions of intergovernmental organisations are creating new norms. In the course of his remarks he posed the following questions –

> Are they legal norms? Are they generally binding legal norms, or are some of them binding and some not? How are the binding norms determined?[5]

A reluctance by States to enter into NAC treaties has already been noted in the previous chapters. Reasons for this are not uniform. In some cases

States apparently prefer to continue with a phase of the arms race in the belief that they can outdistance other States in nuclear arms. On other occasions, there are grounds why one State may deliberately attempt to obstruct other States from reaching accommodation. Alternatively, the conclusion of NAC agreements is inhibited by genuine concerns about, *inter alia,* the precision, universality, verifiability or enforceability of a contemplated treaty. There is a positive aspect to the caution displayed in assuming NAC undertakings. It demonstrates that the utmost weight is attached to treaty obligations in this field. Apparently there is a belief that any public relations advantage that may accrue from acceding to an NAC treaty precipitously, would be outweighed by the possibility that responsibilities undertaken might have to be dishonoured or repudiated.

By contrast, non-binding expressions of opinion by States on NAC issues are given somewhat more readily, although generally care is exercised to convey a responsible attitude. While the voting patterns of States on these issues tend to be fairly consistent, no great loss of face is entailed in a vote change at the United Nations, provided that cogent reasons can be adduced to justify the altered position. The relevant negotiations and deliberations being undertaken in the forums of the United Nations are to be examined below. It will be seen that despite many positive developments *the rate at which NAC agreements are reached*, whether by treaty, by resolution or otherwise, falls far short of what the agendas of those bodies have designated to be desirable targets.

No doubt with such concerns in mind, Professor Suy has put forward six proposals for assisting the conclusion of international agreements to satisfy the requirements of contemporary international life.[6] While the proposals refer to all types of agreements, they also have great relevance to NAC agreements. The following is a summary of the proposals: *first*, that there should be more rapid and extensive codification of international law at international conventions; *second*, that steps ought to be taken to further encourage universal participation during the elaboration of international instruments; *third*, that the timing and venue of international law-making gatherings should be arranged so as to enable States with limited manpower resources to participate effectively; *fourth*, that non-participating delegations at diplomatic conferences be entitled to submit texts for the consideration of delegates; *fifth*, that the importance of the speed with which treaties are concluded and ratified should be recognised; and *sixth*, that more attention be given to the implementation provisions contained in international agreements.

A consideration of the subject matter of proposed NAC agreements is undertaken partly in order to throw light on the reasons why the rate of progress does not meet stated expectations. This involves many subsidiary questions as to the significance of the issues that have been agreed upon so far, the reasons for differing progress in the establishment of NAC norms relating to the various subject areas, and why advice of the kind offered by Professor Suy is not sufficiently put into practice. A central question to emerge is, whether the content of the sought after agreements is insuperably difficult to negotiate and to deliberate upon, or whether the methodology of international negotiation and deliberation is merely inappropriate and out of date for the task at hand.

Multilateral NAC Negotiations in the Committee on Disarmament

The Committee was reconstituted following SSD I, to be the only 'multilateral disarmament negotiating forum' on arms control of the United Nations. It is the successor to the Eighteen Nation Disarmament Committee, established in 1961, and the subsequent Conference of the Committee on Disarmament. During SSD I, it acquired its present format of delegations from 35 United Nations Member States, on the basis of equitable geographical distribution, together with the five permanent Members of the Security Council.[7] In accordance with its mandate, the Committee is required to formulate all recommendations by consensus. At its first session, in 1979, the requirement was incorporated into the Committee's Rules of Procedure.

Issues are referred to the Committee for consideration on the basis of international agreement in principle about the desirability of elaborating each topic into more specific commitments, if not binding treaties. Regarding nearly all of the themes that apppear on the annual agendas it could be fairly said that, at the least, they constitute agreements to formulate agreements. They are an endorsement of the desirability that international norms should prescribe the rights and duties of States in the matters concerned.

During 1980 and 1981, the Committee had four formal *ad hoc* Working Groups on the following topics:

– Effective international assurances to non-nuclear-weapon States against the use or threat of use of nuclear weapons
– A comprehensive programme of disarmament
– Radiological weapons
– Chemical weapons.

This format of negotiation has continued to be acceptable. In a Statement evaluating the work of the Committee in 1981, the Group of 21 comprising the Non-aligned States, expressed the view that –

> . . . *ad hoc* working groups have proved to be the best available machinery for the effective conduct of all substantive disarmament negotiations in the Committee on Disarmament.[8]

In 1979 much of the Committee's time was set aside for drawing up its Rules, but in 1980 and 1981, it had full agendas of substantive items largely oriented towards reaching agreements on NAC issues. The following have been the major NAC topics discussed, as initiated in 1980[9] and 1981[10] –

A. A Comprehensive Test-Ban Treaty
B. New Types of Weapons of Mass Destruction Including Radiological Weapons
C. Cessation of the Nuclear Arms Race and Nuclear Disarmament.
D. Assurances to Non-Nuclear-Weapon States
E. Comprehensive Programme of Disarmament.

While no NAC treaty has emerged, so far, as the outcome of any part of the Committee's work, significant progress has been made on a number of items and many issues have been clarified. In its reports, the Committee has enumerated all of the pertinent recommendations and other sources on which negotiations were based. As well as summarising the conclusions reached where agreement was possible, it has also collated the various arguments put forward regarding those issues that did not produce a consensus. Assessments of the Committee's achievements, by the Chinese delegation, for example, attribute considerable value to those functions, even if they fall short of constituting concrete agreements. As observed by the Chinese delegation in August 1981–

> . . . the statements made by the various delegations during the general debate in the Committee and in the discussion on specific items in the working groups have made clearer the points in common as well as the points of divergence on various issues of disagreements and increased delegations' understanding of each other's positions, which will undoubtedly help the future consultations and considerations . . .[11]

In order to study the effectiveness of this method of norm creation, and to examine the validity of the above assessment, each major NAC issue negotiated by the Committee on Disarmament since its inception will be considered separately.

A. *A Comprehensive Test–Ban Treaty*

Apart from various proposals by States and groups of States, in 1980 the Committee had before it a report on the subject by a Group of Experts,[12] submitted by the Secretary-General, presenting the background to the negotiations as well as making numerous recommendations. Other notable documents were the progress report by the 9th[13] and 10th[14] Sessions of an *ad hoc* Group of Scientific Experts to Consider International Co-operative Measures to Detect and Identify Seismic Events.

During the debates, there was a confirmation of the view, long held in the United Nations, that the conclusion of a treaty banning nuclear tests in all environments was the first priority of all contemplated disarmament measures. Previous negotiations on this subject, discussed in Chapter 2, had spanned a quarter of a century. By 1980, the opinion was over-whelmingly endorsed that all scientific and technical problems relating to the verification of the proposed Treaty had been substantially solved[15] and that only political commitment was outstanding. However, a few notable delegations, including those of the United Kingdom and the United States, maintained that some of the vital verification issues were still unresolved.

From the beginning of the discussions, many delegates claimed that the Soviet Union, the United Kingdom and the United States were not making sufficient effort to promote the conclusion of a Treaty. These three nuclear Powers had been engaged in trilateral negotiation of the subject for over three years without reaching agreement. Committee Members requested that, at the least, the Committee should be given a full report concerning the state of the negotiations. Towards the end of the Committee's 1980 Session this was done[16] and Committee Members had the opportunity to discuss the report. Among several criticisms and proposals, the suggestion was made that the three negotiating nuclear Powers should immediately stop all testing of nuclear weapons, either by way of individual moratoria undertaken by each of them or by a trilaterally negotiated moratorium, pending the conclusion of a multilateral Treaty on the subject.

In the course of 1981, it became further apparent that some States had made only half-hearted efforts towards establishing a global network that could verify a CTB with indisputable accuracy. The Progress Report of the Scientific Experts to Consider International Co-operative Measures to Detect and Identify Seismic Events, made to the Committee and hence to the Working Group, regarding their 11th[17] and 12th[18] Sessions held in February and August 1981, left no doubt that the scientists engaged in the task failed to receive high priority assistance. At the latter meeting, the scientists noted the following areas in which additional scientific and technical progress was needed –

(a) studies on the use of seismographs and hydro-acoustic instruments on the ocean bottom to improve the detection and identification capability for seismic events in the southern hemisphere;
(b) widespread digital recording of data from seismographs;
(c) automation of the extraction of parameters from seismograph data;
(d) automation of the data processing at international data centres. Organisation and co-ordination of the work at these centres;
(e) methods to accommodate reporting of large earthquake sequences and swarms.[19]

Apart from security considerations, there is a major legal disincentive for the conclusion of a Comprehensive Test-Ban Treaty, being the known intention of two nuclear Powers, France and China, to remain aloof from such a Treaty and their consistent non-participation in substantive negotiations on the subject. As noted previously, there is at present not even theoretical justification, let alone formal enforcement machinery that could be brought to bear on these two States to ensure their compliance, even if an overwhelming international consensus were achieved. The attitude of the great majority of States, in favour of the Treaty, has been expressed in resolutions of the General Assembly, notably in the Final Document of SSD I, albeit qualified by some disclaimers in the form of 'explanation of vote'.

The Chinese and French position is not in breach of any recognised principle of international law, nor would it be if those States failed to accede to an existing Treaty on the issue. For example, it has not been alleged that those two States are acting contrary to international law for non-accession to the almost universally adopted Treaty for the prevention of horizontal proliferation, the Non-Proliferation Treaty. Yet, it is very significant that the two States have complied with the applicable provisions of that Treaty, and that China has gone so far as to accede to Protocol II of the Treaty of Tlatelolco.

The international expectation appears to be that, with the endorsement by the Committee on Disarmament of the elements of a Treaty, the resulting Comprehensive Test-Ban Treaty would be adopted by most States. China and France might then decide to conform to the extent of abiding by its provisions.[20] However, the military plans of those States would be directly affected by a ban on nuclear testing. Therefore, in this instance, France and China might decide to defy international consensus in the form of an almost universally adopted Treaty, not only by failing to become Parties but also by refusing to comply with its provisions. The concern of the Soviet Union and its allies on this issue was expressed in a Statement to the Committee on Disarmament in the following terms –

> The socialist States . . . expect that those two nuclear-weapon States which do not take part in the above negotiations determine more clearly their attitudes to the creation of an *ad hoc* working group on a nuclear test ban and express their readiness to take part in the preparation of a treaty on the complete and general prohibition of nuclear-weapon tests and to take over corresponding obligations under that treaty.[21]

To what extent a decision along those lines would depend on the prevailing legal position is difficult to estimate with any degree of confidence. This aspect of the question will be explored in the following Chapters. There it will be suggested that, if a clearly defined legal obligation existed imposing at least a theoretical duty to comply with internationally adopted standards of State conduct, it could substantially influence decision-making by States contemplating defiance of international opinion in such circumstances.

Apart from problems of verification and universal accession by nuclear-weapon States, the two Superpowers and the United Kingdom may be reluctant to conclude a CTB because they wish to continue perfecting nuclear weapons, requiring test explosions to do so. Another weighty consideration is that a treaty would prohibit even the occasional testing of existing nuclear arsenals, so as to establish their persisting efficacy, against the possibility of deterioration or sabotage.

In the opinion of Non-aligned States, even this genre of fundamental objections could be overcome if the Committee on Disarmament were able to assume a greater role in the negotiations. As they see it, the procedure would entail the setting up of a Working Group to deal specifically with the subject, and the exercise of concerted pressures on the trilateral negotiators to report fully and frankly all outstanding differences between them. Contrary to some measure of reporting in 1980, at the conclusion of the 1981 session of the Committee, many delegates felt it was –

> . . .regrettable that the parties which had been engaged in trilateral negotiations on this subject did not respond, either jointly or individually, to the question posed to them . . . on issues which are of vital concern to both nuclear-weapon States and non-nuclear-weapon States alike.[22]

During a debate on the issue, the delegate of Nigeria, Ambassador O. Adeniji, went so far as to question the good faith of the three nuclear-weapon States concerned, by saying that –

> When a commitment to negotiate is coupled with refusal to accept the basic machinery for effectively undertaking the negotiations, we are bound to doubt if good faith is present.[23]

Their inability to obtain the necessary universal consent for additional *ad hoc* Working Groups in 1981, including one on a CTB, led to bitter recriminations during plenary sessions by the States belonging to the

Group of 21. They pointed out that the rule of consensus had its limitations. For example, Rule 25 of the Committee's Rules of Procedure, qualifies the consensus method as follows –

> The approval by consensus of reports shall not be interpreted as affecting in any manner the essential requirement that such reports must reflect faithfully the positions of all the members of the respective organs.

In a Working Paper on the establishment of subsidiary organs of the Committee, the Group of 21 recommended, unsuccessfully, the following addition to Rule 25 –

> The rule of consensus shall not be used either in such a way as to prevent the establishment of subsidiary organs or the effective performance of the functions of the Committee, in conformity with the provisions of rule 23.[24]

This instance of the inability of the great majority of States to exert their influence, even to the extent of determining negotiating procedure, is a telling illustration of the negative aspects of negotiation by universal consensus. In 1982 a Working Group on a CTB was established but with only a very limited mandate. However, similar problems arose regarding the creation of Working Groups in other subject areas.

B. *New Types of Weapons of Mass Destruction Including Radiological Weapons*

An *ad hoc* Working Group was established by the Committee to deal with that portion of the topic relating to the negotiation of a Convention Prohibiting the Development, Production, Stockpiling and Use of Radiological Weapons. As radiological weapons are only at the research and development stage, they are still the subject of argument regarding definition. The weapons being developed could cause destruction, damage or injury by means of radiation produced by the decay of radioactive material that would be disseminated by means other than a nuclear explosive device. The definition, as presently envisaged, would not include particle-beam weapons, which produce radiation in ways other than through radioactive decay. Although by definition, the contemplated weapons are not 'nuclear' weapons, they are in practice akin to those weapons, being non-explosive radioactive weapons.

From the point of view of norm creation by the Committee on Disarmament, it is an interesting case because, by mid-1979, the Soviet Union and the United States had already submitted an agreed Joint Proposal on a treaty prohibiting the development, production, stock-piling and use of radiological weapons.[25] The agreement was in a form that could have been readily endorsed and recommended for plenipotentiary negotiations to conclude a final draft for multilateral signature. The Committee's attention was repeatedly drawn to this fact and a reference to it was eventually included in the end-of-session Statement by the Socialist States, in August 1981, as follows –

> The delegations of the socialist countries believe that in 1981 the Committee on Disarmament could have completed the drafting of a treaty on the *prohibition of radiological weapons.*[26]

This Working Group's approach to its task conclusively demonstrated that it is not only Superpower rivalry or problems of verification, adjudication or enforcement of NAC agreements that inhibit their timely conclusion.[27] The reluctance to commitment in this instance suggests that procrastination may have become endemic in NAC negotiations. Unlike the negotiation of other issues, where the Committee has been faced with irreconcilable positions adopted by the two major Power Blocks, or where overwhelming and imminent security issues were at stake, in this case failure to reach agreement was the result of many diverse and contradictory amendments of marginal significance regarding the definition of terms and the scope of the proposed Treaty.

Uncharacteristically, the most persistent obstruction came from Sweden, which, for no apparent international reason, attempted to link the proposed Treaty with the inviolability of commercial nuclear reactors. The unexceptionable response from Ambassador P. Lukes, of Czechoslovakia, was as follows –

> We share the concern of the Swedish delegation as regards the importance of the protection of civilian nuclear facilities. This problem is not new, and the concern of many countries has already been reflected in the 1977 Additional Protocol to the Geneva Conventions of 12 August 1949, as well as in several other documents of international law . . . With all this in mind we tend, like several other delegations, to be in favour of finding a way of dealing with this very complicated and very specific problem of the enforcement of the existing rules for the protection of nuclear facilities separately from the radiological weapons treaty.[28]

Ambassador de Souza E Silva, of Brazil, objected to the proposed complaints procedure, despite its conformity with complaints provisions in a number of NAC treaties, on the ground that it was discriminatory. It would 'confer a privileged status on some of the parties', he said, 'if the complaints procedure made use of the Security Council of the United Nations', and added –

> We fail to see the merit of establishing a procedure, that can easily be blocked by a handful of nations, among which, incidentally, are included those that possess the technological means to contemplate the production of radiological weapons.[29]

For its part, Romania gave great weight to two issues that had been raised in discussion, of very doubtful relevance to a Treaty on radiological weapons, being 'the peaceful application of nuclear energy' and 'the relationship between the convention and the nuclear disarmament process'. Ambassador M. Malita referred to those issues as 'fundamental problems on which the success of the convention depends'.[30]

Criticism of the Treaty by the Yugoslav delegate, Ambassador M. Vrhunec, concentrated on the definition of radiological weapons. Because the description adopted by the Superpowers excluded nuclear weapons from the definition of radiological weapons, Yugoslavia feared that this would 'imply the direct or indirect legitimation of nuclear weapons'.[31] It was an approach to treaty interpretation, periodically echoed by other States at the United Nations, that would make nonsense of all arms control treaties, because each limitation placed on a weapon could be taken as a licence for the unlimited deployment and use of all other weapons. However, the opposite opinion was also presented to the Working Group, as noted in its 1981 Report.[32]

On any consistent interpretation of the definition, as originally proposed, of radiological weapons, it must be self-evident that the differentiation between the two weapons merely states that weapons having the additional properties possessed by explosive 'nuclear weapons' are to be excluded from the operation of the particular Treaty, not that their use is thereby sanctioned. Further, if there were any doubt about that, it could be stated in a simple explanatory clause.

Notwithstanding the patently pinpricking nature of the objections, Yugoslavia, like the other Non-aligned States, persisted in stalling the conclusion of a Treaty on radiological weapons. Ambassador Vrhunec continued with the assertion that, 'A very important circumstance is that radiological weapons in a concrete, operative and physical form are unknown.' He then proceeded, in the next sentence, to assert that, 'This was the reason why we focused our definition on specific characteristics of radiological weapons', followed by the further contention, regarding the non-existent weapons, that, 'Numerous scientifically-founded facts indisputably confirm that the basic characteristic of a radiological weapon is that it inflicts injury on living beings by its ionizing radiation.'[33]

However, the *coup de grace* was administered by Brazil, with the complaint that –

> It should not be difficult to imagine the dismay of the membership of the United Nations if the Committee on Disarmament cannot go beyond presenting the international community, at the forthcoming General Assembly, with a draft text on weapons that do not exist, and which according to some expert opinion do not stand even the chance of ever existing, and reporting at the same time that no progress has been accomplished on measures deemed vitally urgent by the higher forum on repeated occasions.[34]

It will be noted below, in connection with anti-satellite weapons and exo-atmospheric anti-ballistic missile systems, that radiological weapons do exist, albeit in a form that is still not sufficiently destructive to warrant their deployment in preference to alternative weapons.[35]

During the negotiations in the Working Group, the assessment by Sweden of the impracticality of radiological weapons appears to have carried much weight. The view denigrating the topicality of the subject was restated by Swedish Ambassador C. Lidgard, who declared that –

> Studies which have been undertaken by the competent scientific and technical institutions in Sweden since the early 1950s, and which have now again been carefully examined, show that the development of specific radiological weapons, as defined by the drafters, is a very remote possibility. They could hardly become practical weapons of mass destruction or have any effective use in the battlefield. A radiological weapon of sufficient strength for denying an enemy access to significant areas of terrain would be almost impossible to fabricate, handle or deliver.[36]

The stance adopted by Sweden and the other Non-aligned States overlooked the consideration that, should the weapons remain impractical for a lengthy period, no harm could result from banning them, whereas the converse error of assessment about the 'remote possibility' of their utility, could clearly have the gravest consequences. Further, a Treaty on radiological weapons could serve as a prototype for further treaties banning projected energy weapons of various kinds.

In any event, the point which the Non-aligned States had made in the Committee on innumerable occasions was, that the Superpowers should be encouraged to reach whatever specific items of arms control they could agree to, bearing in mind the adverse political relations between them. Yet, in the case of the agreement on banning radiological weapons the process of accommodation was hindered, above all, by several of the States usually pressing for more NAC measures to be adopted.

The Committee on Disarmament in plenary session considered other types of new weapons of mass destruction (NWMD). It attempted, unsuccessfully, to define 'weapons of mass destruction' and to decide whether an expert study should be commissioned on the subject. It was proposed that a Group of Experts be requested to prepare a draft comprehensive agreement on individual types of weapons of mass destruction and new systems of such weapons, and it was further proposed that the Experts be requested to keep the Committee constantly informed of developments in this field.

In contrast to the negotiations on radiological weapons, where Committee Members failed to adopt a practically ready made agreement, supported by both the United States and the Soviet Union, in the matter of new weapons of mass destruction there was no draft, no outline of the topic or programme of work before the Committee, and even the ambit of the subject matter was in doubt.

In a Working Paper on the subject, Hungary suggested that, pending the establishment of a formal Group of Experts, there should be informal meetings between experts to explore suitable methods of approach. The following headings were proposed on the basis of preliminary expert discussions:

– Review of questions related to the definition of new types of weapons of mass destruction as well as the criteria on the basis of which particular weapons fall under certain categories of NWMD on the basis of the formula of 1948 taking also into account the advance reached in the field of science and technology.

– Review of the trends of the development of technology especially in the military field, identifying particular areas where the progress may contemplate emergence of NWMD.

– Recommendations to the Committee on Disarmament as to the methods of further work and negotiations, including the setting up of an *ad hoc* group of experts.

– Other relevant aspects, experts may deem necessary to bring to the consideration of the Committee.[37]

The scope of the subject matter of new types of weapons of mass destruction is, by definition, limitless, both in terms of possible weapons to be controlled and the duration of the danger posed by the introduction of the weapons. The issues to be addressed under this heading go to the core of the problem of the circumvention of existing NAC agreements, adverted to in Chapter 1. In view of these considerations, the proposal to set up a Group of Experts to monitor the emergence of, *inter alia,* new types of nuclear weapons and systems of weapons, was significant. Had an agreement been reached and implemented on this point in the Committee on Disarmament, it could have had a more far reaching effect on NAC than a formal NAC treaty, duly signed and ratified, on a less significant matter. Concerning the issue of new weapons of mass destruction, agreement on a method of approach could be expected to establish fundamental new principles regarding circumvention.

In the absence of agreement on the establishment of a Group of Experts, the functions envisaged have been fulfilled, to some extent, by several highly respected peace research organisations. Independent assessments regarding the development of nuclear weapons systems, especially those made by the Stockholm International Peace Research Institute, are frequently quoted by States at the United Nations during NAC debates. In September 1980 another expert body was established outside the United Nations, which has fulfilled some of the functions contemplated to be addressed by an Expert Group to the Committee on Disarmament on the subject.

Although that body, the Independent Commission on Disarmament and Security Issues, has no formal connection with the United Nations, many of its members and advisers have represented their respective countries at the United Nations in recent times. Commission members from all five regional groupings, recognised by the United Nations for the application of the principle of equitable geographical distribution, take part in the deliberations. The Commission makes periodic recommendations on NAC issues like the SALT process, the verification of proposed new NAC treaties, and the operation of the ABM Treaty. Regarding the identification of new weapons of mass destruction and appropriate agreements for their control, the Commission has met a need brought to light during the deliberations of the Committee on Disarmament.[38]

When weighing the relative effectiveness of various approaches to the creation of NAC agreements, it is appropriate to take into account all of the threads that constitute the fabric of accommodation. Interaction between the Committee and the Commission, especially in relation to forestalling a new spiral in the nuclear arms race, is a particularly revealing example of the intertwining sub-structure of emerging international opinion.

C. *Cessation of the Nuclear Arms Race and Nuclear Disarmament*

This topic has been a catch-all, especially useful for the introduction of NAC issues not being considered by *Ad Hoc* Working Groups. Apart from proposed treaties for a CTB and the prohibition of radiological weapons, as well as recommendations for the ratification of the SALT II Treaty, the NAC issues discussed by the Committee on Disarmament have presented no immediate prospect of agreement on specific measures. That is not to deny that NAC issues exist that would be amenable to rapid negotiation. For instance, the Indian delegate to the Committee, Ambassador A.P.

Venkateswaran, regarded the following items as falling within that category –

(i) a complete and immediate freeze on the deployment of new types of nuclear weapons and their means of delivery, (ii) a complete and immediate halt to the replacement of existing missiles, aircraft and other nuclear delivery vehicles by new and modernized versions, (iii) a ban on the increase of the megatonnage of existing nuclear warheads, irrespective of the delivery vehicle on which they are mounted.[39]

Negotiating stages usually proceed from the general to the particular, and each stage is of importance towards the achievement of the ultimate goal. However, the greatest political resistance tends to occur towards the final steps, including agreement on all of the elements of a treaty and their incorporation into a binding instrument. There can be input from sources outside the United Nations regarding acceptable formulations at all stages of the NAC negotiating process, from the identification of the general concepts to concurrence about blanket obligations and, finally, the elaboration of specific measures.

The sequence of such negotiations consists of:

(a) *Agreement on the scope of the subject matter and the need to take international action with respect to it;* among the crucial NAC topics still at the stage of general principle was the suggestion for an agreement to prohibit the further flight-testing of strategic delivery vehicles. While agreement was not even reached on the desirability of imposing a prohibition on this activity, it was pinpointed as an issue worthy of intensive negotiation.

(b) *The identification of conflicting interests and outlooks;* for example the negotiation on affective international arrangements to assure non-nuclear-weapon States against the use or threat of use of nuclear weapons revealed eight distinctive standpoints.

(c) *The elaboration, in increasingly more detail, of the scope and consequences of the proposed NAC agreement;* for example the negotiation on the prohibition of radiological weapons, examined the detailed implications of the proposed Treaty.

(d) *Resolution of the areas of disagreement by compromise, the introduction of new machinery provisions, and narrowing of the topic to exclude irreconcilable clauses*; for example, negotiations to overcome the outstanding impediments to the conclusion of a CTB.

Negotiations in the Committee confirmed that the NATO and Warsaw Pact countries persist in their different approaches to the measures to be adopted for the halting of the nuclear arms competition, although the positions are not diametrically opposed. For instance, the Western States favour an agreement for the cessation of production of fissionable material for weapons purposes.[40] The Soviet Union and other Socialist States would prefer wide-ranging negotiations on ending the production of all types of nuclear weapons and gradually reducing their stockpiles until they have been completely destroyed.[41] The Non-aligned States pressed the Committee to establish a further *Ad Hoc* Working Group to undertake intensive negotiations on those specific topics, as well as on additional subjects, such as concrete measures for the prevention of nuclear war and an examination of the doctrines of nuclear deterrence.

A major problem confronting the international community on the subject of the cessation of the nuclear arms race, including the prevention of nuclear war breaking out in the short term, and doctrines of nuclear deterrence delineating long term R & D policies, is that these matters are effectively in the hands of the Superpowers. Irrespective of the theoretical equality of States, it is universally acknowledged that, in practice, the choices lie with the United States and the Soviet Union.

The immutability of this situation in the foreseeable future has given rise to two theoretical corollaries; first, it is asserted that the greater potential to cause nuclear war by the Superpowers has to be accompanied by their commensurately greater responsibility towards mankind; and second, that bilateral processes to this end are the legitimate concern of all other States, because third parties are affected by those processes. During the debate it was emphasized by delegates that, while bilateral and NAC issues were primarily the responsibility of the States concerned, the nuclear arms race has universal implications and is therefore an appropriate subject for multilateral negotiation in all its aspects. Ambassador Venkateswaran of India put it this way –

> Today the worsening state of confrontation among the major Powers makes it even more necessary for the non-aligned and neutral countries to play an active role in the prevention of a nuclear war and the negotiation of urgent measures of nuclear disarmament. This would be in the obvious interest of the major Powers and their allies themselves just as it would be in the interest of the non-aligned and neutral countries.[42]

Contribution by other States to the process for NAC between the Superpowers in the SALT related negotiations has not been excluded from the area of competence claimed by the Non-aligned States for themselves. It is noteworthy that the subject matter of the SALT-related treaties in Table II (see page 28), concerns only weapons possessed by the Soviet Union and the United States, and does not name or directly involve any third State. Therefore, with reference to the principles of international law, the proposition that third parties have an interest in the negotiations, merely because they could be incidentally affected, is a novel one. It is an area where theory may have to yield to the exigencies of technological change. As the Group of 21 commented in a Statement to the Committee –

> . . . all nations, nuclear and non-nuclear alike, have a vital interest in measures of nuclear disarmament, because the existence of nuclear weapons in the arsenals of a handful of Powers directly and fundamentally jeopardizes the security of the whole world.[43]

The Statement further asserted that, 'a nuclear war would affect belligerents and non-belligerents alike'.[44] Finally, the Non-aligned States making up the Group rejected as 'politically and morally unjustifiable that the security of the whole world should be made to depend on the state of relations existing among nuclear-weapon States'.[45] It was therefore recommended that the Committee set up an *Ad Hoc* Working Group to commence 'multilateral negotiations on questions of vital interest to nuclear and non-nuclear-weapon States alike', as follows –

60

(i) the elaboration and clarification of the stages of nuclear disarmament envisaged in paragraph 50 of the Final Document including identification of the responsibilities of the nuclear-weapon States and the role of the non-nuclear-weapon States in the process of achieving nuclear disarmament;

(ii) clarification of the issues involved in prohibiting the use or threat of use of nuclear weapons, pending nuclear disarmament, and in the prevention of nuclear war;

(iii) clarification of the issues involved in eliminating reliance on doctrines of nuclear deterrence;

(iv) measures to ensure an effective discharge by the CD of its role as the single multilateral negotiating body in the field of disarmament and in this context its relationship with negotiations relating to nuclear disarmament conducted in bilateral, regional and other restricted fora.[46]

Nevertheless, the substantive issues of the SALT negotiations were not canvassed, nor was there a move to apportion culpability between the Superpowers for the arrest of the SALT process. The declaration of the principle of a universal right to involvement in the limitation of strategic arms seemed to be intended more as an intimation of positions to be adopted in the future, should the negotiating hiatus continue, than as a signal of imminent international intervention in the bilateral process.

D. *Assurances to Non-nuclear-weapon States*

The *Ad Hoc* Working Group on effective international arrangements to assure non-nuclear-weapon States against the use or threat of use of nuclear weapons, has made only modest headway towards its goal of attaining agreement on a common formula that could be included in an 'international instrument of a legally binding character'.[47]

In Chapter 2 it was suggested that, in the absence of a first strike capability, the practical assurances against first use of nuclear weapons are a fear of retaliation by a nuclear power and/or a universal coalition against the culprit Government, possibly including some of its own citizens. It was also suggested that condemnation could only be avoided if the weapons were used defensively, to escape from an overwhelmingly adverse situation not brought about by the user's own actions.

Although it is not stated in these frankly pragmatic terms, the objective of assurances to non-nuclear-weapon States is to circumscribe, with the greatest possible accuracy, those extraordinary situations when the use of nuclear weapons may be excused and, by a process of elimination, to declare all other possible uses of the weapons to be heinous crimes against humanity. Hence, even the defensive use of nuclear weapons is to be outlawed in most situations.

Both positive and negative security assurances are contemplated. Globally, the most significant positive security assurance was given by the Soviet Union, the United Kingdom and the United States, in Resolution 255(1968), jointly sponsored by them in the Security Council, whereby they undertook to extend immediate aid to any non-nuclear-weapon State attacked or threatened with nuclear weapons.[48] Negative security assurances to the non-nuclear-weapon States have been given by all of the nuclear-weapon States during SSD I and again presented to the Committee on Disarmament in 1980 as follows –

China: Complete prohibition and total destruction of nuclear weapons are essential for the elimination of nuclear war and nuclear threats. We are aware that its realization is no easy matter. This being the case, we hold that the nuclear-weapon States should at least undertake not to use or threaten to use nuclear weapons against the non-nuclear-weapon States and nuclear-free-zones. On its own initiative and unilaterally, China long ago declared that at no time and in no circumstances would it be the first to use nuclear weapons.[49]

France: To negotiate with nuclear-free zones participants in order to contract effective and binding commitments, as appropriate, precluding any use or threat of use of nuclear weapons against the States of these zones.[50]

Soviet Union: To offer a binding commitment in a new international convention not to use or threaten to use nuclear weapons against non-nuclear States Parties to such a convention which renounce the production and acquisition of nuclear weapons and which have no nuclear weapons in their territory or under their jurisdiction or control, and to consult whenever any party to the convention has reason to believe that the actions of any other party are in violation of this commitment.

The Soviet Union, for its part, wishes to state as emphatically as it can that we are against the use of nuclear weapons, that only extraordinary circumstances, only aggression against our country or its allies by another nuclear Power, could compel us to have recourse to that extreme means of self-defence. The Soviet Union is doing and will do all in its power to prevent the outbreak of a nuclear war and to protect the people from becoming the victims of nuclear strikes, whether initial or retaliatory. This is our steadfast policy, and we shall act in accordance with it.

I wish also solemnly to declare that the Soviet Union will never use nuclear weapons against those States which renounce the production and acquisition of such weapons and do not have them on their territory.[51]

(Note – During SSD II in June 1982 the Soviet Union renounced any first use of nuclear weapons.)

United Kingdom: Not to use nuclear weapons against States which are parties to the Non-Proliferation Treaty or other internationally binding commitments not to manufacture or acquire nuclear explosive devices except in the case of an attack on the United Kingdom, its dependent territories, its armed forces or its allies by such State in association or alliance with a nuclear-weapon State.[52]

United States: Not to use nuclear weapons against any non-nuclear-weapon State party to the Non-Proliferation Treaty or any comparable internationally binding commitment not to acquire nuclear explosive devices, except in the case of an attack on the United States, its territories or armed forces or its allies by such a State allied to a nuclear-weapon State or associated with a nuclear-weapon State in carrying out or sustaining the attack.[53]

The diversity and imprecision of the undertakings should be noted. For example, not being 'the first to use nuclear weapons', as undertaken by China and later the Soviet Union, is ambiguous. It could relate to a conflict at a particular time and place with a specific enemy, or to a region, or the whole world. Would the undertaking preclude the use of nuclear weapons by that country after such weapons had been used in a broad conflict beyond its borders? Strictly speaking, having been used on Hiroshima and Nagasaki, 'first use' of nuclear weapons is no longer possible.

The earlier undertaking by the Soviet Union is also ambiguous in several ways, for example, by the failure to enumerate or to define that country's allies, and by referring to countries that do not have nuclear weapons 'on their territory', without elaboration. It is not clear whether the latter exception refers only to countries with permanent nuclear bases or also to those with communications centres or providing refuelling or other temporary facilities to craft armed with nuclear weapons.

Notwithstanding some uncertainties, the Chinese and Soviet negative security assurances regarding the use of nuclear weapons are more extensive and definite than those given by the other nuclear-weapon States. The large land areas and commensurate conventionally armed military forces possessed by the Soviet Union and China, could be contributing factors making the more stringent undertakings feasible.

By comparison, the undertakings given by the United Kingdom and the United States are even less predictable because they countenance the use of nuclear weapons, not only in defence of undefined allies, but also of the armed forces of those nuclear-weapon States wherever they may be in whatever capacity. Furthermore, that right is reserved irrespective of the entirely non-nuclear status of the adversaries against whom the weapon is to be used, provided they are 'associated' with a nuclear-weapon State. In accordance with the terms of these undertakings, the use of nuclear weapons would have been permissible during the Korean and Vietnam wars while United States troops were engaged in military action on the territories of those countries.

The statement made by France does not amount to any kind of undertaking to exercise restraint in the use of nuclear weapons. It is merely an indication of willingness to conduct negotiations with members of nuclear-free-zones. At present these only exist in Latin America and Antarctica, the two continents in respect of which France has already entered into treaty obligations to refrain from the deployment or use of nuclear weapons.

Nuclear-weapon States have, in effect, undertaken to refrain from the use of nuclear weapons aggressively and, by implication, in some situations of self-defence. As the distinction between aggressive and defensive situations is not always obvious,[54] an explicit undertaking not to use nuclear weapons defensively, except in clearly defined extreme circumstances, could have a genuinely restraining effect, especially on the use of tactical nuclear weapons.

Prohibition of aggression and permission for self-defence are already provided for in the Charter of the United Nations. Article 2, requires States to abjure 'the threat or use of force against the territorial integrity or political independence of any State', while Article 51, guarantees 'the inherent right of individual or collective self-defence if an armed attack occurs against a Member of the United Nations'.

The Committee on Disarmament established an *Ad Hoc* Working Group in 1979, to consider security assurances to non-nuclear-weapon States. Since SSD I, three basic attitudes to the issue have emerged. The first was put forward by the Soviet Union in a draft Convention, with operative provisions in Articles I and II, as follows –

Article I

The nuclear-weapon States Parties to this Convention pledge themselves not to use or threaten to use nuclear weapons against non-nuclear States Parties to this Convention which renounce the production and acquisition of nuclear weapons and which have no nuclear weapons in their territory or anywhere under their jurisdiction or control, on land, on the sea, in the air or in outer space.

Article II

The obligations set forth in Article I of this Convention shall extend not only to the territory of non-nuclear States Parties, but also the armed forces and installations under the jurisdiction and control of such States wherever they may be, on land, on the sea, in the air or in outer space.

An alternative formulation of the draft Convention was proposed by Pakistan in the following terms –

Article I

The nuclear-weapon States Parties to this Convention, as a first step towards the complete ban on the use or threat of use of nuclear weapons, pledge themselves not to use or threaten to use nuclear weapons against non-nuclear-weapon States not parties to the nuclear security arrangements of some nuclear-weapon States.

This undertaking is without prejudice to the obligation of States Parties to this Convention arising from treaties establishing nuclear-weapon-free zones.

Article II

The nuclear-weapon States Parties to this Convention also undertake to avoid the possibility of the use or threat of use of nuclear weapons in any contingency and to achieve nuclear disarmament, resulting in the complete elimination of nuclear weapons, in the shortest possible time.

As in the individual security assurances given by the five nuclear-weapon States, restraint in defensive use is tacitly implied in both drafts, but neither draft acknowledges this explicitly. It is noteworthy that similarly non-specific formulations are used in other existing and proposed treaties to ban the use of certain weapons, including biological, chemical, radiological, and excessively harmful conventional weapons. The difference is that, in those instances, the destruction of all militarily significant stockpiles of weapons is contemplated, guaranteeing their non-use in any circumstances, whereas that is not the case with respect to nuclear weapons.

During negotiations, Western States did not favour a multilateral convention of any kind, on the ground that the diversity of the security requirements of the various nuclear and non-nuclear-weapon States would make the operation of any convention inequitable. Concurrently with that position, the Western view has been that the solemn undertakings by States as unilateral declarations carry a genuine, if undefined, element of binding force. In the words of the United States, the individual pledges made at SSD I, 'represent an immediately effective measure of security for the non-nuclear-weapon States'.[55] A Working Paper presented by the United Kingdom in April 1981, claimed that its undertaking, as confirmed at the second NPT Review Conference, was 'fully in force'. The submission of the United Kingdom added that –

> Much of the discussion about security assurances has been concerned with the possibility of making them 'legally binding' . . . In these circumstances attention has focussed on the possibility of enhancing the political status of the various assurances given by Nuclear-Weapon States. The United Kingdom doubts the need for any such enhancement of its own assurance since it already regards it as a solemn undertaking.[56]

Ruling out the possibility of a generally acceptable world-wide treaty, the Western States proposed as a gesture of compromise, that the pledges made by the nuclear-weapon States in the course of SSD I should be incorporated into a General Assembly resolution, in order to formalise them in an internationally recognised manner. As this approach to internationally binding agreements was not acceptable to the Non-aligned and Socialist States, the issues remained unresolved.

A strictly legal evaluation of this dispute would be misleading. The point of contention was not the principles of law as to what constitutes a binding international agreement, or whether States genuinely regarded themselves, as they claimed, to be obligated to observe an undertaking given in one or other form. The essence of the difference of opinion concerned the establishment of a common formula that would greatly alter, in favour of the non-nuclear-weapon States, the substance of the undertakings already given. It may be unfortunate with respect to the development of international law, that the motivations for the dispute were not spelled out and separated from the legal principle that was casually invoked.

During negotiations it was agreed, in general terms, that non-nuclear-weapon States should be assured against the use or threat of use of nuclear weapons. Significant headway was made with the identification of two main questions regarding the application of the proposed arrangements:

(1) the criteria for extending the undertakings; and
(2) the exceptions in the undertakings associated with the right of self-defence.

The Group made significant progress, from general to particular concepts, when it differentiated between the basic elements of several negotiating positions. The analysis highlights the fundamental differences, as well as the many uncertainties, contained in the security assurances offered individually by the nuclear-weapon States. The alternative elements extracted from the undertakings in 1980 were:

– pending nuclear disarmament, a complete prohibition on the use of nuclear weapons;

– the extension of arrangements, pending a complete prohibition on the use of nuclear weapons, to all non-nuclear-weapon States without any conditions or limitations;

– the extension of arrangements to all non-nuclear-weapon States which were not parties to the nuclear security arrangements of some nuclear Powers;

– the extension of arrangements to States which renounce the production and acquisition of nuclear weapons and which have no nuclear weapons on their territories or under their jurisdiction or control;

– the extension of arrangements to non-nuclear-weapon States Parties to the Non-Proliferation Treaty or any other comparable internationally binding commitment not to acquire nuclear explosive devices;

– the extension of arrangements to non-nuclear-weapon States Parties to a nuclear-weapon-free zone.[57]

During 1981 another two elements were differentiated and the formulations were expanded.[58] In view of the demonstrably incompatible positions that emerged, it became necessary to consider the possibility of interim arrangements. An effort to narrow the gap between the varying positions led to a proposal for the Security Council, on the recommendation of the General Assembly, to adopt concrete measures for the assurance of non-nuclear-weapon States. Neither this, nor any other compromise suggestion has been acceptable to all power blocks. The most favourable assessment of the negotiation was made by Ambassador Saw Hlaing of Burma, who stated that –

> In an effort to find [such] a common formula or approach, the *Ad Hoc* Working Group, under the chairmanship of Minister Ciarrapico of Italy, has mobilized all its negotiating power to reconcile different formulations into a cohesive one that would be acceptable to all.[59]

By the end of 1981, although important progress had been made in identifying the points of agreement and disagreement, the terms of a universally acceptable convention could not be formulated, nor could the several unilateral undertakings be given a universally acknowledged legal character.

E. *A Comprehensive Programme of Disarmament*

When first formulated, this topic was envisaged as a long term agenda for the negotiation of arms control issues. It consisted of the restatement of NAC priorities that had already been identified in the Final Document and had been re-evaluated, without any substantial changes, by the Disarmament Commission during its 1979 Session. The substantive issues had also been elaborated, once more, in a Draft Declaration designating the 1980s as the Second United Nations Decade on Disarmament. Nevertheless, the Committee on Disarmament set up an *Ad Hoc* Working Group to prepare a text.

Subsequently, it was decided by the Preparatory Committee for SSD II, that adoption of the Comprehensive Programme was to be the cornerstone of deliberations at the Special Session. As a consequence, during 1981, the subject was addressed with renewed vigour, as indicated by the 41 working papers submitted on the Comprehensive Programme of Disarmament to the Committee on Disarmament during 1981, in addition to the official documents presented to the Committee.[60]

While the submissions contain many variations of the general theme, there was no change in the consensus, repeatedly reiterated in 1980 and 1981, that the Final Document agreed to at SSD I should form the basis of the Comprehensive Programme, and that there should be no departure from its terms. For example, in the draft submitted by Australia, Belgium, Federal Republic of Germany, Japan and the United Kingdom, it was noted that –

> The present draft is based on the Final Document of the First Special Session of the General Assembly devoted to Disarmament, in which the Comprehensive Programme was outlined as encompassing all measures thought to be advisable in order to ensure that the goal of general and complete disarmament under effective international control becomes a reality, and on the Elements of a Comprehensive Programme of Disarmament which have been adopted by the Disarmament Commission. The draft reflects in particular the discussions and negotiations held so far in the Committee on Disarmament and the report of the *Ad Hoc* Working Group on the Comprehensive Programme.[61]

The submission of the Group of 21 on the principles to be embodied in the Comprehensive Programme, assumed as axiomatic that all the principles contained in the Final Document would be included, adding that, 'even those that are not to be found in the Final Document but which may be found appropriate', should be included.[62]

The Socialist States have also maintained a similar position, as stated at the inception of negotiations on the Comprehensive Programme in the Committee by the delegate of the Soviet Union, Ambassador V.L. Issraelyan. He said –

> The Soviet delegation considers, as previously, that in the elaboration of a comprehensive programme of disarmament, States must above all adhere unswervingly to the provisions contained in the Final Document of the special session of the General Assembly devoted to Disarmament and in the Commission's report, and must strictly comply with the balanced formulations which, as we all recall, were arrived at with such great difficulty.[63]

As the Comprehensive Programme, by definition, encompasses all NAC programmes, the discrepancy in proposed formulations of the document under consideration was to be expected. However, the area of most acute contention has been the binding character of the undertaking to be attributed to every State prepared to adopt the text. Many of the States that consented to the Final Document at the conclusion of SSD I, advised the Working Group that they regarded more concrete undertakings, as to the treaties into which they would be prepared to enter in the future, to be impractical. In particular, they objected to the proposal put forward by developing States, that rigid time frames should be set for the completion of the various phases of arms control.

The arguments presented had not persuaded the States belonging to the Group of 21, by the time the Committee rose prior to the commencement of the 36th regular Session of the General Assembly, when the original demands were restated in the following terms –

> The Group of 21 attaches considerable importance to the adoption of the Comprehensive Programme of Disarmament at the second special session of the United Nations General Assembly devoted to disarmament. To be meaningful, the Programme must contain concrete disarmament measures in defined stages leading to the ultimate [goal] of general and complete disarmament within an agreed time frame. In accordance with provisions of paragraph 38 of the Final Document which refers, *inter alia*, to the negotiation of a treaty on general and complete disarmament, a Comprehensive Programme of Disarmament should create obligations on the part of all States to implement the measures included in the Programme.[64]

There is no possibility of the Western States entering into a treaty, or even consenting to a declaration, which requires them to undertake international obligations the terms of which have not been settled. In the domestic jurisdictions of those States, a contract to enter into further contracts that are only vaguely defined in character, would be adjudged void or voidable on account of uncertainty. Indeed the proposition to impose rigid time frames on negotiations runs counter to every known principle of law, domestic and international, because it seeks to make legal entities responsible for events that are, at least in part, beyond their control.

Evaluation of the Committee's Norm Creating Role

Despite frequent references in the Committee to the legal nature of its undertaking to create internationally binding agreements, the formulation of relevant legal principles has been invariably vague, and often subordinated to the exigencies of a particular advantage sought.

The problem has arisen with each major topic discussed. For instance, during negotiations on radiological weapons, the rules of treaty interpretation with respect to the definition of the weapons were disregarded. Concerning the cessation of the nuclear arms race and nuclear disarmament, the existence of any rights of non-nuclear-weapon States to become involved in treaties only applicable to nuclear-weapon States, remained unresolved. In the case of assurances to non-nuclear-weapon States, the 'binding' nature of unilateral undertakings – made at international conferences, in Security Council resolutions, or incorporated into General Assembly declarations – was not determined. In connection with a comprehensive programme of disarmament, the Committee failed to face up to the legal implications of attempting to impose time frames on negotiations.

With respect to a CTB, a legal approach to a non-legal matter could have been beneficial. As it was, no attempt was made to determine the degree of certainty required to amount to an 'adequate' level of verification, although this was the issue said to prevent agreement. There can be little substance in an agreement if there is no possibility of discerning whether or not its terms are implemented. Yet, if the certainty of instant discovery of every possible breach is to be the criterion of adequate verification, then the possibility of further NAC agreements can be dismissed. It would be appropriate, therefore, to delineate the approximate requirements of adequate verification of an agreement.

It is worth noting that the above issues have not been widely discussed by international lawyers beyond the United Nations, which indicates a dichotomy between the theory and practice of international law regarding NAC. Lack of concern to pursue a consistent approach to international law by NAC negotiators, is matched by a corresponding absence of interest by international lawyers to enquire into the legal implications of ongoing NAC negotiations. There are no doubt substantial justifications for this tendency. One reason could be the fragile quality of international discourse on military matters, and the resulting need to put civility and tact ahead of precise formulations that could expose questionable motives too pointedly.

Being the only multilateral negotiating body on arms control, the Committee is a microcosm, burdened with all the problems associated with NAC in the context of a divided world. The prevailing ethos in the Committee is predicated on the interests of power blocks, primarily those of NATO, the Warsaw Pact States and Non-aligned. Negotiating patterns reveal the presumption by each power block that any negotiating position acceptable to the others is likely to be disadvantageous to itself. Whatever sense there may be of common purpose, to escape the physical danger and economic and social burdens posed by the nuclear arms race, appears to be outweighed by the presumption of implacable hostility. This could be the paramount reason why the rate of negotiations is so slow.

The distrust between States is compounded by the technical complexity of the issues being negotiated. Neither concessions nor demands can be readily evaluated in their true colours. Even relatively simple issues, such as the proposal for the cessation of the manufacture of fissionable materials for weapons purposes, can be interpreted by the adversary block to be an excuse for gathering military intelligence under the guise of verification. Alternately, sweeping proposals for halting and reversing the nuclear arms race are looked upon as mere propaganda, designed to weaken the resolve of other peoples to defend themselves.

Concurrently with the above difficulties, co-operation between the Superpowers, as in their joint attempts to inhibit horizontal proliferation, or to conclude a treaty on radiological weapons, is immediately under suspicion by the Non-aligned, who fear a conspiracy against themselves by the militarily and economically powerful North.

Many difficulties can also be traced to internal communications problems shared by legal and technical experts in their contacts with policy-makers within their own countries. Legal analysis of international problems tends not to probe beyond the persona of the State. It is assumed that States conduct themselves in their own best interests *vis-à-vis* other States, on the basis of adequate knowledge and foresight. While not necessarily acting for the benefit of all their citizens, it is also taken for granted that at least the welfare of Governments in power and their supporters are well served. These assumptions are not invariably correct with respect to nuclear arms policies. In reality, the inflexibility of the one party system, preoccupation with domestic politics in the Western democracies, and the absence of stable government prevalent among developing States, prevent administrations from fully utilising expert advice available on NAC issues that could best serve their long term interests.

The most difficult stance for any State to adopt in the long term interests of its people, is to make a magnanimous gesture in its day to day relations with other States. On the other hand, if all of the above-mentioned problems were to be overcome and one of the power blocks, or individual States, were to make an unequivocally generous NAC gesture, it could well be interpreted by all other States as a sign of fear and weakness, to be exploited with more stringent demands, or even covert threats.

Concerning a somewhat analogous case already adverted to, when concessions were repeatedly made by one side, each concession was greeted by a further objection. In that case, for a period of many years, a Comprehensive Test-Ban was ruled out by the United States on the grounds that the Soviet Union refused to permit on site inspections; to include peaceful nuclear explosions in the proposed treaty; to co-operate in a seismological network to monitor nuclear explosions; and because the Soviet Union required that all nuclear-weapon States take part in the agreement from the outset. Having conceded all of those issues, albeit gradually, to the satisfaction of Western arms control experts, the United States and the United Kingdom are still unwilling to end nuclear weapons tests on the ground that verification procedures are not absolutely foolproof.

Conversely, States often adopt extreme negotiating positions with the intention of subsequently making apparent concessions regarding matters that should have been conceded at the outset. Apropos to the above-mentioned case, the United States and the United Kingdom could assert that objections to their various demands over the years were unjustified from the outset.

These difficult circumstances reinforce the short term interests of States to equivocate and to delay decisions. Although the postponement of NAC decisions may be inimical to the long term interests of States, the short term interests usually prevail. It was probably in recognition of the lack of short term incentives for NAC that prompted Ireland, in a submission to SSD I, to propose that such incentives be deliberately devised. [65]

Based on the analogy of the manner in which societies maintain cohesion within the State, Ireland's approach was very apt. The measure of success in any area of endeavour tends to correlate with the extent to which long term interests can be equated with short term satisfactions. For instance, within States, rewards are given to young people long before they are able to contribute productive work. Incentives are given to industry to establish export outlets, and honours are awarded to those who perform tasks that are especially valued by society. The perpetuation of national entities is not only the result of sanctions and commands administered by the sovereign, as Austin postulated, [66] nor imposed by the rest of society. On the contrary, most importantly, the State offers its citizens a series of immediate benefits.

It could well be, that all of the formidable problems associated with speedy conclusion of NAC agreements would be overcome if adequate short term rewards for doing so could be devised. The proposal for direct diversion of a proportion of funds earmarked for armaments to the needy people of the world, especially in the developing countries, which was the cornerstone of the Irish proposal, has the disadvantage that the benefit would go to those who have the least influence in halting the nuclear arms race. Thus, the persuasive influence of the scheme, which has been reiterated many times by other States, has proved to be insufficient.

While there are immediate benefits to be derived from the promotion of friendly relations between States within each of the power blocks, at the inter-block level the stigma of being lenient with a perceived enemy evidently outweighs other considerations from the individual statesman's point of view – at least in most countries. States that have been active in NAC endeavours, in keeping with long term rather than short term interests, like Austria, Mexico, Nigeria, Romania, Sweden and Yugoslavia, have been given the honour of frequently having their nationals elected to sensitive posts in the NAC negotiating process, such as chairmen of working groups, conference preparatory committees, *Ad Hoc* committees etc. But these distinctions are clearly not sufficiently rewarding to induce the overwhelming majority of States to make greater efforts in the NAC field.

Although, judged by historical standards, the Committee on Disarmament has made a notable impact, it has failed to live up to the high expectations that accompanied its foundation, even if the intangible benefits to be derived from its mere existence are taken into account. For instance, the contribution of the Committee cannot be adequately assessed on the basis of its formal meetings alone, because that gives no credit to initiatives taken at informal, exploratory negotiations. During 1980, for example, the Committee held 45 informal meetings regarding which no formal records are publicly available.

Another intangible function performed by the Committee is to consolidate world opinion for the retention of NAC agreements already in existence. This was pointed out by the delegate of Australia, Ambassador R.A. Walker, who, while acknowledging the limitations imposed on the Committee resulting from 'the current international situation', asserted that the work of the Committee was 'more important than ever'. He regarded it as a positive achievement of the arms control process that, despite international stresses –

> The edifice of international disarmament agreements built up over the previous decade survived and there was, moreover, a widespread reaffirmation of these existing agreements.[67]

All of the above factors have to be taken into account when evaluating the Committee's performance. They can also throw light on why, for example, the size of delegations and supportive staff accorded to the Committee are disproportionately small compared with the gigantic task they are required to perform, and why blatant obstruction by some States has been tolerated.

During 1980 obstruction and delay in the work of the Committee mainly took the form of extended procedural interventions. The adverse consequences of this have been partly countered by delegating most of the substantive work of the Committee to *Ad Hoc* Working Groups. The additional delegation of most procedural matters to a further working group, or to a sub-committee, could go a long way towards making the Committee more effective than it is. As the delegate of Mexico, Ambassador A. Garcia Robles, pointed out –

> The lengthy discussions in the Committee this year, on the question of requests for participation received from States not members of the Committee have resulted in a deplorable loss of time which has had a very harmful effect on the substantive negotiations which should constitute the principal function of this multilateral negotiating body on disarmament.[68]

Of course, improved staffing and better machinery provisions could not, in themselves, improve the Committee's performance in the face of widespread determination to stall its work. However, at a time of mere hesitation and vacillation, the prevailing conditions and procedures of work could have a strong influence on the rate and content of NAC negotiations. In those circumstances, under sound procedural conditions, any deliberate obstruction would have to be in blatant opposition to the great majority, which is a stance that States generally try to avoid at the United Nations.

Probably as the result of loss of face by the States mainly responsible for the administrative delays in 1980, this problem was largely overcome in the course of the following year. However, it has been widely acknowledged that during 1981, the Committee's work was seriously impaired by what was referred to as 'the adverse trends in the international situation',[69] which prevented significant progress in negotiations on most items on the agenda, 'especially the items to which the United Nations General Assembly has accorded the highest priority'.[70]

At the commencement of the Committee's 1981 session, the approach by Western medium Powers was to advocate modest but readily achievable goals. The Canadian delegate, Ambassador D.S. McPhail, observed that –

> ... the Committee on Disarmament does not work in a vacuum, but is influenced by the international environment ... We should therefore limit our objectives to realistic proposals lending themselves to items where prospects of agreement are high or where we have reasonable chances of achieving consensus. Only through registering progress can we be confident that the credibility of the CD will be strengthened.[71]

The Socialist view coincided with those sentiments, as advanced by the delegate of the German Democratic Republic, Ambassador G. Herder, saying –

> Mr Chairman, never before has the responsibility that rests with the Committee on Disarmament, as the single multilateral forum for disarmament negotiations, been so apparent as now in view of the complicated and aggravated international situation. The delegation of the German Democratic Republic believes that the Committee should make more vigorous efforts now to achieve tangible progress at least on the most important issues on its agenda.[72]

Yet, by the end of 1981, failure to reach agreement on the contents of any NAC treaty or protocol, demonstrated the limitations of the Committee's influence.

No achievements were attained by the Committee during its two 1982 Sessions[73] to warrant a re-evaluation of its work. The most significant development that occurred did not affect NAC directly, although it signalled a somewhat more constructive general approach. This became evident in the very businesslike negotiations, by members of all the power blocs, with respect to the outlawing of chemical weapons.[74] Determined efforts were also made on all sides to confront the most destabilising aspect of NAC, namely the spread of the arms race to outer space. However, only preliminary discussions, both formal and informal, were held on that subject.[75]

Notes

1 The International Law Commission has not been directly involved in norm creation for NAC. Regarding international norm creation in other (some related) subject areas, see *Review of the Multilateral Treaty-Making Process* A/35/312/Add. 2 of 28 August 1980.

2 Refer to n.1.

3 E.g. Ohlin, Göran, 'Can World Order be Negotiated?' *The Spirit of Uppsala* (JUS 81) Manuscript No. 42 p. 10 – 'It is undeniable that personal qualities matter greatly in international negotiation. In postwar development cooperation the vitality, determination, and charisma of some outstanding personalities is recognized to have been of decisive importance in overcoming the inertia of governments and rallying them to greater commitments in the joint interest.'

4 CD/PV. 146 of 13 August 1981, p. 10.

5 Suy, Erik, 'A New International Law for a New World Order', *The Spirit of Uppsala* (JUS 81) Manuscript No. 43 p. 7.

6 Id. pp. 12-15.

7 *Final Document* of SSD I, A/RES/S-10/2 para. 120; *Report of the Committee on Disarmament* A/34/27 and Corr. 1.

8 CD/222 of 19 August 1981, p. 1.

9 *Report of the Committee on Disarmament* to the General Assembly (1980) CD/139.

10 *Report of the Committee on Disarmament* to the General Assembly (1981) CD/228.

11 CD/221 of 18 August 1981, p. 1.

12 A/35/257.

13 CD/61 of 1980.

14 CD/119 of 1980.

15 Conclusion reached in the study on a *Comprehensive Nuclear Test-Ban* A/35/257 para. 154, endorsed by many States including Sweden, as stated by delegate to the Committee on Disarmament, Ambassador I. Thorsson – 'We are convinced, however, that the means of verification in relation to nuclear tests that exist now are fully adequate to police a three-year moratorium.' CD/PV. 101 of 3 February 1981, p. 26.

16 *Tripartite Report to the Committee on Disarmament* CD/130 of 1980.

17 CD/150 of 12 February 1981.

18 CD/210 of 12 August 1981.

19 Id. p. 3.

20 As a preliminary step, the Canadian delegate to the CD suggested that China and France might sign the Partial Test-Ban Treaty, CD/PV. 156 p. 11 of 1982.

21 CD/194 of 13 July 1981, p. 1; In 1982, when the Working Group on a CTB was formed, China and France refrained from participating in its work.
22 CD/222 of 19 August 1981, p. 1.
23 CD/PV. 94 of July 1980, p. 7.
24 CD/204 of 30 July 1981, p. 1.
25 CD/31 and CD/32 of 1979.
26 CD/224 of 20 August 1981, p. 2.
27 Report of the Working Group on Radiological Weapons CD/218 of 14 August 1981; For 1979-80 negotiations, CD/104 of 1980.
28 CD/PV. 137 of 14 July 1981, p. 8.
29 CD/PV. 122 of 7 April 1981, p. 21.
30 Id. p. 18.
31 Id. p. 13.
32 CD/218 of 14 August 1981, p. 9.
33 Id. p. 13.
34 Id. p. 19.
35 See report of assessment by US Dept. of Defence by Andrews, Walter, 'Soviet Military Space Threat Bared', *Army Times*, 8 March 1982, p. 7., indicating that the weapons may be operational by 1983.
36 CD/218 p. 24.
37 CD/174 of 7 April 1981.
38 The attention of the CD was drawn to the work of the ICDSI by Mexico, in CD/143 of 11 February 1981 and CD/188 of 17 June 1981.
39 CD/PV. 128 of 11 June 1981, p. 15.
40 CD/90 of 1980.
41 CD/4 of 1979 and CD/109 of 1980.
42 CD/PV.128 of 11 June 1981, p. 16.
43 CD/180 of 1981, p. 1.
44 Ibid.
45 Ibid.
46 Id. p. 2.
47 CD/222 of 19 August 1981, p. 3.
48 The resolution was adopted by 10 votes to none, with 5 abstentions – with operative paragraphs as follows:
     '1. Recognizes that aggression with nuclear weapons or the threat of such aggression against a non-nuclear-weapon State would create a situation in which the Security Council, and above all its nuclear-weapon State permanent members, would have to act immediately in accordance with their obligations under the United Nations Charter;
     '2. Welcomes the intention expressed by certain States that they will provide or support immediate assistance, in accordance with the Charter, to any non-nuclear-weapon State Party to the Treaty on the Non-Proliferation of Nuclear Weapons that is a victim of an act or an object of a threat of aggression in which nuclear weapons are used;
     '3. Reaffirms in particular the inherent right, recognized under Article 51 of the Charter, of individual and collective self-defence if an armed attack occurs against a Member of the United Nations, until the Security Council has taken measures necessary to maintain international peace and security.'
49 CD/133 of 1980.
50 CD/139 of 1980.
51 Ibid.
52 Ibid.

53 Ibid.
54 Infra Chapter 7, 'Generally Accepted Principles of International Law'.
55 CD/27 of 1979.
56 CD/177 of 10 April 1981, pp. 1, 2 and 4.
57 CD/125 of 1980.
58 CD/215 of 1981 pp. 4-5.
59 CD/PV. 139 of 21 July 1981, p. 34.
60 CD/217 of 17 August 1981.
61 CD/205 of 31 July 1981, p. 2. (CD/CPD/WP. 52)
62 CD/208 of 10 August 1981, p. 1 (CD/CPD/WP. 55)
63 CD/PV.95 of 31 July 1980, p. 18.
64 CD/222 of 19 August 1981, p. 3.
65 A/S-10/AC. 1/21 of 9 June 1978.
66 Austin, John, *The Philosophy of Positive Law* (J. Murray, London 1885, 5th Ed. by R. Campbell).
67 CD/PV. 102 of 5 February 1981, pp. 12-13.
68 CD/PV. 95 of 31 July 1980, p. 8.
69 CD/222 of 19 August 1981, p. 1.
70 Ibid.
71 CD/PV. 103 of 10 February 1981, p. 15.
72 CD/PV. 102 of 5 February 1981, p. 7.
73 Working Paper No. 74/Rev. 1 of 17 September 1982.
74 CD/334 of 1982.
75 Working Paper No. 74/Rev. 1, paras. 97-105.

CHAPTER 4

Norm Creation by Deliberation for the Control of Nuclear Arms

Multilateral Norm Creation for NAC by Deliberation

The distinction between seeking international agreement by negotiation, on the one hand, and deliberation, on the other, is rather fluid. The term 'negotiation' carries a stronger inference of exploration to find common interests and of bargaining to reach a compromise, whereas the term 'deliberation' connotes decision making with greater reliance on the force of numbers, or other authority, to overcome differences. Yet each function contains elements of the other.

In the course of establishing norms for NAC at the United Nations, the two functions are divided between the Committee on Disarmament, being the negotiating forum, and a number of other bodies, all of which are said to have deliberative functions. A submission by the United Kingdom to a United Nations Study on institutional arrangements relating to the process of disarmament, referred to the relationship between the two functions. The submission stated –

> Deliberation on the political and security aspects of disarmament should be carried out in the established United Nations institutions: the First Committee of the General Assembly and the Disarmament Commission. In the view of the United Kingdom, discussions in the First Committee would be assisted by the introduction of a properly structured agenda; every effort could then be made to concentrate on achieving resolutions which would be directly helpful to the disarmament negotiations, and not merely declaratory statements.[1]

There is also a demarcation of significance within the deliberative function. One type of NAC deliberation (a) is concerned with the establishment of international standards regarding the testing, deployment and use of given nuclear weapons. The other type of NAC deliberation (b) deals with the implementation of those standards in a way that can have exhortative, administrative or adjudicative overtones. Deliberative function (a) usually culminates in a resolution approving the elements of a proposed NAC agreement, say, a CTB Treaty. Deliberative function (b) could take several forms such as a resolution or declaration, calling on States to conclude a treaty in accordance with the agreed elements. Alternatively, it could involve setting up a subsidiary body to assist with NAC verification, for example an International Satellite Monitoring Agency. Or it could entail the adoption of an expert report apportioning the blame for a nuclear explosion contrary to the principles stated in the standard setting resolution (a).

Deliberative NAC functions for standard establishment and implementation overlap in the various United Nations bodies, and several, or all deliberative functions may be accomplished within the scope of one resolution. However, with the streamlining of United Nations activity, it could become necessary to formalise the distinctions, at least between (a) the standard establishing tasks in arms control, and (b) the standard adherence tasks. The United Nations bodies most involved in norm creation by deliberation for NAC are the Disarmament Commission, the First Committee and the General Assembly.

The Disarmament Commission

Like the Committee on Disarmament, the Disarmament Commission was also reconstituted at SSD I, after its suspension as an active forum in 1965. In its earlier capacity it had the hybrid functions of negotiating and planning. On reconstitution, it has retained only its overall planning role, with representation from all State Members of the United Nations.[2] While the Commission may utilise voting procedures for the resolution of differences among delegates, in conformity with the rules of procedure relating to the Committees of the General Assembly, in the words of the Final Document of SSD I, it was requested to make 'every effort' to achieve consensus in its deliberations.

The Commission has the task, *inter alia,* of overall planning for NAC, yet it has marked time with repeated reiteration of disarmament priorities. During 1979 the Commission considered priorities under the heading of the 'Elements of a Comprehensive Programme of Disarmament'.[3] In 1980 it did so, pursuant to a General Assembly directive, in the context of the elements of the Declaration of the 1980s as the Second Disarmament Decade.[4]

In 1981 the Commission at last abandoned its regurgitation of the disarmament priorities, already successfully established during the course of SSD I, and concentrated on three other items largely unrelated to NAC. These were, the elaboration of a general approach to negotiations on conventional disarmament; the reduction of military budgets; and the general approach to the study on disarmament relating to conventional weapons. By the end of 1981, the Commission produced a Background Paper on principles and ideas with respect to the freezing and reduction of military expenditures. The Disarmament Commission Chairman also presented two Working Papers to the General Assembly, both in the form of guidelines relating to conventional disarmament.[5]

In its position of a disarmament norm creating body, so thoroughly overhauled as to be virtually a new organ, the Disarmament Commission has yet to find a useful niche. Its formal mandate is that of a deliberative body, subsidiary to the General Assembly, required to 'consider and make recommendations on various problems in the field of disarmament'.

Since its reconstitution, the Commission has laboured under a fourfold inhibition. It has been obliged to avoid infringing the domain of three United Nations bodies with similar but more specific mandates than its own. These were the Committee on Disarmament, the First Committee and the Preparatory Committee for SSD II. The Committee on Disarmament is charged with the conduct of all specific arms control and disarmament negotiations on a continuing basis. The First Committee debates disarmament and arms control draft resolutions in preparation for their endorsement by the General Assembly. The Preparatory Committee for SSD II, a temporary body functioning during 1981–2, has had the task of collating the agenda for the Session, involving an overview of arms control and disarmament issues. Finally, the Commission had to avoid reopening controversies successfully settled at SSD I, which were negotiated at the time with extraordinary diplomatic skill, to the satisfaction of all concerned.

The reconstitution of the Disarmament Commission had been the result of pressure from the Third World for a disarmament forum where all States would be represented.[6] States that did not expect to participate in the Committee on Disarmament were particularly adamant about the need for the Commission. At present, it is in reality an arms control forum in reserve. An NAC issue could arise at any time, ideally suited for preliminary investigation by the Commission before referral to the overburdened Committee on Disarmament.[7]

The First Committee

This is one of the seven Main Committees serving the General Assembly. The First Committee is the most authoritative recommendatory body on NAC matters, preparing draft resolutions in the form of direct recommendations for consideration by the General Assembly. It does so on the basis of reports referred to it by the Committee on Disarmament, the Disarmament Commission, as well as several expert and procedural reports of the Secretary-General, drawn up or processed by his Secretariat. The recommendations are almost invariably accepted by the General Assembly.

Many of the diplomats who participate in the work of the Committee on Disarmament, also attend the Sessions of the First Committee and the relevant General Assembly debates. Unlike the Committee on Disarmament, the First Committee is not restricted to agreement by consensus. However, the range of subjects discussed is very similar because, since 1978, the First Committee has been required to restrict the range of its deliberations to 'questions of disarmament and related international security questions'.[8] Within the context of that mandate NAC is the Committee's chief preoccupation.

As part of its standard establishing functions, the First Committee prepared many recommendations during 1980 for the General Assembly on topics relating to NAC, including the following significant items:

– *Non-stationing of nuclear weapons on the territories of States where there are no such weapons at present* – requesting the Committee on Disarmament to elaborate an international agreement on the subject.

– *Study on all aspects of regional disarmament* – deciding to transmit a recent Expert Study on the subject to the Disarmament Commission and requesting the Secretary-General to refer the Study to the Committee on Disarmament.

– *Study on nuclear weapons* – inviting regional intergovernmental organisations, the Specialised Agencies of the United Nations and the International Atomic Energy Agency, as well as national and international organisations, to make the report widely known.

– *Conclusion of an international convention prohibiting the development, production, stockpiling and use of radiological weapons* – calling on the Committee on Disarmament to continue negotiations with a view to elaborating a treaty.

– *Prohibition of the production of fissionable material for weapons purposes* – requesting the Committee on Disarmament to pursue its consideration and prohibition of the production of fissionable material for nuclear weapons and other nuclear explosive devices.

– *Strategic arms limitation talks* – urging the two signatory States to ratify the SALT II Treaty and, in the meantime, to refrain from any act which would defeat the object and purpose of the Treaty, in conformity with the provisions of the Vienna Convention on the Law of Treaties; and expressing satisfaction that agreement had been reached on basic guidelines for subsequent negotiations on the limitation of strategic arms.

Further to the requirement, in Article 13 of the Charter, for the General Assembly to 'initiate studies', the First Committee has increasingly devoted more attention to the commissioning of expert reports on NAC related issues.[9] Generally that is done pursuant to the recommendations of the Advisory Board on Disarmament Studies. This has become an effective aspect of the process of norm creation, by helping to overcome difficulties resulting from the complex and technical nature of NAC. From the time that the studies are first contemplated, the choice of the particular issues to be investigated, the formulation and presentation of the terms of reference, and the selection of representative and universally respected experts, all entail a high level of consensus with respect to the goals of NAC.

The reports themselves enjoy an excellent reputation, making both the factual and evaluative findings acceptable as common ground. Exceptionally influential expert reports on NAC in recent years have been the Study on a Comprehensive Nuclear Test-Ban, and the Comprehensive Study on Nuclear Weapons, both submitted to the 35th Session of the General Assembly. For example, the latter report was endorsed by the General Assembly as –

> . . . a highly significant statement on present nuclear arsenals, the trends in their technological development and the effects of their use, as well as on the various doctrines of deterrence and the security implications of the continued quantitative and qualitative development of nuclear-weapon systems and also a reminder of the need for efforts to increase the political will necessary for effective disarmament measures.[10]

Such highly prized evaluations have proved to be effective launching pads for further agreement on NAC principles. The tendency was very pronounced at SSD I, where background papers, prepared largely by disarmament experts and co-ordinated by the Centre for Disarmament, formed the basis for much of the ultimate consensus reached.[11] The groundwork provided by the experts helps to make resolutions on NAC factually non-controversial and sound. Hence, the resulting consensus tends to be based on realistic expectations and is therefore more likely to have long term effectiveness.

As well as preparing the final drafts of resolutions containing NAC initiatives for approval by the General Assembly, standard adherence tasks are sometimes referred to the First Committee regarding the application and enforcement of NAC measures. The Committee's functions have not been prominent, in this regard, with respect to either vertical or horizontal proliferation. In the former case, compliance issues have been negotiated by the Superpowers directly or via the Standing Consultative Commission established for that purpose, while in the latter case, the two Review Conferences of the Non-Proliferation Treaty have been the major forums for compliance issues.

The potential of the First Committee for the initiation of measures to ensure compliance with NAC agreements was reinforced by a prolonged debate in the Committee, in December 1980. It concerned an arms control matter not associated with nuclear weapons, namely, compliance with the 1925 Geneva Protocol for the Prohibition of the Use in War of Asphyxiating, Poisonous or Other Gases, and of Bacteriological Methods of Warfare, which entered into force on 8 February 1928.

The debate concerned the appropriate methods to be employed for the verification of compliance with arms control agreements, in a manner equally relevant to all forms of arms control measures. The debate helped to circumscribe the parameters of United Nations competence for verification and enforcement, as well as to examine the modalities of any actions to be taken.

Positions adopted by the various States are particularly relevant to compliance measures for NAC, as four of the eight multilateral treaties listed in Table I (see page 24) specifically refer to United Nations assistance with compliance problems, while the other four treaties do not exclude United Nations involvement. Further, Non-aligned States assert, with increasing conviction, that even the bilateral treaties between the nuclear-weapon States are not immune from oversight by the United Nations, although neither the theoretical nor the practical implications of the principle have been examined beyond the proposition that anything that directly affects the peace and security of third countries is their rightful concern.

The Protocol under discussion[12] relates to the *use* of chemical and bacteriological weapons, to be distinguished from the Draft Convention on Chemical Weapons, which refers not only to the use of such weapons but also to the research, development, manufacture, stockpiling and transfer of the weapons. The operative paragraphs of the Protocol provide that –

Whereas the use in war of asphyxiating, poisonous or other gases and all analogous liquids, materials or devices has been justly condemned by the general opinion of the civilized world,
Whereas the prohibition of such use has been declared in Treaties to which the majority of Powers in the world are parties,
And to the end that this prohibition shall be universally accepted as a part of international law, binding alike the conscience and the practice of nations,
The undersigned Plenipotentiaries, in the name of their Governments,

80

declare that the high contracting parties, so far as they are not already parties to Treaties prohibiting such use, accept their prohibition, agree to extend this prohibition to the use of bacteriological methods of warfare and agree to be bound as between themselves according to the terms of this declaration.

No provision is made in the Protocol for the establishment of machinery to investigate reports about the activities prohibited by it. In November 1980, Canada, France, the Federal Republic of Germany, the Netherlands, New Zealand, Norway, Turkey and Spain, sponsored a draft resolution in the First Committee requesting the Secretary-General to carry out an investigation, concerning 'the alleged use of chemical weapons and to assess the extent of the damage caused by the use of chemical weapons'.[13]

The allegations were referred to as 'recent reports' of use of the weapons 'in recent years', 'in various parts of the world'. It was contended in a preambular paragraph of the resolution that, 'the continued authority of the Protocol and relevant rules of customary international law' required that all reports regarding alleged breach should be properly investigated, notwithstanding the absence of verification clauses in the Protocol.[14]

The investigation was to be carried out by the Secretary-General, a procedure that in practice means the United Nations Secretariat, to be aided by medical and technical experts. By the terms of the draft resolution, the Secretary-General was to collect and examine evidence, including on-site evidence, but only with the consent of the countries concerned. Information was to be sought from Governments, international organisations, and any other sources deemed 'necessary' after consulting 'the States on whose territories the use of chemical weapons has been reported', with reference to their proposals on how the investigation should be carried out. The precise aim of the investigation was to be the ascertainment of the facts regarding the allegations and the assessment of the extent of the damage caused. The Secretary-General was called on to submit a report on the matter at the following Session of the General Assembly.[15]

The draft resolution was adopted with some amendments after a week-long debate, by 62 votes to 17, with 32 abstentions, the remaining States having refrained from participation in the vote. However, while the particular issue was thus settled, several important questions have remained undecided. The debate had been acrimonious and highly politicised, with much more attention devoted to scoring debating points than to constructing an enduring framework for promoting compliance with arms control agreements. In this connection the Mexican representative, Ambassador A. Garcia Robles, remarked that 'I do not believe we have had any topic which has been as controversial in all our deliberations and has given rise to such strong statements as this one'.[16]

Nevertheless, some significant principles were advanced regarding, for instance, the circumstances in which alleged breach of arms control agreements should be investigated by the United Nations, and the most desirable form that such investigations should take.

The United States put forward the view that all 'reports that cast doubt on solemn international agreements' should be investigated 'to make certain that no accusations are made without solid foundation in fact and to clarify ambiguous situations . . .'[17] Other Western States largely concurred with that point of view. For example, the United Kingdom supported the investigation of 'numerous reports' of breach, in circumstances 'where the facts cannot be ascertained through generally available information'.[18]

France concurred that it was appropriate and necessary to conduct an investigation, because information existed 'from various sources regarding the possible use of chemical weapons'.[19] Sweden also supported the investigation on the ground that, 'in principle, every request from a State Member of the United Nations for clarification of the reality behind allegations of such a serious character' deserved support.[20] New Zealand, which introduced the proposal for an enquiry, similarly took the position that it is necessary 'to look into all reports of alleged use' of the prohibited weapons, and to conduct a 'speedy' and 'impartial' investigation by a 'respected body'.[21]

States that opposed the resolution contended that it would constitute a dangerous precedent to initiate an enquiry based on 'so-called information of a more than dubious character',[22] as stated by the German Democratic Republic. Even more scathingly, Vietnam referred to the evidence prompting the investigation to be 'fables invented by the radio broadcasting service of the so-called Democratic Kampuchea . . .'[23] In a similar vein, the representative of the Lao People's Democratic Republic accused the resolution's sponsors of seeking to set up the enquiry merely as an excuse for intervening in the internal affairs of States by the use of 'unreliable information'. He further contended that –

> If they have been unable to name or identify the countries which are contravening the Geneva Protocol, with solid proof in support of the allegation, it would be entirely futile to spend any length of time on this draft resolution.[24]

Legal arguments opposed to the draft resolution were presented mainly by Non-aligned and Socialist States, stated in their most succinct form by Madagascar. The delegate of Madagascar claimed that 'any violation of the Protocol should be referred to a conference of the contracting parties'.[25] It was argued that State participation in any treaty, more particularly a disarmament treaty, is substantially influenced by procedures to ensure compliance, and that therefore it is unfair to change those procedures. Furthermore, even if the United Nations were to substitute new methods for the verification of complaints, Madagascar claimed that referral to a committee of enquiry would not be an appropriate method.

Elaborating this point further, the delegate referred to the verification and adjudication of complaints pursuant to the provisions of the Convention on the Prohibition of Military or Any Other Hostile Use of Environmental Modification Techniques, which was opened for signature in 1977.[26] Madagascar found that to be a preferable method of investigation. In addition to the other disadvantages of the verification procedure proposed in the draft, Madagascar asserted that the 'independence of the functions of the Secretary-General' would be placed in jeopardy if the Secretariat were required to conduct the enquiry, and that the procedure would establish an unfortunate precedent.

The representative of the Byelorussian Soviet Socialist Republic presented the main objection raised by Madagascar in the form of a general principle, stating that, 'any question connected with the status of an international legal instrument is exclusively a matter for the parties to that instrument'.[27] That outlook, which is consistent with the Vienna Convention on the Law of Treaties, would exclude United Nations involvement altogether. However, the provisions of NAC treaties, as well as the predominant view presented at the debate, favour a United Nations role at some stages in promoting arms control compliance, although there is no accepted procedure as to which organs should initiate or carry out the function.

In practical terms, an investigation by the Secretary-General with the aid of experts, at the request of the General Assembly, would not be very different from an investigation by the Security Council, having overcome the veto provisions of that body. The personnel engaged to conduct the investigation are likely to be the same and a report back to the General Assembly, instead of the Security Council, would not preclude the Security Council from taking any action flowing from the report.

Article 11(2) requires the General Assembly to refer any question on which *action* is needed to the Security Council. The meaning of 'action', in this context, has been interpreted by the International Court of Justice to refer only to issues where enforcement is contemplated.[28] In accordance with that Opinion of the Court, the General Assembly may set up 'commissions or other bodies' in connection with the implementation of its recommendations on peace and security issues. The Court qualified the Assembly's competence to do so only to the following extent –

> The functions of the General Assembly for which it may establish such subsidiary organs include, for example, investigation, observation and supervision, but *the way in which such subsidiary organs are utilized depends on the consent of the State or States concerned.*[29]

While in accordance with Article 10, the General Assembly may *discuss* any issues; Article 11(3) especially empowers the Assembly to 'call the attention of the Security Council to situations which are likely to endanger international peace and security'. The parallel provision with respect to the Security Council, in Article 34, empowers that body to *investigate* any dispute and to evaluate whether it poses a threat to peace and security.

Several Non-aligned States, among them both those that voted for the resolution, like Sweden, and those that abstained, like Mexico, voiced deep concern regarding the dearth of agreed principles, as well as machinery provisions, to cope with issues of the kind confronted in the debate. The representative of Sweden maintained, regarding the exchange that had just taken place in the First Committee that it was –

> . . . shown beyond any doubt how well founded is the demand of the neutral and non-aligned countries for a strengthened complaints procedure in matters of this kind, so that what we have experienced here this year can be avoided in the future.[30]

It may indeed be preferable that the mode of establishing any investigatory group on compliance matters should be predetermined by national vote, rather than left to decisions within the Secretariat, although such decisions are also made on the basis of international consensus. The ultimate discretion for all decisions of the Secretariat, which in theory rests with the Secretary-General, is usually not exercised by him personally. Decision-making bodies of the Secretariat are selected on the basis of equitable geographical distribution, taking into account major political alignments. Due to their composition, those bodies tend to reflect national attitudes, notwithstanding the provisions of Article 100 of the Charter, prohibiting Governments from seeking to influence persons employed in the Secretariat.

Thus, the most important factor is not which body sets up the enquiry, but the existence of machinery provisions, and the acceptance of operating principles, on a permanent basis. If those provisions were to apply to appropriate NAC issues, it would preclude the exacerbation of disputes with conflicts over implementation procedures, whether they be the task of the Secretariat or of other organs of the United Nations.

The General Assembly

At its normal Sessions, the General Assembly predominantly acts as a rubber stamp to approve the NAC and other disarmament related recommendations of the First Committee. Its vast agenda, encompassing all the areas of endeavour of the United Nations, leaves little opportunity for substantive input with respect to NAC. However, the Assembly has an important role as publicist for the dissemination of information and advocacy of NAC related problems.

Resolutions of the General Assembly, as the apex of the United Nations norm creating system, have often laid the groundwork for NAC agreements. For example, the Partial Test-Ban Treaty was preceded by many General Assembly resolutions on the subject, including Resolutions 1648 (XVI) and 1762A (XVII). The Outer Space Treaty closely followed the principles laid down in the Declaration of Legal Principles Governing the Activities of States in the Exploration and Use of Outer Space, in Resolution 1962 (XVIII), together with associated principles laid down in Resolution 1884 (XVIII). The Treaty of Tlateloclo was preceded by United Nations consensus as expressed in Resolution 1911 (XVIII), while both that Treaty, and the Non-Proliferation Treaty, were in keeping with United Nations deliberations, for instance as expressed in Resolution 808 (IX), advocating 'the total prohibition of the use and manufacture of nuclear weapons and weapons of mass destruction of every type'. International opinion demanding limitation of the vertical nuclear arms race, which eventually led to the SALT Treaties, was expressed long before in Resolution 2028 (XX), establishing the principle of balanced responsibilities between nuclear and non-nuclear-weapon States for the implementation of NAC.

The General Assembly assumes a more significant initiating role in the creation of norms during its Special Sessions. So far, only one of those has concerned NAC, under the general aegis of disarmament. The world-wide consensus arrived at in the course of the five weeks of SSD I, held in May-June of 1978, has restructured both the theoretical approach and the organizational machinery of NAC negotiation.

The Special Session was preceded by protracted negotiations of the agenda and of draft documents. These preliminary negotiations were conducted by a Preparatory Committee, composed of a globally representative group of States, which considered proposals and draft formulations from all Member States of the United Nations wishing to contribute. The intractable nature of the issues that had to be resolved was demonstrated by extensive disagreements, many of which remained contentious at the beginning of the Special Session, evident from the large number of bracketed alternative formulations in the draft documents.[31]

Ultimate resolution of all controversies by the General Assembly on that occasion, in the form of a consensus Final Document,[32] was an extraordinary achievement. At the time, the dilution of substance for the sake of consensus was regarded by many statesmen and commentators as a failing, but the passage of time has demonstrated the paramount importance of universal endorsement of fundamental arms control precepts.

The document consists of 126 paragraphs, being in the format of an Introduction, a Declaration, the Programme of Action, and a collation of Machinery Provisions. While it is directed to arms control issues in all their aspects, attention is predominantly focused on the solution of NAC problems including general principles, accepted negotiating positions, priorities, and guiding precepts. Interrelationships are noted and steps to be taken for the attainment of solutions are indicated. The document concludes with 33 arms control proposals submitted by Member States, which could not be debated at the Session due to insufficient time, but which are gradually being more fully elaborated.

The most notable aspect of this concise document is the Programme of Action, which, in the terms of Article 44 –

. . . enumerates the specific measures of disarmament which should be implemented over the next few years, as well as other measures and studies to prepare the way for future negotiations and for progress towards general and complete disarmament.[33]

The Programme of Action designates the following priorities for negotiation: nuclear weapons; other weapons of mass destruction, including chemical weapons; conventional weapons, including any which may be deemed to be excessively injurious or to have indiscriminate effects; and reduction of armed forces.[34]

The achievement of having reached universal agreement in favour of the document can be measured less in terms of the arms control achievements that have flown from it, than in the fervent adherence to its provisions over the years. In the period between the two Special Sessions on disarmament there has been no substantial departure, in any negotiating or deliberating organ of the United Nations, from the objectives, priorities and methods designated in the Final Document.

The Final Document is the best demonstration of both the strengths and the weaknesses of the General Assembly in its approach to NAC. To acknowledge that the document contains a fundamental and irreconcilable theoretical flaw, is not tantamount to a denial of its pioneering and overwhelming significance. In 1978 no higher consensus could have been reached regarding the theoretical-legal basis of disarmament. Yet, for the achievement of positive NAC measures greater commitment would be required, generally referred to as 'political will'. *The General Assembly has, so far, failed to acknowledge that the measure of political will is the extent of the sacrifices that a State is prepared to incur in the short term, in order to attain the long term benefits of arms control and disarmament.*

Consequently, an erroneous juxtaposition of objectives and possibilities permeates the Final Document, which was not queried by any State at the Special Session or since but which, nevertheless, excludes the possibility of substantial progress in NAC if the defective principle is to set the standard of international conduct.[35] The defect lies in the concept of disarmament, in particular NAC, without sacrifice in the short term. The various manifestations of the erroneous principle in the Final Document will be examined in turn.

First, arms control and disarmament conducted on 'the principle of undiminished security of the parties', in paragraphs 22, 29, 49 and 83, is often not possible. At the least, there is usually an element of uncertainty about the operation of an NAC agreement. The equivalent operation of arms control measures can virtually never be ascertained with accuracy, while the difficulty of so doing is exacerbated by inevitable partisan assessments of security interests by potential enemies. As a theoretical concept, the aim of *minimising* security imbalance that may be temporarily, and unavoidably, caused by arms control measures, would be far more constructive. Simultaneously, and most importantly, there should be an expression of accolade for States prepared to proceed with arms control measures despite their possible short term drawbacks. This is not feasible while the fiction of 'undiminished security' persists.

Second, the Final Document lays down the theoretical requirement, in paragraph 31, of 'adequate measures of verification satisfactory to all parties concerned'. Such measures of verification have not been found in practice, nor are they likely to become possible in the future. Again, the formulation should have been to strive for those objectives not to make their non-attainment an excuse for delays in arms control measures, especially in the control of nuclear arms.

Third, paragraphs 36, 68, 69 and 70, advocate the principle of the 'inalienable right of all States' to the acquisition of all levels of nuclear technology and proclaim this to be consistent with non-proliferation goals. The 'appropriate' safeguards, referred to in those paragraphs, do not exist and will become even less appropriate when the more sophisticated reactors come into operation, to be described in Chapter 8.

Fourth, paragraph 40 states the self-evident principle that universality of multilateral disarmament agreements would make those agreements more effective. It would seem necessary to take that concept one step further by proclaiming that it is the duty of each State to make whatever concessions it can, without flagrantly jeopardising its own security, to comply with applicable multilateral arms control agreements.

Fifth, as a corollary to the concept of undiminished security and strictly equivalent obligations in arms control, the Final Document belittles the importance of unilateral measures, especially relevant in the field of NAC. Paragraphs 41 and 114 merely refer in passing to that method of arms control. However, as a confidence builder, as a means of overcoming an impasse, and as a method of shaming other States into emulating the initiative, unilateral steps in arms control warrant greater emphasis.

Sixth, the document offers no satisfactory formula, even in theory, for measuring the equitable rate of NAC or any type of arms control, while acknowledging, in paragraph 49, the various stages of armament attained by different States. It is merely observed in paragraphs 48 and 81, that the most heavily armed States have the greatest responsibility in that regard. The imprecision countenanced has resulted in a variety of arms control formulae, with all States contending that the others should be first to practice arms limitation. China and France, in particular, have explained their refusal to accede to multilateral NAC agreements on the grounds that they are entitled to maintain a relativity with the Superpowers.

Since the acquisition of nuclear weapons capability by the United States, to the present day, the Soviet Union has asserted that it feels threatened unless it can attain and maintain approximate parity with the forces of the United States and the nuclear prowess of other nuclear-weapon States. The United Kingdom has not claimed a right to parity, but the constant upgrading of that State's nuclear forces, including the envisaged replacement of the existing *Polaris* with *Trident* missiles, is in itself an assertion that the nexus between the strength of its nuclear forces and those of other States is to be retained.

The two subsequent nuclear Powers, France and China, have persistently asserted that they have a right to maintain a nuclear weapons capability proportionate to that of the two Superpowers. In the case of France, it is sought merely not to fall behind the rate of development pursued by the other Powers, as stated during SSD I by the French Minister for Foreign Affairs –

> As for France, it would take appropriate action on the basis of such reductions only if there were a change in the extent of the disparity persisting between those two arsenals and its own arsenal, which France keeps at its disposal to ensure the security and credibility of its deterrent.[36]

China, on the other hand, does not only assert the right to ensure that the gap between its own nuclear prowess and those of other nuclear-weapon States is not increased but claims the right to *close* the gap.

The proposition that all States have an equal right to weapons, including nuclear weapons for defence, is theoretically unassailable. Fortunately, non-nuclear-weapon States have so far refrained from giving it practical application, no doubt in appreciation of the appalling practical consequences that it would have. The Chinese position in mid-1981 was explained in *Beijing Review* by Mu Youlin, the International Editor, as follows –

. . . we demand that the two super powers, the Soviet Union and the United States, should be the first to reduce their armaments. When the huge gap between them and the other nuclear states and militarily significant states is closed, the latter should then join them in reducing armaments proportionately. This is fair and reasonable.[37]

In this exposition only the *militarily significant* were designated as having the right to nuclear-weapons parity with the Superpowers, with no attempt to define which States may be included in that category.

Nothing would be gained from re-writing every clause of the Final Document which reflects the notion that disarmament and, in particular, the NAC component of disarmament, can be accomplished without risks and generous gestures. Nor does acknowledgement of the unavoidability of short term imbalances in the NAC process have to be presented in the form of amendments. The appropriate changes could be adopted in the course of applying the various arms control measures, by making the neccessary additions to and elaborations of the concepts contained in the Final Document.

The General Assembly could again contribute to such developments at subsequent Special Sessions on disarmament, when time is provided and world leaders are available to discuss the issues in some depth. Otherwise, the General Assembly is in a position to collaborate with other United Nations bodies, like the Committee on Disarmament, the Disarmament Commission, the First Committee, and other bodies referred to at the commencement of Chapter 3, by putting the stamp of approval on proposals emanating from them.

Notes

1 A/36/392 of 11 September 1981, p. 70.
2 Final Document of SSD I, A/RES/S-10/2, para. 118.
3 Pursuant to A/RES/33/91A.
4 Pursuant to A/RES/34/75.
5 These were only interim reports, see A/36/752 p. 19.
6 See *Disarmament: a Periodic Review by the United Nations* May 1979, Vol. II No. 1 p. 53.
7 Reports of the reconstituted disarmament Commission, Supplement No. 42.
8 Final Document of SSD I, op.cit. Art. 117.
9 Since SSD I the following studies on NAC or relating to it have been completed:
   - All the Aspects of Regional Disarmament, A/35/416.
   - Comprehensive Study on Confidence Building Measures, A/36/474.
   - Comprehensive Nuclear Test-Ban, A/35/257.
   - Comprehensive Study on Nuclear Weapons, A/35/392.
   - Implications of Establishing an International Satellite Monitoring Agency, A/AC.206/14.
   - Institutional Arrangements Relating to the Process of Disarmament, A/36/392.
   - Israeli Nuclear Armament – A/36/431.
   - Reduction of Military Budgets: International Reporting of Military Expenditures, A/35/479.

- Relationship Between Disarmament and Development, A/36/356.
- Relationship Between Disarmament and International Security, A/36/597.
- South Africa's Plan and Capability in the Nuclear Field, A/35/402.
10 In accordance with the *Report of the First Committee* A/35/699 para. IIF. II.
11 See series A/AC. 187/- of 1977-8.
12 See A/C. 1/35/PV. 47, p. 26.
13 A/C.1/35/L. 43, Rev. 2.
14 Ibid.
15 Ibid.
16 A/C. 1/35/PV. 44, p. 31.
17 Id. PV. 49, p. 2.
18 Id. PV. 48, p. 56.
19 Id. PV. 45, p. 26.
20 Id. PV. 48, p. 56.
21 Id. PV. 43, pp. 5-6.
22 Id. PV. 47, p. 40.
23 Id. PV. 43, p. 11.
24 Id. PV. 43, p. 26.
25 Id. PV. 47, p. 35.
26 As appears in Table I, the Treaty, *inter alia*, empowers the Security Council to investigate the evidence supporting a complaint of breach.
27 A/C. 1/35/PV. 47, p. 37.
28 *Expenses* case, I.C.J. Rep. 1962, p. 153.
29 Ibid. emphasis added.
30 A/C. 1/35/PV. 48, p. 56.
31 E.g. see A/S-10/AC. 1/37 adopted on 23 June 1978 by the *Ad Hoc* Committee of SSD I, only one week prior to the end of the Session when the Final Document was adopted
32 A/RES/S-10/2.
33 Id. p. 11.
34 Id. Art. 45.
35 C.f. the view of Finland in a submission to the Preparatory Committee for SSD II, A/AC. 206/12 of 12 May 1981, pp. 2-3 – 'Irrespective of the type of approach and extent of measures envisaged, i.e., whether comprehensive or sectorial, regional or universal, bilateral or global, the fundamental principles for negotiations incorporated and elaborated in the Final Document of the first special session retain their validity. They include, *inter alia*, the following:
- All States have the obligation to contribute to efforts in the field of disarmament, and all States should benefit from them;
- They have the right to participate on an equal footing in the multilateral negotiations which have a direct bearing on their security;
- Disarmament measures should ensure, in an equitable and balanced manner, the right of all States to security; all States and groups of States should obtain equal advantage at every stage;
- Success of disarmament efforts presupposes a balance and a strict observance of mutual obligations;
- Adequate measures for verification satisfactory to all parties should be provided for in order to attain the confidence of all parties in the implementation of agreements.'
36 SSD I, Ninth Plenary Mtg. ref. *The United Nations Disarmament Yearbook* Vol. 4 of 1979 (New York 1980) p. 117.
37 *Beijing Review*, 20 July 1981, No. 29, p. 3.

CHAPTER 5

The International Legal System
and Nuclear Arms Control

International Law in a Changing World

The practice of negotiating, entering into, and adhering to the NAC agreements in Tables I and II (see pages 24 and 28), has been undertaken by all parties at all times on the understanding that those actions were within the framework of a system of international law. It is the existence of international law which induces the expectation that an agreement between States will be adhered to, together with other shared expectations regarding the consequences that will flow from its adoption, such as the predictable interpretation of forms and expressions used.

Changes in the international legal system can therefore affect international agreements, as can the responsiveness or lack of responsiveness of international law to economic, political, social and technological changes throughout the world. The interrelationship between individual international agreements, and the milieu in which they operate, has been noted by the General Assembly. For example, the influence of changing social, economic and political conditions on the development of international law has been considered by the General Assembly in relation to drawing up the programme of the International Law Commission.[1]

In practice, international law has responded more or less adequately to the needs of many of the growth areas of interaction at an international level,[2] as, for example, in maritime law, civil aviation, diplomatic law, communications, and a variety of commercial transactions. As a result, the theoretical basis of international law is rarely examined with respect to agreements between States regarding these and many other areas of activity. By contrast, the nature and domain of international law become matters of concern and analysis in relation to those aspects of international life which have so far eluded regulation by adequate and predictable rules,[3] including issues of international security, peace and war. As NAC is among the least satisfactory areas of contemporary international endeavour, it is appropriate that the difficulties encountered in the negotiation of NAC agreements should lead to reappraisals of the precepts of international law applying to them.

The advent of nuclear weapons and other weapons of mass destruction has introduced a fundamental new element into international law, namely, the exclusion of all-out war as the ultimate method for resolving intractable hostilities between States. The traditional maxim of *jus ad bellum*, the right to resort to war, was already seriously challenged during the period between the world wars, but it was only after World War II that it was abandoned altogether.[4] Elaborating on provisions in the Covenant of the

League of Nations, the General Treaty for the Renunciation of War, known as the Briand-Kellog Pact, was signed in 1928. Article I of the Treaty states –

> The High Contracting Parties solemnly declare in the names of their respective peoples that they condemn recourse to war for the solution of international controversies, and renounce it as an instrument of national policy in their relations with one another.

The sixty-three States, currently Parties to the Treaty in 1939, included the belligerents in the war which broke out at that time. Clear words of the Treaty had been interpreted only five years previously, by the International Law Association, to mean that –

> A signatory State which threatens to resort to armed force for the solution of an international dispute or conflict is guilty of a violation of the Pact.[5]

The United Nations Charter of 1945, in Article 2, paragraphs (3) and (4), requires all Members, being Parties to the Treaty of the Charter of the United Nations, to 'settle their international disputes by peaceful means' and to 'refrain in their international relations from the threat or use of force'. Article 2, by itself, could be interpreted to outlaw armaments other than those required for the maintenance of internal order. However, Article 51, which gives Members the right of individual or collective self-defence until such time as the Security Council may be able to protect them from armed attack, has been relied upon as justification for the maintenance and unprecedented growth of armed forces, and the stockpiling of armaments, including nuclear arms.

One of the four stated aims of the United Nations Charter is –

> . . . to establish conditions under which justice and respect for the obligations arising from treaties and other sources of international law can be maintained . . .

Since the Charter was signed in San Francisco, on 26 June 1945, the avoidance of world war has been generally attributed to the fear of 'unacceptable damage' from enemy nuclear weapons, rather than obedience to the undertakings pledged at the inception of the United Nations and subsequently. Foreseeably, States will continue, in the main, to be motivated by considerations of self-preservation and self-advancement until a condition of much greater international cohesion is attained than at present.

International law merely facilitates methods to be devised for the attainment of those national objectives that are shared by States at the international level. As the avoidance of nuclear war is the most ardently shared objective of the current era, the appropriate utilisation of the international legal system in that endeavour becomes uniquely relevant. Existing NAC treaties, and innumerable General Assembly resolutions, bear witness to the expectation that the elaboration and observance of international law will be able to prevent nuclear confrontation in the short term, and facilitate the conversion of a fragile balance of terror into a secure system of assurances in the long term.

Traditional Approaches to International Law

Due to the ossification of the basic tenets of *jus gentium*, the Greek, Roman and mediaeval approach to international law still carry definitive influence. The age and continuity of the system are regarded as virtues by many contemporary jurists, one of whom expressed this widely held sentiment with the observation that, 'the structure of the international system . . . appears to be still tremendously solid since its distant origins back in the Middle Ages'.[6]

While there are countless divergencies regarding the finer points of international legal theory, it is generally assumed that international law is an entity with inevitable characteristics and that it only remains to establish what those characteristics are. For example, Professor Eric Suy, Legal Counsel of the United Nations, asks some of the most fundamental questions confronting international law today, but he asks them as if the answers merely had to be *discovered* and not *invented*. In 1981, speaking of the status of resolutions adopted by the United Nations and its specialised agencies, he said –

> Contemporary international law must deal with these new 'prescriptive norms'. There are a number of questions that must be examined. For example, to what extent *are* the decisions of those various inter-governmental organizations creating new norms? *Are* they legal norms? *Are* they generally binding legal norms, or *are* some of them binding and some not? How *are* the binding norms determined?[7]

The attributes of international law are enumerated and analysed as if they were the properties of a specific object known to exist, whose chemical and physical composition have not yet been adequately identified and measured. Consequently, questions about reconciling contemporary needs with persisting traditions are invariably posed within a static framework.

It is asked, 'How can resolutions of the General Assembly becomes rules of customary international law in order that they may be incorporated into the international legal system?'. It is not asked, 'How could international legal theory be recast so as to accommodate recommendations of the General Assembly in a way that would attribute to those resolutions a normative influence on international conduct commensurate with their *de facto* authority?' and 'How could this be achieved without ascribing to the States that voted for those resolutions an intention to create positive law which they patently did not envisage?'. In other words, the possibility of remoulding the basic principles of international law, in order to make them convenient tools for the attainment of current objectives, has not been adequately confronted.

The conduct between States in their dealings with each other at the time of the Greek and Roman Empires, and later, in the Middle Ages, consisted of rules that were so obvious and elementary as to be identifiable with the rules of nature *jus naturale*.[8] With the spread of religious concepts during the Middle Ages, the law of nature was equated with the Divine Law in the writings of theologians such as Saint Thomas of Aquinas. Christian and Moslem[9] religious writers and *naturalists* as they came to be called, shared the view that law, including international law, was part of an immutable body of precepts waiting to be discovered. European scholars, who developed and refined this concept, included Thomas Rutherford,[10] Jean Jacques Burlemaqui[11] and De Rayneval.[12]

As international contacts become more frequent and increasingly complex, subjective evaluations of what the natural or Divine Law was, inevitably conflicted with different evaluations made by other individuals. Telling examples can be found among the views propounded by Samuel Pufendorf,[13] Professor of Law at the University of Heidelberg, Germany, in the mid-Seventeenth Century. The reputed foremost exponent of the naturalist school, Pufendorf claimed, for instance, that no mercy should be shown in war, as this would merely delay a return to a condition of peace, being the natural state of existence. Predictably, the proposition did not meet with universal concurrence.

In response to the untenable conflicts arising from the naturalist interpretation, there emerged an approach to international law which, after theoretical elaboration, became known as the *positivist* school. Cornelius Van Bynkershock,[14] Johann Jacob Moser[15] and George Friedrich von Martens[16] are regarded as the founders of the positivist school, which maintained that the sources of international law are international obligations explicitly undertaken by sovereign States.[17] This view proved to be much less tenable in the Eighteenth Century than it would be today, due to the sparseness of treaties and other overt undertakings. Technical difficulties, including rudimentary communications and the absence of efficient bureaucratic structures, made the conclusion of treaties and the ascertainment of other agreements very difficult. Hence, it was not possible to adhere to the positivist principle because often no agreements existed to guide the resolution of new international conflicts as they arose.

The theory that best suited the requirements of Euro-centred international life from the Seventeenth Century to modern times, made a pragmatic compromise between naturalists and positivists, without acknowledging its pragmatic origins. The compromise approach relied on the obscure language of treaties; whatever scant evidence there was of international customs; together with naturally fertile imaginations, to adduce the rules and principles of international law. The followers of this compromise approach were the first to state their views in detail. They became known as the *Grotians*, after Hugo Grotius[18] who is regarded as the 'father' of international law. The theory on which the Grotian school was based differentiated between what was believed to be *necessary* law, and merely *voluntary* law. The former was believed to be the law of nature and God, while the latter consisted of treaties and customs made by men to suit the exigencies of given situations. These views were further elaborated by Christian Wolff and Emmerich de Vattel.

Seventeenth and Eighteenth Century doctrines still form the basis of international law as it is known today. These vague and jumbled concepts, with generations of elaborations and qualifications haphazardly appended, provided the basis of the jurisdiction of the Permanent Court of International Justice. In 1945 they were incorporated into the Statute of the International Court of Justice which, in Article 38 (1) designates the terms of reference of international law to be –

a. international conventions, whether general or particular, establishing rules expressly recognized by the contesting States;
b. international custom, as evidence of a general practice accepted as law;
c. the general principles of law recognized by civilized nations;
d. subject to the provisions of Article 59, judicial decisions and the teachings of the most highly qualified publicists of the various nations, as subsidiary means for the determination of rules of law.

The drafters of the Court's Statute deliberately chose to establish no hierarchy of precedence to be attributed to paragraphs a, b and c of Article 38 (1), on the ground that this would be self-evident to international lawyers.

The aforementioned exposition of sources, in the light of the meanings that those concepts have acquired over the centuries, is the only guide to the nature and content of international law to be applied under the Statute, which enjoys the concurrence of 157 Member States of the United Nations pledged by Treaty. In practice, relevant treaties are usually given *precedence* over other sources as the best evidence of State consent in any matter, while as between treaties, obligations under the Charter are claimed, by Article 103, to prevail in case of conflict with 'any other international agreement'. However, the Statute does not recognise the theoretical *supremacy* of treaties.

According to the West European tradition of international law, enshrined in the Statute, the most highly respected source of international law is *custom*.[19] Therefore, when Professor Bo Johnson, legal adviser of the Ministry for Foreign Affairs of Sweden, claimed in 1981 that 'the first and most important source of this "international law" is the custom of states',[20] he was describing the contemporary factual situation consistent with the provisions of the Charter.

International Custom and Nuclear Arms

We have seen that international agreements for NAC are an integral part of the international legal system, and that the international legal system is inextricably bound up with 'international custom as evidence of a general practice accepted as law'. It is not immaterial, therefore, that both the applicability of custom and the theoretical basis of the whole international legal system of which custom is a part, are in disarray. As Professor Grahl-Madsen said when opening the Joint UNITAR-Uppsala University Seminar on International Law –

I cannot see that we have any alternative to attempting to develop new and more efficient machinery for the progressive development of international law.[21]

Later in the Seminar, Professor Grahl-Madsen observed that –

Like the old Law of Nature, a customary law and legal principles developed in Europe can no longer serve as a solid basis for international law.[22]

Much of the criticism of international custom as applied by the International Court of Justice, is not of the concept of custom, but its affinity to West European values and approach to legality. While this is no doubt the case, criticism of this kind, emanating from the Socialist and recently independent States, has somewhat obscured more fundamental problems. When some of this criticism surfaced in 1974, during a debate in the Sixth Committee on the efficacy of the International Court of Justice, the United States, Canada, and Italy complained that –

> . . . the uncertainty of the content and scope of the rules which were applicable in the international sphere was a weakness; the Court's role and the law it applied should be clarified and strengthened.[23]

Uncertainty regarding the content of the rules of international custom, unless they are interpreted by a Court, can lead to difficulties. There is also uncertainty, *inter alia*, about how custom comes into being, its relevance to United Nations resolutions, how it can be renounced, and what States are bound by it.

It is well established that, in order to determine the existence of a rule of international custom, it is necessary to prove that States have acted in conformity with the rule, and that they have done this in the belief that they were legally obliged to do so.

There are several uncertainties, however, concerning what constitutes the required acts of States. For instance, it would be necessary to have a clear understanding as to what is regarded a sufficient number of States applying the rule. In the *Fisheries Jurisdiction* case, the Court declared that –

> States are on record as not supporting in fact and by their conduct the alleged maximum obligatory 12-mile rule. In these circumstances, the limited State practice confined to some 24 maritime countries cited by the Applicant in favour of such a rule cannot be considered to meet the requirement of generality demanded by Article 38 of the Court's Statute.[24]

Yet, in the *Anglo-Norwegian Fisheries* case, the Court relied largely on the practice of one State, the United Kingdom, stating –

> The notoriety of the facts, the general toleration of the international community, Great Britain's position in the North Sea, her own interest in the question, and her prolonged abstention would in any case warrant Norway's enforcement of her system against the United Kingdom.[25]

Another uncertainty is whether pronouncements of States accompanying custom creating acts should be taken into account. As the Court put it –

> There is at the moment great uncertainty as to the existing customary law on account of the conflicting and discordant practice of States. Once the uncertainty of such a practice is admitted, the impact of the aforesaid official pronouncements, declarations and proposals must undoubtedly have an unsettling effect on the crystallization of a still evolving customary law on the subject.[26]

In the circumstances it was thought unreasonable to discard official statements as to 'what States are prepared to claim and to acquiesce in . . .'[27]

In the *Asylum* case, the Court entertained the possibility of a rule of customary law developing in a region. The Court did not disapprove that –

> The Colombian Government has finally invoked 'American International Law in General'. In addition to the rules arising from agreements which have already been considered, it has relied on an alleged regional or local custom peculiar to Latin-American States.[28]

Provided that other necessary conditions were met, the Court took the view that recognition of a regional custom falls within the provisions of Article 38 of the Statute of the Court.[29]

The required duration of the State practice establishing the rule is also subject to wide variations. Whereas the original fiction was that the rules had been observed from time immemorial, contemporary writers speak of the possibility of 'instant custom' arising from United Nations resolutions, while in the dissenting Opinion of Judge Tanaka it was suggested in the *South West Africa* cases that –

> . . . the establishment of such a custom would require no more than one generation or even far less than that.[30]

Requirements regarding proof of the belief that a legal obligation exists are even more subject to doubt. The tortuous reasoning of the Permanent Court of International Justice in the *Lotus* case, is a pertinent illustration –

> Even if the rarity of the judicial decisions to be found among the reported cases were sufficient to prove in point of fact the circumstance alleged by the Agent for the French Government, it would merely show that States had often, in practice, abstained from instituting criminal proceedings, and not that they recognized themselves as being obliged to do so; for only if such abstention were based on their being conscious of having a duty to abstain would it be possible to speak of an international custom.[31]

A modern statement of the requirement appears in the judgment of the International Court of Justice in the *North Sea Continental Shelf* cases. There it was laid down that –

> Not only must the acts concerned amount to a settled practice, but they must also be such, or be carried out in such a way, as to be evidence of a belief that this practice is rendered obligatory by the existence of a rule of law requiring it. The need for such a belief, i.e. the existence of a subjective element, is implicit in the very notion of the *opinio juris sive necessitatis*. The States concerned must therefore feel that they are conforming to what amounts to a legal obligation.[32]

There are numerous further refinements and distinctions in relation to international custom, with a variety of views as to their exact application.[33] In one instance, it has been remarked with some exasperation that –

The complexity of the question of customary law is not diminished by the tension which exists between the application and interpretation of *general* principles and rules versus the creation and subsequent application of *detailed* rules.[34]

Indeed, the labyrinth of uncertainty that surrounds the concept of 'international custom, as evidence of a general practice accepted as law' is endless.

The above illustrations demonstrate that international law, as it relates to the notion of custom, is not suited for the establishment of the rights and duties of States in relation to NAC, or any other vital issue of international peace and security. Perhaps international custom is a useful concept with respect to subject areas where agreements are sparse and any definitive ruling is more important than the detailed content of a rule, as in demarcation and border disputes. In these and similar instances of moderate concern to States, where there is scant evidence of the law, customary rules may be helpful.

In regard to NAC, the most insidious aspect of international custom, as presently understood, is its possible admixture with treaty law. There have been suggestions that, providing a State does not expressly object to a 'norm creating' treaty in force among other States, and does not act in contravention of that treaty, it may be bound by the rules established in the treaty in the form of a rule of international customary law. Such an interpretation could be given, for example, to the States that have abided by the terms of the Non-Proliferation Treaty but which have not acceded to it.

Discussing the question as to what constitutes 'consent' and 'opposition' to an international custom, Professor Allan Rosas contended that –

> It seems pertinent to speak of *presumed* consent, which means that a state can become bound by a rule the creation of which it has not participated in as long as it has not clearly voiced its opposition. Perhaps this is better terminology than the often used expression 'tacit agreement', which despite the word 'tacit' seems to connote the idea of specific 'understandings' between the parties to a customary norm, something which might not correspond to reality.[35]

In modern national administrations, contemporary treaties that are relevant to a State, especially treaties relating to peace and security like NAC treaties, are continuously and carefully assessed. If they are not acceded to, that is positive proof that the State concerned does not wish to be bound. However, that State may agree with some aspects of the treaty and therefore comply with some or all of the provisions of the treaty, or it may be persuaded by one means or another to comply, despite fundamental reservations.

Although perhaps indistinguishable in terms of acts performed, there is a profound difference in principle between a State *acting as if* it were bound by an NAC treaty, and *giving its explicit consent* to be bound. Any legal fiction that may blur that distinction must be counterproductive in the longer period. That is so because, unless the theory reflects reality, it cannot change that reality constructively when the time for change has arrived. Even in the short term, all that the fiction of notional consent to NAC agreements could achieve, would be to add to the scepticism about the relevance of international law.

To assert the above is not to deny the beneficial influence that treaties can exert on third parties in standardising State conduct. The problem would only arise if it were sought to *bind* States to a course of action with a ruling of the Court. For example, Professor Thomas Franck pointed out –

> Also, when treaty provisions or law-declaring resolutions are adopted by consensus, these may so affect national conduct as to create 'instant' customary law. An example is the concept of the 200-mile economic zone, adopted by consensus at the Law of the Sea Conference, which immediately entered into the repertory of practice of enough states to raise the question whether, quite aside from the treaty, it does not thereby become universally sanctioned as customary law.[36]

While ineffective in its positive tenets to come to terms with the realities of contemporary inter-State relations, the general theory of international law, as far as it can be ascertained, also suffers from several important omissions. For example, it contains no coherent principles to distinguish between emerging norms and existing norms. Further, not only is no legal status accorded to non-procedural United Nations resolutions, but the current and potential adjudicative functions of the Security Council and General Assembly are ignored. It is little wonder then that Professor de Nascimento e Silva thought it appropriate, in 1981, to describe the present time as being –

> ... a period when international law is being subjected to challenge from so many quarters, when its very existence is being questioned not only by laymen but even by some lawyers, and when its relevance to international relations and to the regulation of concrete problems between States is constantly belittled.[37]

The anachronisms and uncertainties of international legal theory prejudice attempts to control nuclear arms. They detract from the authority of the International Court of Justice[38] and respect for the whole system of international law. Not surprisingly, only a small percentage of States has accepted the compulsory jurisdiction of the Court, and that percentage is shrinking. Today there are only forty-seven States that have made declarations under Article 36, paragraph (2) the Court's Statute, or made declarations under Article 36, paragraph (2), of the Statute of the Permanent Court of International Justice that are currently operative. It is about 30% of the present membership of the United Nations, whereas in 1950, 60% of United Nations Members had accepted the compulsory jurisdiction of the Court. Moreover, States that have done so, have mostly attached such rigorous conditions to their acceptances that they have little practical import.

A statement touching on these issues by Judge Robert Ago of the International Court of Justice, made in the course of an address to the International Law Commission in mid-1981, has been reported as follows –

> He said it would, in particular, be very dangerous to lose sight of the fact

that, following the profound changes that had occurred in the composition of the community of States, it had become both essential and urgent to define anew and with the participation of all concerned, the old customary law, to redefine it, to supplement it, and to invest it with the *clarity* characteristic of written, conventional law.[39]

The imprecision of the international legal system leaves the judges of the Court, as well as any arbitrators or negotiators who may wish to rely on the principles of international law, with vast areas of personal discretion. Few contemporary treaties, and none of the NAC treaties now in existence, require disputes to be adjudicated by the International Court of Justice. On the contrary, several of the multilateral NAC treaties specifically indicate that recourse to the Court is to be by mutual consent, while many NAC treaties designate alternative modes of settling disputes.

Notes

1 Res. 1505 (XV) of 12 December 1960.
2 C.f. Stone, Julius, *Of Law and Nations: Between Power Politics and Human Hopes* (William S. Hein and Co. Inc., Buffalo, New York 1974) p. 211 – 'I may recall here the astonishing observation of the late Sir Hersch Lauterpacht (with which I venture to agree) that "once we approach at close quarters practically any branch of international law we are driven, amidst some feeling of incredulity, to the conclusion that although there is as a rule a consensus of opinion on broad principle – even this may be an over-estimate in some cases – there is no semblance of agreement in relation to specific rules and problems".'
3 Schachter, Oscar, 'Towards a Theory of International Obligation', *The Effectiveness of International Decisions: Proceedings of the Conference of the American Society of International Law* (Oceana, Dobbs Ferry, NY 1971) p. 11. The author argues that the theory of international law has great relevance. With reference to 'conceptions as to the basis of obligation' he states – 'They come up in concrete controversies as to whether a rule of law has emerged or has been terminated; whether an event is a violation or a precedent; and whether practice under a treaty is accepted as law. They are involved in dealing with situations in which solemn declarations, couched in legal terminology, are adopted by official bodies which had no formal authority to lay down prescriptive rules. They come up when there is substantial variance between what is preached and what is practiced; or when consensus (or expectations) are limited in geographical terms or in duration. These are not, of course, new problems and over the years they have been the subject of much jurisprudential writing. But in the last few years the general problem has assumed a new dimension. The peculiar features of contemporary international society have generated considerable normative activity without at the same time involving commensurate use of the formal procedures for international legislation and adjudication.'
4 Arangio-Ruiz, Gaetano, *The United Nations Declaration on Friendly Relations and the System of the Sources of International Law* (Sijthoff & Nordhoff, Maryland 1979) p. 106. The author considers it an open question whether the loss of the right occurred between World Wars I and II or only as a consequence of the UN Charter.
5 *Report of the 38th Conference of the International Law Association*, Budapest 1934, p. 67.

6 Arangio-Ruiz, op.cit. p. 301.

7 Suy, Erik, 'A New International Law for a New World Order', *The Spirit of Uppsala* (JUS 81) Manuscript No. 43 p. 7., emphasis added.

8 Kronman, Anthony, 'Aristotle's Idea of Political Fraternity', *The American Journal of Jurisprudence*, 1979, Vol. 24 p. 114, *re*. the relationship between friendship and justice in political life.

9 See Rechid, Ahmed, *Islam and Jus Gentium*, The Hague Academy of International Law (1937); see also dissenting judgment of Judge Tarazi in the *Hostages* case p. 59.

10 Author of *Institutes of Natural Law*, 1754, England.

11 Author of *Principes de Droit de la Nature et des Gens*, Switzerland.

12 Author of *Institutions de Droit de la Nature et de Gens*, France.

13 Author of *De Jure Naturae et Gentium*, 1672, Germany.

14 Holland 1673-1743.

15 Germany 1701-1785.

16 Germany 1756-1821.

17 See Rumble, Wilfrid E., 'Divine Law, Utilitarian Ethics, and Positivist Jurisprudence: A Study of the Legal Philosophy of John Austin', *The American Journal of Jurisprudence*, 1979, Vol. 24 p. 139.

18 Holland 1583-1645.

19 For an examination of the relationship between formal and material sources of law and the foundation of international obligation see Schachter, Oscar, 'Towards a Theory of International Obligation', *The Effectiveness of International Decisions: Proceedings of the Conference of The American Society of International Law* (Oceana, Dobbs Ferry, NY 1971). The author lists the concepts that have been advanced as constituting the foundation of international obligation thus – Consent of states; Customary practice; A sense of 'rightness' – the juridical conscience; Natural law or natural reason; Social necessity; The will of the international community (the 'consensus' of the international community); Direct (or 'stigmatic') intuition; Common purposes of the participants; Effectiveness; Sanctions; 'Systemic' goals; Shared expectations as to authority, Rules of recognition.

20 Johnson, Bo, 'Changes in the Norms Guiding the International Legal System – History and Contemporary Trends', *The Spirit of Uppsala* (JUS 81) Manuscript No. 44 p. 23.

21 Grahl-Madsen, Atle, 'International Law for Our Times', *The Spirit of Uppsala* (JUS 81) Manuscript No. 41 p. 9.

22 Id. Background Paper on 'International Law and Organization for a New World Order', Manuscript p. 1.

23 *U.N. Yearbook* 1974 p. 833.

24 *Fisheries Jurisdiction* case (United Kingdom of Great Britain and Ireland v. Ireland) I.C.J. Rep. 1974 (Joint Sep. Op.) p. 50 para. 15.

25 *Anglo-Norwegian Fisheries* case (United Kingdom v. Norway) I.C.J. Rep. 1951, p. 139.

26 *Fisheries Jurisdiction* case (Joint Sep. Op.) I.C.J. Rep. 1974, p. 48 para. 12.

27 Ibid.

28 *Asylum* case (Colombia/Peru) I.C.J. Rep. 1950, p. 276.

29 Id. p. 276-7.

30 *South West Africa* case (Ethiopia v. South Africa; Liberia v. South Africa) I.C.J. Rep. 1966, p. 291.

31 The *Lotus* case (the Case of the S.S. 'Lotus') P.C.I.J. Ser. A. Judgment No. 9 (1927) p. 28.

32 *North Sea Continental Shelf* cases (Federal Republic of Germany/Denmark; Federal Republic of Germany/Netherlands) I.C.J. Rep. 1969 p. 44 para. 77.

33 E.g. those of Akehurst, M.B., *A Modern Introduction to International Law* (Allen & Unwin, London, 2nd Ed. 1971); D'Amato, A.A., Falk, R.A., and Weston, B.H., *International Law and World Order*; (St Paul, Minn. West 1980); Greig, D.W., *International Law* (Butterworths, London, 2nd Ed. 1976); Tunkin, G.I., *Theory of International Law* (Harvard Uni. Press, Cambridge, Mass. 1974); and Wolfke, K., *Custom in Present International Law* (Wroclaw, 1964).

34 Rosas, Allan, 'Customary Law: from "Universal" in a European System to "Regional" in a World System', *The Spirit of Uppsala* (JUS 81) Manuscript No. 56 p. 8.

35 Id. pp. 5-6.

36 Franck, Thomas M., 'Growth of the International Community and Qualitative Shift in International Legal Relations', *The Spirit of Uppsala* (JUS 81) Manuscript No. 54 p. 3.

37 Id. Nascimento e Silva, G.E., 'New Ways for Treaty-Making and International Legislation', Manuscript No. 71 pp. 1-2.

38 Gross, Leo, *The Future of the International Court of Justice* (Oceana, Dobbs Ferry, NY 1976), for an overview of the problems besetting the Court.

39 Report of the International Law Commission on the work of its thirty-third session, 4 May – 24 July 1981, Supp. No. 10 (A/36/10) p. 384; emphasis added.

CHAPTER 6

The Adjudication of Nuclear Arms Control Agreements

Settlement of NAC Disputes by the International Court

Two recent cases have been brought before the International Court of Justice, with attributes that indicate the extent of the Court's ability to settle international disputes involving NAC type issues. Although Article 59 of the Court's Statute provides that, 'The decision of the Court has no binding force except between the parties and in respect of that particular case', in practice the decisions and reasoning of the Court have been accorded high authority in subsequent cases. In Opinions handed down, judges have referred to passages from previous Opinions much more frequently than warranted by the tentative wording of Article 38(1) (d) of the Court's Statute.[1]

The cases to be examined are relevant to the adjudication of NAC disputes, not only on account of the persuasive influence likely to be exerted by the decisions reached and the principles enunciated, but also because the Court's evasion of substantive issues demonstrates the limits of its genuine competence.

The issue of nuclear testing in the atmosphere, in *Nuclear Tests (Australia v. France)*[2] and *Nuclear Tests (New Zealand v. France)*[3] (the *Nuclear Tests* case), concerned similar facts, relating to the detonation of nuclear devices in the South Pacific area by France. The other case was *United States of America v. Iran* (the *Hostages* case),[4] which concerned the capture of United States diplomatic and consular staff in Tehran. The last mentioned case was not related to nuclear arms in any way but it involved the interpretation of significant contemporary treaties under circumstances likely to prevail in relation to the breach of an NAC agreement.

The Nuclear Tests Case

In the *Nuclear Tests* case, Australia and New Zealand instituted proceedings against France, on 9 May 1973, alleging that the carrying out of atmospheric nuclear weapons tests in the South Pacific Ocean was not consistent with applicable rules of international law. The two States sought orders prohibiting the French Republic from carrying out any further nuclear tests of that nature. The Court's jurisdiction was invoked by the Applicants on the basis of the General Act for the Pacific Settlement of International Disputes,[5] and Articles 36 and 37 of the Statute of the International Court of Justice.

France failed to file a Counter-Memorial and did not appear at the hearing, informing the Court by letter that it did not intend to submit to the

Court's jurisdiction. France asked for the summary removal of the case on the basis that the Parties were not in conflict as to their legal rights and that nuclear tests did not violate any rules of international law.

Refusing to accede to the request by France, the Court made a Provisional Order, on 22 June 1973, requesting France to avoid nuclear tests that could deposit radioactive fallout on Australian and New Zealand territories. In defiance of the Provisional Order, France continued to conduct nuclear tests in the atmosphere in the prohibited area. The gesture could only be interpreted as a severe blow to the Court's prestige and it underlined the precarious nature of the Court's authority. However, a measure of lost ground was retrieved when, in mid-1974, a series of verbal and written statements were made by the President of the French Republic, French delegates at the United Nations and French Embassy officials to the effect that France was about to conclude its tests of nuclear weapons in the atmosphere. None of the statements by France indicated that the cessation of the tests was to be in response to the cases before the Court. On the contrary, it was pointed out that the change to underground nuclear tests was to be undertaken 'in the normal course of events'.[6] Nor did the statements give any undertaking that atmospheric tests would not be resumed at some future date.

By a majority of nine votes to six, the Court decided to attribute to the equivocal statements of intention by France the status of existing commitments to be recognised by international law[7] and asserted, on that basis, that the alleged dispute did not exist. In this way the Court avoided the necessity to adjudicate upon its own jurisdiction; the legal standing of the Applicants as members of a much wider class of States that may have incurred damage; and an assessment of the merits of the case.

In a closely argued and eminently logical joint dissenting Opinion, Judges Onyeama, Dillard, Jimenez de Arechaga and Sir Humphrey Waldock, argued that the Court had jurisdiction – both as to the legal nature of the dispute, and the legal standing of Australia and New Zealand to present their case in accordance with the practice of *actio popularis*. Further, the joint dissenting Opinion contended that the statements made by French officials, although accepted by the four judges as 'the French Government's unilateral undertaking', were not capable of 'affording the Applicant legal security of the same kind or degree as would result from a declaration by the Court specifying that such tests contravened general rules of international law applicable . . .'[8] Most importantly, the dissenting judges held that no undertaking could dispose of the dispute as to the general issue of the legality of nuclear testing in the Pacific region. The Applicants were therefore still entitled to a judgment. Hence, the judges who delivered the joint dissenting Opinion formed the view that the Court should have proceeded to hear and to adjudicate upon the merits of the case.

The majority of the Court put expediency before logic. Had the Court proceeded to adjudicate on the merits it would have been faced with an untenable situation. The Court would have been required to make pronouncements on various aspects of the applicability of customary international law to an NAC issue. This would have entailed the evaluation of several multilateral NAC treaties, a large number of General Assembly resolutions, the decisions of a World Conference of the United Nations,[9] as well as the findings of national and international scientific bodies.[10] There is no disrespect for judicial integrity in the proposition that the above, unstated but weighty considerations, may have prompted the decision reached by the majority of the Court.

The evidence presented in the written Pleadings referred to the large majority of eligible States Parties to the Partial Test-Ban Treaty, the Treaty of Tlatelolco and the Non-Proliferation Treaty, as well as to General Assembly Resolutions 1148 (XII) 1957, 1252 (XIII) 1958, 1379, 1402 (XVI) 1959, 1578 (XV) 1960, 1632 (XVI) 1961, 1948 (XVI) 1961, 1762A (XVII) 1962, 1910 (XVIII) 1963, 2032 (XX) 1965, 2163 (XXI) 1966, 2343 (XXII) 1967, 2455 (XXIII) 1968, 2604B (XXIV) 1969, 2661A (XXV) 1970, 2663B (XXV) 1970, 2828 (XXVI) 1971, and 2934A to C (XXVII) 1972,[11] all of which, in one way or another, condemned atmospheric nuclear tests. A resolution and a declaration were also cited from the United Nations sponsored Stockholm World Conference on the Human Environment, which deplored the tests on the grounds of environmental damage allegedly caused by them. In addition, references were made to the findings of the International Commission on Radiological Protection and the United Nations Scientific Committee on the Effects of Atomic Radiation. However, with respect to none of the Treaties, resolutions or evaluations just referred to, had France committed herself to the views expressed by the overwhelming majority of mankind.

If the concept of customary international law is to have any practical meaning as an expression of international opinion and commitment, then the conclusiveness of the evidence prepared by the Applicants, that customary international law prohibited the testing of nuclear devices in the atmosphere, was unassailable. The evidence could have withstood any reasonable test, irrespective of the precise view taken regarding the mode of creation and the applicability of international custom. Therefore, had the case been decided on the merits, the Court would have been obliged to make a clear-cut ruling on whether or not a State had the right to withhold its consent to be bound by a general rule of customary law. The only way to avoid the issue with a substantive argument, would have been to maintain the untenable assertion that the existence of the rule had not been established. Faced with such a dilemma, the majority of judges chose to evade the substantive issues.[12]

The prudence of that decision can be demonstrated by exploring in greater detail the problems that would have confronted the Court had it proceeded to consider those substantive issues. For the Court to do so, would have entailed a determination as to whether France was bound by treaty, by custom, or otherwise to observe the putative rule of general customary international law prohibiting the detonation of a nuclear device in the atmosphere.[13] Had the Court decided that France was not bound, it would have done so in defiance of the overwhelming weight of world opinion. On the other hand, had the Court decided that France was bound, the decision, while favoured by world opinion on the particular issue, would have rested on contentious legal grounds. Further, at the time it seemed uncertain whether France could be persuaded to desist permanently from atmospheric testing of its nuclear weapons, in obedience to the Court or otherwise, while the possibility of persuading China to conform to such a ruling was remote. Finally, there was no realistic prospect of compensating States that may have suffered damage as a result of the tests, to be designated by the Court as having been in breach of the rule.[14]

The first issue for the Court to consider would have been whether France could be required to adhere to the terms of the Partial Test-Ban Treaty, a Treaty to which it had not acceded. A decision that an almost universal treaty, like the Partial Test-Ban Treaty, is *ipso facto* binding on non-Parties would be counter to the rule of international law that treaties confer no rights or duties on States not parties to them. That rule has been recently confirmed with its incorporation into the Vienna Convention on the Law of Treaties, in Articles 34 to 37. Nevertheless, the Convention leaves the supremacy of custom untrammelled by providing, in Article 38, that 'Nothing in articles 34 to 37 precludes a rule set forth in a treaty from becoming binding upon a third State as a customary rule of international law, recognised as such.'

Continuing to assess the merits, the Court would have been required to make a decision on whether the testing of nuclear devices in the atmosphere had become unacceptable as the result of a rule of customary law. The Court's Opinion in the *North Sea Continental Shelf* cases[15] would have been directly in point. In that Opinion, the elements of a putative customary rule were assessed in the light of various criteria and were found, in the main, to lack the attributes required. However, the putative rule in the *Nuclear Tests* case would satisfy all of the following five criteria advanced by the Court in its earlier Opinion. Although not stated in precisely these terms, the criteria invoked can be identified as follows –

(i) The rule must be sufficiently significant to be of a *fundamentally* norm creating character.[16]

(ii) The rule must be of a *potentially* norm creating character with respect to precision as to its meaning and scope.[17]

(iii) State practice constituting the subject matter of the rule should be extensive and virtually uniform.[18]

(iv) The passage of a considerable period of time is not necessary, provided there is widespread and representative participation in the observance of the rule, particularly among States having a direct interest in the issue.[19]

(v) The States that adopt the practice constituting the rule must do so because they feel legally compelled to comply.[20]

A rule prohibiting atmospheric nuclear explosions would patently satisfy criteria (i) and (ii). Criteria (iii) and (iv) would also have been satisfied because, apart from France, with the only exception of the then minor nuclear-weapon State of China, all nuclear-weapon States had observed the rule, as had all non-nuclear-weapon States. In confirmation of their commitment, by 1973 more than a hundred States were Parties to the Partial Test-Ban Treaty, including the three original nuclear-weapon States. Further, as the States observing the ban were predominantly bound to do so by treaty, there can be no doubt that they believed themselves to be under legal compulsion to comply, thus satisfying criterion (v).

Yet the putative rule in the *Nuclear Tests* case would have failed to satisfy the further two criteria posed by the Court in the *North Sea Continental Shelf* cases, nor could any foreseeable NAC rule satisfy those criteria. They can be stated as –

(vi) The States that observe the rule because they feel legally compelled to do so, must believe themselves to be bound by a custom as representing law, not merely by treaty obligation.[21]

(vii) The treaty embodying the rule in question must have been, at its inception, declaratory of a then existing rule of customary international law.[22]

Regarding the application of *opinio juris sive necessitatis* in (vi), it is not only 'extremely difficult' to obtain evidence of its existence, as stated in the dissenting Opinion of Judge Tanaka,[23] but it is entirely impossible with respect to NAC issues. It would be reasonable to suppose, however, that States obeyed the test-ban so as to comply with the Treaty, to which they acceded probably because they approved of its terms as being in their own national interest.

Prior to the Partial Test-Ban Treaty, all nuclear-weapon States conducted nuclear tests in the atmosphere, except for periodic suspensions in pursuance of agreed moratoria. Thus, there was conclusive evidence that criterion (vii) was not satisfied, as there had been no existing mandatory rule prior to the Treaty.

On reaching agreement for a test-ban, or any other NAC related issue, States do not enter into a treaty because it gives expression to an existing custom but because they believe it to be imperative to prescribe future conduct in the light of new technological advances in armaments. States parties to NAC treaties make every effort to persuade all eligible States to accede to the treaties or, at least, to abide by their terms. Had the Court been prepared to state explicitly that an NAC treaty, embodying a novel breakthrough in arms control was, by reason only of its acceptability in the form of a treaty, and its originality, precluded from engendering a customary rule, it would not have been possible to conceal the absurdity of the proposition.

However, the Court could have concluded that a rule of customary international law existed, by giving a different interpretation to the seven criteria advanced in the *North Sea Continental Shelf* cases, and by invoking so much of the contradictory theories of international custom as might have been regarded sufficient to attribute a legally binding quality to the rule in question.

With respect to (vi) and (vii), regarding the requirement to comply with the putative norm for legal reasons other than treaty obligation, a contrary point of view has been expressed from time to time. For example in his dissenting Opinion Judge Lachs, in the *North Sea Continental Shelf* cases, said that not only could provisional international instruments, like unratified treaties, give rise to general rules of international law, but that –

Treaties binding many States are, *a fortiori* capable of producing this effect, a phenomenon not unknown in international relations.[24]

Adjudication on the merits of the *Nuclear Tests* case would have required that the Court, as well as examining treaty provisions and customary rules, to take into account any applicable general principles of law. In that connection, the Court would have been obliged to assess the principle-creating function of the numerous General Assembly resolutions and other expressions of international opinion exhorting States, with a cumulative authority, to refrain from nuclear testing in the atmosphere.

Conclusively to dismiss these pervasive expressions of international opinion as not indicative of principles of law recognised by civilised nations, would have been difficult to justify with the usual arguments. In academic analysis the most frequently advanced reason for not accepting General Assembly resolutions as capable of establishing binding principles and rules, beyond the very limited express rule making powers ascribed to them by the Charter, is that the States voting for the resolutions do not make institutional arrangements confirming their commitment.[25] However, with respect to the testing of nuclear weapons in the atmosphere, the large number of accessions to the Partial Test-Ban Treaty, as well as the actual cessation of the testing of nuclear weapons in the atmosphere by the United Kingdom, the United States and the Soviet Union, demonstrated the determination to abide by the rule on the part of the vast majority of States.

However, in order to justify a finding that Assembly resolutions were relevant to the outcome, would have required at least some indication as to the legal status of those resolutions. Did they establish custom? Were they to be regarded as quasi-legislative? In what ways and by whose authority were they to be so regarded? To answer those questions would have disposed of many of the major controversies presently confronting the whole discipline of international law. Recent Opinions handed down by the judges suggest that the Court has not been sufficiently united in its views to make pronouncements on those fundamental questions in a credible manner.

Yet, if despite all obstacles, the putative rule had been accepted as law, the Court, on the discretion of a handful of individuals, would have challenged the perceived vital security interests of several States, notably those of both France and China. The judges who handed down the majority Opinion were no doubt aware that this would not have been an acceptable solution in the eyes of the international community.

Finally, the Court may have been required subsequently to adjudicate on the issue of *actio popularis* with far reaching consequences.[26] If Australia, New Zealand and other South Pacific States had been found to have a legal interest based on damage suffered, this would have give them a right to compensation. Consequently all States in the world, especially those in the Northern hemisphere which have received far larger amounts of radioactive fallout from nuclear testing than Southern hemisphere States, would have been given the right, by inference, to receive compensation for damage sustained during the previous series of nuclear tests in the atmosphere. Alternatively, the Court would have been required to pinpoint a time when the international custom forbidding tests in the atmosphere came into being.

It is difficult to envisage any contravention of international law relating to NAC which would not affect all States in the world, or at least in a region. This would be equally true regarding the breach of bilateral agreements between the Superpowers. For that reason uncertainty about the applicability of *actio popularis* and rules for the apportionment of damages, if any, could be serious obstacles to the predictable outcome of any litigation.

The dilemma faced by the International Court of Justice in the *Nuclear Tests* case was not one that arose as the result of the particular facts involved, nor was it related to the individual judges who happened to constitute the Court. It was a dilemma that would foreseeably arise with every NAC related case to be brought before the Court, unless the applicable law were entirely unambiguous. Moreover, the situation is likely to apply equally to cases brought before any independent court or arbitrator, not only to the International Court of Justice.

The case discussed here, highlights the discrepancy between the significance of the disputes in terms of contemporary world politics and human survival, and the anachronistic and vague notions to be invoked in any judicial attempt to settle those disputes.

With respect to the case in question as in possible future NAC related cases, the weight of international opinion as expressed in United Nations forums, perhaps translated into overt or thinly disguised sanctions by member States, can put pressure on racalcitrant States to conform to the accepted norms of international conduct. Since the *Nuclear Tests* case, France has in fact ceased to conduct nuclear tests in the environments prohibited by the Partial Test-Ban Treaty and condemned by the various General Assembly resolutions. What appears to be unacceptable is to entrust issues of such magnitude to the unpredictable discretion of individuals, however highly regarded they may be as to their personal integrity. A recognition of such attitudes by States was implicit in the Court's unobtrusive stance on this occasion.

It has been contended from time to time, that predictable outcome in international law is not necessary because, if it existed, there would be no point in referring cases for adjudication.[27] The argument is erroneous first, because the objective is not to increase the number of cases but to settle or prevent international disputes. Second, States may refer predictable cases to the Court so as to obtain judicial confirmation of their rights, just as they present such issues to a General Assembly vote, in order to attract more determined enforcement procedures. With each case brought before the Court, no matter how unambiguous, the Court would have an opportunity to further clarify and confirm the principles of international law.

The Hostages Case

The *Hostages* case[28] presented the International Court of Justice with somewhat different problems. In this case the Court's jurisdiction, as well as the substantive issues to be decided, were essentially based on two Treaties clearly in force at the relevant time between the United States of America and the Islamic Republic of Iran. These were the Vienna Convention on Diplomatic Relations of 1961, and the Vienna Convention on Consular Relations of 1963, together with the Optional Protocols of each Convention concerning the compulsory settlement of disputes. The Treaty of Amity, Economic Relations and Consular Rights of 1955, was also invoked in relation to a side issue regarding two hostages who were not members of the consular staff of the United States of America.

In this case, the problems arose from an element of Superpower rivalry due to the strategic implications of Iran's political affiliations, leading to the intense involvement of the Security Council in mediating efforts to settle the dispute. These, as well as several other major issues in the case, are likely to be features of any NAC dispute that may be referred to the Court.

The *Hostages* case resulted from an incident on 4 November 1979, when several hundred citizens of Iran invaded the United States Embassy compound in Tehran, taking diplomatic personnel and other persons present hostage by detaining them in the Embassy. The United States sought the release and repatriation of all United States hostages and reparations from Iran for the alleged violations of her international legal obligations. It was claimed that the breach of obligations by the Iranian State consisted of 'tolerating, encouraging, and failing to prevent and punish the conduct described', relating to the capture and detention of the hostages.

It was alleged that the breach of obligations had been compounded by specific undertakings by the Government of Iran that the United States Embassy staff would be defended by Iranian Security Forces against the frequent demonstrations that were taking place throughout the country. The undertaking was to apply despite any adverse political developments between the respective countries, notably the permission given by the United States for the entry into its territory of the deposed Shah of Iran for medical treatment.

The issue of State responsibility for the unauthorised acts of individuals could well arise in a dispute involving an NAC agreement. It could relate to illegal modes of production of nuclear energy. Or it could arise in connection with the manufacture of certain types of nuclear weapons by a company engaged in armaments manufacture where the particular weapons are in breach of international obligation.

The reasoning of the Court in the *Hostages* case gives cause for concern in this regard. While the judges were unanimous in the view that, in all the circumstances, the State of Iran was responsible for the actions of the captors, the many arguments adduced in the majority Opinion to support this proposition indicates that, in a less factually clear-cut case, problems could be encountered. However, in NAC, State responsibility for the acts of individuals or entities within the State has to be absolute in order to make agreements appropriately reliable.

Like the *Hostages* case, NAC cases are likely to create international crisis situations. The United States instituted proceedings in the Court on 29 November 1979, a little over three weeks after the events complained of took place in Iran. However, many decisive international actions concerning the dispute had been taken in the interim. On 9 November 1979, the President of the Security Council was requested by a letter addressed to him from the Permanent Representative of the United States to the United Nations, to secure the release of the hostages. *Before the end of that day*, the President of the Security Council had already made a public statement asking Iran to release the hostages. Still on the same day, the President of the General Assembly was able to announce that he was sending a personal message to the Ayatollah Khomeini, making a like appeal. On 25 November, the Secretary-General of the United Nations requested the President of the Security Council to call an urgent meeting of that body in order to seek a peaceful solution to the dispute.

After the institution of proceedings, but before the case was heard, the Security Council on 4 December and 31 December, respectively, adopted resolutions 457 and 461 of 1979,[29] calling on the Iranian Government to release the hostages. At the instigation of the Security Council, the Secretary-General visited Tehran on 1–3 January 1980, and he established a fact-finding mission to Iran on 20 February 1980. In the meantime the United States imposed a number of economic sanctions against Iran on a unilateral basis.

On 13 January 1980, a draft resolution introduced into the Security Council by the United States, calling for economic sanctions against Iran by the international community, received ten votes in favour, two against, and two absentions, with one Member not participating in the voting. The negative vote of a permanent Member, the Soviet Union, having had the effect of a veto, the resolution was defeated. Despite the veto, the United States and some other States continued with the economic sanctions directed against Iran, and the United States Government broke off diplomatic relations with the Government of Iran on 7 April 1980.

Hence, by the time the Court delivered its judgment in May 1980, all the issues of the case had been explored in other forums, negotiating initiatives and sanctions had been implemented, and international opinion had crystallized regarding the merits of the case.

It is foreseeable that if a breach of a treaty occurred involving NAC, a similar sequence of events would follow. In 1978, in the *Aegean Sea Continental Shelf* case, the Court had already found that 'the fact that negotiations are being actively pursued during the present proceedings is not, legally, any obstacle to the exercise by the Court of its judicial function'.[30] The unanimous confirmation by the Court that intensive involvement by the Security Council is no bar to legal proceedings, could be a valuable guide to the decision-makers of Governments involved in an NAC dispute.

The Court demonstrated its ability to respond with some speed, by having made an Interim Order concerning the return of the hostages as early as 15 December 1979, barely two weeks after proceedings were instituted. This was undoubtedly largely the result of the existence of 'multilateral conventions codifying the international law governing diplomatic and consular relations'.[31]

Despite the indisputable breach of treaty obligations, and accession by both States to the Optional Protocols, Iran failed to submit to the jurisdiction of the Court[32] on the grounds that: (a) the issue was an internal matter for the State of Iran, and (b) the existence of alleged breaches of international obligations by the United States, being of overwhelming weight and consequence, were not before the Court in its deliberations on the matter.

The failure of Iran to acknowledge the jurisdiction of the Court was not given the opprobrium in the judgment that might have been expected to result from so clear a breach of treaty obligations. Iran's absence from the proceedings was noted chiefly in the context of rebutting the contention that the Court should have examined alleged political actions in Iran by the

110

United States during the preceding quarter century. The Court claimed that it would not be in a position to investigate those issues unless Iran appeared to present its case. Taken as a whole, the judgment conveyed the impression that little significance attaches to the acceptance of compulsory jurisdiction and that the only sanction for failure to appear formally before the Court is the inability to fully present an alternative argument. This would suggest that the absence of clauses requiring submission to the compulsory jurisdiction of the Court in NAC treaties is of no practical importance. However, the case has no bearing on the situation regarding those NAC treaties which specify that recourse to the Court is to be by consent of the parties. The plain words in those treaties indicate that, unless all concerned parties agree, the Court has no jurisdiction in relation to claims arising from obligations under the treaty in question.

In the *Hostages* case it was fortuitous that Iran refused to take its counter-complaints to the Court, as the issues raised in its informal communications with the Court by letter, telegram and telex, would have presented insurmountable difficulties. Iran alleged 'more than twenty-five years of continual interference by the United States in the internal affairs of Iran'.[33] The Court would not have been in a position to examine the merits of that claim due to the nature of the evidence required, the breadth of the value judgments involved, and the gravity of the allegations at issue. No matter how ideally impartial the judges might be, a pronouncement by the Court on such matters would be regarded by most, if not all States, as a political evaluation either in favour or opposed to their particular point of view.

Although the Opinion handed down made reference to the wide jurisdiction of the Court notwithstanding the political implications of cases brought before it, had the Court felt obliged to examine Iran's claims in greater detail, it may well have found that it did not have jurisdiction with respect to those matters. Similarly, in an NAC dispute, the Court would not be a suitable organ to adjudicate upon the relevance of any overriding political consideration that may have prompted a party to an NAC treaty to act in breach of its treaty obligations.

In the *Hostgages* case, even presuming that Iran had presented its arguments before the Court in a defence Memorial or by way of a counter-claim, the Court would have avoided adjudicating upon the substance of those arguments. In passing, the Court adverted to the grounds that would have been adduced, namely, that the State of Iran could have invoked other means of countering unwarranted United States diplomatic influence with the use of appropriate sanctions against illicit activities by any member of a diplomatic mission. While adeptly avoiding to consider the substance of major political issues, the Court still claimed competence to deal with issues involving significant political overtones, stating –

> Yet never has the view been put forward before that, because a legal dispute submitted to the Court is only one aspect of a political dispute, the Court should decline to resolve for the parties the legal questions at issue between them. Nor can any basis for such a view of the Court's functions or jurisdictions be found in the Charter or the Statute of the Court; if the Court were, contrary to its settled jurisprudence, to adopt

such a view, it would impose a far-reaching and unwarranted restriction upon the role of the Court in the peaceful solution of international disputes.[34]

With this observation, the designation of 'a legal dispute' as distinct from 'a political dispute' was avoided.

Perhaps the most important principle enunciated in the judgment was the decisive weight given, by all judges, to the express words contained in the relevant Treaties, resulting in a unanimous decision for the immediate return of the hostages. Although the Court did not base its conclusions exclusively on the binding force of the Treaties involved, but on the more general 'imperative character of the legal obligation',[35] the ultimate importance of treaty commitments is conveyed by the overall import of the judgment.

The inference to be drawn is that unequivocal treaty commitments are justiciable even in politically complex and strategically sensitive situations. These are the conditions likely to prevail in disputes involving NAC.

Eventually, the Applicants in the *Nuclear-Tests* case, as well as in the *Hostages* case, were all successful in that the matters they had complained of were resolved largely to their satisfaction. Furthermore, contrary to fears prevalent at the time that each case was heard, the conduct complained of has not been repeated. With respect to the testing of nuclear weapons in the atmosphere since the judgment, these have only been conducted by China, with a negligible average of one weapon per year on that State's own territory. Likewise, contrary to predictions, the capturing of diplomatic hostages by States has not become a favoured method of extracting concessions from other States. The nations of the world did succeed in imposing their common will on the deviating States. They defined their purpose primarily through resolutions and negotiations undertaken via the Security Council and the General Assembly, and, in the *Hostages* case, with the aid of the provisions of treaties in force, upheld by the International Court of Justice.

Nevertheless, there are some negative conclusions to be drawn from the conduct of the two cases. These relate to the cumbersome nature of the international machinery for determining and imposing justice at the international level, and the haphazard decisions that are entailed in activating the process.[36] *Central to the dilemma is that the theoretical ambit of the Court's competence to deal with matters of the kind that would be involved in NAC disputes, greatly exceeds the authority that the Court actually enjoys in practice.* The discrepancy tends to lead to the mistaken perception that the Court, and the system of international law identified with it, are not very relevant. Therefore, in order to make the international legal system effective in ways that promote respect for NAC agreements, leading to their observance and the more expeditious negotiation of new agreements, it would be advantageous if the Court's ostensible functions could be brought into line with its actual authority to prescribe the conduct of States *inter se*.

A corollary of the Court's inflated jurisdiction, is a corresponding lack of legal recognition for the vast normative and mediating potential of the Security Council and the General Assembly. Yet it is only these bodies with their subordinate committees and backup facilities which have, by virtue of their constituent nationally accredited representatives, *de facto* authority and power to modify international conduct on the most vital issues such as NAC.

Notes

1 This is not to say that the Opinions handed down by the Court have been consistent. For example, in the view of Georg Schwarzenberger – 'To attempt to harmonize the judgment of the International Court of Justice in the South West Africa (Preliminary Objection) cases (1962) with that in the Second Phase of the same case (1966) and both with the advisory opinion on Namibia (South West Africa) (1971) would be evading the real issue; to understand the ideological significance of the break that has occurred in the Court's practice' – Schwarzenberger, Georg, *International Law as Applied by International Courts and Tribunals* (Stevens, London 1976) p.168.

2 I.C.J. Rep. 1974, p.253.

3 Id. p.457.

4 *Case Concerning United States Diplomatic and Consular Staff in Tehran* (United States of America v. Iran), I.C.J. Reps. 1979, 1980.

5 Geneva, 1928.

6 On 10 June 1974 the French Embassy in Wellington sent a Note to the New Zealand Ministry of Foreign Affairs, including the following passage – 'France, at the point which has been reached in the execution of its programme of defence by nuclear means, will be in a position to move to the stage of underground tests, as soon as the test series planned for this summer is completed. Thus the atmospheric tests which are soon to be carried out will, in the normal course of events, be the last of this type.' I.C.J. Rep. 1974, pp. 265-6.

7 The Opinion expressed by the majority of judges goes so far as to give unilateral declarations the same status as treaties. Hence it was stated by the Court that 'Just as the very rule of *pacta sunt servanda* in the law of treaties is based on good faith, so also is the binding character of an international obligation assumed by unilateral declaration. Thus interested States may take cognizance of unilateral declarations and place confidence in them, and are entitled to require that the obligation thus created be respected.' I.C.J. Rep. 1974, p.268. The Court advanced this view despite its acknowledgement of the statement by 'the French Ambassador in Canberra to the Prime Minister and Minister for Foreign Affairs of Australia, that it has the conviction that its nuclear experiments have not violated any rule of international law, nor did France recognize that it was bound by any rule of international law to terminate its tests . . .' p.270.

8 I.C.J. Rep. 1974, p.320 para. 20.

9 U.N. World Conference on the Human Environment, Stockholm, June 1972.

10 *Inter alia*, the U.N. Scientific Committee on the Effects of Atomic Radiation, and the International Commission on Radiological Protection.

11 See annual records of *Resolutions and Decisions Adopted by the General Assembly*.

12 *Contra:* comment on the case has concentrated on the issue of the binding force in international law of unilateral declarations, not on the practical considerations that may have motivated the Court. Nevertheless, the Court's Opinion has been viewed as inconsistent with precedent. E.g. Rubin, Alfred P., 'The International Legal Effects of Unilateral Declarations', *American Journal of International Law*, January 1977, Vol. 71 No. 1 p. 24 – 'It may be concluded from this review of doctrine, that as of the time the ICJ produced its Judgment in the *Nuclear Tests*

cases there was no real support in theory for the proposition that a unilateral declaration, not made in a negotiating context and provoking no reaction from second states, created an obligation or, to the extent that it created legal effects, put them beyond reach of cancellation by the declarant state.'

13 This was the ruling sought. See para. 19 of the Application of Australia which stated that, 'The Australian Government will seek a declaration that the holding of further atmospheric tests by the French Government in the Pacific Ocean is not in accordance with international law . . .'

14 As pointed out in the Joint Dissenting Opinion, I.C.J. Rep. 1974, p.318 para. 16 – 'It is true that the Applicant has not asked for compensation for damage in the proceedings which are now before the Court. However, the Australian Government has not waived its right to claim them in the future.'

15 *North Sea Continental Shelf* cases (Federal Republic of Germany/Denmark; Federal Republic of Germany/Netherlands) I.C.J. Rep. 1969.

16 Ibid. Judgment of the Court, p.41 para. 72.

17 Id. p.42.

18 Id. p.43 para 74.

19 Id. p.42 para. 73.

20 Id. p.44 para. 77.

21 Id. pp.44-5 para. 78.

22 Id. p.45 para. 81.

23 *North Sea Continental Shelf* cases, I.C.J. Rep. 1969, p.176. Regarding 'the factors required for the formulation of customary law' in the case, Judge Tanaka added, 'The appraisal of factors must be relative to the circumstances and therefore elastic; it requires the teleological approach.'

24 Id. p.225.

25 E.g. Arangio-Ruiz, Gaetano, *The United Nations Declaration on Friendly Relations and the System of the Sources of International Law* (Sijthoff & Nordhoff, Maryland 1979). The author repeatedly claims that there is a tendency for States not to act in conformity with UN resolutions. Therefore, he describes the resolutions as only 'skin deep', p. 109 – 'What would matter . . . is not whether Assembly members felt legally bound *to vote* for the declaratory resolution but, rather, whether they felt legally *bound by the rules* they proclaimed', p. 48.

26 See *Barcelona Traction, Light and Power Company Limited* case, Second Phase, I.C.J. Rep. 1970, p. 32.

27 E.g. '[If] the outcome of litigation were predictable, there would be no cases at all for any court lacking compulsory jurisdiction, save where one party had by chance been uncommonly badly advised.' Jennings, R.Y., 'The Discipline of International Law', *Lord McNair Memorial Lecture*, International Law Association, 57th Conference, 1976, p. 12.

28 *Case Concerning United States Diplomatic and Consular Staff in Tehran* (United States of America v. Iran), I.C.J. Reps. 1979, 1980.

29 Resolutions and Decisions of the Security Council.

30 *Aegean Sea Continental Shelf* case (Greece v. Turkey) I.C.J. Rep. 1978, p. 12 para. 29.

31 I.C.J. Rep. 1979, p. 16 para. 25.

32 Non-appearance by a defendant is now commonplace, see *Fisheries Jurisdiction* case, I.C.J. Rep. 1974; *Nuclear Tests* case, I.C.J. Rep. 1974; *Aegean Sea Continental Shelf* case, 1978.

33 I.C.J. Rep. 1980, p. 20 para. 37.

34 Ibid.

35 Id. p. 41 para. 88.

36 From 1970 onward, concerted efforts have been made in the United Nations to increase the utility of the International Court of Justice in the settlement of international disputes. In 1974 exhaustive debate on the subject in the Sixth Committee, culminating in a General Assembly resolution on 'Review of the Role of the International Court of Justice' (Res. 3232 (XXIX)), failed to make a noticeable impact on the rate of utilisation of the Court; See also *U.N. Yearbook 1974* p. 833.

CHAPTER 7

International Law and International Precept

Generally Accepted Principles of International Law

The endeavour to reach agreement so as to control the spread and perfection of nuclear arms is one of the most recent international endeavours, without traditions of its own and with no history of contribution to the basis, nature, and methodology of international law during its formative period. The rules that govern NAC were not founded on natural law, customary law or existing international norms.

International law applying to NAC is in the form of treaties or other specific written agreements, or is embodied in declarations and resolutions of the United Nations. Whenever discussing the negotiation of NAC agreements at the United Nations, States continually emphasize the distinction between non-binding and binding agreements, the latter being in the form of treaties duly signed and ratified. Since the beginning of the nuclear era, vigilant, streamlined bureaucracies have regularly and meticulously weighed the advantages and disadvantages of signing or ratifying NAC treaties, and they have prepared elaborate reservations to qualify the extent of their commitment. Deliberateness and precision are the hallmarks of undertakings relating to NAC.

By contrast, in traditional approaches to fundamental issues, like aggressive and defensive military postures, the principles of international law tend to be diffuse and contradictory, deliberations are usually ponderous in style, and *ad hoc* methods are often invoked. The inappropriateness of the principles and methods of international law to satisfy many of the contemporary requirements of interaction among States in several subject areas is universally recognised. It has led to many serious efforts to rectify the position,[1] especially by international lawyers themselves.

The most extensive endeavour for improvement is conducted by the International Law Commission, which was established by the General Assembly in 1949, with the express objective of promoting the progressive development of international law and its codification.[2] A number of very significant treaties have been concluded on the basis of Draft Articles prepared by the Commission. However, its recommendations concerning fundamental rationalisations of the principles and basic tenets of international law have failed to gain acceptance.

The recommendations have consisted of a Draft Declaration on the Rights and Duties of States, prepared in 1949; a formulation of the principles of international law contained in the Charter and in the Judgment of the Nuremberg Tribunal, in 1950; and a Draft Code of Offenses Against the Peace and Security of Mankind, in 1954. All three drafts were prepared by the Commission at the request of the General Assembly but none has been adopted. At the time, the orientation of the Commission was still focused on the problems of the international situation prevailing prior to and during World War II, as revealed at the Nuremberg Tribunal. Nevertheless, some contemporary issues were addressed, notably, the Draft Code in Article 2 (7) lists the following offences against the peace and security of mankind –

Acts by the authorities of a State in violation of its obligations under a treaty which is designed to ensure international peace and security by means of restrictions or limitations on armaments, or on military training, or on fortifications, or of other restrictions of the same character.

Personal responsibility for the acts is proclaimed by Article 4, which states –

The fact that a person charged with an offence defined in this code acted pursuant to an order of his Government or of a superior does not relieve him of responsibility in international law if, in the circumstances at the time, it was possible for him not to comply with that order.

Believing that the International Law Commission was at fault for the unacceptability of its recommendations, the General Assembly set up a Special Committee on Principles of International Law, to draft a 'Declaration on Principles of International Law Concerning Friendly Relations and Co-operation Among States in Accordance with the Charter of the United Nations', to be submitted for adoption on the twenty-fifth anniversary of the Organisation. The Declaration[3] was duly adopted on 24 October 1970.

The seven principles of international law embodied in the Declaration are still referred to with favour as representing 'a generally accepted interpretation of the provisions of the Charter'.[4] They were cited, for example, in the New Delhi Appeal and Declaration, issued at the 1981 Conference of Non-aligned foreign ministers, condemning the Iraq-Iran war for being in contravention of those principles, yet failing to name the aggressor.

No doubt due to the vagueness of their terms, neither the New Delhi statement, nor the United Nations Declaration which it invoked, has made an appreciable impact. The 1970 Declaration added nothing new to existing principles and procedures while disregarding practical considerations. For example, with respect to arms control the Declaration lays down that –

All States shall pursue in good faith negotiations for the early conclusion of a universal treaty on general and complete disarmament under effective international control and strive to adopt appropriate measures to reduce international tensions and strengthen confidence among States.

With respect to the fulfilment of State obligations, the Declaration merely reiterates that –

Every State has the duty to fulfil in good faith its obligations under the generally recognized principles and rules of international Law.

No attempt is made to identify the so called 'generally recognized principles and rules'. Ten years later, but no nearer to identifying the relevant principles of international law, the Disarmament Commission in its Report to the 35th Session of the General Assembly, obliquely links the *generally accepted principles of international law* with certain objectives often reiterated in the United Nations, in the following terms –

> All States Members of the United Nations have, in the Final Document, reaffirmed their full commitment to the purposes of the Charter of the United Nations and their obligation strictly to observe its principles as well as other relevant and *generally accepted principles of international law* relating to the maintenance of international peace and security. *Disarmament*, relaxation of international tension, respect for the right to self-determination and national independence, sovereignty and territorial integrity of States, the peaceful settlement of disputes in accordance with the Charter and the strengthening of international peace and security are directly related to each other. Progress in any of these spheres has a beneficial effect on all of them; in turn, failure in one sphere has negative effects on others.[5]

In the light of that construction, it is perhaps opportune to examine the nexus between the various principles of international law as they impinge on the above-listed interrelated issues.

The facility for reaching agreements under the prevailing international legal system affects NAC not only as regards agreements for the qualitative and quantitative limitation of nuclear weapons, but also as it relates to the prevention and settlement of all major international disputes. Agreements concerning the development, stockpiling, transfer and deployment of weapons, especially nuclear weapons, at all stages of their negotiation, conclusion and implementation, share all of the shortcomings which also result in the failure to settle other vital international disputes.

At the same time, in so far as there are stronger inducements for the elimination of genocidal force than lesser types of force, it has been possible to conclude NAC agreements, amounting to the resolution of international disputes as to the disposition or equivalence of nuclear forces, perhaps more readily than the settlement of less immediately threatening disputes. Yet the two processes interact, so that failure of the international legal system to resolve disputes involving geopolitical conflicts, seriously inhibits the process of NAC.

In its legal context, the utilisation of nuclear armaments is generically an aspect of war, pertaining to the threat or use of force, while the control of nuclear armaments is part of the maintenance of international peace and security. Although there are plausible theories that the threat and use of force, at all levels, often has bio-psychological origins of an irrational nature, the direction into which that belligerence is channelled in the international arena usually relates to genuine conflicts of interests. The conflicts take the form of international disputes involving the territorial,

118

economic and social aspirations adopted by States, or reflecting the interests of influential groups within States.[6]

Hence, the efficacy of settlement of the international disputes is an important factor in the process of eliminating the threat or use of force, including the most extreme force entailing weapons of mass destruction. International disputes caused by the clash of territorial, economic and social interests could be termed *primary disputes*. Increasingly, there are conflicts about the manner in which conflicts should be resolved, including the principles and procedures of peaceful settlement, as well as the legitimate methods of self-defence and the assertion of international rights. Disputes concerning these matters, which could be termed *consequential disputes*, include all outstanding NAC issues. Failure to differentiate between primary and consequential disputes can give rise to negotiating postures inconsistent with a State's fundamental objectives.

Three basic methods are utilised for the settlement of major primary and consequential disputes. There is a judicial method, a direct method and a institutional method, all of which contain legal elements.

Judicial settlement of both primary and consequential disputes threatening international peace and security rests with the International Court of Justice, as presently provided by the Charter of the United Nations. With respect to issues other than NAC, arbitration could be classified as a judicial function. In regard to NAC matters, it is not foreseeable that settlement of a substantial NAC dispute would be entrusted to any arbitrator. Possibly an arbitrator may be empowered at some time to determine a point that is minor, by NAC standards, perhaps in conjunction with a wider mediating role. The direct method includes negotiation, mediation and conciliation. In accordance with the variants of this method, the parties arrive at an accommodation among themselves, with or without the assistance of third parties selected by them. It is an essentially *ad hoc* procedure, whereby the rules governing the mode of settlement can be varied on each occasion in conformity with the agreed wishes of the parties.

The institutional method of resolving disputes relies on the facilities and authority of an institution, other than a Court, enjoying international confidence. Foremost among these are the General Assembly and the Security Council, representing world opinion. The Security Council has the primary responsibility in this regard, as provided in Chapters VI and VII of the Charter. Both the General Assembly and the Security Council are empowered to set up subsidiary bodies to assist them in these tasks, on a permanent or *ad hoc* basis.

Attempts to create permanent bodies to help with institutional dispute settlement have not succeeded so far. In 1947 the General Assembly established an Interim Committee[7] with a view to organising ongoing machinery for enquiry tasks. The Committee adjourned *sine die* in 1952. In 1949 the General Assembly set up a Panel of Inquiry and Conciliation,[8] whereby Member States were invited to nominate suitable persons for appointment to enquiry and conciliation work, at the request of organs of the United Nations or individual States. No use was made of the Panels, which were abandoned after 1961.

However, several important United Nations quasi-legal enquiries have been conducted on an *ad hoc* basis. Some examples of General Assembly enquiries were the United Nations Special Committee on Hungary, of 1957,[9] and the Commission of Investigation into the death of Patrice Lumumba,[10] of 1961.

It is common knowledge that attempts to settle disputes involving international peace and security by the three methods, judicial, direct, and institutional, have often failed, leading to many instances of hostility and armed conflict between States. Therefore, especially since the end of the Second World War and the advent of nuclear weapons, persistent efforts have been made by international lawyers to improve the theoretical basis, as well as mechanisms, for the prevention and settlement of international disputes impinging on the security interests of States. By Western States, these efforts consisted largely of theories for the stimulated growth of customary international law, while the other States frequently reaffirmed and attempted to expand the relevant provisions of the Charter by means of declarations of the General Assembly.

As has been already noted, three unsuccessful attempts were made by the International Law Commission, within the first decade after World War II, to strengthen the principles of international law for the maintenance of peace, in accordance with the experience of the 1930s and 1940s. During the next quarter century, the General Assembly made numerous recommendations on the subject, the following eight being the most comprehensive. They were mostly initiated by the Non-aligned and Socialist States. Despite the more lengthy description of the issues, the content of these documents does not, in essence, go beyond the provisions of the Charter.

Western States predominantly opposed or abstained from voting in five out of the eight resolutions, while three resolutions were carried by consensus. These were the Resolution approving the Declaration on Principles of International Law Concerning Friendly Relations and Co-operation Among States in Accordance with the Charter of the United Nations, of 24 October 1970,[11] referred to above; the Resolution on the Definition of Aggression, of 14 December 1974;[12] and a Declaration on the Deepening and Consolidation of International Detente, of 19 December 1977.[13]

The Resolution on the Definition of Aggression does enlarge on the *description* of aggression as laid down in Article 2(4) of the Charter, by citing self-evident instances of aggression, such as bombardment, blockade, etc. However, also listed are less straight-forward forms of aggression, including 'the use of armed forces, such as a State permitting another State to use its territory for the perpetration of an act of aggression against a third State', which would apply to aggression via foreign bases. Another prohibition listed is the incursion of armed bands from one State into another, which would apply to infiltration by guerilla forces, referred to in Article 3(f) and (g) of the Resolution. Article 5 also introduces a new element by proclaiming that 'no consideration of whatever nature, whether political, economic, military or otherwise, may serve as a justification for aggression.' Nevertheless, the Resolution does not attempt to derogate from the right of individual and collective self-defence provided by Article 51 of the Charter.

The Declaration on the Deepening and Consolidation of International

Detente, disclaims any intention to 'detract from' the provisions of the Charter and the existing principles of international law, and does not claim in any way to 'alter' those provisions. Yet, without adding to the *obligations* of member States, the Resolution does *encourage* Members to permit freer international travel and to promote cultural exchanges.

The non-consensus declarations are even less significant in elaborating the general principles of international law, as they may apply to NAC or to other areas of interaction that could affect NAC. The Declaration on the Inadmissibility of Intervention in the Domestic Affairs of States and the Protection of their Independence and Sovereignty, of 21 December 1965,[14] reiterates that no State may intervene either directly or indirectly into the affairs of another State and that no type of coercion is permissible including economic, political, subversive, etc.

The Declaration on the Strengthening of International Security, of 16 December 1970,[15] lists several provisions of the Charter, including the primacy of obligations assumed under the Charter, and 'the principle that States shall settle their international disputes by peaceful means in such a manner that international peace and security and justice are not endangered'. The Declaration also seeks to enhance the authority of decisions reached by the Security Council and urges the establishment of subsidiary organs of the Council in conformity with Article 29 of the Charter.

The resolution on the Non-Use of Force in International Relations and Permanent Prohibition of the Use of Nuclear Weapons, of 29 November 1972,[16] enunciates 'the permanent prohibition of the use of nuclear weapons'. The Resolution on the Conclusion of a World Treaty on the Non-Use of Force in International Relations, of 8 November 1976,[17] calls on States Members to give consideration to a Draft Treaty[18] on the subject, submitted by the Soviet Union; while the Resolution on the Inadmissibility of the Policy of Hegemonism in International Relations, of 14 December 1979,[19] describes the concept of hegemonism and condemns 'the creation of spheres of influence and the division of the world into antagonistic political and military blocks'.

The most recent international effort in this field, the draft Manila Declaration on the Peaceful Settlement of Disputes,[20] shows no more promise of effectiveness than its predecessor resolutions in the General Assembly. It restates the relevant principles already contained in the Charter and draws attention to various Chapters and Articles of that document, as if they were likely to be overlooked in the absence of reiteration. Perhaps the only sentence that comes to grips with a concrete issue is the proposed item stating –

> It is recalled that whenever States have accepted a binding means of settlement of disputes, they are obliged to comply strictly with the decision taken.[21]

Principles embodied in the above United Nations resolutions are still too vague to cover many contingencies. For instance, no appreciable headway has been made to define and outlaw *quasi-aggression*, posing as defence assistance to allies, hot pursuit or forward defence, as the case may be.

Thus, while overt aggression has been clearly outlawed, there are no guidelines for the designation and condemnation of that type of military activity whereby one Government gives assistance to another Government in order to resist so called 'aggression', in cases when civil disaffection within the besieged State is a factor in the unrest. Yet it is this type of activity, or the threat thereof, involving both Superpowers, that has precipitated the most bitter primary international disputes in recent years,[22] and which presents the scenario for nuclear conflict at any time.

So long as existing disputes and potential conflicts of such magnitude remain unsolved, and apparently insoluble, the temptation to settle them by force is overwhelming, leading to the acceptance of extreme risks in the escalation of the nuclear arms race, with a corresponding reluctance to enter into NAC agreements.

International Agreement by Resolution

In the attempt to formulate adequate rules of conduct for the avoidance or settlement of primary international disputes, the international community faces a dilemma. The possibilities of advance by way of treaty law are limited. Unlike arms control agreements, treaties for the designation of specific rights and duties related to the avoidance of primary disputes would be necessarily too limited in scope for the ongoing maintenance of international security. On the other hand, existing principles are insufficient. Yet, while the broad objectives for peace and justice contained in the Charter have stood the test of time and fundamentally changed circumstances, any attempt to elaborate them further would amount to a quasi-legislative function.

Nevertheless, it is evident that the resolutions of the General Assembly have to be incorporated into the international legal system, especially as they relate to principles for the maintenance of peace and security, because agreement in the form of those resolutions is the only process capable of sufficiently rapid development to make a timely impact over a wide range of major issues. For instance, the Legal Counsel of the United Nations, Professor Erik Suy, has noted the norm creating authority of General Assembly resolutions, claiming that –

> It is therefore no exaggeration to say that the general will of the international community has acquired a certain legislative status when manifested through formal actions of international institutions. In this sense the General Assembly resolution is becoming a useful modern tool for standard-setting and rule-creation in an expanded international society that requires more rapid formulations of standards governing the conduct of its members.[23]

However, Professor Suy did not indicate the jurisprudential nature of the process. Failure to resolve this impasse in international norm creation and conflict resolution, involving matters vital to State interests, has a strong indirect influence on the success of NAC. It also has a direct bearing on NAC, to the extent that States do not avail themselves of the opportunites to conclude the appropriate NAC treaties.

Unable to devise a solution, international lawyers from the Socialist States tend to ignore that a theoretical dilemma exists beyond acknowledging that the principles of international law need to be further elaborated by agreement, based on the concept of co-existence. Lawyers from the newly independent States of the Third World are understandably uneasy that West European oriented international law is dominant, drawing attention to its weaknesses, while refraining from advancing comprehensive alternatives. They take the pragmatic stance of attaching great importance to Assembly resolutions without feeling the need to explain their position in terms of a general theory.

By contrast, many international lawyers of the West, although showing no marked enthusiasm for the content of General Assembly resolutions, have suggested that, in one way or another, Assembly resolutions should be accorded a theoretically consistent status. Basically two modes of achieving this aim have been envisaged by them.

According to one school of thought, the Assembly's recommendatory powers are quasi-legislative, or should be transformed into explicitly legislative powers; while others believe that Assembly recommendations can form part of the evolutionary process of the law.

The *legislative* school of thought has several variants. Professor Richard Falk asks in this context, 'How can there be legislative change without a legislature?'.[24] He answers the question by proposing that Assembly resolutions should be regarded as creating 'weak' legislative norms. However, he does not elaborate in detail how these weak norms are to influence international conduct, except to observe that –

> . . . the resolution joins, admittedly to an imperceptible degree, with other tendencies that together create some legal basis for the argument that an obligation exists . . .[25]

It then becomes necessary to determine how 'weak' a norm may be without altogether losing its normative character. Professor Falk suggests the minimum support required to be a two-thirds majority in the General Assembly, including the Superpowers. A different assessment is made by Rosalyn Higgins, who postulates the possibility of a General Assembly resolution emerging more or less intact as a norm of general international law, without the support of any of the permanent Members of the Security Council, although she recognises that, '. . . exclusion of *all* the Big Powers may in present circumstances render the new custom ineffective'.[26] The suggestion may possibly have validity in a regional context.

Similarly indeterminate qualities have been attributed to Assembly resolutions by Gaetano Arangio-Ruiz. Using somewhat different terminology, he claims that –

> The Assembly has a law determining, interpreting and developing function in a 'non-technical' sense.[27]

Taking a somewhat stronger stand, B.V.A. Röling claims that, 'National sovereignty must give way to international co-operate action . . .'[28] without specifying the *modus operandi* for its attainment. Taking the extreme position on the *legislative* spectrum are those who see a need for overt legislation by the General Assembly under a system of world government, advocating world peace through world law, world federalism etc.[29]

Academic writers who support what could be termed the *evolutionary* school, envisage the metamorphosis of General Assembly resolutions into customary international law by a gradual transformation. It has been already concluded above that international law relating to NAC is not amenable to evolution by means of customary international law. Hence, it remains to consider whether the principles and rules of international law, especially as they may affect the settlement of international disputes pertaining to the basic security interests of States, could be advanced by some variant of the evolution of resolutions into custom.

The first prerequisite of the evolution of Assembly resolutions into customary international law would be the frequent interpretation of the law by the International Court of Justice, or like judicial body, in order to indicate in what manner development is taking place. Yet, as noted in the previous Chapter, very few cases are referred to the Court even by States with a West European tradition. It has been frequently observed that the most prevalent reason for avoiding the Court is the unreliability of the law which it applies. Hans Blix put it in these words –

> What are the reasons for this reluctance to submit to the Court's jurisdiction? One reason, applying generally, is that the rules of customary international law are often so uncertain, that states may be inclined in their disputes to rely rather upon their bargaining position than upon what they believe is – but cannot be quite sure is – their right.[30]

If the International Court of Justice were at fault, rather than the law it dispenses, then States could be expected to use arbitration facilities. However, with the exception of commercial transactions, relying on quasi-contractual agreements involving States,[31] international arbitration has not gained favour.

During the early 1950s a concerted effort was made to encourage arbitration. In pursuit of that aim the International Law Commission drafted a Convention on international arbitration and agreed on a set of model rules. These were considered by the General Assembly which decided to circulate the model rules to Member States for their comments.[32] Governments showed their disinterest in arbitration by their failure to comment on the draft rules, leading to their abandonment.

Therefore, the formulation used by M. K. Nawaz in describing the situation is more apt in this context because it emphasizes the reluctance of States to submit to *any* judicial ruling that would rely on imprecise concepts of international law. He said –

> Time and again states have expressed a view that in the absence of agreement on the precise scope and content of international law, they cannot submit their disputes to compulsory judicial settlement.[33]

Yet, if the principles of the evolutionary school were adopted, there would have to be constant uncertainty as to which Assembly resolutions were evolving into law and, if so, to what extent they had evolved. Without constant Court rulings it would be impossible to determine the rights and duties of a given State at a particular time. Therefore, whenever a judicial body were called upon to adjudicate on any issue involved, the judges or arbitrators concerned would have to take upon themselves a wide personal discretion similar to that necessitated by the imprecision of the general principles and rules of international customary law.

Further, as has been noted with respect to NAC issues, the Charter, with the exception of a few subject areas, only gives the General Assembly power to make recommendations. Therefore, States must be assumed to rely on the express provisions of the Charter. Hence, far from the possibility of assuming their intention to be bound, the opposite presumption must prevail short of clear evidence to the contrary. Nevertheless, several academic writers have expressed a contrary view. For example, Professor Arangio-Ruiz states that –

> ... the resolutions of international bodies are certainly among the elements of states' practice that many contribute to the creation of rules of customary law or of contractual rules.[34]

The widely held view is also presented by Dr Higgins, in these words –

> Resolutions of the Assembly are not *per se* binding; though those rules of general international law which they may embody are binding on member states, with or without the help of the resolution. But the body of resolutions as a whole, taken as indications of a general customary law, undoubtedly provide a rich source of evidence.[35]

Apart from the theoretical difficulties of the evolutionary school, it should be observed that its adherents would find it difficult to produce recent examples of the development of international law by these means, especially involving issues that concern the vital security interests of States. This is not to deny that some aspects of the above cited formulations are both valid and significant, but merely to observe that they are so vague as to be impractical in their present form.

As the International Law Association concluded at its Workshop on the *Theory and Methodology of International Law*, 'The fact that international law is in a state of incoherence and confusion needs no further elaboration.'[36] The conclusion which emerges from that fact, notwithstanding persistent efforts to make improvements is, that the traditional framework of the theory of international law can no longer accommodate the necessary changes.

Restructuring the International Legal System

In previous Chapters, and the earlier part of this Chapter, an examination was undertaken of the shortcomings of the international legal system in relation to agreements for NAC. Subsequently it was noted that the international legal system is similarly deficient in the prevention and resolution of primary conflicts of interest which constitute the major plausible inducements fuelling the nuclear arms race. Whether or not those apparent inducements are valid grounds for nuclear armament is immaterial, so long as they are perceived to be so by decision makers. It has also been noted that the operation of NAC agreements cannot be separated from the general principles of international law imparting their particular status, and prescribing all other relationships between States. Further, it was asserted that, in several ways, those general principles have proved to be inadequate for present needs and for the tasks ahead.

It follows that NAC is inhibited by the present structure and content of the international legal system and, implicitly, that if that system were to be improved NAC agreements would become more effective. Therefore it is pertinent to advert to the type of improvements that might take place, and to propose an outline for a restructured international legal system. The conclusions reached by the United Nations *Study on the Relationship Between Disarmament and International Security* present the issues thus –

> Even in a climate of co-operation and detente, some basic political and other differences among States will remain. It is important to contain these by developing and utilizing more effectively procedures for the peaceful settlement of disputes in accordance with the Charter of the United Nations, and by the establishment and faithful respect for principles of international conduct in relations among States. In the long run, only consistent adherence by all States to such principles would provide a solid basis for lasting detente, far-reaching disarmament and sustained international security. Over the years, the United Nations General Assembly has been elaborating such principles in relevant expressions of the political will of States to act accordingly in international relations. *However, their full potential as means for developing an international legal order is not realized unless they are developed, as appropriate, into recognized norms of international law.* Such norms should, wherever possible, include procedures for the settlement of disputes that may arise out of the implementation of the terms of such agreements and treaties.[37]

There are also non-legal impediments to the NAC process, briefly adverted to in the Introduction and previous Chapters, which could become so inhibiting as to make the adequacy of the international legal system irrelevant to the inevitable loss of control over the nuclear arms race. Proceeding on the assumption that other obstacles to NAC are not insurmountable, the following changes are required in the international legal system to create a climate in which NAC can become more effective –

First: in order to win the confidence of the great majority of States to an acceptance of third party adjudication of international disputes, the law applied by the International Court of Justice would have to be so unambiguous that the outcome of cases presented to it would be largely predictable. In order to achieve this, the obligations recognised by the Court of Justice would have to be restricted to those that had been unequivocally undertaken by the parties to the dispute under consideration.

Likewise, the methods of interpretation of those undertakings would have to enjoy the widest possible acceptance, and such discretion as remained with the judges would have to be exercised with reference to norms approved by the various forums of the United Nations. The inevitable consequences of such changes would be that the Court would have to abandon any pretention of being able to adjudicate all international conflicts hitherto regarded as legal disputes. Therefore, it would be necessary to have the means for transferring all inappropriate cases, or aspects of cases, from the ambit of the Court's jurisdiction to organs more suited for dealing with them.

Second: major international disputes not amenable to speedy negotiated settlement by the parties themselves, with or without mutually accepted third party assistance, and excluded from the Court's jurisdiction, would have to be automatically referred to the Security Council as the only world body with the theoretical right to take action, and the practical capacity to do so. However, the Security Council could not assume the administrative burden of this task without backup facilities. Further, it would be of paramount importance for the whole membership of the United Nations to participate in the adjudicative process, but only in a recommendatory capacity, in keeping with the spirit of the Charter and the contemporary alignment of power and influence which it represents.

The procedure would not have to entail the abandonment of the legal process or the sacrifice of the expertise contributed by international lawyers. It would merely require the institution of a system whereby lawyers could exercise their competence as accredited delegates of States, instead of sitting in their individual capacities. Nor would the change have to entail the diminution of impartiality. The standard of adjudication would be predicated on whether States wish to conduct a system of consistent international justice or whether they do not. If not, it would be futile to attempt to foist justice on them surreptitiously by any means whatever. All that can be done is to devise an administrative system for the dispensation of justice that is seen to be the nearest possible approximation, under present circumstances, to the impartial application of international norms. Viewed in that light, the relevant comparison is not between the operation of the Court and an ideal Court, but between the marginal impact on major international disputes that has been exerted by the Court, juxtaposed against the relatively successful day to day functioning of the General Assembly and the Security Council.

Third: so as to foster the development of international law as a universally accepted standard of conduct, all States must have the opportunity to participate in the establishment of its norms, as well as in determining the manner of their observance. Likewise, possibilities should be created for States to have a direct input with respect to the legal principles and rules governing their relationship *inter se* in keeping with the changing requirements of international life, including the designation of the legal consequences that are to flow from their deliberations and agreements at the various levels of formality.

As some of these functions do not lend themselves to decision by deliberations of the General Assembly, a more flexible system should be instituted. At the same time, in keeping with the balance of powers inherent in the United Nations system, the Security Council, with the concurrence of its permanent Members, must remain the final arbiter. Where appropriate, of course, the method of approval by resolution, based on recommendations of the International Law Commission and/or the Sixth Committee, as the case may be, would be utilised.

Fourth: in all but the most pedantic sense, the provisions of the Charter are the embodiment of customary international law at this time. If there exists a State that does not believe itself bound by the principles and rules of the Charter, it can be confidently asserted that none of that State's accredited representatives would be prepared to acknowledge that perception. Also, the Charter is a Treaty in force, duly ratified by nearly all sovereign States in the world. Its rules are sufficiently detailed to create contractual relations. Its principles are broad enough to encompass all the significant endeavours of the international community.

Albeit technically a part of the Charter, Article 38 of the Statute of the International Court of Justice is not consonant with the principles of the Charter and the division of powers created by it. It has already been argued in the previous Chapter that the provisions of Article 38 lead to consequences out of step with contemporary State practice; that they enshrine a Eurocentric orientation; and that they imply the willingness of States to entrust their most vital interests to a few individuals with legal qualifications acquired in other, sometimes potentially hostile, States.

The aforementioned inappropriate attributes of Article 38 are reminiscent of the failed League of Nations regime of international law. The provisions transposed in their entirety from the Statute of the Permanent Court of International Justice are the heritage of an alien era, that not only hinders the settlement of current disputes but also stands in the way of the development of viable alternative modes of settlement.

For the above reasons, in order to achieve the requisite improvement in the international legal system, it would be imperative to devise a general theory of international law in harmony with the outlook prevalent in the main groups of States, that would be acceptable to all. Such a general theory would have to differentiate between legal consequences flowing from matters to which States have given their explicit consent, and legal consequences flowing from those matters to which they have given only tacit or implied consent.

Code of General Principles of International Law

The Code would be adopted by consensus in the General Assembly on the basis of a draft prepared by the International Law Commission, and revised by the Sixth Committee, or a Legal Revision Committee appointed by the Assembly in accordance with the principles of equitable geographical distribution. Subsequently the draft could be incorporated into the Charter in the form of an amendment. Alternatively, an Assembly Resolution or Declaration could form the basis or a separate Convention. Another solution would be for States to act in accordance with a consensus Declaration of the subject without other formal endorsement. The following elements might be considered when preparing the Code:

1. Affirmation of the supremacy of the United Nations Charter as the ultimate source of international law for the foreseeable future.
2. Declaration that two kinds of international law exist –
    a. *treaty law*, being international agreement by explicit consent of the

parties, to be created, observed and interpreted in accordance with the Vienna Convention on the Law of Treaties, and

b. *precept law*, being *precepts of international co-operative conduct*, to be defined and applied in accordance with the Code.

3. Definition of precept law as being those principles and rules of international co-operative conduct to which Member States of the United Nations have implicitly given their consent.

4. Confirmation that the International Court of Justice be retained as provided in the Court's Statute, including the scope of the Court's jurisdiction as laid down in Article 36, provided that the sources of law to be invoked in the Court's ordinary jurisdiction shall be as follows –

a. treaties in force that were concluded or confirmed after the Charter was adopted

b. to the extent necesssary for the interpretation of treaties –
i. precept law
ii. in the absence of relevant precept law, such international norms, hitherto called customary rules of international law, as have already been cited in cases decided by the International Court of Justice or by the Permanent Court of International Justice.

5. Identification of –
a. the sources of precept law, as being principles and rules of international co-operative conduct contained in –
i. widely accepted treaties in force
ii. resolutions of United Nations bodies
iii. in the absence of i and ii, such international norms, hitherto called customary rules of international law, as have already been cited in cases decided by the International Court of Justice or by the Permanent Court of International Justice.

b. the content of precept law, as being those principles and rules of law that can be deduced from i, ii and iii, having been implicitly recognised as constituting international co-operative conduct required of Members of the United Nations.

6. Exposition of the operation of precept law, establishing that it can only be applied by –
a. the Security Council
b. the International Court of Justice in its treaty interpreting capacity.

7. The designation of *jus cogens* as being the body of principles contained in the Charter.

8. Provison that –
a. legal issues referred to the Secretary-General by the Security Council, the General Assembly or the International Court of Justice, not being adjudicable by the Court in its amended jurisdiction in accordance with paragraph 4 , are to be transferred for assessment to Legal Panels;

b. States entitled to nominate delegates to the Legal Panels are to be selected by the General Assembly on the basis of equitable geographical distribution, provided that, if the issue relates predominantly to the observance of treaty provisions, the Legal Panel to assess it shall be composed of representatives of States parties to the relevant treaty, or those of them that wish to avail themselves of the opportunity to participate;

c. in the event that the participation of States representatives exceeds a given number, being representatives of the parties to a treaty under consideration, then those representatives are to be empowered, by decision among themselves, to appoint an appropriate lesser number to sit on the Panel.

9. Pronouncement that the mandate of the Legal Panels is to be the submission of recommendations to the Security Council, in accordance with the assessment of Panel members as to whether a State has acted contrary to treaty law or precept law or both, as the case may be. Further, that in accordance with paragraph 6, the Panel be required not to determine the content of precept law by reliance on any individual resolution of the United Nations, but only on an overall appraisal of the relevant treaties, resolutions, and their observance by States, indicating the creation of an accepted standard of international co-operative conduct.

10. Indications of the procedure to be followed by the Legal Panels, requiring them to –

a. Receive submissions from the parties and, when appropriate, from the Sixth Committee;

b. At any stage of the proceedings to recommend interim action by the Security Council;

c. Recommend referral of any issue of treaty interpretation to the International Court of Justice, provided that in the opinion of the Panel the Court has jurisdiction to hear the case;

d. Specify the relevant treaty law, and establish the nature and extent of the consensus that allegedly constitutes the precept law to be invoked, (for example that there shall be no testing of nuclear weapons in the atmosphere) citing evidence of the consensus;

e. Investigate the facts complained of, allegedly constituting the breach;

f. Assess whether the breach has occurred and its significance in all of the circumstances, including –

i. whether specific damage has resulted or could result from the breach

ii. the existence of any aggravating or mitigating circumstances;

g. Report its findings or interim recommendations, made jointly or severally and presented in a public document to the Security Council, preferably not in a discursive style but concisely, under the various headings.

11. Reaffirmation that the Legal Panels are to be entirely subordinate to the Security Council and that their creation is not to be interpreted as establishing a practice requiring the Security Council to desist from debating and deciding upon issues concurrently under consideration by a Legal Panel.

Notes

1 E.g. see G.A. Res. on the *Peaceful Settlement of International Disputes* 3283 (XXIX) of 12 December 1974, in operative paragraphs as follows –

'1. *Draws the attention* of States to established machinery under the Charter of the United Nations for the peaceful settlement of international disputes;

2. *Urges* Member States not already parties to instruments establishing the various facilities and machinery available for the peaceful settlement of disputes to consider becoming parties to such instruments and, in the case of the International Court of Justice, recognizes the desirability that States study the possibility of accepting, with as few reservations as possible, the compulsory jurisdiction of the Court in accordance with Article 36 of the Statute of the Court;

3. *Calls upon* Member States to make full use and seek improved implementation of the means and methods provided for in the Charter of the United Nations and elsewhere for the exclusively peaceful settlement of any dispute or any situation, the continuance of which is likely to endanger the maintenance of international peace and security, including negotiation, inquiry, mediation, conciliation, arbitration, judicial settlement, resort to regional agencies or arrangements, good offices including those of the Secretary-General, or other peaceful means of their own choice;

4. *Requests* the Secretary-General to prepare an up-to-date report concerning the machinery established under the Charter relating to the peaceful settlement of international disputes, inviting his attention in particular to the following resolutions of the General Assembly:

(a) Resolution 268 D (III) of 28 April 1949, in which the Assembly established the Panel of Inquiry and Conciliation;

(b) Resolution 377 A (V) of 3 November 1950, Section B in which the Assembly established the Peace Observation Commission;

(c) Resolution 1262 (XIII) of 14 November 1958, in which the Assembly considered the question of establishing arbitral procedure for settling disputes;

(d) Resolution 2329 (XXII) of 18 December 1967, in which the Assembly established a United Nations register of experts for fact-finding;

(e) Resolution 2625 (XXV) of 24 October 1970, in which the Assembly approved the Declaration on Principles of International Law concerning Friendly Relations and Co-operation among States in accordance with the Charter of the United Nations . . .'

See also *Report of the Special Committee on the Charter of the United Nations and on the Strengthening of the Role of the Organization*, A/36/33 Supp. No. 33; and *Report of the Working Group on the Peaceful Settlement of Disputes* A/C. 6/36/L. 19, known as the draft Manila Declaration on the Peaceful Settlement of International Disputes.

2 *Report of the International Law Commission* covering its First Session, 12 April – 9 June 1949, Supp. No. 10 (A/925) of 1949; also *Review of the Multilateral Treaty-Making Process* A/35/312/Add. 2 of 28 August 1980, esp. p. 16.

3 Res. 2625 (XXV).

4 Sahovic, Milan, 'The Nonaligned and International Law', *Review of International Affairs*, May 1981, Vol. XXXII p. 12.

5 A/35/42 para. 18, emphasis added.

6 International instruments for the peaceful settlement of international disputes concluded prior to the nuclear arms race included – the First Hague Convention on the Peaceful Settlement of International Disputes (18 October 1907), the General Act for the Pacific Settlement of International Disputes

(26 September 1928), the Revised General Act (28 April 1949); and regional treaties concluded among Western European States (29 April 1957).

7 Res. 111 (II).
8 Res. 268 (III).
9 By Res. 1132 (XI).
10 By Res. 1601 (XV).
11 Res. 2625 (XXV).
12 Res. 3314 (XXIX).
13 Res. 32/155.
14 Res. 2131 (XX).
15 Res. 2734 (XXV).
16 Res. 2936 (XXVII).
17 Res. 31/9.
18 A/31/243 and Annex.
19 Res. 34/103.
20 A/C. 6/35/L. 5 and A/C. 6/36/L. 19.
21 A/C. 6/36/L. 19 p. 5.
22 E.g. in Afghanistan, Angola, Chile, El Salvador, Ethiopia, Kampuchea, Korea, Vietnam.
23 Suy, Erik, 'A New International Law for a New World Order', *The Spirit of Uppsala* (JUS 81) Manuscript No. 43 p. 11.
24 Falk, Richard A., *The Status of Law in International Society* (Princeton University Press, New Jersey, 1970) p. 29.
25 Id. p. 180.
26 Higgins, Rosalyn, *The Development of International Law through the Political Organs of the United Nations* (Oxford University Press, London 1963) p. 6.
27 Arangio-Ruiz, Gaetano, *The United Nations Declaration on Friendly Relations and the System of the Sources of International Law* (Sijthoff and Nordhoff, Maryland 1979) p. 77.
28 Röling, B.V.A., *International Law in an Expanded World* (Amsterdam 1960) p. 77.
29 E.g. Galtung, Johan, *The True Worlds: A Transnational Perspective* (The Free Press, NY 1980).
30 Blix, Hans, 'The Principle of Peaceful Settlement of Disputes', *The Legal Principles Governing Friendly Relations and Co-operation Among States*, WFUNA Seminar (A.W. Sijthoff, Leyden 1966) p. 64.
31 Convention on the Settlement of Investment Disputes between States and Nationals of Other States, of 14 October 1966. There were 79 contracting States at 30 June 1980.
32 By Res. 1262 (XIII).
33 Nawaz, M.K., 'An Inquiry into the Historical Development of Certain Cardinal Principles of International Law', *The Legal Principles Governing Friendly Relations and Co-Operation Among States*, op.cit. p. 27.
34 Arangio-Ruiz, op.cit. p. 36.
35 Higgins, op.cit. p. 5.
36 Report of the Working Group on 'Theory and Methodology of International Law', *Fifty-eighth Conference of the International Law Association*, 1980, p. 198.
37 Report of the Secretary-General, A/36/597 of 19 November 1981, p. 56 para. 236; emphasis added.

CHAPTER 8

Preventing an Increase in Nuclear Armed States

The Horizontal Non-Proliferation Regime

Horizontal proliferation is the acquisition of nuclear weapons capability by additional States. Nuclear weapons capability could be a few crude bombs manufactured or obtained by clandestine means, or the declared stock-piling of several hundred weapons, with correspondingly sophisticated delivery systems, or any other level of nuclear weapons preparedness between those extremes. The stationing of nuclear weapons, owned and controlled by one State, into the territory of another State, is regarded as a part of vertical proliferation as between States that have control over nuclear weapons.

The horizontal non-proliferation regime has been created by the international community to prevent or inhibit the spread of nuclear weapons to additional countries. It is based on the operation of three treaties: the Statute of the International Atomic Energy Agency (IAEA), the Treaty of Tlatelolco, and the Non-Proliferation Treaty.[1] The last named Treaty sets out the measures to be adopted for the prevention of horizontal proliferation as follows –

Article I

Each nuclear-weapon State Party to the Treaty undertakes not to transfer to any recipient whatsoever nuclear weapons or other nuclear explosive devices or control over such weapons or explosive devices directly, or indirectly; and not in any way to assist, encourage, or induce any non-nuclear weapon State to manufacture or otherwise acquire nuclear weapons or other nuclear explosive devices, or control over such weapons or explosive devices.

Article II

Each non-nuclear-weapon State Party to the Treaty undertakes not to receive the transfer from any transferor whatsoever of nuclear weapons or other nuclear explosive devices or of control over such weapons or explosive devices directly, or indirectly; not to manufacture or otherwise acquire nuclear weapons or other nuclear explosive devices; and not to seek or receive any assistance in the manufacture of nuclear weapons or other nuclear explosive devices.

The corresponding Article I of the Treaty of Tlatelolco only refers to the obligations of non-nuclear-weapon States in the maintenance of the horizontal non-proliferation regime, in the following terms –

Article I

1. The Contracting Parties hereby undertake to use exclusively for

peaceful purposes the nuclear material and facilities which are under their jurisdiction, and to prohibit and prevent in their respective territories:

(a) The testing, use, manufacture, production or acquisition by any means whatsoever of any nuclear weapons, by the Parties themselves, directly or indirectly, on behalf of anyone else or in any other way, and (b) The receipt, storage, installation, deployment and any form of possession of any nuclear weapons, directly or indirectly, by the Parties themselves, by anyone on their behalf or in any other way.

2. The Contracting Parties also undertake to refrain from engaging in, encouraging or authorising, directly or indirectly, or in any way participating in the testing, use, manufacture, production, possession or control of any nuclear weapon.

Both Treaties require extensive verification procedures to be undertaken in co-operation with the IAEA. Such verification primarily consists of entering into safeguards agreements with the IAEA, whereby the Agency is supplied by the relevant non-nuclear-weapon State with the necessary information concerning nuclear activities to be safeguarded, including the disposal of all special fissionable material. The agreements to be concluded with the Agency also require the contracting State to permit periodic inspection of *all* of its nuclear materials and facilities (full scope safeguards) by designated inspectors employed by the Agency.[2]

The Treaty of Tlatelolco, which preceded the Non-Proliferation Treaty, does not rely entirely on the operation of the safeguards system with the Agency. That Treaty contains provisions for additional controls, requiring States Parties to submit biannual reports confirming that no activity prohibited by the Treaty has occurred within their borders, and permitting special inspections in given circumstances.[3] Another notable difference is that the Treaty of Tlatelolco, unlike the Non-Proliferation Treaty, permits nuclear explosions for peaceful purposes under its Article 18. If the Article is to be observed to the letter, it is not likely to have any practical application because it requires a peaceful nuclear explosion to be in accordance with prior Articles 1 and 5. The relevant portion of Article 5 defines a nuclear weapon as –

. . . any device which is capable of releasing nuclear energy in an uncontrolled manner and which has a group of characteristics that are appropriate for use for warlike purposes.

Since there is no known or contemplated method whereby peaceful nuclear explosions can be differentiated from explosions suited to warlike purposes, the provisions of Article 18 appear to be redundant. This does not exclude the possibility of tortuous interpretations to suit the purposes of some Latin American States not Parties to the Non-Proliferation Treaty, which may be determined to explode nuclear devices without acknowledging nuclear-weapon status. However, world public opinion could not be deceived by such a ruse, least of all in Latin America itself where the issue has been the subject of some concern.

The second Review Conference of the Parties to the Treaty on the Non-Proliferaton of Nuclear Weapons, during August-September 1980, afforded a good opportunity to evaluate the effectiveness of the IAEA safeguards system in relation to the entire horizontal non-proliferation regime. While the Review Conference naturally concentrated on issues directly bearing on the conduct of the Parties to the Treaty, the operation of the safeguards system in relation to the Treaty of Tlatelolco, and also in connection with safeguards agreements entered into with States not members of either Treaty, came under scrutiny. Although the Conference concluded without reaching agreement on any substantive issue,[4] due to the dissatisfaction of Parties with the lack of progress by nuclear-weapon States in halting vertical proliferation, many important assessments were made by individual States and groups of States.

The caucus of developing nations, known as the Group of 77, submitted their assessment in the form of two Working Papers.[5] Relying on the report of the IAEA, as well as their own evaluations, these States maintained that in the past five years there had been no diversion of nuclear material subject to the IAEA safeguards system. Yet, in the same context, they pointed out that there have been reports alleging 'significant quantities of special nuclear material unaccounted for in a non-nuclear-weapon State party to the Treaty'.[6] However, it was felt that in broad terms, the verification procedures undertaken in co-operation with the IAEA,[7] and implemented in accordance with the Agency's Statute, were quite adequate. IAEA provisions were found to be satisfactory, not only to the extent that they verified the non-diversion of sensitive materials, but also with respect to the manner in which they were applied, so as not to hamper 'economic, scientific or technological development of the Parties to the Treaty'.

The Group of 77 also drew attention to serious flaws in the horizontal non-proliferation regime. While it was conceded that there had been no *direct* transfer of nuclear weapons to non-nuclear-weapon States in breach of Article I, it was implied that the spirit of the Treaty had not been altogether complied with. The Group noted the loophole in the Treaty whereby non-nuclear-weapon States Parties are not expressly forbidden to export nuclear material, equipment and technology to other non-nuclear-weapon States, in a manner that could lead to their utilisation for the acquisition of nuclear weapons capability by the recipient. The members of the Group did not recommend an amendment of the Treaty to rectify this omission. Instead, they called on the Parties to the Treaty to interpret its provisions so as to infer an extension of the obligations of nuclear-weapon States to non-nuclear-weapon States, whenever applicable.

The Group was particularly concerned about the transfer of nuclear materials and skills to States not Parties to the Treaty whose nuclear-weapon status has been in doubt, in particular South Africa and Israel.[8] They referred to these two States by name but omitted to mention some other similarly ambivalent importing States, as well as all the exporting States so implicated.

Mexico and Yugoslavia were critical of the alleged deficient implementation of Article V of the Treaty.[9] They claimed that there had been insufficient effort, on the part of the IAEA, to inform non-nuclear-weapon States Parties about the potential benefits to be derived from the peaceful application of nuclear explosions allegedly obtainable from the nuclear-weapon States. Efforts to keep open the lines of communication for passing on information of this kind might be intended to forestall any moves among the Parties to the Treaty of Tlatelolco from insisting on the right to detonate nuclear explosions of an ostensibly peaceful kind.

The United States drew attention to a very significant problem, arising from the vast increase in the volume and type of safeguarding activities that the IAEA will have to undertake in order to keep pace with the growing nuclear industry and with changed methods of operation among sections of that industry.[10] The United States cautioned that, unless additional human and financial resources were made available for the refurbishment of the Agency's safeguards procedures, they could become inadequate in the near future. It was also suggested that States planning new commercial nuclear installations should design and construct them in such a manner as to facilitate safeguards measures.

The Implications of Horizontal Proliferation

The consequences of horizontal proliferation would undoubtedly vary depending on the sequence in which States acquired the capability, the overt or clandestine nature of the capability, and the degree of sophistication attained by the various States. None of these variables are foreseeable with any certainty, although the level of nuclear technology for industrial energy production is acknowledged to be the best guide of a State's ability to produce nuclear weapons, if it so wished.

Taking into account both technological development and a possible political motivation, the following States have come into contemplation as likely threshold or Nth States in the foreseeable future: Algeria, Argentina, Australia, Brazil, Egypt, Germany (Federal Republic of), India, Indonesia, Iran, Iraq, Israel, Japan, Korea (South), Libya, Nigeria, Pakistan, South Africa, Sweden, Syria, Taiwan and Zaire.[11]

While several of these States are subject to the Non-Proliferation Treaty or the Treaty of Tlatelolco, their renunciation or breach of those Treaties cannot be ruled out in the event of the breakdown of the non-proliferation regime. Such an eventuality must be contemplated in any prediction about the likely consequences of horizontal proliferation.

Bearing in mind the difficulty of foreseeing what any one State may do in an altered international environment or as the consequence of an internal change of Government, it is evident that across-the-board prediction about the consequences of a cataclysmic upheaval, such as horizontal proliferation might produce, can only qualify as guesswork. Nevertheless, many predictions of this kind are being confidently made.[12]

Soviet commentators have said little about the expected consequences of horizontal proliferation, but the actions of the Soviet Union indicate that it is committed to a stringent policy of preventing the emergence of more nuclear-weapon States. The Soviet Union has been extremely reticent about the transfer of nuclear technology,[13] even at the expense of serious political disadvantage in its relations with the States friendly towards it.[14] Further, it has foregone the very considerable political advantages to be attained from offering nuclear technology and materials to countries rebuffed in their efforts to obtain these from the United States and other Western States. Whenever supplying special fissionable materials, the Soviet Union insists on the return of all spent fuel, thus preventing any possibility of its misuse.[15]

Although not as commercially stringent as the Soviet Union, the United States has so far followed a determined policy opposed to horizontal proliferation. This policy coincided with Government and academic assessments concerning the dangerously destabilising consequences that the emergence of additional nuclear-weapon States would produce. The introduction of the Nuclear Weapon Non-Proliferation Act in 1977 by President Carter, and its subsequent adoption in 1978, marked the zenith of that policy and that outlook.

When attempting to apply the legislation by renegotiating supply agreements with countries like India and Japan, the United States encountered much stronger opposition than it had anticipated. In addition, Western allies like France and Germany did not close ranks on the issue. Instead, they permitted commercial interests in their States to take advantage of the strict supply conditions imposed by the United States, by offering more favourable terms.[16] Naturally this was received with disfavour by the United States nuclear industry, which has resulted, since 1978, in a powerful backlash opposed to strict anti-proliferation measures.

Since that time there has been a number of assessments in the United States predicting that an increase in nuclear-weapon States is (a) inevitable, (b) manageable, or (c) decidedly advantageous. There is a notable contrast between the attitudes that prompted the introduction of the 1977 Act, and subsequent official attitudes to horizontal non-proliferation. For instance, a *Nuclear Proliferation Fact-book*, prepared in 1977 by the Congressional Research Service of the Library of Congress,[17] took the objective of non-proliferation for granted and concentrated on methods for achieving this purpose. By 1979, however, a collation of assessments by the Central Intelligence Agency and the Department of Defence,[18] assumed large-scale proliferation within a decade or so to be unavoidable.

Without over-estimating the significance of the 1979 collation, it is interesting to note that all of the assessments in that study tend to be optimistic and no grossly destabilising consequences of horizontal proliferation are predicted. On the contrary, it is postulated that the known possibility of possession of nuclear weapons by sub-national groups would tend to stabilise otherwise unstable regimes;[19] that horizontal proliferation could undermine Third World solidarity in its economic confrontation with the North;[20] that acquisition of the weapons is not likely to result in their use;[21] that, alternatively, the use of nuclear weapons by the newly emerged nuclear-weapon States could have a salutory effect by bringing about a code of good behaviour regarding nuclear weapons;[22] and, above all, that horizontal proliferation would disadvantage the Soviet Union *vis-à-vis* the United States. The last-mentioned assessment is the most significant from a policy point of view, and is presented in the following unequivocal terms –

To recapitulate, nuclear proliferation would have adverse effects on the

Soviet Union, increasing the threat to its national security, diminishing its ability to project power and influence through military means, and reducing its stature as a global power. To counteract these effects and remain as actively competitive in world affairs as possible, the Soviet Union would modify some of its traditional strategies and tactics which would tend to become increasingly counterproductive in an era of nuclear proliferation, replacing them with others, more suitable to cope with the tasks at hand. The style and method of Soviet foreign policy would become less abrasive. The content of Soviet foreign policies would be less confrontationally oriented, emphasizing co-operation and accommodation instead. Moderation, reasonableness, a high sense of responsibility, and, perhaps, even responsiveness to the sensitivities of others would characterize Soviet behaviour. In sum, under the impact of nuclear proliferation the Soviet Union would become a more sensible member of the global community and play a more constructive role in it.[23]

In all of the assessments, the possible adverse consequences in the West of uncertainty, social disillusionment, rapid political realignments, and perhaps public fear verging on panic if nuclear weapons were used by anyone, have been omitted from calculation. Neither is it apparent, for example, why Soviet leaders should react so positively in a situation of unprecedented complexity and stress, unless they are expected to be endowed with superhuman qualities. As there is no suggestion of confidence in the Soviet leadership in other connections anywhere in the collation, there appears to be no reasonable explanation for this expectation of extraordinary prudence. Similar criticisms could be levelled at other highly optimistic conclusions reached by the study, which derives its significance from the fact that the views presented coincided with United States policy changes indicating diminished commitment to non-proliferation.

One example of the change was the acceptance, within the framework of the International Nuclear Fuel Cycle Evaluation (INFCE), of the arguments supporting the construction of fast breeder reactors on a commercial scale, despite the well known proliferation risks involved. Other examples of relaxation could be found in the easing of uranium supply conditions, as in the case of continuing supplies to India, notwithstanding that country's non-compliance with United States export conditions. There has also been a slackening of United States diplomatic and economic pressures to compel all States to submit their nuclear facilities to full scope IAEA safeguards.[24]

Interestingly, the diminished concern shown by the United States in non-proliferation, spurred many Third World countries to adopt the non-proliferation cause. Since SSD I, there has been a growing appreciation of the likely security and economic consequence to the Third World of the acquisition of nuclear weapons capability by some of them. While longer term destabilisation in Superpower relations is anticipated, it has not been overlooked that the first casualties of horizontal proliferation could be the political rivals within the Non-aligned group of nations.

At the Second Review Conference of the Non-Proliferation Treaty, had the participating members of the Group of 77 decided to end the non-proliferation regime, they had an excellent opportunity to do so.[25] With political divisions and economic competitiveness holding sway among the nuclear-weapon States, the re-emergence of cold war attitudes between the Superpowers, and adequate justification provided by the clear breach of their obligations under Article VI by the nuclear-weapons States, especially the Superpowers, the Non-Proliferation Treaty could have been repudiated there and then.

There was no repudiation. On the contrary, the nations of the Group of 77 affirmed their adherence to the principles of the Treaty in the strongest terms used to date. They did so by quoting from the conclusions reached by SSD I in the Final Document, which warned of 'the threat to the very survival of mankind posed by the existence of nuclear weapons and the continuing arms race', and cautioned that 'mankind today is confronted with an unprecedented threat of self-extinction arising from the massive and competitive accumulation of the most destructive weapons ever produced . . .'[26]

The upshot was that, although the Review Conference ended without agreement on any substantive issue, commitment to the Treaty and the principles it embodies remained intact – no longer primarily in response to active persuasion by the West but rather as an expression of the autonomous evaluation of the Third World, including would-be Nth countries.

Since the end of the Conference, there has been a partial swing back of the pendulum in the United States towards a reassertion of the non-proliferation commitment. The reappraisal has been at the behest of long-standing opponents of horizontal proliferation, like Senator John Glenn, who was a sponsor of the 1978 Nuclear Non-Proliferation Act, and who continues to warn about the propensity of peaceful nuclear technology to diversion for the production of nuclear weapons.[27] Other traditional advocates of anti-proliferation measures, like Joseph Nye, Deputy Under-Secretary of State responsible for non-proliferation policy during the Carter Administration, now take an intermediate position, cautioning against both 'purism' and 'cynicism' in supply policy.[28]

The trend was confirmed in the Presidential Statement on Non-Proliferation, made on 16 July 1981, in which it was reiterated that –

> Further proliferation would pose a severe threat to international peace, regional and global stability, and the security interests of the United States and other countries.

Regarding the contentious issue of supply policy, President Reagan undertook to 'seek' agreement on full scope safeguards in non-nuclear-weapon States, 'as a condition for any *significant new* nuclear supply commitment'. On the issue of reprocessing, the Statement declared that the Administration will 'not inhibit or set back . . . breeder reactor development abroad in nations with advanced nuclear power programs where it does not constitute a proliferation risk'.[29] No guidelines were set out for the objective determination of the existence of a 'proliferation risk'.

Continuing Development of the Horizontal Non-Proliferation Regime

Convention on the Physical Protection of Nuclear Material [30]

Following several years of negotiations, the Convention was opened for signature on 3 March 1980. As stated in the text, which was adopted at the Vienna Conference of Government representatives, the chief aim is to prevent the diversion of nuclear materials for weapons purposes, although the prevention of other kinds of misuse is also contemplated, whether in the course of domestic use, storage or transport. The Convention refers to any illegal manner of appropriating nuclear material, including illegal receipt, possession, use or alteration of materials.[31]

The first international effort to give protection against theft or other unauthorised diversion of nuclear material, and against sabotage of nuclear facilities, was made in 1972 under the auspicies of the IAEA. It was in the form of a report by a panel of experts convened by the Director-General, under the title 'Recommendations for the Physical Protection of Nuclear Materials'. These Recommendations were revised and published in 1975.[32] Subsequently the Director-General of IAEA convened a Standing Advisory Group on Physical Protection of Nuclear Material, which proposed some modifications that were incorporated into the document in 1977.[33]

The Convention is a further extension of the original IAEA Recommendations. By its provisions, physical protection is to be applied during the transportation of the materials across international borders, and also across the territories of individual States. Pursuant to the Convention, Parties undertake responsibility for materials carried on ships or aeroplanes under their jurisdiction, and they are required to impose agreed terms on any import or export authorisation of such materials. The types of physical protection that are to be applied to nuclear materials have been determined in accordance with the technical standards of the IAEA.

States Parties have also agreed to co-operate in the retrieval of missing or illegally appropriated material and to prosecute or extradite the perpetrators of criminal offences prohibited by the Convention. Provisions relating to the prosecution and extradition of offenders have been based on the Hague and Montreal Conventions on Suppression of Terrorism in Air Traffic and on the Convention and Punishment of Crime Against Internationally Protected Persons including Diplomatic Agents.[34]

International Nuclear Fuel Cycle Evaluation (INFCE)

The International Nuclear Fuel Cycle Evaluation was undertaken during 1978-80 by forty supplier and consumer States of nuclear materials and technology. It was an attempt to reconcile the perceived economic benefits of nuclear energy with the belatedly acknowledged propensity of such use to spread the capability of manufacturing nuclear weapons. The suitability of all nuclear technology, and all weapons-grade material however obtained, to utilisation for the manufacture of nuclear weapons, has long been denied or underrated. It has been correctly pointed out, particularly by spokesmen for the developing nations, that there are more efficient ways of acquiring nuclear weapons capability than by clandestinely diverting materials and technological expertise ostensibly required for peaceful use. While that argument is sound from an economic standpoint, there are persuasive political reasons why the more devious path to proliferation may be preferred.[35]

Concerns of this genre prompted a number of supplier States, consisting of Western and Socialist industrial States, to form themselves into the so-called 'London Suppliers Club'. They agreed to a set of guidelines regarding the conditions under which transfer of sensitive materials and technologies for peaceful purposes were to be conducted. These guidelines were reproduced in IAEA document INFCIRC 254, imposing substantially stricter conditions of transfer than those agreed upon by all IAEA Members, as set out in INFCIRC 209 and Addenda. Some consumer Members of the IAEA bitterly attacked the sectional approach by the 'London Suppliers Club', whose members were accused of restricting supply for economic gain, rather than a measure to prevent proliferation.

Developing countries have argued, convincingly enough, that if the supplier States were truly concerned about the horizontal proliferation problem, they would ensure that States Parties to the Non-Proliferation Treaty received preferential treatment over non-Parties[36] – whereas the converse position tends to prevail whenever economic conditions favour the non-Party. Some supplier States have even failed, so far, to require the acceptance of full scope IAEA safeguards as an invariable condition of supply, on the inconsistent and spurious ground that the requirement would constitute unwarranted interference in the internal affairs of sovereign States.

Another area of contention has arisen with respect to the measures to be adopted to enable the IAEA to maintain the high standard of its inspections. Of particular concern were the newly developed fast-breeder reactors being constructed in Germany and Japan as prototypes, with a view to their introduction on a commercial scale, and the growing volume of nuclear material being produced by an increasing number of facilities. Plans have been under consideration by the Agency for the construction of regional nuclear fuel-cycle centres and for the international management of surplus plutonium.

It was the accumulation of problems such as these which prompted the organising of INFCE. The essentially technical and analytical study afforded opportunities for international diplomatic consultation and the informal negotiation of outstanding issues. The evaluation was conducted in the following Working Groups –

Working Group 1 – Fuel and Heavy Water Availability (Co-Chairmen: Canada, Egypt, India);

Working Group 2 – Enrichment Availability (Co-Chairmen: France, Federal Republic of Germany, Iran);

Working Group 3 – Assurances of Long-Term Supply of Technology, Fuel and Heavy Water and Services in the Interest of National Needs Consistent with Non-Proliferation (Co-Chairmen: Australia, Philippines, Switzerland);

Working Group 4 – Reprocessing, Plutonium Handling, Recycle (Co-Chairmen: Japan, United Kingdom);

Working Group 5 – Fast Breeders (Co-Chairmen: Belgium, Italy, USSR);

Working Group 6 – Spent Fuel Management (Co-Chairmen: Argentina, Spain);

Working Group 7 – Waste Management and Disposal (Co-Chairmen: Finland, Netherlands, Sweden);

Working Group 8 – Advanced Fuel Cycle and Reactor Concepts (Co-Chairmen: Republic of Korea, Romania, USA).

The above designation of Working Groups accurately indicates that the emphasis was on economic considerations, especially the assurance of supply, the efficiency and safety of reactors, and the implementation of more productive technologies with respect to reprocessing, spent fuel management etc. However, all of these matters are inexorably bound up with the problems of diversion and proliferation. Hopes were expressed during the earlier part of the Evaluation that a breakthrough in technologies might result in the construction of nuclear fuel cycles that are diversion-proof. While it was found that such innovations would be feasible, it was concluded that they are not, at present, economically competitive.

During the course of the evaluation, the activities most prone to risk were identified as fuel fabrication, uranium reprocessing, and plutonium handling. However, it was acknowledged at various times that some risks of proliferation exist in relation to fresh nuclear fuel containing enriched plutonium, uranium enrichment, all reactors, spent fuel storage – especially plutonium storage, mixed oxide fuel fabrication, waste disposal, and the dismantling of old nuclear plants.

The findings of the participating countries, and five international organisations which contributed to the evaluation, were largely inconclusive.[37] It was envisaged by the participants that, following INFCE, dialogue concerning the subject would continue within the framework of the IAEA. One kind of follow-up measure was expected to be the conduct of tests to evaluate a number of proposals presented at INFCE for proliferation-resistant technology.

Ongoing Conflicts and their Resolution

Neither INFCE nor any other forum has yet provided satisfactory solutions for reconciling the often quoted, so called 'inalienable right' of all non-nuclear-weapon States to carry out their own programmes for the peaceful use of nuclear energy,[38] with the objectives of preventing horizontal proliferation. Nevertheless, many improvements have been made with an important cumulative effect. The least publicised, but probably most effective steps have been the continuing improvements in the safeguards system applied by the IAEA. Increasingly stringent conditions imposed by the supplier countries, although open to charges of undemocratic and discriminatory conduct, have no doubt had an inhibiting effect on proliferation tendencies.

The several anti-proliferation proposals in Working Papers and other contributions to the inconclusive second Review Conference of the Non-

142

Proliferation Treaty, together with the many tentative suggestions arising from the INFCE studies, have provided the basis for far-reaching measures. Clandestine diversion of nuclear materials for whatever purpose, including their utilisation by terrorist groups, perhaps with the connivance of some non-nuclear-weapon States, will be inhibited as the result of the Convention on Physical Protection of Nuclear Material. Technological initiatives undertaken by States, singly or in co-operation, for the perfection of economically viable yet proliferation-resistant technologies also hold promise. Alternatively, the utilisation of nuclear fusion techniques in energy production, such as those being investigated through the International Tokamak Reactor Project,[39] could have an important future impact.

Likewise the proposed institutional barriers to proliferation, notably the scheme for international plutonium storage and international spent fuel management, as well as regional reprocessing and similar co-operative measures,[40] present possibilities for reconciling economic objectives with non-proliferation objectives. Current projects have a predominantly European commercial orientation.[41] Plans for international projects proposed to be undertaken chiefly to inhibit proliferation, are not sufficiently developed for legal issues to have emerged clearly. They could be established along the lines of the Statute of the IAEA, only participating States would have much greater economic interests in their operation.

The above matters will remain under constant review by the IAEA. There will be further opportunities for the elaboration of the appropriate agreements at several forthcoming conferences. The most significant of these will be a world Conference, in 1983, for the Promotion .of International Co-operation in the Peaceful Uses of Nuclear Energy.[42]

It should be borne in mind, however, that neither the technical possibilities for further international action to inhibit horizontal proliferation, nor administratively contrived opportunities, could be automatically converted into concrete measures. That will depend on the extent of concurrence of all relevant States to take the definitive steps. Likewise, existing agreements regarding safeguards are only as firm as the determination to enforce them. If other political objectives override that determination, particularly by one or other of the Superpowers, then the non-proliferation regime must suffer to that extent. The gradual erosion of the non-proliferation regime could be slowed down by the strict imposition of the requirement for full scope safeguards of all nuclear activities by non-nuclear weapon States wishing to acquire nuclear technology, equipment or materials.

It may be preferable for the international community to moderate disapproval of the existence of a few quasi-nuclear-weapon States whose security is under special threat, like India, Israel and South Africa, until the political situation eases, than to make their presence an excuse for the further relaxation of standards. Yet both Third World and developed Western States are prone to the latter interpretation of the situation.

There is a tendency for countries of the Third World to accept proliferation under the slogan of non-discrimination. China has been the foremost proponent of this approach, in outright opposition to the Non-Proliferation Treaty. Three years before that Treaty was concluded, the

Chinese position was stated in these words by Marshal Chen Yi –

> China hopes that Afro-Asian countries will be able to make atom bombs themselves and it would be better for a greater number of countries to come into possession of atom bombs.[43]

Since rapprochement with the United States, China has modified its public statements on horizontal proliferation but has made no statement in favour of non-proliferation goals. It appears, however, that China has not supplied nuclear technology to other States. For example K.N. Romachandran claims that –

> Firstly on the question of transferring nuclear-weapon technology to other countries – a tangible act in support of proliferation – Beijing's unwillingness is similar to that of other nuclear powers. When Libya sent a secret mission to China and expressed a desire to buy a nuclear bomb late Premier Chou politely but firmly rejected the request.[44]

Yet it has been claimed by M. Goryanov that a statement made by Chinese Premier Zhao Ziyang in Pakistan, during his visit there in 1981, 'implies assistance in the manufacture of the "Islamic atom bomb" '.[45]

It has been noted that there are also some Western theorists who postulate the alleged benefits to be derived from the possession of nuclear arsenals by States friendly to the Western Alliance. What they overlook is that if such a process gained momentum, the transfer of counterveiling nuclear weapons to their antagonistic competitors could be achieved in a very short period of time. A clear example of the speed with which a developing nation can acquire a nuclear weapons capability is that of Iraq, an oil-rich State which has no need of nuclear energy for industry and has had no peaceful nuclear facilities. Nevertheless, a sophisticated research reactor would have been ready for operation in that country by 1982, had it not been destroyed by Israel.[46] There can be no doubt that Iraq was in the process of acquiring the capability to manufacture nuclear weapons. The only matter open to question is whether there had been an intention to divert fissionable materials in contravention of commitments entered into under the Non-Proliferation Treaty.[47]

As we have seen, the horizontal non-proliferation regime requires States to adopt and adhere to treaties, contractual arrangements, and gentlemen's agreements, and to do so by following the spirit as well as the letter of the agreements. In a subsequent Chapter the further need to monitor observance of the agreements, and to apply formal sanctions or economic disincentives, will also be examined. The success of the regime depends on these, together with some other factors.

As with vertical proliferation, the impetus towards horizontal proliferation is constantly spurred by technological advances. The nexus between the spread of technology and the danger of proliferation was presented in the following terms by United States Senator John Glenn –

> A nation with fairly low sophistication in nuclear matters can make a bomb from 10 kilograms of plutonium. If they really know what they're doing, they can make a bomb from 5 kilograms. That means you could have between 25 and 50 bombs made from the leftover fuel of each

gigawatt each year. If you multiply all that, the potential from 247 peaceful nuclear reactors is between 4,000 and 8,000 bombs per year.[48]

Technological advances also make safeguarding more difficult due to the quantity of materials to be inspected and the presently seeming impossibility of verifying the quantity of fissionable materials in the more advanced nuclear reactors.

In common with all NAC, horizontal proliferation is also dependent on the general international situation, especially the relationship between the Superpowers and their progress, or lack of it, to curb vertical proliferation. Much more than other NAC issues, horizontal proliferation is influenced by economic considerations. These involve competition for nuclear markets by the developed nations and the condition of North-South relations, especially disputes about the implementation of a New International Economic Order and the claims of erstwhile colonial peoples to the rapid transfer of technology.

Maintenance and extension of the institutional framework of IAEA is crucial. For example, the future ability of IAEA to assume control over the storage and reprocessing of nuclear materials could be decisive for the long term success of horizontal non-proliferation. In the short term, the person of the Director-General of the IAEA, as well as the composition of the Board of Governors, exercise a considerable influence over the maintenance of the regime. Apart from its planning duties, the Board is a quasi-judicial panel when investigating a breach or threatened breach of its Statute, and when recommending sanctions or warnings accordingly.[49] Therefore, the election in September 1981 to the position of Director-General of Hans Blix,[50] a committed opponent of proliferation, is a signal that, for the immediate future at least, the international consensus is to persist with a stringent approach to the horizontal spread of nuclear weapons.

Notes

1 See Table I. (page 24); Indirectly, the Partial Test-Ban Treaty also inhibits horizontal proliferation.
2 Infra Ch. 10.
3 Arts. 10 (5) and 16 (1).
4 *Final Document of the Second Review Conference of the Parties to the Treaty on the Non-Proliferation of Nuclear Weapons*, NPT/CONF. II/22 of 7 September 1980.
5 NPT/CONF. II/C. I/2 and NPT/CONF. II/C. II/34.
6 NPT/CONF. II/C. II/34 p. 1.
7 INFCIRC/153 (Corr.), *The Structure and Content of Agreements Required in Connection with the Treaty on the Non-Proliferation of Nuclear Weapons.*
8 NPT/CONF. II/C. I/2 p. 2.
9 NPT/CONF. II/C. II/39.
10 NPT/CONF. II/C. II/35.
11 E.g. discussion by Fischer, D.A.V. (former Assistant Dir.-Gen. of IAEA) in unpublished Paper on *Preventing the Spread of Nuclear Weapons*, delivered at the Australian National University on 2 April and 9 April 1981; See also *The Annual Report* of the IAEA, esp. for 1980 and 1981.
12 For recent predictions initiating the trend, see Gompert, D.C., Mandelbaum,

M., Garwin, R.L., and Barton, J.H., *Nuclear Weapons and World Politics* (McGraw-Hill, New York 1977).

13 Fischer, D.A.V., *Nuclear Issues: International Control and International Co-operation* (ANU, Canberra 1981) p. viii – 'As far as the writer is aware, there is no sensitive plant (reprocessing plant or enrichment facility) or significant quantity of plutonium or highly enriched uranium in any of the countries which have received nuclear supplies from the Soviet Union.'

14 E.g. refusal to provide Egypt with a nuclear reactor prior to that country's alignment with the West.

15 Fischer, loc. cit. – 'Spent fuel from Soviet reactors is returned to the Soviet Union.' See also Nogee, Joseph L., 'Soviet Nuclear Proliferation Policy: Dilemmas and Contradictions', *Orbis*, Winter 1981, Vol. 24 No. 4 p. 751.

16 Regarding the most ambitious project of this kind see Krugmann, Hartmut, 'The German-Brazilian Nuclear Deal', *The Bulletin of the Atomic Scientists*, February 1981, Vol. 37 No. 2 p. 32.

17 Transmitted to Congress on 23 September 1977, (US Govt. Printing Office, Washington 1977).

18 King, John K., (Ed.) *International Political Effects of the Spread of Nuclear Weapons* (US Govt. Printing Office, Washington 1979).

19 Ibid. p. 57.

20 Id. p. 37.

21 Id. p. 143.

22 Id. p. 146.

23 Id. p. 122.

24 Fischer, D.A.V., (1981) op. cit. p. 27 – '. . . the reprocessing and enrichment restrictions of the Act have had no visible impact upon Pretoria, Islamabad, Tel Aviv or New Delhi'.

25 See *Final Report of the Preparatory Committee* of the Conference, NPT/CONF.II/1 of 2 April 1980 esp. Background Papers prepared by the UN Secretariat for the Conference, ref. NPT/CONF.II of 1980; and other background material collated by the Preparatory Committee ref. NPT/CONF. II/PC. II of 1979 and 1980.

26 NPT/CONF. II/C. 1/2 p. 1.

27 *New York Times*, 26 April 1981, Section IV p. 3.

28 Nye, Joseph, 'Prospects for Non-Proliferation', *Survival*, May-June 1981, Vol. XXIII No. 3 p. 107.

29 Presidential Statement on Non-Proliferation (United States, 16 July 1981) *Survival*, Sept.-Oct. 1981, Vol. XXIII No. 5 p. 232. Emphasis added.

30 INFCIRC/274/Rev. 1 of May 1980.

31 It has been argued that this type of NAC agreement is inimical to personal freedom: Sieghart, Paul, 'Nuclear Power and Human Rights', *International Commission of Jurists*, June 1977, No. 18 p. 49 – 'In short, the price of "safe" nuclear power could prove to include a slow but inexorable erosion of civil liberties, human rights and the rule of law.'

32 INFCIRC/225 Corr.

33 INFCIRC/255/Rev. 1 of June 1977.

34 See Mitic, Miodrat, 'Convention on Physical Protection of Nuclear Materials', *Review of International Affairs* (Belgrade) March 1980, Vol. XXXI pp. 24-6.

35 Dahlitz, J., 'Proliferation and Confrontation', *Australian Outlook*, April 1979, Vol. 33 No. 1 p. 34.

36 NPT/CONF. II/C. II/34 p. 5.

37 INFCE/PC/2/1-9 of 29 February 1980, reproduced in IAEA publication STI/PUB/534.

38 A/RES/32/50, A/RES/34/63, and Report of the Secretary-General A/34/197 and Adds. 1 and 2.

39 Regarding the construction of a demonstration fusion reactor, the International Tokamak Reactor (INTOR) Workshop published its first report in June 1980.

40 For a comprehensive discussion see *Internationalization to Prevent the Spread of Nuclear Weapons*, Stockholm International Peace Research Inst. (Taylor & Francis, London 1980).

41 Apart from the IAEA, the following are the major international institutions for assisting the nuclear power industry, chiefly established for commercial purposes but with a proliferation inhibiting dimension – *Eurochemic* consisting of 13 States was initiated by the Nuclear Energy Agency of the OECD for training, research and development with the aid of a minor reprocessing plant. *Urenco* was created by the Federal Republic of Germany, the Netherlands and the United Kingdom to promote centrifuge technology. *Eurodif* is a European joint stock company operating a commercial gaseous diffusion plant. *Joint European Torus (JET)* is a research and development project to investigate fusion energy.

42 To be held in Geneva 29 August – 9 September 1983, A/RES/36/78.

43 Press conference on 29 September 1965, reported in *Peking Review*, 8 October 1965, Vol. 8 No. 41.

44 'China and Nuclear Non-Proliferation Issues', *Institute of Defence Studies and Analyses*, July-September 1980, Vol. 13 No. 1 p. 99.

45 'Cause for Concern', *New Times*, June 1981, No. 24 p. 11.

46 See A/RES/36/27.

47 See Perera, Judith, 'Was Iraq Really Developing a Bomb?' *New Scientist*, 11 June 1981, Vol. 90 No. 1257 p. 688; Also Day, Peter, *The Australian*, 23 June 1981, p. 6.

48 *New York Times*, 26 April 1981, Section IV. p. 3.

49 Statute of the IAEA, esp. Art. VI F.

50 Former Deputy Foreign Minister for Development and Co-operation of Sweden.

CHAPTER 9

The Bilateral Process in Nuclear Arms Control

Stabilising the Balance of Terror

As the nuclear weapons prowess of each Superpower greatly exceeds the nuclear weapons capability of all other States combined, the bilateral process is the most significant aspect of NAC. The bilateral NAC process consists of public agreements in the form of the ratified and unratified treaties listed in Table II (see page 28), public statements and, presumably, some confidential understandings. It is evident from Table II that basically two kinds of public agreements have been concluded in efforts by the Superpowers to stabilise the nuclear arms race.

The first kind of agreement is in the form of ratified treaties that aim to prevent the accidental outbreak of nuclear war, essentially by improving communications. These agreements encompass the so-called 'Hot Line' treaties which establish telegraphic, radio-telegraph, teleprinter and satellite communications between the Parties, especially for use in times of crisis. This type of agreement includes the only bilateral NAC agreements that are not between the Superpowers, namely agreements, concluded by the Soviet Union with the United Kingdom and France respectively. The other communications agreements are the Nuclear Accidents Agreement and the Agreement on the Prevention of Incidents On and Over the High Seas, both between the Superpowers. These Treaties require that immediate notification be given in ambiguous situations that could be mistaken for hostile action, and the taking of preventive steps in order to forestall misunderstandings that could lead to unpremeditated nuclear exchanges.

The second kind of bilateral NAC agreement sets limits on the number and type of nuclear weapons and delivery systems that may be tested or deployed by either Superpower. Most of the relevant agreements have been the outcome of the Strategic Arms Limitation Talks (SALT), of which only the agreements in the SALT I group of Treaties have been ratified. These comprise the Treaty on the Limitation of Anti-Ballistic Missile Systems (SALT ABM Treaty); the Interim Agreement on Certain Measures with Respect to the Limitations of Strategic Offensive Arms (SALT I Interim Agreement); and a Memorandum of Understanding Concerning the Establishment of a Standing Consultative Commission on Arms Limitation.

Several other bilateral agreements of the second kind have also been signed but have not been ratified. The most important among these has been the Treaty on the Limitation of Strategic Offensive Arms, including a Protocol, a Memorandum of Understanding, and a Joint Statement, together known as the SALT II Treaty. There is no evidence to suggest that there has been a breach of any of the currently relevant, but still unratified, bilateral NAC treaties. Regarding the SALT II Treaty, there have been repeated public statements by the United States, the Party unwilling to ratify the Treaty, that its terms will be observed on a reciprocal basis.

Multilateral NAC treaties listed in Table I (see page 24) also play a part in the bilateral NAC process, as they have a special relevance for the Superpowers. In particular, the Outer Space Treaty[1] is at present only applicable to the Superpowers, as only they have the means to carry out the activities contemplated by the Treaty. Although with the possible broadening of the terms of the Treaty other powers may also be affected, the Treaty would still retain a predominantly bilateral application.

The envisaged bilateral NAC programme entails a three-pronged strategy. *First*, there is need for the maintenance and continued supervision of existing ratified treaties and those agreements which, although unratified, have so far been observed on a mutual basis. *Second*, it is sought to prevent a new spiral in the bilateral nuclear arms race that could disturb the existing essential equivalence of nuclear armed forces. *Third*, there is the aspiration to achieve an eventual dismantling and destruction of nuclear weapons and weapons systems on a mutual basis, maintaining equal security at progressively lower levels of nuclear armament.

The principles agreed upon to govern the bilateral NAC process have been elaborated in their most comprehensive form by the SALT II Treaty, in the terms of a Joint Statement of Principles and Basic Guidelines. The Statement, despite its title, does not refer to principles but merely to broad objectives. These include the avoidance of the outbreak of nuclear war; the attainment of strategic stability; the outlawing of strategic offensive arms most destabilising to the strategic balance; the quantitative and qualitative reduction of strategic arms, including their development, testing, deployment and modernisation; and the future continuation of the SALT process.

These so-called principles avoid the issue of time frames, or the specification of any indices of asymmetrical equivalence for the guidance of negotiators. There are also other shortcomings. For example, while affirming the principle of equality and equal security, the Statement fails to specify whether equality refers only to strategic equality or to full military equality. Nor does it indicate whether equality is sought with reference to the two Superpowers, the NATO and Warsaw Pact Powers, or the whole Western and Eastern alignment of States. Yet even a rough approximation of equivalence would require such distinctions to be made.

A constructive feature of the Statement is the precedence given to strategic stability, ahead of contemplated reductions in strategic arms, acknowledging a concept of growing significance in arms control. It is often assumed that the chief aim of arms control is the reduction in the number and destructiveness of weapons. However, in the bilateral NAC context, the regulation of strategic arms for the sake of stability does not necessarily entail their reduction, and may even require a temporary increase.

For instance, one of the destabilising aspects of the bilateral nuclear arms race at the present time is the growing vulnerability of the command, control and communications (C^3) systems of the Superpowers.[2] It could prevent subsequent escalation to conclude bilateral NAC agreements for strengthening the C^3 systems of both the United States and the Soviet Union in order to guarantee the survivability of verification, early warning and retaliatory mechanisms. Similarly, an increase of missile sites protected by BMD could make mutual deterrent systems more secure, thereby enhancing their deterrent effect.

The view has also been advanced that certain arms cuts would result in propelling the arms race forward. *Prima facie* it would appear that a freeze on nuclear weapons systems, or their reversal to a prior stage of equilibrium, would promote stability. Yet it has been suggested that the proposition would only apply in the absence of continuing R & D, because the nature of the balance is irreversibly altered with the availability of new techniques, even if they remain only a latent option. The argument has been advanced, for instance, that –

> The recent history of SALT has only augmented the powerful hold that substantial reductions have had on the popular imagination. Yet proposals for deep cuts seldom deal with the forces that most endanger stability – improvements in accuracy; some forms of mobility; antisubmarine warfare capabilities; ABMs; and the possibility of more exotic systems such as lasers. Indeed, deep cuts may only stimulate development in these areas.[3]

The above formulation gives a misleading impression because it is not the quantitative freeze, or reduction of nuclear weapons, that could endanger stability but the failure to conclude concurrent agreements so as to control qualitative improvements in nuclear weapons systems. For NAC to be effective in the long term, each new refinement in the weapons and every new weapons system that becomes technically feasible, would have to be the subject of additional agreements forestalling their deployment.

Thus, the obsolescence of strategic stability gives rise to the need for advances in NAC merely for the maintenance of strategic equilibrium. As each Superpower is prone to conceal its genuine vulnerabilities with disputes about relatively inconsequential imbalances, such as numbers and throw weight of missiles, it is incumbent on the other Superpower or on third States to advance proposals for solutions to problems arising from disproportionate developments.

For the day to day application of current agreements, as well as for the continued monitoring of the overall balance, it is imperative to have an ongoing dialogue between the Superpowers in addition to the negotiation of major new SALT treaties. This requirement was recognised with the establishment of the Standing Consultative Commission (SCC)[4] in conjunction with the conclusion of the SALT I group of Treaties. The Commission, established by a Memorandum of Understanding between the United States and the Soviet Union,[5] was originally given the task to promote and implement the Nuclear Accidents Agreement of 30 September 1971, the SALT ABM Treaty of 26 May 1972, and the SALT I Interim Agreement, also of 26 May 1972.

By the terms of the Treaty setting up the Commission, each side is entitled to representation by a commissioner, deputy commissioner, and such staff as may be deemed necessary from time to time. The original regulations agreed upon for the conduct of the Commission, laid down that the commissioners were to preside over meetings alternatively. They also provided that, on all occasions, each side could submit for consideration any issue within the competence of the Commission to determine, preferably after prior notification.

The Treaty requires the Commission to meet at least twice yearly, in addition to which the regulations facilitate the exchange of written or oral communications by commissioners during the intervals between sessions. While the original rules did not specify the numbers of advisers and experts whom either side was permitted to invite for participation at meetings, references to the work of the Commission indicate that efforts have been made to attain reciprocity in the number of participants.

Express directives were given identifying methods of work, including the setting up of *Ad Hoc* Working Groups and the written recording of proceedings, English and Russian texts being equally authoritative. Regarding all aspects of Commission work, each side bears its own expenses.[6]

In the main, the work of the SCC can only be adduced from the results attained, as the meetings have been held in private since its inception.[7] Regulation 8 immediately provided that the proceedings were not to be made public unless expressly agreed to by both commissioners. Report by consent has rarely occurred, and then only in very general terms.

Substantial expansion in the work of the Commission was contemplated in March 1977, when the two Superpowers agreed to convene joint Working Groups on the following subjects: chemical weapons, radiological weapons, conventional arms transfers, civil defences, anti-satellite capabilities, missile test flights, the Indian Ocean, and a comprehensive test-ban. The United Kingdom was invited to join the last-mentioned Group in July of that year. It is notable that the Working Groups established by the Commission relate to most of the major subject areas also under consideration by the Committee on Disarmament.[8] In the case of radiological weapons, the consultations have led to the formulation of the elements of a treaty, although there has been less success in other subject areas. For example, it is known that the Working Group on anti-satellite capabilities has only met three times.[9]

The SALT II Treaty envisages a greatly expanded role for the SCC in the conduct of Superpower relations.[10] Although the Treaty has not been ratified, minimal compliance with its terms is being observed on the basis of reciprocity.[11] However, there is no evidence that such observance has included the envisaged expansion of the Commission's role. In the longer term, with the continuation of the SALT process, the intensification of the Commission's work seems inevitable for the maintenance of strategic stability between the Superpowers.

Competition, Reciprocity and Linkage

Whether in the Standing Consultative Commission or in the course of SALT negotiations, Superpower dialogue on the limitation of nuclear weapons is founded on the reluctant acceptance of a military stalemate that could only be resolved by mutual destruction. In its simplest form it has been stated as 'co-existence or non-existence'. Co-existence, as envisaged a decade ago, was to rest on strategic equilibrium together with other military restraints, some economic co-operation[12] and cultural exchanges.[13] It was thought possible to pursue this course in the face of undiminished competition for eventual supremacy, which each side believed would result from the ultimate non-viability of the social system espoused by the other. Unfortunately, the experience of the past decade has demonstrated grave contradictions implicit in the concept of co-existence.

In the first instance, the balance of terror is not based on the nuclear arsenals possessed by both sides but on the perception that the other side will respond to the threat, and will do so reasonably. Apprehensions persist in the West that, due to their indiscriminate destructiveness, the weapons are perceived to be unusable.

Concern has also been expressed that a reckless leadership could gain control in either State, prepared to countenance vast destruction as 'acceptable damage'.[14] Fears about the ascendancy of extremists in the opposite camp could, within each Superpower, weld coalitions between individuals who are motivated entirely by considerations of self-defence and those who desire to exploit military advantages for aggressive purposes.[15] Further, nuclear weapons are clearly useless without the projection of an image of extreme viciousness that makes their possible use credible. This is in direct contrast to the calm reasonableness that is required for NAC dialogue.

The objective of maintaining equivalence in one sphere whilst seeking superiority in other spheres is also a direct contradiction, entailing simultaneously threatening and co-operative behaviour. Contradictions in detente, as hitherto understood, are exemplified by definitions of the concept from the leaders of the Superpowers during the zenith of the period of accommodation. Gerald Ford, then President, said in 1975 regarding the meaning of detente –

> It means maintaining the strength to command respect from our adversaries and to provide leadership to our friends, not letting down our guard or dismantling our defenses, or neglecting our allies. It means peaceful *rivalry* between political and economic systems, *not the curbing of our competitive efforts* . . . Detente means moderate and restrained behaviour between the two superpowers, not a license to fish in troubled waters. It means mutual respect and reciprocity, not unilateral concessions or one-sided agreements. With this attitude I shall work with determination for a relaxation of tensions.[16]

Likewise, Leonid Brezhnev said in 1972 that –

> . . .while striving for the confirmation of the principle of peaceful coexistence, we recognize that successes in this important matter in no way signify the possibility of weakening *the ideological struggle*. On the contrary, it is necessary to be prepared that this struggle will intensify, will become a still sharper form of the *antagonism between the two social systems*. And we do not have any doubts about the outcome of this struggle, for the truth of history the objective laws of social development are on our side.[17]

In the course of their endeavours it is constantly demonstrated to practitioners that success in one aspect of their conduct diminishes returns in the other aspect. In a situation of overall confrontation, every concession is interpreted as a sign of weakness. Yet NAC consists of reciprocal concessions.

Both Superpowers have great difficulty in coming to terms with the abovementioned contradictions. The United States finds it especially burdensome to adjust to the loss of its outright nuclear weapons superiority. It is faced with the spectre that the Soviet Union will continue its rate of ascendancy unrestrained by public scrutiny or the means of societal censure. Restraint in the nuclear arms competition is particularly irksome in view of the overall technological superiority enjoyed by the United States and its allies, and because the arms race is financially rewarding to some sections of the private sector.[18]

Another, more aggressive strand in the United States anti-SALT syndrome is motivated not so much by concern about ultimate defeat but rather by expectations of imminent victory over the Soviet Union. That approach rests on the conviction that a continuing strategic nuclear arms race with the Soviet Union would soon exhaust the lesser resources of that country, leading to its spontaneous disintegration.[19] The Soviet Union, in turn, faced with domestic problems as well as simultaneous hostility in North America, Western Europe, Japan and China, is not well placed to make concessions at the present time without giving an impression of outright capitulation.[20] Whether, and if so to what extent, concessions would be made by the Soviet Union if the tables were turned, is a matter of conjecture.

So long as the confrontation mentality exists, the contradictions in the bilateral NAC process are likely to persist. The wish, if not the active promotion, of the disintegration of the political system in the adversary State is the diametrical opposite of the restraint and the predictability required for the reliable observance of NAC agreements. Failure to face this problem frankly and realistically has led to disillusionment with detente, the name allotted to the imprecise notion of 'peaceful competition' between the Superpowers.

During the 1960s and 1970s, the NAC agreements enumerated in Tables I and II (see pages 24 and 28) were concluded, and various measures of economic, social and cultural co-operation, were undertaken between States having a socialist economic system and those with a free enterprise system. These measures succeeded in lessening antagonisms, but not sufficiently to give either Superpower the assurance that its security and the security interests of its allies would be safe from the other in the absence of constant military readiness. The Soviet Union gave expression to the dilemma with the vain slogan that detente should be made 'irreversible', while United States leaders have increasingly decried the whole concept of detente.

Nevertheless, before the objective of detente is discarded, it is as well to recapitulate that the only alternative is mutual annihilation. This situation cannot be materially changed by measures such as the prohibition by the United States on the sale of some electronic equipment to the Soviet Union, imposed with increased vigour in 1982. Any suggestion that such steps could be significant in the balance of terror is entirely inconsistent with the often repeated United States assessment that the military strength of the Soviet Union is approximately equal, if not superior, to that of the United States.[21] It is similarly inconsistent with the assessments of the Soviet Union and its allies, that the forces of the Soviet Union are inferior to those of the United States, but only marginally so.[22]

Thus, it becomes prudent to re-examine the concepts of detente and co-existence, to ascertain whether the methods of their implementation could be altered so as to reduce the contradictions inherent in notions of 'peaceful competition'. It is relevant to the present study to enquire how the fierce antagonism between the Superpowers could be reconciled with the continuation of the NAC process.

At the basic conceptual level, it would no doubt be helpful if the future of mankind ceased to be perceived in terms of a competition to demonstrate the 'correctness' of the two unrealised and increasingly unrealisable nineteenth century objectives concerning proletarian inspired communism and free enterprise.[23] It is suggested that a more realistic approach, in preparation for the twenty-first century, would be to envisage an era of rapid constructive evolution of all national systems of government for the benefit of citizens in conformity with the principles laid down in the Charter, taking into account historical, social and current resource factors, as well as the demands of the cataclysmic technological and demographic changes to be anticipated.

In the day to day management of Superpower disengagement an obvious approach would be to expand, and to make more precise, the concepts in the Joint Statement of Principles and Basic Guidelines contained in the SALT II Treaty. The principles and rules of the bilateral NAC process have to serve the implementation of a wide range of tasks, the most prominent of which are now briefly to be considered.

Primarily, agreement is required on the demarcation of categories of nuclear arms, for example, as to what are to be designated strategic nuclear arms, and whether grey area weapons should be included in calculations of strategic weapons parity. Simultaneously there is the problem of measuring equivalence among a range of varied weapons, taking into account features like speed, accuracy, destructive power, capability to evade detection, and durability.

A further vital consideration is verifiability, such as adherence to externally observable design features. There is the need to consider how suspected breaches are to be dealt with. Attention must be paid to the functioning of early warning systems, so as to keep them inviolate against new weapons designed to evade detection; and to ensure that false alarms will not provoke mistaken retaliatory responses. It is also necessary to plan ahead so as to forestall the development of destabilising systems, complicating deterrence by the introduction of further weapons into space, or the perfection of a first strike capability by whatever means.

At the same time, there is the problem of the scope of the SALT process – whether it should take into account non-strategic nuclear weapons, conventional weapons, and non-nuclear weapons of mass destruction, namely whether, and if so under what circumstances, cognizance should be taken of issues extraneous to the strategic nuclear balance. The relevant principle of both theoretical justice and military practicality on which the bilateral NAC process was based, has been that of reciprocity. The concept has been translated into words like 'essential equivalence', 'balanced reductions' and 'mutual benefit'. The problem then arises of the boundaries within which reciprocity should operate. The notion of 'linkage' propounded by former United States Secretary of State Henry Kissinger,[24] is a form of reciprocity. It differs from the reciprocity of the SALT process, as hitherto understood, in that it advocates that the reciprocal acts, bargaining positions, rewards and punishments meted out by the Superpowers towards each other, should extend to the whole gamut of East-West relations.

The greater fairness of the proposed wider scope for the operation of reciprocity is beyond doubt. The problem is whether it is feasible, given the methods of auto-legislation and auto-adjudication that are essential and foreseeably unalterable ingredients of the bilateral NAC process. For instance, could it be realistically argued that the United States is entitled to an X number of additional ICBM, provided that it supplies Y tonnes of grain per annum to the Soviet Union? Or that the Soviet Union may station twice the number of SS-20 missiles aimed at Europe, provided that a trade union organisation in Poland is given access to certain media outlets?[25]

Records of the seven-year negotiation of the SALT II Treaty provide ample evidence of the difficulty of measuring equivalence and ensuring reciprocity, even within very confined parameters. In particular, the debates in the United States prior to the signing of that Treaty, and in connection with the advisability of its ratification, demonstrate the immense complexity of the measurement of military strategic equivalence. That conclusion is confirmed by the varied assessments adduced by the two Superpowers in their pre-SSD II update, published by the United States under the title *Soviet Military Power*,[26] and countered by the Soviet Union in a response entitled *Whence the Threat to Peace*.[27]

Similarly, with respect to compliance, one can only conjecture about the chaos that would result if, say, the United States decided to suspend the Hot Line Treaties as punishment for the jamming of 'Voice of America' broadcasts in Europe, or if the Soviet Union shot down a United States verification satellite in retaliation for that country's co-operation with South Africa in defiance of United Nations directives.

Hence, linkage between the bilateral NAC process and other forms of interaction between the Superpowers can only be envisaged in relation to a suspension of the bilateral norm creating process. However, as has been shown in connection with the consideration of recent technological advances, and as will be discussed subsequently relating to projected nuclear arms programmes, the suspension of the norm creating process will shortly render existing NAC agreements obsolete. Therefore, by exercising the option to suspend bilateral norm creation for NAC, a Party must inevitably bring about a situation in which the entire bilateral process of NAC is put into jeopardy.

Perhaps wishing to increase public confidence, or perhaps due to fundamental misconceptions, the spokesmen of both Superpowers occasionally make statements indicating that they could defend themselves in a military contest should bilateral agreements on NAC be abandoned.

Whatever the motivation, such statements are misleading. As previously indicated, the strategic balance is not a policy option but an inescapable necessity.[28] Therefore, an element of choice only impinges on whether that balance is to be stable or unstable, in the knowledge that any instability poses roughly equally catastrophic dangers to all. In order to have predictability and reliability, and to adhere to a set of consistent norms capable of auto-application, it is essential to maintain a self-contained system. Within that framework, the general principles of conflict resolution have relevance.[29]

Conflict Resolution and Quasi-Judicial Negotiation

Negotiation has emerged as the most favoured method of conflict resolution in the NAC process. It is applicable to both multilateral and bilateral situations, and is suited to the elaboration of new NAC agreements, as well as to the settlement of disputes that arise in relation to the manner of their observance.

With respect to the conclusion and observance of NAC agreements between the Superpowers, bilateral negotiation has been the only method employed, without the benefit of third party assistance in any arbitral or mediating capacity. Even good offices have never amounted to more than a general encouragement. Hence, the nature of the negotiating process, notably its potential for harmonising Superpower relations, is of crucial importance.

The confrontational nature of bilateral NAC negotiations is not in question. For instance, the chief SALT negotiator appointed by the Reagan Administration, Paul H. Nitze sees the overall situation in these terms –

> In seeking each specific objective within their global policy, the Soviet rulers use the lowest level of pressure or of violence necessary and sufficient to achieve that objective. The purpose of their capabilities at the higher levels of potential violence, all the way up to intercontinental nuclear war, is to deter, and if necessary control, escalation by us to such higher levels.
> It is a copybook principle in strategy that, in actual war, advantage tends to go to the side in a better position to raise the stakes by expanding the scope, duration, or destructive intensity of the conflict. By the same token, at junctures of high contention short of war, the side better able to cope with the potential consequences of raising the stakes has the advantage. The other side is the one under greater pressure to scramble for a peaceful way out. To have the advantage at the utmost level of violence helps at every lesser level. In the Korean war, the Berlin blockades, and the Cuban missile crisis the United States had the ultimate edge because of our superiority at the strategic nuclear level. That edge has slipped away.[30]

Leading Soviet theoretician on bilateral NAC negotiations, Henry Trofimenko, has a different view of the matter –

> To sum up, then, throughout the entire post-World War II period, it is the United States that has tried to impose on the 'potential adversary' rules of the game (i.e., rules of conflict behaviour) which would

maximize the one-sided technical advantage enjoyed by the United States at any given moment and minimize the capabilities of the adversary. That is what the entire American doctrinal progress boils down to.[31]

There has been so little trust between the two States that it sometimes appears from their dialogue that they are hardly discussing the same problems. For example, the Deputy Director of the Institute of United States and Canada Studies in Moscow, R.G. Bogdanov, speaks of –

. . . the illusion that it is possible to wage nuclear war and to survive sufficiently intact to make it other than completely senseless.[32]

Paul Nitze, on the other hand, states that –

The Soviets do not follow a strategy of deterrence and retaliation. In their doctrinal writing, they spell out their belief in a strategy of first strike, and their weapons have been designed with that use in mind. Therefore, in their case, a condition of parity plus their policy of strategic initiative gives them superiority.[33]

The partners in the bilateral dialogue have had negative attitudes towards each other regarding negotiating style as well as credibility. A typical view was that of Arthur H. Dean, Ambassador in the post-armistice negotiations in Korea; Chairman, of the United States delegation at the Disarmament and Nuclear Test-Ban negotiations in Geneva, 1961-3; and former member of his country's delegation to the UN General Assembly. In 1964 he claimed that –

In considering Soviet diplomacy as a whole, two major characteristics stand out: a dogmatic expectation of hostility from the outside world and an iron determination to carry out a program previously determined in Moscow and not subject to change by the diplomat in the field.[34]

In the same year, Thomas W. Wolfe, of the Sino-Soviet Institute, George Washington University, elaborated further on the theme of both the unwillingness and the inability of the Soviet side to conduct fruitful negotiations.

Publicly expressed Soviet views of the West more often than not are meant to serve propaganda ends of one sort or another, such as demonstrating aggressive intent in every Western move. The private Soviet assessment, on the other hand, may vary from one case to another. Thus, image of the West reflected in Soviet public statements does not necessarily correspond in all respects with what Soviet leaders may think privately about the strategies and intentions of their opponents . . .

He went on to add –

It would be premature in the extreme to suggest that the Soviet image of the West now mirrors reality with reasonable fidelity. Soviet perception of the West is still filtered through ideological and parochial suspicions that produce a woefully distorted picture, particularly of Western motives and intentions.[35]

Yet the treaties concluded and observed during the past two decades indicate that these assessments were, at the least, exaggerated and of limited application. The possibility of acquiring a changed outlook resulting from dialogue and experience, is illustrated by the remarks in 1979 of Senator Charles Percy, later to become Chairman of the Senate Foreign Relations Committee under the Reagan Administration. Commenting on the testimony of General Rowny during the SALT II ratification hearings, the Senator said –

> It is interesting that the two most credible and strongest opponents of this treaty have both come to the same conclusion. In an off-hand comment this morning, I am sure well thought through, Paul Nitze came to the conclusion that he did not believe that the Soviet Union wanted to wage a nuclear war. This is an utterly responsible statement. It is so easy to demagogue this issue, to wave the flag and imply that the motive of the Soviets is to make a nuclear first-strike on the United States of America. That position has no credibility.
>
> The last trip I took to the Soviet Union was with Hubert Humphrey. We walked through the Leningrad Cemetery where a half-million Soviet men are buried. The Soviets lost 20 million people in a war that was waged entirely with conventional weapons. We realized at the time that the deep-seated desire to avoid an all-out confrontation goes from the most humble Soviet citizen right straight through the top.[36]

Conflict resolution theories based on experiences from other fields such as management-labour disputes or inter-personal relations, could give too much weight to psychological considerations. Significantly different conditions prevail at bilateral NAC negotiations. As the Canadian Professor, Edward McWhinney, has pointed out –

> The rival Soviet and American negotiating teams in the area of disarmament and arms control seem to have had superb professional qualifications and an unusual degree of technical expertise in strategic armaments limitation. . . .[37]

Thus, when debating the relative destructive capabilities of contending nuclear weapons, the parties can at least have confidence in their own assessments and a thorough comprehension of the legal and technical nuances involved in the day to day discussions.

Superpower negotiation for NAC in the framework of the Standing Consultative Commission has all the elements of the classical bipolar model for conflict resolution. Although it is doubtful whether theories and models of conflict resolution have reached a standard that could beneficially influence a negotiating process of such complexity, the converse might very well apply so as to inhibit and discourage negotiation due to a misconception and under-estimation of its possibilities by political decision-makers.

The negative impact of conflict resolution models chiefly arises from the projection of various game theories,[38] which postulate two adversaries with diametrically opposed interests seeking to defeat one another by all means available within given bounds. In the light of this projection, negotiation is seen as a kind of game or battle, being a set arena of conflict where each player must beat the other or be beaten. It gives rise to the notion of 'negotiation from a position of strength',[39] which implies negotiation by threat. Negotiation by threat is a contradiction in terms and is merely an excuse for the avoidance or the postponement of negotiation. It is the converse of the concept of mutual benefit envisaging, as it does, a series of victories by one side and capitulation by the other.

A similarly negative approach is engendered by the postulate that a negotiation is a type of market place for bargaining over two relatively fixed sets of beneficial attributes. It implies that any shift from the status quo is likely to be to the advantage of one party and to the disadvantage of the other.

Another approach to negotiation is to see it as a process of compromise, in the sense that each side gets less than it would wish, on the understanding that the other is similarly deprived. The outcome is always represented as an overall loss. In accordance with this outlook, instead of making increasing threats, the parties need to make inflated claims, to ensure that the compromise struck will appear to be more of a sacrifice to them than it is in reality.[40]

The Marxist concept of conflict and its resolution by thesis, antithesis and synthesis could also be applied to negotiating postures, but this would imply that both parties have to change their position fundamentally in the process.[41] In the present climate of Superpower relations such an outcome would be, even theoretically, unacceptable to both sides.

Negotiation can be treated in the manner of a holding operation, as an empty gesture for marking time. Or it can be used as a form of camouflage, providing a benign facade to conceal preparations for hightened aggressive conduct. Negotiations can also be envisaged as a form of intelligence activity, facilitating the extraction of information concerning the strengths, weaknesses and objectives of the other side. Alternatively, a negotiation can be used as a propaganda weapon, by treating it as a forum for the dissemination of misleading information or, perhaps correct information, disconcerting to the other party.

All of the above negotiating postures are predicated on the premise that each side occupies distinctly circumscribed economic, social, ideological, and hegemonistic positions.[42] Admittedly, some representations of conflict resolution postulate an evolutionary movement to take place as a result of sitting at one table and talking, but there is no suggestion of where the input will come from to propel the evolutionary development. For example, NAC negotiation between the Superpowers is mostly represented as an essentially closed system, not with respect to the precise nuclear weapons available, but in regard to the existence of two distinct ideological-military entities.

The most belligerent conceptualisation envisages the two 'positions' to be entirely disparate, while more conciliatory outlooks picture the positions as overlapping at various points. Negotiation cannot alter whether the positions overlap or whether they do not, because that is given fact. The overlap could only increase, in this representation, if one or both sides changed their positions. To the extent that they would be prepared to do that, they would have to compromise their chosen ideology or abandon the most advantageous power-seeking military, or quasi-military posture.[43]

It is possible that with the further advance of conflict resolution theory the process of negotiation, notably by the Superpowers, will become substantially more effective.[44] In particular, it is suggested that there are prospects for the development of negotiation theory in two main directions. One approach could be called *the theory of the unstated third position*, and the other, *quasi-judicial negotiation*.

The Theory of the Unstated Third Position

In accordance with this proposed theory, the positions adopted by the two adversaries in bilateral NAC negotiations – and by the various parties in most negotiations – do not accurately reflect either the real interests of the parties or the full import of their respective ideologies. This observation does not refer to deliberate deception but to genuine misconceptions by the parties due to stereotyped thinking, the constraints of language, the clumsiness of State bureaucracies, and other similar factors that limit and distort the perception of reality.

Therefore, there generally exists a reservoir of conciliatory factors not at first fully recognised by either side. These factors are not the kind that would necessarily become manifest with more thorough self-appraisal by each side. Slothful appraisal tends not to arise as a significant problem in NAC issues.[45] These misconceptions are more fundamental and have the character of blind spots, which result in an inability to ask the right questions.

The theory differs from other models of conflict resolution, in that the 'third position' is not envisaged as any variant of compromise, deceit, conquest or synthesis, but of mutual discovery. Without denying that compromise and synthesis can be beneficially utilised in the resolution of conflict, the emphasis is on the opportunity afforded by the negotiating process for two or more parties, having different conceptual frameworks, to interact with a view to discovering areas of mutual benefit. Those areas represent the unstated third position.

The most significant example of an unstated third position that was subsequently identified, is the ideology and strategy of co-existence. Co-existence here is used in the sense of a permanent political condition for the foreseeable future, not merely an interim condition that was predicted by Lenin to persist until the so-called 'inevitable' victory of international communism had been achieved.

Neither free enterprise nor socialist ideology has much to say about it, yet it is implicit in both ideologies that physical and cultural survival are indispensable conditions for their success. However, the notion of co-existence is only the tip of the iceberg. The detailed aspirations contained in the concept of the wish to survive, and the modalities to be elaborated for the attainment of those aspirations, form the subject matter of the future unstated third position.

The unstated third position is, by definition, the position of realism. It reveals the necessary, often unwelcome – that is why it is overlooked – preconditions necessary for the realisation of the stated material and moral objectives of the parties. The identification of the unstated third position in NAC has consisted of perceptions concerning mutual benefits arising from the preservation of the environment, the desirability of legalised and co-operative espionage in the form of verification, the need for faster and more reliable communication between adversary leaders in times of crisis etc. Such measures have become the subject matter of the agreements listed in Tables I and II (see pages 24 and 28), although the concepts on which they are based were foreign to the ideological and military postures of the parties in the not too distant past.

Quasi-Judicial Negotiation

This form of negotiation relates mostly to the auto-interpretation and auto-adjudication of treaties, although it is also applicable to the elaboration of agreements on the basis of precepts such as equivalence and equal benefit. It is a process whereby the parties apply mutually accepted principles and rules to a subject in order to resolve the differences between them.

It has often been claimed that the judicial process, to be effective, requires a common ideological-cultural base.[46] The overall ineffectiveness of the International Court of Justice has been attributed partly to the alleged absence of such a base. The contention overlooks the fact that even national entities are, to various degrees, culturally and ideologically heterogeneous. What does appear to be indispensable is a *bridging ideology*, consisting of a set of intellectual concepts and sincerely held beliefs concerning the legal precepts to be utilised.[47] An internationally bridging ideology has to include fundamental concepts like the inviolability of treaty undertakings, reciprocity, essential equivalence, and the various norms of international conduct including those referred to above as international *precept*.[48] While the existence of some common ground is necessary for any international judicial function, the need for a consistent and plausible bridging ideology is more pronounced in the tenuous environment of a bilateral negotiation.

The absence of a judge or any judicial figure is the chief distinguishing feature between quasi-judicial negotiation and an overtly legal procedure. It can be compensated for by meticulous precision in the rules to be applied. The terms of the SALT II Treaty indicate that the need to formulate exact rules and definitions has been recognised by both Superpowers.

However, it must happen in all complex evaluations that occasionally individual judgments have to be made, when existing rules do not extend to a particular situation. The decision could be of marginal importance and still cause inordinate delays. In such situations, a relatively impartial, respected individual could be asked to adjudicate regarding, say, the military equivalence of two somewhat similar weapons. These and like stratagems could also be useful to save face, when the point at issue is not so much the content of a concession, although preparedness to make the concession could be construed as a defeat. In those circumstances, third party adjudication could greatly accelerate bilateral NAC negotiation.

Unlike other judicial proceedings, quasi-judicial negotiations are best conducted in secrecy, otherwise public opinion could usurp the position of the absent judge. In other words, the parties would be tempted to address their submissions to an extraneous audience that has no opportunity to gain access to all the relevant facts, thereby only further complicating the difficult task.

One possibility exists for the utilisation of public opinion in quasi-judicial negotiation, namely in case of a stalemate. A party could advise the other that, unless agreement is reached by a given date, the negotiating position of that side would be divulged. For example, the Soviet Union could declare that, unless the United Kingdom and the United States agree to a Comprehensive Test-Ban Treaty by, say, September 1983, its own position would be made public at the 38th Session of the General Assembly. Or, the United States could declare that, unless the Soviet Union were prepared to accept certain substantial cuts in armaments by a given date, details of the refusal would be revealed.

In those circumstances, the threat of adjudication and sanction by public opinion might accelerate the negotiation. On the other hand, it could lead to increased resentment and intransigence. A more beneficial variant might be if the parties were to agree to such a procedure as a prior stipulation at the commencement of negotiations. However, there are other, more effective sanctions to induce the Superpowers in the bilerateral NAC process to adhere to NAC agreements, which will be discussed in the next Chapter.

When assessing the likely future effectiveness of NAC agreements in the maintenance of international peace and security, it would be misleading to exclude from consideration the possibilities for innovation that could accompany the increasingly acute danger of nuclear war. The elaboration of conflict resolution theory in this context is sought to provide an indication of the available outlets for development that might emerge with the passage of time, in the light of the successes and failures of NAC agreements so far negotiated and presently operative.

It would seem that with stronger commitment by States for negotiated arms control, especially on the part of the two Superpowers, negotiating techniques could be improved. It is also possible that a theoretical basis of NAC negotiation could be established, with a view to creating a consistent discipline that would impart much greater speed and predictability to the process.

Preventing the Next Spiral in the Bilateral Nuclear Arms Race

After consideration of various nuclear weapons strategies in previous chapters, it was concluded that the weapons could be used in a non-self-destructive way only in two situations, either in an extreme case requiring self-defence, or in an almost totally disarming first strike.[49] The next spiral in the nuclear arms race involves chiefly the development of weapons to serve those two purposes.

In the one instance, additions to arsenals consist of local war fighting weapons, like the neutron bomb and other tactical nuclear devices, together with hard-to-detect delivery systems, like the cruise missile and low flying manned bombers. Yet it is noteworthy that, while these weapons could be used defensively in local conflicts, they could also be employed aggressively although, as has been observed previously, such use could lead to unlimited escalation.

The other kind of development taking place is the perfection of weapons systems leading to the possibility of a disarming first strike capability, together with weapons designed to thwart such an outcome. The main arena for that contest is in outer space.[50] In this regard it has been noted previously that the most dangerous international situation could arise at a time when either Superpower appeared to be approaching a first strike capability, because the other Superpower might be induced to take extreme measures in order to prevent the attainment of that objective.

It may be appropriate to recapitulate that in view of the abovementioned considerations, no State stands to gain militarily, or in any other way for that matter, from developments that would constitute the next spiral of the nuclear arms race.

There are two impediments that appear to be particularly difficult to overcome in the limitation of tactical nuclear weapons. Firstly, verification of any treaty to limit their manufacture and deployment may be difficult to achieve by the ususal verification methods. The other impediment to the limitation or elimination of tactical nuclear weapons is that the United States is thought to be disadvantaged, in some contemplated military confrontations, if restricted to conventional weapons and combat troops. Therefore, there is a powerful body of opinion within the United States and, to a lesser extent, among the NATO allies, that nuclear weapons should be on hand for use in those situations.[51]

With respect to arms control agreements to restrict the arms race in outer space, a major difficulty is to establish, with an acceptable degree of certainty, the level of R & D attained by the other side at any given time. The prevalent attitude is that any slackening in the pace of R & D might give the other side a lead that could not be made up. In addition, with respect to many relevant technologies, it would be impossible to differentiate between those that have a military application, and those that are developed exclusively, or predominantly, for civilian purposes.

The strategic nuclear balance is closely bound up with the arms race in outer space. ICBM delivering nuclear warheads must travel through outer space during part of their trajectory. Also most of the backup systems enabling the use of nuclear missiles are conducted via satellite. For instance, the pinpointing of targets is largely by satellites; homing guidance can be augmented by satellite; and commands for activating nuclear weapons systems rely, to a considerable extent, on satellite transmission.[52]

Many defensive systems against nuclear weapons are also based in outer space. Early warning networks utilise satellite mounted reconnaissance systems, and verification by NTM is conducted by the Superpowers chiefly with the aid of remote sensing and other satellite connected methods of surveillance. A contemplated development is a space-based ballistic missile defence (BMD) system. In case of an impending first strike, anti-satellite (ASAT) weapons could be used to disrupt the command, control and communications (C^3) networks of the opponent.[53]

The abovementioned defence systems could also be used aggressively. A combination of exact pinpointing of targets – even moving targets, accurate guidance of missiles, instantaneous transmission of commands, elimination of the opponent's satellites with anti-satellite weapons, and the use of BMD against any vestige of retaliatory capacity could, conceivably, result in a counterforce strike able to disarm the other Superpower.

Apart from effective BMD, the systems referred to are already operational, although they have not been perfected to the point that would enable either Superpower to mount a disarming first strike against the other. The most significant aspect of the next spiral in the nuclear arms race could provide such a capability although, on the available evidence, this could not be achieved by stealth.[54] The new technologies giving rise to these developments will be considered briefly below.

It should not be overlooked that the technological revolution in the perfection of nuclear weapons systems has another dimension. While attention is directed to the novel technological feats of the Superpowers, it is all too easy to discount the immense technological strides of the other nuclear-weapon States, as well as the nuclear threshold States. Seven States are now said to have observation satellites in space, including those of two 'developing' countries, namely China and India.[55] For instance, the placement of weapons of mass destruction in space may not be far from the technical capabilities of these States. It is therefore disconcerting to note that China has not acceded to the Outer Space Treaty, which forbids the placement of weapons of mass destruction into outer space.[56]

Failure by third parties, with military capabilities that have been the subject of bilateral NAC agreements between the United States and the Soviet Union, to adhere to the terms of those agreements, could exert a negative influence on the whole NAC process between the Superpowers. In the same way, by refusing to abide by multilateral NAC agreements with hitherto special application for the Superpowers, third States could prejudice the bilateral efforts for accommodation.

Several of the Treaties referred to in Table I (see page 24) have an application for arms control in outer space. The Partial Test-Ban Treaty of 1963, forbids the detonation of nuclear devices in outer space. The Outer Space Treaty of 1967, in Article IV, provides that the moon and other celestial bodies are to be used 'exclusively for peaceful purposes'. The Treaty also requires the Parties to –

> ... undertake not to place in orbit around the Earth any objects carrying nuclear weapons or any other kinds of weapons of mass destruction, install such weapons on celestial bodies, or station such weapons in outer space in any other manner.

The SALT Treaties[57] also have relevance to arms control in outer space. The SALT ABM Treaty of 1972, and Protocol of 1976, forbid all ballistic missile defence with the exception of one site each in the Soviet Union and in the United States, which may be so defended.

The SALT II Treaty of 1979, in Article IX provides that –

> Each party undertakes not to develop, test or deploy . . . systems for placing into Earth orbit nuclear weapons or any other kind of weapons of mass destruction, including fractional orbital missiles. . . .

In addition, Article XV of the SALT II Treaty provides that –

> For the purpose of providing assurance of compliance . . . each party

undertakes not to interfere with the national technical means of verification of the other party . . .

The import of the provision is that it forbids interference with satellites used for verification.

It has been noted already that all of the unambiguous provision of the above treaties have been observed. What the treaties fail to prohibit is the development of structures, instruments and techniques that could be used to destroy satellite-borne C^3 systems, or to intercept nuclear warheads in the early stages of their trajectories.[58] So far there is no evidence to demonstrate that 'weapons' as presently defined, have been utilised in outer space in the course of developing the aforementioned technologies. With the exception of weapons support systems and earth-targeted missiles, all space-related weapons are tested on the ground or in aerospace.

The technologies currently being perfected include 'real time' calculations, with the aid of vast satellite formations some of which are already in their correct orbits.[59] They will facilitate exact pinpointing of all potential targets on earth and in aerospace – and perhaps in outer space – together with precise home guidance systems for weapons to destroy them. Another facet of the development is the perfection of directed energy weapons (DEW), including both particle beam weapons (PBW) and high energy lasers (HEL).[60] Unhampered by an atmosphere, the speed and accuracy of those beams would make them ideal ASAT weapons, as well as exo-atmospheric BMD weapons. Continuing perfection of the manoeuvrability of satellites could also be turned to military use, both for approaching enemy satellites and for evading them.

The next stage in the testing of these systems would be to undertake experiments for actually destroying targets with the weapons in outer space. While any State that commenced such activities would be acting in defiance of the general principles of the Charter urging peaceful conduct, it is not entirely clear whether the Outer Space Treaty forbids the conduct. In accordance with Article III of the Treaty, activities in outer space are to be carried out –

. . . in the interests of maintaining international peace and security and promoting international co-operation and understanding.

However, in specific terms, Article IV of the Treaty only prohibits the testing of weapons and the carrying out of military manoeuvres *on* 'celestial bodies'. No definition is given of a 'celestial body', but presumably the Treaty refers to naturally occurring celestial bodies indicated by various references in the Treaty, including a provision in Article I that 'there shall be free access to all areas of celestial bodies'.

The Antarctic Treaty, in wording similar to that used in the Outer Space Treaty, provides in Article 1(1) that –

Antarctica shall be used for peaceful purposes only. There shall be prohibited, *inter alia* any measures of a military nature, such as the establishment of military bases and fortifications, the carrying out of military manoeuvres, as well as the testing of any type of weapons.

In that instance, the spirit as well as the letter of the Treaty has been observed. Not so with the Outer Space Treaty, which has been strictly interpreted by the Superpowers so as to permit the *projection* of weapons into space, as well as the stationing of military support systems on satellites. Keeping in mind the important bearing that those military activities have on the strategic balance, it would be entirely impractical to dismantle those systems at the present time. Likewise, continuation of the legal debate as to the correctness of the interpretation that permitted those military activities,[61] could only serve as a distracting diversion from efforts to implement further arms control measures in outer space.

The crucial question is still outstanding, namely whether all space-targeted weapons, discharged from earth, aerospace or outer space, are to be outlawed. Countenancing tests of that kind would be consistent with the interpretation that the Superpowers have given the Treaty provisions, rightly or wrongly. Yet it appears from the literature that, so far, both Superpowers have been very restrained about weapons tests in space. Hence the next step for NAC in this field is to foreclose the option of deploying space-targeted weapons, either with a Protocol to the Outer Space Treaty or with the conclusion of a further treaty.

An additional treaty has been proposed by the Soviet Union, and a draft Treaty has been presented to the United Nations to that end. In two separate resolutions, one with the support of Western States and the other with the support of Socialist States, the General Assembly decided in December 1981 to explore the means of preventing an arms race in outer space. Western States gave priority to the negotiation of 'an effective and verifiable agreement to prohibit anti-satellite systems',[62] while the Socialist States called for a treaty on 'the prohibition of the stationing of weapons of any kind in outer space',[63] taking into account the draft presented by the Soviet Union.[64]

Support given to both General Assembly resolutions by the Non-aligned States suggests that the obstructive, albeit theoretically plausible argument that the existing Treaty is adequate, has been abandoned.

No resolutions or treaties regarding the arms race in outer space, or any other aspect of the bilateral NAC process, could be so worded as to guarantee implementation. At best, the agreements are tools of trade that make NAC *possible*, provided the two Superpowers genuinely wish them to succeed. Their interests in so doing have already been adverted to, and will be further elaborated in the next chapter.

Notes

1 Treaty on Principles Governing the Activities of States in the Exploration and Use of Outer Space Including the Moon and Other Celestial Bodies.
2 Karas, Thomas H., 'Implications of Space Technology for Strategic Nuclear Competition', *Occasional Paper 25*, Periodical of the Stanley Foundation (Iowa USA) July 1981, p. 10 – 'The paradox of the force-multiplying satellites is that they and their associated ground facilities become valuable military assets which are tempting targets for preemptive attack. Except for the danger of sabotage, most ground stations would probably be safe from attack during a

conventional war. In a central strategic crisis, however, these facilities could supply one reason for the Soviets to consider preemption. In the years to come the proliferation of mobile ground stations could reduce this tempting vulnerability.' This emerging threat to a stable strategic balance was identified by the mid-70s, e.g. Vlasic, Ivan A., cites a US Library of Congress Study, *c* 1976, thus – 'Voicing a suspicion that the USSR might be developing a system similar to the NavStar, he [US Navy Secretary] called for accelerated efforts on the part of the United States to produce instruments which could "neutralize" such Soviet spacecraft "through the use of chaff [to 'blind' them] or by interdiction [i.e., destruction]". It is, therefore, obvious, that, even in non-combat conditions, the temptation will be great to interfere with space vehicles regarded as strategic threats, and so will the prospects of uncontrollable escalation.' 'Disarmament Decade, Outer Space and International Law', *McGill Law Journal* 1981, Vol. 26 No. 2 p. 157.

3 Sigal, Leon V., 'Kennan's Cuts', *Foreign Policy*, Fall 1981, No. 44 p. 80.

4 Not to be confused with the Special Coordination Committee (SCC) of the National Security Council, which has engaged in the task of advising the US Govt. on SALT issues.

5 TIAS 7545.

6 Protocol establishing Regulations TIAS 7637.

7 Minimal information is released from time to time, e.g. *The Department of State: Selected Documents* (Bureau of Public Affairs, Office of Public Communication) February 1978, No. 7 p. 4; Remarks of a 'White House official', *Aviation Week and Space Technology*, 25 May 1981, p. 15.

8 *Arms Control* (US Arms Control and Disarmament Agency, May 1978) Publication 96 p. 13.

9 During 1978-9, see Vlasic, op.cit. p. 159.

10 'Article XVI [SALT II]

1. To promote the objectives and implementation of the provisions of this Treaty, the parties shall use the standing consultative commission established by the memorandum of understanding between the Government of the United States of America and the Government of the Union of Soviet Socialist Republics regarding the establishment of a Standing Consultative Commission of December 21, 1972.

2. Within the framework of the Standing Consultative Commission, with respect to this Treaty, the parties will:

(a) Consider questions concerning compliance with the obligations assumed and related situations which may be considered ambiguous;

(b) Provide on a voluntary basis such information as either party considers necessary to assure confidence in compliance with the obligations assumed;

(c) Consider questions involving unintended interference with national technical means of verification, and questions involving unintended impeding of verification by national technical means of compliance with the provision of this Treaty;

(d) Consider possible changes in the strategic situation which have a bearing on the provisions of this Treaty;

(e) Agree upon procedures for replacement, conversion, and dismantling or destruction of strategic offensive arms in cases provided for in the provisions of this Treaty and upon procedures for removal of such arms from the aggregate numbers when they otherwise cease to be subject to the limitations provided for in this Treaty, and at regular sessions of the Standing Consultative Commission, notify each other in accordance with the aforementioned procedures at least twice annually, of actions completed and those in process;

(f) Consider, as appropriate, possible proposals for further increasing the viability of this Treaty including proposals for amendments in accordance with the provisions of this Treaty;

(g) Consider, as appropriate, proposals for further measures limiting strategic offensive arms.

3. In the Standing Consultative Commission the parties shall maintain by category the agreed data base on the numbers of strategic offensive arms established by the memorandum of understanding between the United States of America and the Union of Soviet Socialist Republics regarding the establishment of a data base on the numbers of strategic offensive arms of June 18, 1979.'

11 For a comprehensive account of the stance adopted by the two Superpowers regarding compliance with the terms of SALT II and the actual conduct pursued, see *Strategic Survey 1980-1981* (Published by the International Institute of Strategic Studies, London 1981) p. 107 – 'Officially, the United States said she would take no action to defeat the purpose of the treaty. Though the Soviet Union did not take a parallel position and insisted that an unratified agreement is not binding, she reaffirmed her desire to have the treaty ratified by the United States, implying that she will not act against the principles of the agreement while some prospect of its coming into force remains. As 1981 began both sides were acting so as not to prejudice future implementation of SALT II's terms.' The position of the United States has been reiterated by President Reagan, Secretary of State Haig and CD Delegate, Ambassador Flowerree. It was originally released by the Dept. of State as follows – 'While we are reviewing our SALT policy, we will take no action that would undercut existing agreement so long as the Soviet Union exercises the same restraint.' CD/PV. 122 p. 11.

12 For one of the foremost Western proponents of co-existence and inter-block trade, see Pisar, Samuel, *Coexistence and Commerce* (New York 1970).

13 A formal recognition of the endeavours constituting co-existence was achieved in the framework of the Conference on Security and Co-operation in Europe, commenced in September 1973, culminating in the Helsinki Accords and subsequent East-West dialogue in the context of Review Conferences.

14 Then U.S. Secretary of Defence, Harold Brown, was quoted as saying – 'But if deterrence of nuclear war is our most fundamental defense objective – and it surely is – what counts is what Soviet civilian and military leaders believe. On that score, we face another uncertainty. What we see as sufficient may appear as something else to them. What would deter us might not deter them. What some consider credible as a deterrent, they may dismiss as bluff.' *SALT II: An Interim Assessment* – Report of the Panel of the Committee on Armed Services, House of Representatives, Second Session, 23 Dec. 1978 (US Govt. Printing Office, Washington 1978) p. 26.

15 The observation that some NAC policies strengthen the position of the more belligerent decision makers on the other side of the negotiating-table, while other policies strengthen the less belligerent ones, was made by Ambassador Averell Harriman. He called the latter 'the more sensible people who are more interested in the development of Russia than in international adventure.' *The SALT II Treaty*, Hearings Before the Committee on Foreign Relations, U.S. Senate, July 1979 (US Govt. Printing Office, Washington 1979) p. 311.

16 Quoted by Mally, Gerhard, *Interdependence: The European - American Connection in the Global Context* (D.C. Heath, Massachusetts 1976) p. 78, emphasis added.

17 Id. p. 77, emphasis added.

18 For a Soviet view see Ovinnikov, R., 'How the USA Orchestrated the Attack on Detente', *International Affairs* August 1980, No. 8 pp. 92-6.

19 This world view is usually implied rather than directly stated, e.g. Newton, Maxwell, 'The West Helps Russia to Arm: US strategists plan financial pressure as Soviet block economies begin to crumble', *The Australian* newspaper, 5 April 1982, p. 9; Also supra p. 18.

20 Contra, alleging Soviet superiority, 'International Reports and Comments', *Beijing Review*, 9 Nov. 1981, No. 45 p. 12.

21 *Soviet Military Power* (US Govt. Printing Office, Washington) undated, approx. December 1981 - January 1982.

22 E.g. statement of Ambassador I. Kömives of Hungary, CD/PV.153 of 11 February 1982 p. 30 –
'. . . the atomic bomb was introduced in 1946 by the United States and only four years later by the Soviet Union;
. the hydrogen bomb was introduced in 1953 by the United States and one year later by the Soviet Union;
. the strategic bomber: introduced in 1953 by the United States, four years later by the Soviet Union;
. the intermediate-range ballistic missile (IRBM): in 1953 by the United States, four years later by the Soviet Union;
. the tactical nuclear weapon: in 1955 by the United States, one year later by the Soviet Union;
. the intercontinental ballistic missile (ICBM): in 1955 by the United States, two years later by the Soviet Union;
. the nuclear submarine: in 1956 by the United States, six years later by the Soviet Union;
. the submarine-launched ballistic missile (SLBM): in 1959 by the United States, nine years later by the Soviet Union;
. the anti-ballistic missile (ABM): in 1960 by the United States, one year later by the Soviet Union;
. the MRV warhead: in 1964 by the United States, six years later by the Soviet Union;
. the MIRV warhead: in 1970 by the United States, five years later by the Soviet Union;
. the cruise missile: in 1976 by the United States;
. the neutron weapon: in 1981 by the United States.'

23 *European Security and Co-operation: Premises, Problems, Prospects* (Progress Publishers, Moscow) Eng. Translation 1978, p. 53, emphasis added – 'Despite some sensible ideas put forward by these bourgeois analysts, their views and doctrines are essentially limited, for in philosophical and political terms these are usually based on the idea that under the deepening general crisis of the capitalist system, the class, social and political foundations of capitalism should be strengthened *to the detriment of socialism*. The Marxist-Leninist doctrine makes it possible to give an all-round analysis of present-day international development and a deep assessment of the possibilities and prospects of detente under the *contest* between capitalism and socialism, the chief contradiction of our day.' Emphasis added.

24 'Out of office, Henry Kissinger has critized more forcefully what he sees as the lack of Soviet cooperation in building a "web of common interests" with the United States. Early in 1979 he told an interviewer "I'm not saying we should link SALT to every Soviet action that we do not approve of." He went on, however, to enumerate Soviet actions which, in his opinion, violate the general

spirit on which the SALT process eventually depends:

... We have had Cuban troops in Angola, Cuban troops in Ethiopia, two invasions of Zaire, a Communist coup in Afghanistan, a Communist coup in South Yemen, and the occupation of Cambodia by Vietnam, all achieved by Soviet arms, with Soviet encouragement and in several cases protected by the Soviet veto in the United Nations. In addition, Soviet-advanced aircraft piloted by Soviet personnel are protecting Cuba – presumably against us – so that Cuban pilots and aircraft are operating all round Africa – also presumably against us. That cannot go on and have SALT survive. It is doing no favor to Soviet-American relations to pretend that these areas are unrelated. Sooner or later it will lead to a confrontation.' *SALT II: Some Foreign Policy Considerations*, Congressional Research Service (US Govt. Printing Office, Washington June 1979) p. 7; [Parallel Soviet grievances for the relevant period included – 1954, Guatemala; 1958, Lebanon; 1961, Cuba; 1962-72, Indochina; 1965, Dominican Republic; 1973, Chile. *Whence the Threat to Peace* p. 75, n 27 infra.] See Also Kissinger, Henry, *The White House Years* (Wiedenfeld and Nicholson, London 1979).

25 An argument akin to Secretary Kissinger's view was advanced by E.V. Rostow to the CD on behalf of the United States. Quoting a remark by 'the Soviet Foreign Minister, Maxim Litvinov' that 'peace is indivisible', Mr Rostow said that – 'The United States has high hopes for a fair and reasonable outcome of the crisis in Poland. Such a turn in Soviet policy could make many other agreements possible, and help prepare the way for a genuine improvement in the climate of world politics and the fabric of the international community. One of the principal means on which we rely to achieve that goal is the negotiation of fair and balanced agreements for the reduction of nuclear arms, particularly of offensive nuclear arms.' CD/PV.152 of 1982, pp. 11-12. The remarks were countered by Ambassador D. Erdembileg of Mongolia, who said that – 'The Government of the Mongolian People's Republic, together with other socialist States, firmly believes that questions relating to the sovereign rights of socialist Poland should cease to be used as a pretext for increasing international tension and diverting the attention of peoples from the solution of the vital problems of strengthening peace and security, ending the arms race and achieving disarmament. Equally disturbing is the continued aggression of South African racists against the freedom-loving African peoples. As in the Middle East, the source of tension in South Africa would already long since have been eliminated and all Africa would have been free, had it not been for the direct assistance of the United States and other imperialistic States – assistance which has already been repeatedly condemned by the United Nations General Assembly.' CD/PV. 153, p. 22.

26 *Soviet Military Power* (US Govt. Printing Office, Washington) undated.

27 *Whence the Threat to Peace* (Military Publishing House, USSR Ministry of Defense, Moscow 1982).

28 Steinbruner, John D., 'Nuclear Decapitation', *Foreign Policy*, Winter 1981-2, Vol. 45 p. 16. Describing the vulnerabilities of the C^3 systems of both Superpowers the author concludes (at p. 28) – 'The United States can ill afford emotions or illusions of any sort in dealing with the problems of command vulnerability. Purging security policy of such influences and establishing a realistic grasp of the circumstances in which the United States finds itself should be the overriding commitment of the coming decade.' Also, the issue is squarely confronted by Panofsky, W.K., *Arms Control and SALT II* (Uni. of Washington Press, Seattle and London 1979) p. 52 – 'Signing a SALT agreement is not a

reward for good conduct on the part of the Soviet Union, nor does it imply approval of decisions made by this or past administrations of various actions in weapons procurement or military policy. *The merit of SALT must be judged on the basis of whether U.S. security and world security would be greater or less with SALT – and by that test the answer is clearly positive.'* A similar formula may be applicable to the policy options of the Soviet Union.

29 Beres, Louis Rene, 'Steps Toward a New Planetary Identity: the 1980 Rabinowitch Essay', *The Bulletin of the Atomic Scientists*, Feb. 1981, Vol. 37 No. 2 p. 43 – 'As we go on and on with our seemingly important day-to-day concerns, the planet moves inexorably toward nuclear war. Just a few more years, perhaps, and there will remain no conceivable way of averting humankind's last paroxysm. The people of Earth will draw their last fitful, convulsive gasps. And they will do so, incredibly, with incredulity.'

30 Nitze, Paul H., 'Is SALT II a Fair Deal for the United States', (1979) reproduced in *SALT Hand Book: Key Documents and Issues 1972-1979* ed. Labrie, Roger P., (American Enterprise Institute for Public Policy Research, Washington, D.C.) p. 669.

31 Trofimenko, Henry, 'The "Theology" of Strategy', *Arms and Control and Security: Current Issues* (Westview Press, Boulder, Colorado 1979) p. 101.

32 Bogdanov, R.G., 'Strategic Arms Limitation and Reduction – an Urgent Problem', *Disarmament*, May 1981, Vol. iv No. 1 p. 21.

33 *SALT Hand Book* op. cit. p. 680.

34 Dean, Arthur H., 'Soviet Diplomatic Style and Tactics', reprinted from *Test Ban and Disarmament: The Path of Negotiation*, in *The Soviet Approach to Negotiation*, compiled by the Subcommittee on National Security and International Operations of the Senate Committee on Government Operations (US Government Printing Office, Washington 1969) p. 61.

35 Id. p. 58.

36 *The SALT II Treaty*, Hearings before the Committee on Foreign Relations US Senate, July 1979 (US Govt. Printing Office, Washington 1979) p. 565.

37 McWhinney, Edward, *The International Law of Detente* (Sijthoff and Nordhoff International Publishers, 1978) p. 184.

38 See Wyer, R., 'Prediction of Behaviour in Two-Person Games', *Journal of Personality and Social Psychology*, 1969, Vol. 13 p. 222; Szulc, T., 'How Kissinger Did It', *Foreign Policy*, 1974, Vol. 15 p. 21; Shubik, M., *Game Theory and Related Approaches to Social Behaviour* (John Wiley, New York 1964).

39 E.g. '. . . I believe that under current circumstances it will not be possible to negotiate reductions unless we are seen to be building.' Testimony of Henry Kissinger, *The SALT II Treaty*, Hearings before the Senate Foreign Relations Committee, July 1979 (US Govt. Printing Office, Washington 1979) p. 196. This approach to negotiation was subsequently adopted by the Reagan Administration.

40 Shea, G.P., 'The Study of Bargaining and Conflict Behaviour', *Journal of Conflict Resolution*, Vol. 24, 1980, pp. 706.

41 Engels, Frederick, *Anti-Dühring* (Lawrence & Wishart, London 1942) Ch. XIII; *Short History of the CPSU (Bolsheviks)*, (Corbett Publishing House, London 1943) esp. p. 94; Politzer, George, *An Elementary Course in Philosophy* (Current Book Distributors, Sydney 1950) p. 155.

42 See Lee, J.M., 'Opening Windows for Arms Control', *Foreign Affairs*, Vol. 58, 1979, p. 121; Also Kiselyak, C., 'Round the Prickly Pear: SALT and Survival', *Orbis*, Vol. 22, 1979, p. 815.

43 Baldwin, David A., 'Inter-Nation Influence Revisited', *Journal of Conflict*

Resolution, December 1971, No. 15 p. 471.

44 So far, the practical application of these theories to NAC has been very limited. See Lall, A., *Modern International Negotiation: Principles and Practice* (Columbia University Press, New York 1966); Ikle, F.C., *How Nations Negotiate* (Harper and Row, New York 1964).

45 E.g. As well as numerous assessments by United States Govt. personnel of the SALT II Treaty, when considering ratification of the Treaty during the second half of 1979 more than 100 expert witnesses gave testimony, mostly at public hearings, to the Senate Committee on Foreign Relations.

46 For a range of Western views on the subject see Tunkin, G.I., *Theory of International Law* (Harvard Uni. Press, Cambridge, Mass. 1974) pp. 23-8.

47 Id. Ch. 3., Professor Tunkin identifies the new principles of international law during the period of co-existence to be – nonaggression; peaceful settlement of disputes; self-determination of peoples; peaceful co-existence; disarmament; respect for human rights; and the prohibition of war propaganda.

48 Supra Chapter 7.

49 The further remote possibility was suggested in Chapter 2 supra, of the use of nuclear weapons against a third State found to be acting in defiance of the whole international community.

50 Christol, C.A., 'International Space Law and the Use of Natural Resources: Solar Energy', *Revue Belge de Droit International*, 1980-1, Vol. XV p. 28, for a discussion of the definition of outer space, and sovereignty issues regarding space objects.

51 Ellsberg, Daniel, 'Will We Use Them?', *Current*, June 1981, No. 233 p. 41, claims that documentary evidence exists to prove that the US has contemplated use of nuclear weapons on four occasions – 1950 at the Chosin Reservoir in Korea; 1953 at Panmunjom, Korea; 1954 for the defence of Dienbienphu, Viet Nam; and 1968 in defence of Khe Sanh in Viet Nam. – In *Whence the Threat to Peace* op. cit. p. 75, the Soviet Union claims that 'In 19 instances Washington discussed in earnest the employment of nuclear weapons, the USSR being directly threatened four times.' The preponderance of Soviet conventional weapons is acknowledged on p. 69 – 'True, the USSR has more divisions in its ground forces than the USA. But this is quite natural because owing to its geographical and strategic position the Soviet Union has to maintain the balance of forces not only in Europe but also in other regions adjoining its borders.'

52 Dahlitz, J., 'Arms Control in Outer Space', *The World Today*, April 1982, Vol. 38 No. 4 p. 154.

53 Ibid.

54 E.g. Andelman, David A., 'Space Wars', *Foreign Policy*, Fall 1981, No. 44 p. 106 – 'Although ground-based testing of a laser system intended for use in space could conceivably be concealed, space-based testing could not. And a weapon system involving such exotic new technology could not be deployed without extensive experimentation in space. Otherwise, there would be no assurance whatsoever that the system could meet operating standards either defensively or offensively.'

55 'India Rockets Ahead with Observation Satellites', *New Scientist*, 11 June 1981, Vol. 90 No. 1257 p. 691; Ghosh, S.K., 'China's Space Programme', *IDSA Journal*, April–June 1980, Vol. XII No. 4 p. 364, esp. p. 373 – 'To sum up, while a successful operational military satellite system takes a long time to develop and deploy, and to reach the level of the two Super Powers in this regard takes even a longer time, there is no doubt that China's stepped up space activity signifies its determination to advance towards this goal.'

56 But cf. Vlasic, Ivan A., 'Disarmament Decade, Outer Space and International Law', *McGill Law Journal* 1981, Vol. 26 No. 2 p. 151 – 'Professor Harrison Brown of the California Institute of Technology foresaw the possibility of orbiting nuclear devices of 1000 megatons which could, on command, incinerate six Western states within minutes if exploded at an altitude or three hundred miles. The concept of orbital nuclear bombers was eventually rejected as impractical and less efficient than the more conventional means of delivery . . .'
57 See Table II (page 28).
58 The latter loophole in the Outer Space Treaty may be impliedly covered by the ABM Treaty for the time being.
59 Dahlitz, J., 'Arms Control in Outer Space', *The World Today*, April 1982, Vol. 38 No. 4 pp. 156–9, *re.* current technological advances.
60 Ibid.
61 See Vlasic, op. cit. esp. pp. 168–9.
62 A/RES/36/97C.
63 A/RES/36/99.
64 A/36/192.

CHAPTER 10

Supervision of Compliance and Enforcement of the Agreements

Verification of Multilateral NAC Agreements

Supervision of compliance with NAC agreements and, in case of reluctance to comply or outright breach, the enforcement of those agreements, are essential components of the NAC process. There is no ambiguity in international law concerning the obligation to observe treaties on the basis of the universally uncontested maxim of *pacta sunt servanda*. Despite the assumption that all international agreements will be carried out in good faith, it is acceptable practice to supervise performance. The observance of compliance for the purpose of detecting any breaches of NAC agreements is referred to as *verification*. Methods of persuasion or coercion used to ensure that States abide by their obligations – whether pursuant to an Order or Opinion of the International Court of Justice, an arbitrated or negotiated settlement, or otherwise – are referred to as *enforcement*.

Apart from the *Nuclear Tests* case, discussed in Chapter 6, there is no case law relating to NAC. In accordance with the general principles of treaty interpretation, it can be adduced that the obligation to abide by an NAC agreement requires compliance with the letter and spirit of its terms, although it does not forbid circumvention of the agreement by extraneous means even if that entails the attainment of unilateral advantage over another party. NAC provisions appear to be prone to ambiguity regarding distinctions between a breach and a permissible circumvention.

Verification has assumed a new importance with the advent of arms control agreements. In the case of other international agreements, such as commercial arrangements, protection of diplomatic personnel and aliens, or border dispute settlements, the observance or non-observance of the agreement is generally obvious. By contrast, in NAC agreements there is often a substantial possibility that extensive preparations for breach, should they occur, would not be detected and, possibly, that actual and repeated breach of the terms of the treaty would be overlooked. For this reason, the final document of SSD I refers to the need for *adequate* verification of arms control agreements.

'Adequate verification' could be defined as the intensity of surveillance necessary to ensure that discovery of an irregularity would be sufficiently likely as to make breach of the particular undertaking by subterfuge an unacceptable risk to the State concerned. As accidental discovery is usually a possibility, the risk of discovery does not rest entirely on deliberately instituted 'measures'.

When assessing 'unacceptable risk' of discovery of breach, especially by United States Government Agencies, emphasis is often placed on the *likelihood* of discovery rather than the *consequences* of discovery. Yet it is reasonable to suppose that the latter consideration weighs more heavily with Governments than the former one. The consequences of discovery of breach would no doubt depend to a large extent on the steadfastness of the NAC regime. So long as open breaches can be avoided, as they have been so far, then a breach of an NAC agreement by a party could lead to ostracism by other States or, if perpetrated by a Superpower, to the collapse of the entire NAC process.

The possibility of adequate verification can be prejudiced by ambiguities in drafting, often deliberately countenanced, in order to paper over irreconcilable differences among negotiating partners. A typical instance is the imprecise wording of Article IV of the NPT.[1] Another example is a provision in the Statute of the IAEA requiring the deposit with the Agency, for the purpose of temporary storage, of 'any excess of any special fissionable materials' being the by-products of safeguarded materials. The Treaty does not state by whom or by what criteria it is to be determined whether any nuclear material not in current use is 'excess', requiring IAEA storage. Neither does it indicate in what manner or at whose cost such transfers of superfluous nuclear materials should occur.[2] Hence, several non-nuclear-weapon States are building up large stockpiles of weapons grade nuclear materials. So far, no nuclear material whatever has been deposited with the IAEA for safekeeping, and the Agency has no facilities to accommodate a State that may wish to transfer its excess special fissionable material for storage.[3]

In addition to ambiguities, several of the treaties have loopholes. Some of these are acquiring greater significance with the passage of time, such as the absence of any provision in the Non-Proliferation Treaty to prevent a non-nuclear-weapon State Party from supplying special fissionable material or relevant equipment to another non-nuclear-weapon State for military purposes.[4] A further example is to be found in the Outer Space Treaty which is in urgent need of overhaul for the rectification of substantive omissions, for instance, failure to outlaw the stationing of weapons, that are not weapons of mass destruction, on satellites or on space stations.[5]

Methods of Verifying Multilateral NAC Treaties:

In some respects, international verification is comparable to search, interrrogation, inspection of records, and similar procedures in domestic jurisdictions designed to ensure that the laws are being observed. Verification measures provided for in multilateral NAC Treaties are in addition to such other methods as States may themselves devise, without transgressing the rights of other States. For example, nuclear explosions in the atmosphere can be detected visually; by measuring fallout levels of radioactive substances; and by the nature and sequence of shock waves caused, referred to as the 'signature' of the blast.[6] Observations of this kind can be made by NTM without receiving co-operation from other States, by using photographic, electronic, chemical and other sensors.[7] The Partial Test-Ban Treaty, banning nuclear explosions in the atmosphere, makes no provision for internationally co-operative verification, thus leaving the Parties with only NTM as the method of verification.

175

The other multilateral NAC treaties do make some provisions for co-operative verification. To do so, they utilise several techniques, the most substantial being the institutional method employed by the IAEA, which will be considered in greater detail under the next sub-heading. The IAEA also provides the verification mechanism for the Non-Proliferation Treaty, by requiring all non-nuclear-weapon States Parties to enter into full scope safeguards agreements with the Agency.[8] Adherence to the Treaty of Tlatelolco is also verified by the IAEA,[9] in addition to on-site inspections undertaken by the Agency for the Prohibition of Nuclear Weapons in Latin America (OPANAL).[10]

Another verification system being utilised is that of mandatory notification. For instance the Antarctic Treaty requires notification to be given to all Parties of any expedition undertaken to the Antarctic Continent.[11] Likewise, by the terms of the Outer Space Treaty, a Party is obliged to notify all other Parties of any potentially harmful activities in outer space that it plans to undertake.[12] By contrast, the Sea-Bed Treaty only requires notification of Parties after a dispute has occurred, in order to facilitate co-operative verification procedures.[13]

Observation provisions for the verification of NAC treaties authorise general observation of procedures, specific observation under given circumstances, as well as designating appointed observers and investigators. The Antarctic Treaty permits the appointment of observers by the Parties to scrutinise the whole Continent and all traffic flowing to and from it. On the other hand, the Outer Space Treaty only permits observation of activities and installations belonging to another Party after reasonable notice has been given. A different provision has been adopted in the Sea-Bed Treaty, which permits continuous observation of relevant activities, without requiring the designation of special observers.

Co-operative verification is provided for in both the Sea-Bed Treaty and the ENMOD Convention, but only at the request of the Parties when they, presumably, suspect irregularities. It is always implied, while in the Outer Space Treaty and the Sea-Bed Treaty it is overtly stated, that observation procedures must not interfere with the activities of the Parties being observed.[14]

Contemplated Methods of Verifying Future NAC Treaties:

Efforts to improve the verification of multilateral NAC treaties take several forms. While States continuously endeavour to update existing techniques involved in methods such as remote sensing, and air and water sampling to detect nuclear waste products, novel proposals are constantly put forward for the verification of treaties still under negotiation. For instance it has been proposed that a Comprehensive Test-Ban Treaty could be verified by periodic inspection perhaps aided with the installation of recording instruments in 'black boxes' and/or inspection by challenge in the event of suspected irregularity.[15] Likewise, an International Seismic Monitoring Network is under contemplation.[16]

Another type of endeavour in multilateral NAC verification is to give more States access to verification techniques, if need be by utilising a joint operation. The most ambitious programme of this kind is the proposed

International Satellite Monitoring Agency (ISMA).[17] It is anticipated that through participation in the Agency, States would acquire access to remote sensing instruments and techniques by pooling their resources to launch the necessary satellites, and to analyse and interpret the resulting data. Until now, the procedure has been available only to the Superpowers.

When ISMA was proposed by France at SSD I, both Superpowers were strongly opposed to it, fearing that it would merely add to the grounds for international dispute, misunderstanding and competition. However, with the rapid development of launching techniques, particularly by the Europeans and the Chinese, remote sensing will soon be within the competence of several States. Therefore, the options today are only between haphazard additions to the space 'club', or the introduction of an organised international system. Nevertheless, the successful operation of this form of joint verification is not a foregone conclusion. Difficult questions are still unresolved regarding the equitable allocation of management responsibilities, the basis of cost-sharing, the criteria for participation and access to data, together with problems related to the interpretation and divulgence of the information to be gained.

The legal status of the proposed ISMA is also undecided and will, no doubt, depend on whether it is to be a United Nations body or whether only regional or other selective participation is achieved. In the meantime, the international community is obliged to place great reliance on the verification of multilateral NAC treaties by the Superpowers, a situation that is not altogether satisfactory. There is no recognition in international law that the Superpowers have a responsibility to divulge breaches of multilateral NAC treaties observed by them as a consequence of their developed surveillance systems. Nor are they required to report on conduct contrary to General Assembly resolutions, even if they alone are able to verify it. The adverse repercussions of this situation were strongly felt at the time of the suspected nuclear explosion off the coast of South Africa in 1979, known as the 'September event', when records of observations of the event could not be elicited as of right.[18]

The IAEA Safeguards System

The verification of multilateral and bilateral international treaties regarding nuclear activities, referred to as the safeguards system of the International Atomic Energy Agency (IAEA), is by far the most extensive verification system for horizontal nuclear arms proliferation control. The objective of the IAEA verification system, as described in the Statute of the Agency, is –

> To establish and administer safeguards designed to ensure that special fissionable and other materials, services, equipment, facilities, and information made available by the Agency or at its request or under its supervision or control are not used in such a way as to further any military purpose . . .[19]

It was originally envisaged that the Agency's safeguards would be applied chiefly pursuant to *project agreements*, whereby material and technical assistance in nuclear projects is supplied by or through the Agency to a recipient State.

The IAEA is also authorised to apply safeguards at the request of its Members 'to any bilateral or multilateral arrangement'. These are referred to as safeguards *transfer agreements,* which enable States to confer on the Agency the task of supervising safeguards responsibilities undertaken in various nuclear co-operation agreements between them.

There is a further provision in the IAEA Statute which permits the application of safeguards 'at the request of a State, to any of that State's activities in the field of atomic energy'. The provision regarding these *unilateral submissions* has enabled the Agency to verify the commitments of States under the Treaty of Tlatelolco and the Non-Proliferation Treaty.

It was only in 1962 that the first safeguards inspection occurred. During the next four years, the safeguards system was substantially revised and extended as the result of strong co-operation on the issues between the United States and the Soviet Union. It has been suggested that increased support by the Soviet Union for safeguards during that era was consequent upon the acquisition of a nuclear weapons capability by China.[20]

Details of the safeguards system were elaborated in two Agency documents.[21] The specific aim of safeguards is described as –

> . . . the timely detection of diversion of significant quantities of *nuclear material* from peaceful nuclear activities to the manufacture of nuclear weapons or of other nuclear explosive devices or for purposes unknown, and deterrence of such diversion by the risk of early detection.[22]

The Agency's Standing Advisory Group on Safeguards Implementation, has considered the meaning of 'significant quantities of nuclear material'.[23] A 'threshold amount' of nuclear material was defined as the approximate quantity of special fissionable material needed for a nuclear explosive device, namely, in general terms, 8 kg of plutonium, 8 kg of uranium 233 or 25 kg of uranium 235. The phrase 'for purposes unknown', has been interpreted to mean that the Agency is not required to enquire into the purposes for which diverted material may be intended, provided it is shown to be a diversion from the peaceful nuclear activities ostensibly undertaken.[24] The Agency seeks an above 90% probability of detecting a diversion.[25]

All Agency safeguards are based on a State System of Accountancy (SSAC), as well as national physical control of radioactive material. In accordance with this system States accept the obligation to maintain comprehensive records, based on the method of material balance areas to facilitate verification at key measurement points. They are required, *inter alia,* to submit monthly reports to the Agency concerning all nuclear inputs, outputs, production and losses of nuclear material. The State is also obliged to provide the results of all physical inventories of nuclear materials and to draw the Agency's attention to any discrepancies.

Inspectors appointed by the Agency have the task of ascertaining that such records supplied are consistent with the records appearing at the relevant plant and with the quantities of special fissionable material actually present. It is assumed that potential diverters could be States, facility operators, individuals or groups of individuals. Therefore, all information supplied by the State has to be independently verified in the course of *ad hoc, routine* and *special* inspections.[26]

According to IAEA estimates concerning the efficacy of its safeguards on nuclear fuel cycle facilities, as submitted to the second Review Conference of the Non-Proliferation Treaty, the great majority of reactors, being *light water reactors*, are effectively safeguarded. The Agency has greater difficulties with *on-load fuelled power reactors*, including the Magnox and Candu type reactors, which are refuelled continually without reactor shutdown. Also, in these reactors storage may be in 'close-packed three-dimensional arrays', which does not facilitate fuel element counting.

It is claimed that *conversion* prior to fuel fabrication can also be satisfactorily safeguarded, as the facilities are usually shut down several times a year. On those occasions all the material can be tagged for later identification.[27]

The Agency admits to only 'limited experience' in safeguarding *reprocessing* plants and no experience with large reprocessing plants. Only 'some preliminary work' has been done regarding proposed methods for safeguarding the plants. Each of these plants can produce 10 to 14 tonnes of plutonium annually, so that expected measurement errors and uncertainties would be too great for the successful use of the customary material accountancy method. One suggestion has been the installment of monitoring barriers around critical parts of the plant. As safeguards for large reprocessing plants would have to be based mainly on containment techniques, these would have to be built in during the construction of the plant.[28]

Likewise, the Agency has had no experience with *uranium enrichment* plants – or even pilot plants in this case. The first enrichment plants to be safeguarded by the Agency are of the *centrifuge* type. Commerical *diffusion* plants to be safeguarded are still under construction, while the *nozzle* process and other new processes are merely at the experimental stage. *Gaseous diffusion* plants are as yet only operated in the nuclear-weapon States.

The chief verification problem of the Agency at the present time, is to prevent the possibility of converting a high production rate at low enrichment to a low production rate at high enrichment levels, between periods of observation. However, in the near future, larger scale diversion of special fissionable material, namely weapons grade material, could become possible.

Fast breeder reactors are the most proliferation-prone. In those reactors the irradiated fuel, and even part of the fresh fuel assemblies, are 'virtually inaccessible'. Nor can the quantity of material in the core be verified at any stage. Similarly, spent fuel cannot be identified for at least several months.

The Agency has only had experience in safeguarding pilot plants of the liquid metal fast breeder reactor type. At present prototypes are being perfected, while commercial plants are to commence production in the next few years. It is anticipated that containment and surveillance with the aid of inbuilt design features, could make safeguarding possible. The Agency claims that the necessity could arise for new concepts of safeguarding to be utilised as the larger plants and the new fuel cycles of fast breeders come into operation.[29]

Already the Agency has the use of seals; electronic sensors to detect the movement of various grades of nuclear material; 'tamper-proof' cameras; and sound recorders. The possibility of inbuilt measurement and containment features sought to be incorporated, gives some prospect of verifiability of the more sophisticated plants. The responsibility of non-nuclear-weapon States, under the relevant treaties and agreements, to ensure that all nuclear facilities subject to their jurisdiction are so constructed as to facilitate appropriate verification, is an issue of international law that, so far, has not been fully confronted.[30]

Compliance Enforcement of Multilateral NAC Treaties

Enforcing Compliance Pursuant to the IAEA Safeguards System

The function of IAEA safeguards, pursuant to the two non-proliferation treaties and the various bilateral safeguards agreements concluded in compliance with those treaties, is to report on the diversion of special fissionable material suitable for the manufacture of nuclear weapons, from facilities ostensibly required to produce radioactive material for peaceful purposes. The mere knowledge that a breach of treaty obligations has occurred, or is about to occur, would be pointless unless it is assumed that divulgence of the facts would lead to deterrence. The relevant NAC treaties contain only minimal direct sanctions provisions. These consist largely of withholding materials and assistance for further nuclear activities[31] and making the facts of the breach known to those directly concerned, as well as to the world community through the United Nations. It would then be possible for States individually, collectively, or universally to apply economic, social, or military sanctions.

However, pressures in support of upholding the non-proliferation regime do not have to await a finding that an NAC treaty has been breached. International sanctions and inducements can be applied irrespective of treaty obligations.[32] For instance, the offer of economic assistance or military aid can be made, in the first instance, with a view to persuading a State to accept obligations with respect to the prevention of horizontal proliferation. Moves to admit Spain into the European Economic Community, and concurrent acceptance by that State of full scope safeguards, may be a case in point. Conversely, South Africa and Israel have resisted economic pressures and are prepared to forego imports of enriched uranium for commercial use in preference to accepting full scope safeguards. Undoubtedly even those States could be persuaded to conform if Western States were prepared to apply more stringent economic and military inducements or, alternatively, perhaps if the security problems of the non-complying States ceased to be so pressing.

It would be mistaken to conclude from the above considerations that the relevant treaties are either ineffectual or irrelevant. Their role in the non-proliferation regime could be characterised as the main strands in a wider fabric. In accordance with that analogy, the precise objectives and standards set by those treaties, and the support they enjoy, represent the strength and resilience of the binding strands that hold the fabric together.[33]

How well is this horizontal anti-proliferation fabric likely to endure?[34] The present spread of proliferation-prone technology in the world has resulted from the pursuit of short term goals in preference to long term non-proliferation objectives. It began at a time of acute Soviet-American rivalry for influence among emerging Third World nations. In 1954, a United States Atomic Energy Act was passed, enabling that country to supply nuclear research reactors to more than twenty States, including several that were economically underdeveloped and politically unstable. However, as well as extending Western influence to the recipient States, the transactions were commercially profitable.[35]

With the perfection of nuclear technology in additional developed Western States, the commercial incentive gained the upper hand. The nuclear industries of Canada, France and the Federal Republic of Germany, in particular, entered into competition with the United States for the sale of nuclear plant, materials and technology.[36] This occurred simultaneously with growing demands by the Third World for economic and political justice in the international arena.[37]

The demand for commercial reactors for power generation, as well as for research reactors, is invariably justified on economic grounds, while the concomitant creation of a nuclear technology infrastructure, providing at least a potential for weapons capability, tends to be dismissed as an insignificant by-product of the process.

In recent years the argument for supplying sensitive technologies, for example, by Germany to Brazil[38] and by France to Pakistan, has been that the consequent reliance by those States on the supplier for materials, spare parts and consultancy, would integrate them into the economic and legal non-proliferation system. The strategy appears to have succeeded, for the time being, with Brazil which has accepted full scope safeguards. Pakistan, on the other hand, which, as a result of a change of heart by France has been ultimately denied assistance, has decided to refuse full scope safeguards.

These two instances hardly justify a conclusion that the transfer of nuclear technology restrains proliferation while its refusal tends to promote proliferation. Such reasoning fails to take account of the different geopolitical situations of Brazil and Pakistan. More generally, the argument ignores the relevance of the time factor in the spread of proliferation-prone technologies, namely that the mere postponement of nuclear weapons prowess may be beneficial. It also overlooks the propensity for early self-sufficiency in nuclear processes by assisted States, destined to reduce the influence of original suppliers.

Although the spread of nuclear technology was inevitable as the result of world-wide technical development, the *rate* of spread has been artificially increased stemming from Superpower confrontation, economic rivalries among the technologically advanced States, and the desire to acquire a future nuclear weapons option by developing States. The current issue is whether the nuclear weapons option is to be exercised by the twenty or more developed and developing States ripe for it, and at what rate additional States are to acquire the option.

Pakistan has often maintained at the United Nations that horizontal proliferation is not a technological question but a political question. While at present this is still not true for most States, it is becoming an increasingly

181

valid claim. Restraint due to verification and the threat of sanctions, whether imposed pursuant to treaty obligations or as the result of international opinion independently of treaty obligations, in conformity with the general principles of non-proliferation, still only applies to a limited number of countries. It applies especially to those that have large commercial plants capable of rapidly producing militarily significant amounts of weapons-grade material, or the early prospect of enrichment, reprocessing and fast breeder facilities. Those are also the countries that could not only produce increasingly large quantities of the sensitive materials but also, as has been noted previously, are installing reactors that are difficult, if not impossible, to safeguard. As well as undisguised production of weapons-grade material in reactors constructed for that purpose, research reactors and pilot plants can also be utilised to produce significant quantities of weapons-grade material.

At present only four non-nuclear-weapon States possessing nuclear facilities are not under full scope IAEA safeguards. These are India, Israel, Pakistan and South Africa.[39] Several of the countries under full scope safeguards have accepted safeguards not as the consequence of treaty obligations, as they are not parties to either the Non-Proliferation Treaty or the Treaty of Tlatelolco, but under bilateral co-operation agreements. Unlike the requirements of the Treaties referred to, full scope safeguards undertaken pursuant to commercial treaties do not necessarily anticipate the safeguarding of any future nuclear plants.

However, the distinction between safeguards pursuant to a treaty and those in compliance with a co-operation agreement is of limited significance. First, the repudiation of the relevant treaties only requires three months' notice.[40] Second, recent bilateral nuclear co-operation agreements generally contain fallback safeguards, should IAEA safeguards no longer apply, and they can also require prior consent by the supplier to the recipient regarding reprocessing, enrichment and transfers to third countries. In addition, several agreements restrict indirect proliferation routes, including copying and the use of subsequent generations of nuclear fuel. Third, safeguards agreements entered into with the Agency consequent upon co-operation agreements probably have an independent operation and would continue even if the co-operation agreement were repudiated.[41] A situation where it was sought to terminate Agency safeguards resulting from the suspension of a bilateral co-operation agreement has not occurred so far.

The emergence of renewed Superpower antagonisms coincidental with the growing nuclear autarchy of developing nations, could place the task of policing the horizontal non-proliferation regime increasingly with the Third World. Rather than withdrawing from the IAEA supply and safeguards system, these countries may prefer to exercise their voting strength in that institution in order to secure the election of a majority to the Board of Directors. In the meantime, the possibility can be used as a bargaining lever. Having acquired a voting majority, whether they would turn a blind eye to the emergence of some of their number as nuclear-weapon States is not predictable on the basis of present indicators. The wish to gain nuclear-weapon status by some of the developing States could well be offset by the growing apprehensions of their less ambitious colleagues.

At present, the only nuclear-weapon States in the world are the five permanent Members of the Security Council. It is an indication of the astuteness with which the permanent Members were chosen, at a time when the architects of the United Nations were still unaware of the military potential of nuclear reactions. Yet, should the five veto-carrying nuclear-weapon States fail to provide an acceptable modicum of security to non-nuclear-weapon States, as well as continuing to slacken non-proliferation standards, they could be faced with nuclear challenges not only from developing States but also from technologically advanced States. For instance, the Federal Republic of Germany and Japan have vast stockpiles of nuclear material suitable for insertion into missile warheads, the possibility of sophisticated delivery systems, and the technical prowess to turn these capacities to immediate military advantage.[42]

In the absence of concerted world opinion opposed to horizontal proliferation, it would also be possible for less powerful States to become thinly disguised latent or quasi nuclear-weapon States, such as Israel and South Africa are reputed to be. It is a stance that may afford a measure of deterrence while minimising ostracism and the embarrassment of allies.

Over the longer term, the non-proliferation regime could be substantially fractured with the emergence of additional overtly or reputedly nuclear-weapon States. It has been repeatedly put forward that such a situation might galvanize world opinion into enforcement of the non-use of nuclear weapons, thus preventing their further spread.[43] This view is open to conjecture. The successful restraint exercised, so far, by the nuclear five is not proof that nuclear weapons can be stockpiled as a deterrent indefinitely without precipitating their use. The relatively brief time involved and the exceptional stability and competence of the bureaucracies of those States, compared with those of many other States, were no doubt contributing factors in averting nuclear war. Even so, the use of nuclear weapons is known to have been seriously contemplated by at least one of the nuclear-weapon States in the post second World War period, while the other Superpower is also thought to have proposed such use on at least one occasion.[44] Hence, complacency about horizontal proliferation, in the belief that non-use of the weapons in a proliferated world could be more easily enforced than the prevention of proliferation, does not appear to be justified.

General Principles of Compliance Enforcement

It has been observed in previous Chapters that the standard of compliance with the provisions of all the treaties listed in Table I (see page 24) has been very good. No situation has arisen when it would have been appropriate to consider the application of sanctions for non-compliance with an NAC treaty. Therefore, when assessing the likely effectiveness of sanctions that may have to be administered in the future, it becomes necessary to extrapolate from experience gained in the application of measures to enforce non-NAC agreements.

The only experience in relation to the enforcement of NAC provisions has been in the form of consultations between the Parties to a treaty. There has also been conduct inconsistent with United Nations NAC resolutions, perpetrated by States that had not undertaken treaty obligations in the relevant matters, for instance, in relation to conducting nuclear tests in the atmosphere, or refusal to accept IAEA safeguards.

Apart from consultations concerning compliance that take place in the IAEA or in OPANAL, formal consultations have been conducted in the framework of Review Conferences. If any breaches were to occur and in case of suspected breaches, the exposure of such conduct at Review Conferences or by direct communication to the parties, as provided by the disputes procedures of the various NAC treaties, would itself carry the sanction of ill-repute. By comparison, it is noteworthy that in other areas of international law more formal and regular procedures have been devised for the monitoring of compliance with international standards.

For instance, under Article 22 of the Constitution of the International Labour Organisation (ILO), States are obligated to supply annual reports regarding measures adopted by them to give effect to the Conventions they have ratified. Those reports have to supply particulars requested by the Governing Body of the ILO. Further, in accordance with Article 19 of the ILO Constitution, States Members are required to give an account of such circumstances as may have prevented them from ratifying ILO Conventions to which they are not parties. A Committee of Experts on the Application of Conventions and Recommendations, examines the reports submitted by Governments, a summarised version of which is presented at each annual session of the ILO.

Another example of enforcement by persuasion, on the basis of disclosure of non-compliance, is to be found in procedures pursuant to Articles of Agreement of the International Monetary Fund (IMF). For example, Article XII, Section 8 provides that 'the Fund shall at all times have the right to communicate the views informally to any member on any matter arising under this Agreement'. The Article further provides that the Fund is empowered to publish a report concerning matters within its control, if the balance of payments situation of Members has been adversely affected by the activities of another Member, provided there is strong international commitment regarding the matter. In the knowledge that it could be exposed for non-observance of an obligation by the reporting methods just referred to, any State that may be tempted to perpetrate a breach would tend to be dissuaded from so doing.

Yet another form of sanction for breach of an international obligation, under a treaty or otherwise, is to take retaliatory action commensurate with the breach. For example, Article XIX:3(a) of the General Agreement on Tariffs and Trade (GATT), permits the suspension of 'substantially equivalent concessions or other obligations' in certain circumstances as retaliation for breach. Likewise, the Contracting Parties to GATT may, under the said Article, retaliate against the withdrawal of some tariff concessions.

A further kind of retaliation is countenanced by the International Civil Aviation Organisation (ICAO) which, pursuant to the ICAO (Chicago) Convention of 1973, permits the exclusion of aircraft from the airspace of any State that has been adversely affected by a breach of the anti-hijacking provisions of the Convention.

Different considerations apply in the field of NAC. It is difficult to envisage retaliatory sanctions for the breach of NAC agreements that would not be self-defeating in their operation, by permitting the deployment or use of nuclear arms. An exception is the retaliation authorised by the Statute of the IAEA, which provides that a State that receives Agency assistance may be denied further assistance for its nuclear industry as the result of breach of an undertaking with the Agency. In accordance with Article XII (A)7 of the IAEA Statute, the Board of Governors has the discretion under such circumstances to either suspend or terminate assistance to the offending State.

Some formal sanctions for non-compliance with the provisions of NAC treaties are available. For example, the Outer Space Treaty, by Article VII, makes any State Party, 'from whose territory or facility an object is launched' into outer space, liable for damage caused by the space object. Similarly, in case of breach of safeguards Agreements with the IAEA the Board of Governors is empowered to apply several formal sanctions in addition to the retaliatory measures of suspension or termination of assistance. These include the right to recall the return of materials and equipment supplied, and the suspension of all membership privileges, while requiring the continued observance of membership obligations.

The Annual Reports of the Board of Governors indicate that none of the abovementioned sanctions have been applied, so far, by the IAEA in pursuance of Article XII(A)7. Nevertheless, it is relevant to the operation of the horizontal non-proliferation regime that the retaliatory measures available under the Statute of the IAEA, as well as the other sanctions provisions, would pose no administrative difficulties in their application, with the exception that the return of materials and equipment already supplied may be difficult to enforce.

The most onerous formal sanctions that could be administered for breach of NAC obligations, would be applied in accordance with the provisions of Chapter VII of the United Nations Charter. Those sanctions are not available for the enforcement of most international obligations, as they may be invoked only on occasions when there is a 'threat to the peace, breach of the peace, or act of aggression', in circumstances when the maintenance or restoration of 'international peace and security' are at stake. .

As non-compliance with NAC obligations could well give rise to a situation jeopardising international peace and security, the sanctions that may be imposed by the Security Council are very pertinent to this area of international law. The sanctions under Article 41 include the severance of international communication by rail, sea, air, postal, telegraphic, and radio contact, partial or complete interruption of economic relations, and severance of diplomatic relations. Article 42 authorises the Security Council to take whatever military measures are necessary 'to maintain or restore international peace and security'.[45]

While attempted sanctions for non-compliance with NAC undertakings could be frustrated by any permanent Member of the Security Council, the use of the veto to block sanctions against a State that had violated clear-cut treaty obligations would be a very serious step to take, which could damage the whole international legal system impinging on the observance of the United Nations Charter. This conclusion could be drawn from the deterioration of the international situation that occurred at the time when the Soviet Union used the veto power to prevent the application of sanctions against Iran, despite that country's clear violation of treaty obligations with respect to the safety of diplomatic personnel. The use of the veto on that occasion was sought to be justified on the ground that, although the taking of diplomatic hostages was reprehensible and a breach of treaty obligation, it did not represent a danger to international peace and security authorising the application of sanctions under Chapter VII of the Charter. However, the military significance of NAC treaties would foreseeably preclude a similar argument as a plausible excuse for refusal to apply sanctions in the event of breach.

The United Nations can apply the further disincentive of expulsion from United Nations membership under Article 6 of the Charter and, in particular, under Article 5 authorising such action with respect to a Member 'against which preventive or enforcement action has been taken by the Security Council'. Expulsion entails suspension from the 'exercise of the rights and privileges of membership' but does not absolve from the obligations of membership. Such action can only be taken by the General Assembly on the recommendation of the Security Council, which has so far failed to agree on the imposition of that sanction. A similar result can be attained by the General Assembly acting alone under Rule 27 of its Rules of Procedure,[46] regulating the Assembly's exercise of power to accept or reject the credentials of delegations that purport to represent the Government of a Member State. Non-approval of credentials by the Credentials Committee of the General Assembly has been used by that body for several years as a sanction against South Africa, on account of its refusal to repeal its *apartheid* laws.

Neither accession to NAC treaties, nor any other form of international agreement is a necessary prerequisite for the application of United Nations sanctions in a case that is deemed, by the world body, to be a sufficiently serious breach of international obligation under the Charter. Theoretically at least, in any conflict between the provisions of the Charter, no matter how imprecise, and other treaty obligations of Member States, however explicit the latter may be, the provisions of the Charter prevail by virtue of its Article 103.[47] Hence, on the basis of possible imposition of formal United Nations sanctions in the nuclear arms race, the benefits to be derived from the existence of specific treaties is obscure.

It is not possible to prove by cogent argument that treaty obligations for NAC, in addition to the obligation under the Charter for the maintenance of international peace and security, have any practical effect for enhancing the relevant enforcement procedures of the United Nations. Nevertheless, although there is no unassailable legal dictum to that effect, the breach of a precise undertaking is a more obvious affront than failure to perform a nebulous duty, like the maintenance of international peace and security, and is therefore more likely to attract censure. To that extent, a more precise obligation is more binding.

Despite the vast legal powers of the United Nations by virtue of the provisions of the Charter, in practice, the imposition of sanctions and rewards to induce States to pursue a desired line of action is mostly of an informal nature, imposed by one State or a group of States. These inducements usually involve trade or other economic benefits and disincentives.[48] Occasionally, of course, there has been an assault by armed force, as was the case with the attack by Israel on the Iraqi nuclear reactor, on the alleged ground that the reactor was to be used for the manufacture of nuclear weapons with which to bombard Israel.[49] At the other end of the scale, light sanctions can be imposed that mainly have nuisance value, such as restrictions on travel by diplomatic personnel of the State to be punished, and the imposition of other deliberate inconveniences to its citizens.

It is a moot point to what extent the successful imposition of such informal sanctions is dependent on an international sense of justice that deems the conduct being enforced to be consonant with the imposition of international law. For instance, the suspension of nuclear tests in the atmosphere by France, and the release of the United States hostages by Iran, were carried out under the threat of economic sanctions in the former instance, and in response to actual severe sanctions imposed in the latter instance. Nevertheless, it would be plausible to suggest that those sanctions and threatened sanctions could only succeed because the relevant treaties and United Nations resolutions had firmly established the principles of justice which they sought to apply.

Verification and Enforcement of Bilateral NAC Agreements

Supervision of compliance with bilateral NAC agreements is inseparable from the day to day performance of obligations under the relevant agreements.[50] For this reason the main verification procedures, including the provisions in the two SALT Treaties facilitating verification, as well as the verification-related activities of the SCC, have already been alluded to in Chapter 9.

The reliability of verification procedures for establishing requisite compliance by the Soviet Union to bilateral NAC treaties is a matter of contention in the United States, on which expert opinion is sharply divided. In particular, assessments concerning the efficacy of national technical means of verifying the SALT Treaties are often contradictory, despite the sophisticated methods being used. Former Deputy Director of the CIA, Herbert Scoville, gave an indication of the prowess of NTM when he said –

> Satellites can now locate, count and measure modern weapons from 100 miles away, while radar-sensitive radio receivers and infrared sensors on ships, on planes and on land can determine their characteristics and the number of warheads they carry. Limits on armaments can be verified so that pacts such as SALT II do not depend upon Russian co-operation.[51]

For example, in testimony to the Committee on Foreign Relations of the United States Senate, former Secretary of State, Harold Brown, stated the position thus –

> Our capacity for the monitoring is spread among ground stations, some of them in foreign countries, satellite systems, and other detection techniques, some of them deployed aboard ships and aboard aircraft that stay in international air space. If we lost all of our overseas, our non-US sites, our ability to monitor SALT would be degraded some-

what. But our ability to monitor Soviet strategic and other military programs in general and our indications and warning capability for potential Soviet actions would be degraded very much more than that.[52]

When asked whether the United States would know when there was concealment or the impeding of verification by NTM, the Secretary replied –

We will be able to see when that happens. We will not always be sure, but we will always know enough to be able to raise it as an issue . . . It is easier to tell that they are trying to hide something than it is to tell what they are trying to hide.[53]

He added that the chance of the Soviet Union being able to develop a weapons system without the United States being aware of the fact was 'substantially less than 1 out of 1 million'.[54]

Senator Jess Helms has adopted a rather different approach. He maintained during the Senate hearings that, with respect to SALT II –

Technology has overtaken the supposed benefits of this treaty . . . We have no way of knowing whether the Soviet production lines have, in fact, been shut down . . . But, if missiles can be reloaded or launched without a silo launcher, the threat, Mr Chairman, simply cannot be verified. We thought that we were counting guns and that the ICBM's were just the ammunition. Now we see that we have been counting holsters, and we have no idea how many guns they have pointed at us.[55]

More recently, the views of a number of well known writers on the subject were collated in a volume entitled *Verification and SALT: the Challenge of Strategic Deception*.[56] For example, while contributors Bruce C. Blair and Garry D. Brewer are of the opinion that SALT compliance can be adequately verified by national technical means, Senator Gordon H. Humphrey and Amrom H. Katz reach the opposite conclusion, while several others adopt intermediate positions.

A United States Government background briefing in February 1978, regarding compliance with SALT I, disclosed that 'the U.S. does not feel that the Soviet Union has violated either the letter or the spirit of the Treaty since it was signed on May 26, 1972'.[57] At the same time, the briefing also stated that the United States had made eight specific enquiries challenging Soviet activities as to their consistency with the provisions of the Treaty, suggesting that there may have been deliberate concealment of activities. The briefing concluded that by 1975 the situation had improved. It was not alleged that any actual breach of Treaty provisions had occurred.

In April 1978 Secretary of State, Cyrus Vance, made a report on SALT compliance issues to the Chairman of the Senate Foreign Relations Committee. The introduction to the report, reproduced in a Department of State Bulletin, draws attention to '. . . how carefully the United States has raised promptly with the Soviets any unusual or ambiguous activities which could be or could become grounds for concern'. It is further observed that, pursuant to the queries raised by the United States in the SCC –

In each case, the activity in question has ceased or additional information has allayed the concern.[58]

None of the questions posed involved other than possible minor transgression of the agreements. For example, in 1973 United States officials came to the conclusion that the radar associated with FA-5 surface-to-air missiles were being tested by the Soviet Union in 'an ABM mode' contrary to the provisions of the ABM Treaty. Although the Soviet Union denied this, the disputed activity was abandoned. On another occasion the Soviet Union admitted that there had been failure to dismantle old ICBM launchers and SLBM at a sufficiently fast rate to comply with SALT I. When challenged they accelerated the dismantling.

The Soviet Union has also challenged certain activities engaged in by the United States with respect to the observance of the SALT I Treaty. For instance, they enquired whether missile silos for old Atlas and Titan missiles could be reactivated, and they queried the purpose of installing a new United States radar in Alaska, on the basis of its possible usefulness in anti-ballistic missile defence.

The marginal nature of these queries, and their satisfactory resolution in each instance within the framework of the SCC, supports the conclusion that the bilateral NAC treaties are being strictly observed and meticulously verified.[59]

Methods of application and effectiveness of verification procedures under the SALT II Treaty are extensively analysed in the 1980 Yearbook of the Stockholm International Peace Research Institute (SIPRI).[60] Notable features of the verification measures cited include the prohibition of interference with national technical means of verification, and the prohibition of deliberate concealment of objects or activities that could impede observation, such as denial of access to flight-test telemetry of missiles that may be required for verification of compliance. For purposes of verification, the Study also attaches importance to the agreed data base provided by both sides regarding their existing strategic arsenals, to be updated semi-annually.[61]

The manner of defining the various weapons to be limited by the Treaty, taking account of their characteristics observable by NTM, contributes substantially to the effectiveness of verification. The characteristics whereby the various weapons are described, were summarised in the SIPRI study as follows –

(a) ICBMs, by range and land-based launcher;
(b) SLBMs, by their deployment on 'modern' submarines and, in the case of Soviet SLBMs, by the date of initial flight tests;
(c) heavy bombers, by their mission capabilities, including the capability to carry long-range cruise missiles (CMs), with specific exceptions to this definition; and
(d) CMs by their mode of launch, weapon delivery mission, and by use of aerodynamic lift.

Notification provisions under SALT II also add to the reliability of the verification of the Treaty. The Parties are required, *inter alia*, to notify each other of replacement, conversion, dismantling, or destruction of arms limited by the Treaty; they are required to designate new types of light ICBM and SLBM equipped with MIRV; they have to warn 'well in advance' of certain flight-testing of ICBM which is to extend beyond national territory, as well as new ICBM test ranges; advise the number of aeroplanes used for testing cruise missiles; and draw attention to the flight-testing of some unarmed aircraft that might otherwise be identified as cruise missiles, or other weapons limited by the Treaty that could be confused with them.

The backbone of SALT verification techniques is provided by the standards established in the Treaties for distinguishing the various weapons to be banned or, more usually, limited in numbers and performance.[62] There is no verification problem where there are functionally related observable differences (FROD). Where, on the other hand, the observable features do not indicate performance capability, the Parties are required to differentiate between the weapons by creating externally observable design features (ODF).

The United States Arms Control and Disarmament Act of 1978,[63] by Section 37 provides that 'adequate verification of compliance should be an indispensable part of any international arms control agreement'. United States concern about verification of NAC treaties, especially the existing SALT Treaties and those envisaged in a continuation of the SALT process, stems from the belief that it is much more difficult for the United States to supplement verification by NTM with information gleaned from Government and other sources available in the Soviet Union, than it is for the Soviet Union to gain similar information regarding compliance with NAC agreements in the United States.[64]

The danger feared is that a sudden revelation could occur of unsuspected stockpiles of weapons giving the other side a clear advantage, referred to as 'strategic breakout'. However, the SIPRI assessment, as well as much expert opinion in the United States, suggest that verification of NAC agreements by NTM precludes the possibility of strategic breakout, due to the necessity for repeated testing of sophisticated weapons before they become reliably operational. While a Panel advising the United States *Intelligence and Military Application of Nuclear Energy Subcommittee* reached a different conclusion, at least publicly, it did not rebut the arguments put forward in the dissenting testimony of Panel-member John Carr, who drew attention to the following point –

> The panel expresses concern that SS-16 third stages could be secretly produced and stockpiled, and that 'A determined evader could clandestinely MIRV missiles or increase the number of MIRVed warheads with a high degree of confidence that this would not be detected.' This is sophistry. A determined evader could maintain this 'high degree of confidence: that his cheating was undetected *only if he did not test the violating systems*, in which case he would have a very low degree of confidence that the products of his cheating would work. And as I have pointed out elsewhere (see my dissent to HASC No 95-90) the counterforce first strike mission is absolutely intolerant of low-confidence weapons. Thus, cheating of this type would not give the Soviets a weapon of any use to them and would not be worth the risk of exposure.[65]

In view of the many-faceted developments necessary to give a disarming first strike capability to either Superpower, a strategic breakout of that magnitude would not be possible. However, as has been observed in earlier

Chapters, no other kind of military advantage between the Superpowers is meaningful, except in a purely psychological context regarding uninformed persons.

At various times, spokesmen for both the United States and the Soviet Union have made threats of retaliation, predicting military supremacy for their side should breaches of the SALT Treaties occur, or in the event of the breakdown of the bilateral NAC process. Such statements can only be regarded as bravado, because it is self-evident from an understanding of the weapons under consideration, that neither Superpower could attack the other without incurring similarly devastating damage in response.

Nevertheless, a very powerful sanction exists which induces compliance with bilateral NAC agreements, and which propels the Parties towards continuing their NAC negotiations. This sanction could be referred to as the *ultimate consequences sanction.* The sanction consists of the negative consequences that would flow to both Parties if they failed to reach substantive agreement.

The most notable feature of the sanction that exists between the Superpowers is that each interim failure to reach agreement makes subsequent failure more likely which, if it persists, would ultimately invoke the sanction of nuclear war. Hence, although the sanction is liable to be exercised only once, with each setback and delay of the bilateral NAC process, the threat of the sanction becomes more acute.

Notes

1 See Greig, D.W., 'The Interpretation of Treaties and Article IV. 2 of the Nuclear Non-Proliferation Treaty', *Australian Yearbook of International Law* (Faculty of Law, ANU, Canberra 1978) Vol. 6 p. 77.

2 Art. XII (5); See Nathason, Eugene, 'International Management of Radioactive Wastes', *Environmental Affairs*, Spring 1976, Vol. 5 p. 363; Coleman, J.P., 'International Safeguards Against Non-Government Nuclear Theft: a Study of Legal Inadequacies', *The International Lawyer*, Summer 1976, Vol. 10 p. 493.

3 The matter has been under investigation by the IAEA since 1976. An Expert Group on International Spent Fuel Management, established by the Agency, held two meetings during 1980. *The Annual Report for 1980* of the IAEA, p. 6.

4 Art. III (2) only regulates such transfers if they are for 'peaceful purposes', while Art. I, forbidding transfers to non-nuclear-weapon States for military purposes, only applies to nuclear-weapon State transferors.

5 Supra, Chapter 9.

6 Spence, Jack, 'South Africa's "Bomb in the Basement" ', *Armament and Disarmament Information Unit*, October/November 1980, Vol. 2 No. 4 p. 4, for a typical instance when an event can be deduced from several indicators.

7 *Verification: the Critical Element of Arms Control*, US Arms Control and Disarmament Agency (Publication 85, Washington, March 1976): *Compendium of Arms Control Verification Proposals* (Dept. of National Defence, Ottawa June 1980); See also *Statement by the Soviet Government*, dated 19 April 1962, ENDC/32 – 'After all, it is a fact that all nuclear explosions conducted so far, whether by the Soviet Union, the United States, the United Kingdom or France, have been recorded by national systems of detection in various countries – no other systems have existed or exist up to now. Nor do underground nuclear explosions constitute an

exception in this respect. Very convincing in this connexion was the detection of the underground nuclear explosion, recently conducted in the Soviet Union, by the United States Atomic Energy Commission – and not by means of any international control or the despatch of inspection teams into USSR territory, but exclusively by means of national systems. This means that the United States has at its disposal detection systems which are adequate for recording underground nuclear explosions, however far from the United States these explosions were carried out. The Soviet Union also has such detection systems at its disposal, as have many other States.'

8 Art. III (4).
9 Art. 13.
10 Art. 16 (1).
11 Art. VII (5).
12 Art. IX.
13 Art. III (2).
14 Art. XII and Art. III (1) respectively.
15 Study on a *Comprehensive Nuclear Test-Ban*, A/35/257 pp. 20-21.
16 Supra pp. 74-5.
17 See *Study on the Implications of Establishing an International Satellite Monitoring Agency*, Report of the Secretary-General, UN Doc. A/AC. 206/14 of 6 August 1981.
18 Spence, Jack, 'South Africa's "Bomb in the Basement" ', op.cit. p. 4.
19 Art. III (5).
20 Fischer, D.A.V., *Nuclear Issues: International Control and International Co-operation* (Dept. of International Relations, ANU, Canberra 1981) p. 14.
21 INFCIRC/66/Rev. 2 and INFCIRC 153. The latter document forms the basis of all agreements with non-nuclear-weapon States pursuant to the NPT, while the former document forms the basis of project agreements, transfer agreements and unilateral submission agreements. The former document is being applied more stringently than hitherto. Fischer, op. cit. p. 38 no. 24 – 'The Secretariat, with the approval of most members of the IAEA Board of Governors has, however, gradually introduced several amplifications and new clauses into safeguards agreements based on INFCIRC/66/Rev. 2 so as to make the safeguards more water-tight and comprehensive.'
22 INFCIRC/153, Part II Art. 28.
23 *IAEA Safeguards on Nuclear Fuel Cycle Facilities*, Reprinted for the second Review Conference of the NPT (Geneva 1980) DPI/I p. 5.

Quantities of Safeguards Significance

Material		Quantity of Safeguards Significance (SQ)	SQ applies to:
	Pu	8 kg	Total element
'Direct-use'	^{233}U	8 kg	Total isotope
material	U (^{235}U× 20%)	25 kg	^{235}U
	Plus rules for mixtures where appropriate		
	U(^{235}U <20%*	75 kg	^{235}U
'Indirect-use'	Th	20 t	Total element
material	Plus rules for mixtures where appropriate		

* Including natural and depleted uranium.

24 Ibid. p. 4; See also Szasz, P., *The Law and Practices of the International Atomic Energy Agency* (1970) Legal Series No. 7 of the IAEA and 1981 update.

25 *IAEA Safeguards on Nuclear Fuel Cycle Facilities*, op. cit. p. 8; *IAEA Activities Under Art. III of the NPT*, NPT/CONF. II/6 and Add. 2 of 1980.

26 Fischer, D.A.V., *Preventing the Spread of Nuclear Weapons*, Unpublished Paper (Dept. of International Relations, ANU, Canberra April 1981) pp. 19-21; See also the Annual Report of the Board of Governors of the IAEA, and *The Annual Report* for 1980 of the Agency, p. 40 paras. 174, 178 – and p. 41 para 182; *viz* – '174. In 1980, as in previous years, the Secretariat, in carrying out the safeguards programme of the Agency, did not detect any anomaly which would indicate the diversion of a significant amount of safeguarded nuclear material – or the misuse of facilities or equipment under certain agreements – for the manufacture of any nuclear weapon, or to further any other military purpose, or for the manufacture of any other nuclear explosive device. In the light of the report which the Director General submitted to the Board on the implementation of safeguards in 1980, it is reasonable to conclude again that nuclear material under Agency safeguards remained in peaceful nuclear activities or was otherwise adequately accounted for.'

'178. In 1980, safeguards agreements were in force with 11 non-nuclear-weapon States which were not party to NPT – namely, Argentina, Brazil, Chile, Colombia, Cuba, the Democratic People's Republic of Korea, India, Israel, Pakistan, South Africa and Spain . . . In four of the six States, as in nuclear-weapon States, the unsafeguarded facilities were capable of producing weapons-grade material.' [*viz* India, Israel, Pakistan and South Africa.] The report also disclosed that the quantities of nuclear material under safeguards changed during 1980 as follows – separated plutonium decreased by 38% to 5 tonnes; plutonium contained in spent fuel rose by 30% to 78 tonnes; low-enriched uranium rose by 18% to 13,872 tonnes; and source material rose by 24% to 19,097 tonnes. The quantity of highly enriched uranium under safeguards remained at 11 tonnes.

27 *The Annual Report for 1980* of the IAEA, p. 44 Table 7-

Nuclear Installations under Agency Safeguards or Containing Safeguarded Material

Nuclear installations	End of 1980*					
	NPT		Non-NPT			Total
Facilities	103	(94)	24	(23)	127	(117)
Power reactors						
Research reactors and critical assemblies	147	(140)	28	(31)	175	(171)
Conversion plants	3	(4)	1	(0)	4	(4)
Fuel fabrication plants	31	(28)	7	(5)	38	(33)
Reprocessing plants	4	(4)	3	(1)	7	(5)
Enrichment plants	4	(4)	0	(0)	4	(4)
Separate storage facilities	15	(14)	6	(5)	21	(19)
Other facilities	40	(40)	0	(0)	40	(40)
	347	(328)	69	(65)	416	(393)
Other locations	340	(289)	18	(18)	358	(307)
Total	687	(617)	87	(83)	774	(700)

* The figures in brackets indicate the status at the end of 1979.

28 *IAEA Safeguards on Nuclear Fuel Cycle Facilities*, op. cit. pp. 16-36, *re.* satisfactory safeguards possibilities, pp. 37-50 *re.* plants and procedures causing safeguards difficulties.

29 Id. pp. 50-62 *re.* plants and procedures that will require new inspection measures.

30 Ibid; The US Arms Control and Disarmament Agency has carried out investigations on safeguarding the more elaborate commercial nuclear power facilities coming into operation – e.g. – 'Our largest safeguards research project is the design, development, and demonstration of a system to provide nearly instantaneous information to the International Atomic Energy Agency on the status of sensors at safeguard facilities. For example, it should enable the IAEA to check at any time on the status of seals placed on equipment or on stocks of nuclear material and thus materially help provide timely warning of any diversion.' Testimony on behalf of ACDA to the Subcommittees on International Security and Scientific Affairs of the Committee on Foreign Affairs, Ninety-sixth Congress, First Session *Progress in U.S. and International Nonproliferation Efforts* (US Govt. Printing Office, Washington 12 March 1979) p. 22.

31 Statute of the IAEA, Art. XII (A) 7, is the most comprehensive; see Dalhitz, J., 'Proliferation and Confrontation;, *Australian Outlook*, April 1979, Vol. 33 No. 1 p. 32.

32 Holsti, K.J., *International Politics: A Framework for Analysis* (Prentice-Hall, New Jersey 3rd Ed.) p. 181 – 'Acts of influencing may take many forms, the most important of which are the offer and granting of rewards, the threat and imposition of punishments and the application of force.' The author considers the exercise of inducements under the following headings: Persuasion; The offer of rewards; The granting of rewards; The threat of punishment; The infliction of nonviolent punishment; and Force.

33 E.g. Gangl, Walter T., 'The *Jus Cogens* Dimensions of Nuclear Technology', *Cornell International Law Journal*, Winter 1980, Vol. 13 No. 1 p. 63. In the author's opinion the development and sale of peaceful nuclear technology is conducive to horizontal proliferation which is inherently illegal because it is in breach of the norms of *jus cogens*. He asserts (at p. 87) that '. . . the prohibition of nuclear weapons proliferation shares the status of the *jus cogens* prohibitions of slavery, genocide, and aggression.'

34 See Fischer, D.A.V., *Nuclear Issues: International Control and International Co-operation* (ANU, Canberra 1981), pp. 61-4.

35 Doubb, William O., and Fidell, Eugene R., 'International Relations and Nuclear Commerce: Developments in United States Policy', *Law and Policy in International Business*, 1976, Vol. 8 p. 913.

36 For the United States position during the latter 1970s see, Nye, Joseph S., 'Non-Proliferation: a Long-Term Strategy', *Foreign Affairs*, April 1978, p. 601.

37 E.g. see A/RES/36/140, 'United Nations Conference on an International Code of Conduct on the Transfer of Technology'.

38 INFCIRC/237 of 26 May 1976.

39 See n. 26 supra.

40 The Treaty of Tlatelolco and the NPT. The Statute of the IAEA provides for prompt withdrawal on notice but some obligations of membership do not cease thereby.

41 Supra, p. 247 *re.* safeguards agreements.

42 Fischer, op. cit. p. 61, expresses the plausible view that, a situation 'that would persuade countries like Japan and the Federal Republic of Germany that their

national security requires them to abandon the [non-nuclear-weapon] policies they have followed since the war', could only arise as a sequel to 'a catastrophic collapse of the present world power structure'.

43 Gompert, David C., 'A Proliferated World: Would the Flashpoint be Lowered?', *Nuclear Weapons and World Politics*, op. cit. p. 231.

44 See Chapter 9 supra, n. 51.

45 The use of armed force by the UN is considerable although it falls far short of preventing or ending all instances of international aggression, as originally envisaged. E.g. see Sommereyns, Raymond, 'United Nations Peace-Keeping Forces in the Middle East', *Brooklyn Journal of International Law*, Spring 1980, Vol. VI No. 1 esp. pp. 1-3.

46 A/520/Rev. 12 of 1974.

47 Art. 103 – 'In the event of a conflict between the obligations of the Members of the United Nations under the present Charter and their obligations under any other international agreement, their obligation under the present Charter shall prevail.'

48 Doxey, Margaret P., *Economic Sanctions and International Enforcement*, Published for the Royal Inst. of International Affairs (London 1980) esp. Chapters 3 and 6.

49 Supra Chapter 8 n. 47.

50 By Sec. 37 of the United States *Arms Control and Disarmament Act* of 1 January 1978 (22 U.S.C. 2577) '. . . adequate verification of compliance should be an indispensable part of any international arms control agreement'.

51 Quoted by Senator George McGovern, *The SALT II Treaty*, Hearings Before the Committee on Foreign Relations, Part 2, July 16, 17, 18 and 19, 1979 (U.S. Govt. Printing Office, Washington 1979) p. 264.

52 *The SALT II Treaty*, Hearings Before the Committee on Foreign Relations Part 2, July 16, 17, 18 and 19, 1979 (U.S. Govt. Printing Office, Washington 1979) p. 254.

53 Id. p. 255.

54 Id. p. 258.

55 Id. Part 6, October-November 1979, p. 445.

56 Potter, William C., Ed. *Verification and SALT: the Challenge of Strategic Deception*, (West View Press, Boulder, Colorado 1980).

57 Muir, Hugh, *Keeping a Check on Compliance With SALT I*, (United States Information Service, 2 March 1978).

58 'Compliance With the SALT I Agreements', *Department of State Bulletin* (US Govt. Printing Office, Washington) April 1978, Vol. 78 No. 2013 p. 10.

59 See Einborn, Robert J., 'Treaty Compliance', *Foreign Policy*, Winter 1981-2, No. 45 p. 29. At p. 31 the author states that 'A highly vocal group of critics has challenged these assessments, contending that the United States was too hesitant in raising troublesome issues with the Soviets, too weak in objecting to Soviet actions, and too expedient in minimizing the significance of Soviet misconduct.' Yet no example is given of contravention of any NAC undertaking.

60 'Verification of the SALT II Treaty', *World Armaments and Disarmament: SIPRI Yearbook 1980* (Taylor & Francis, London 1980) pp. 285-311.

61 SALT II Treaty –

Statement of Data on the Numbers of Strategic Arms as of the Date of Signature of the Treaty

The United States of America declares that as of 18 June 1979 it possesses the following numbers of strategic offensive arms subject to the limitations provided for in the Treaty which is being signed today:

Launchers of ICBMS   1,054

Fixed launchers of ICBMS	1,054
Launchers of ICBMS equipped with MIRVS	550
Launchers of SLBMS	656
Launchers of SLBMS equipped with MIRVS	496
Heavy bombers	573
Heavy bombers equipped for cruise missiles capable of a range in excess of 600 kilometres	3
Heavy bombers equipped only for ASBMS	0
ASBMS	0
ASBMS equipped with MIRVS	0

The Union of Soviet Socialist Republics declares that as of (date of signature of the Treaty) it possesses the following numbers of strategic offensive arms subject to the limitations provided for in the Treaty which is being signed today:

Launchers of ICBMS	1,398
Fixed launchers of ICBMS	1,398
Launchers of ICBMS equipped with MIRVS	608
Launchers of SLBMS	950
Launchers of SLBMS equipped with MIRVS	144
Heavy bombers	156
Heavy bombers equipped for cruise missiles capable of a range in excess of 600 kilometres	0
Heavy bombers equipped only for ASBMS	0
ASBMS	0
ASBMS equipped with MIRVS	0

The Treaty further provides that – '. . . at each regular session of the Standing Consultative Commission the parties will notify each other of and consider changes in those numbers in the following categories: launchers of ICBMS; fixed launchers of ICBMS; launchers of ICBMS equipped with MIRVS; launchers of SLBMS; launchers of SLBMS equipped with MIRVS; heavy bombers; heavy bombers equipped for cruise missiles capable of a range in excess of 600 kilometers; heavy bombers equipped only for ASBMS; ASBMS; and ASBMS equipped with MIRVS . . .'

62 These include the definitions set out in Art. II of the Treaty and in the Agreed Statements and Common Understandings Regarding the Treaty Between the United States of America and the Union of Soviet Socialist Republics on the Limitation of Strategic Offensive Arms.

63 22 U.S.C. 2577.

64 However, the Soviets also claim to have verification concerns about SALT II. See Arbatov, Georgi, Director of the USSR Institute of US and Canadian Studies – 'Obviously, the agreement does not and cannot resolve all the problems or remove all the reasons for concern. We are worried about the development of some US weapons systems not covered by the agreement. We, like the Americans, would like to ensure the complete invulnerability of our ICBMS and have even more than 100 per cent confidence in verification. But I fail to understand how wrecking SALT II can help solve such problems. Take, for example, the issue of verification. The agreement provides a whole system of verification measures: special counting rules, a pledge not to interfere with each other's technical means, an obligation not to conceal telemetric data that are needed for verification, a special commission to deal with questions in dispute. Let the Americans ask themselves whether they will know more about our strategic forces without this system.' 'The Soviets on SALT', *Newsweek*, 28 May 1979, p. 22.

65 *Report of the Panel on SALT and the Comprehensive Test-Ban Treaty*, Intelligence and Military Application Subcommittee of the Committee on Armed Services, House of Representatives, 28 December 1978 (US Govt. Printing Office, Washington 1978) p. 42, emphasis added.

CHAPTER 11

The Second Special Session Devoted to Disarmament

The Decisions of SSD II

The ten foregoing Chapters which, together with the Introduction and Conclusion were written prior to SSD II,* contain many references to preparations undertaken for the Session. Although the Agenda[1] of the Session mainly referred to 'disarmament' in general, that objective was interpreted to relate primarily to the prevention of nuclear war by measures to limit or prohibit the production, deployment and use of nuclear weapons. For this reason, and also because SSD II became the focus for NAC-related proposals and undertakings, it is necessary to refer to the outcome for a comprehensive view of the current situation.

Matters not yet considered include the decisions reached at the Session, still pending initiatives launched in connection with it, as well as collateral consequences flowing from the event. It is pertinent to estimate the likely influence of these matters on the future course of NAC.

While the decision-making function of SSD II has been widely pronounced a failure, including by this writer,[2] the Session was bound to have an impact of some kind on NAC. As it happened, what SSD II achieved was to prevent the abandonment of the process of NAC – a state of affairs that might have occurred in its absence as a consequence of the deteriorating international situation in mid-1982. However, the holding of the Session may have only delayed that eventuality, while it certainly did not advance NAC in a manner to give it an improved chance of ultimate success. No new principles were agreed upon regarding NAC; nor was any progress made in relation to the settlement of escalation-prone international disputes; the mode of NAC negotiations; the responsibilities of States towards each other in the nuclear age; or any similar issue.

Nothing happened during SSD II to require a reassessment of the conclusions adduced from the first ten Chapters, based on events that occurred prior to the Session. Nevertheless, it should be noted that modest progress was made in some areas. Most importantly, by submitting approximately eighty proposals and by making some very significant unilateral declarations, many States demonstrated a growing recognition of the importance of unilateral initiative and the occasional necessity for short-term imbalance of sacrifice in the interests of NAC.

It has been the aim of the Session to arrive at a consensus expressed in the form of a document along the lines of the Final Document of SSD I, adding to the principles and methods enunciated there. The centrepiece of that consensus was to have been a Comprehensive Programme of Disarmament relating to a period of some twenty years, by which time the process of

---

* Only a few sentences have been added subsequently.

disarmament was to have been completed. As stated in Chapter 3 above, the Committee on Disarmament was required to submit a draft text[3] of the Programme, to form the basis of deliberations. Also for the reasons there stated, it was found to be impossible to reach agreement, so that the text that was eventually submitted for the approval of delegates at SSD II was largely still in brackets. The brackets signified wide-ranging dissent on the wording, while no version added significantly to the priorities already contained in the Final Document and subsequent restatements.[4]

The only important innovation was the continuing insistence by Non-aligned States that the resulting document be given binding legal status, requiring participating States to conclude further treaties in conformity with the Programme, within specified, so called 'rigid' time frames. Attainment of consensus on that basis was never a possibility. If the objective was to use those requirements merely as bargaining levers they did not achieve the sought after concessions. Perhaps the requirements should have been abandoned sooner than they were in fact abandoned during the course of the Session. By then it was too late to arrive at a revised wording. Yet, had it been possible to do so, as a result of earlier withdrawal of the contentious requirements supported by the Non-aligned States, the resulting document would have been of only limited significance.

Another substantive item on the Agenda was the Review of the Implementation of the Recommendations and Decisions Adopted by the General Assembly at its Tenth Special Session. The draft text[5] drawn up by the Preparatory Committee for SSD II was, at the time of submission for the approval of delegates, no closer to finality than the draft Comprehensive Programme for Disarmament had been. While there was general agreement that the little progress that had occurred toward imple-mentation of the Final Document, had failed to keep pace with both the quantitative increase and qualitative improvement of armaments, no consensus could be reached either before or during the Session with respect to attributing responsibility for inadequate performance.

This outcome was also foreseeable and is not significant in itself. Consensus in the apportionment of blame would require States publicly to assess some of their own conduct as blameworthy – a procedure that is neither politically feasible nor necessary for the successful pursuit of NAC or any other aspect of disarmament or arms control.

The Session did succeed in producing a brief consensus document, being the Report of the Ad Hoc Committee[6] (also referred to as the Committee of the Whole) based on a draft prepared by its Chairman, Ambassador Olu Adeniji. It contains a record of the proceedings of the Session as well as the decisions reached, including the launching of the World Disarmament Campaign.[7] The entirely constructive mandate of the Campaign, as agreed by consensus, ensures that it is certain to have a positive impact on NAC by making achievements and problems better known world-wide. Although the extent of the Campaign still remains to be seen, it is not impossible that in conjunction with indigenous information efforts the Campaign could, in time, exert a considerable influence on world public opinion.

Ten paragraphs of the Report are devoted to a statement of Conclusions reproduced below which, in essence, amount to the emphatic reaffirmation of the Final Document. Given the adverse international climate that prevailed during the Session, this outcome was by no means a foregone certainty. It came about as the result of strong determination by the great majority of States to preserve the largely sound formulations contained in that document. In the circumstances, any State that might have wished to defy the reaffirmation would have had to accept the consequences of being labelled a self-proclaimed war-monger. Fortunately, it was a stance that none chose to adopt.

The norm creating function of the Final Document, despite its dubious standing in international law, is a very interesting phenomenon. Disarmament by way of consecutive treaties, the priority of NAC, the unacceptability of horizontal proliferation, maintenance of strategic parity between the Superpowers etc. have become accepted to be axiomatic principles akin in authority to the norms established by the United Nations Charter itself. Today these principles could not be challenged even by a Superpower without profound loss of prestige, not unlike the odium that would result from the breach of a major treaty obligation.

The pervading influence of the Final Document was demonstrated by the nature of the Conclusions reached and included in the Report of the Ad Hoc Committee, subsequently adopted by the final plenary meeting of SSD II, as follows —[8]

'The tenth special session of the General Assembly, the first special session devoted to disarmament, held in 1978, was an event of historic significance. The special session was convened in response to a growing concern among the peoples of the world that the arms race, especially the nuclear-arms race, represented ever-increasing threats to human well-being and even to the survival of mankind. At that session the international community of nations achieved, for the first time in the history of disarmament negotiations, a consensus on an international disarmament strategy, the immediate goal of which was the elimination of the danger of nuclear war and implementation of measures to halt and reverse the arms race. The final objective of the strategy was to achieve general and complete disarmament under effective international control. The conviction that all peoples had a legitimate right to expect early and significant progress in disarmament and a vital interest in its success led to the United Nations being given a central role and primary responsibility in the field of disarmament.

The historic consensus embodied in the Final Document of the Tenth Special Session of the General Assembly (Resolution S-10/2) was rooted in a common awareness that the accumulation of weapons, particularly nuclear weapons, constituted much more a threat to than a protection of mankind. It was also based on recognition that the time had come to put an end to that situation, to abandon the use of force in international relations and to seek security in disarmament, that is to say, through a gradual but effective process beginning with a reduction in the present level of armaments. The Final Document recognized that in the contemporary world the security of States could greatly be enhanced by effective action aimed at preventing nuclear war, ending the arms race and achieving real disarmament. Progress in disarmament would significantly contribute to pursuing the goals of economic and social development, particularly of developing countries. The consensus embodied in the Final Document sought to place disarmament negotiations in a unified perspective and became a most significant and integral part of the context within which negotiations on disarmament have been pursued.

In the course of the twelfth special session, the second special session devoted to disarmament, the General Assembly has noted that developments since 1978 have not lived up to the hopes engendered by the tenth special session. Despite the efforts that have been made by the international community to implement the decisions and recommendations of that session on a multilateral, bilateral and regional level, including action in the General Assembly and the Committee on Disarmament, and steps that have been taken on some specific measures contained in the Final Document, the objectives, priorities and principles there laid down have not been generally observed. The Programme of Action contained in the Final Document remains largely unimplemented. A number of important negotiations either have not begun or have been suspended, and efforts in the Committee on Disarmament and other forums have produced little tangible result. There has been some progress in certain negotiations and bilateral negotiations in the nuclear field have been initiated. The arms race, however, in particular the nuclear-arms race, has assumed more dangerous proportions and global military expenditures have increased sharply. In short, since the adoption of the Final Document in 1978, there has been no significant progress in the field of arms limitation and disarmament and the seriousness of the situation has increased.

The Final Document stated that disarmament, relaxation of international tension, respect for the right to self-determination and national independence, the peaceful settlement of disputes in accordance with the Charter of the United Nations and the strengthening of international peace and security are directly related to each other. Progress in any of these spheres has a beneficial effect on all of them; in turn, failure in one sphere has negative effects on others. The past four years have witnessed increasing recourse to the use or threat of use of force against the sovereignty and territorial integrity of States, military intervention, occupation, annexation and interference in the internal affairs of States and denial of the inalienable right to self-determination and independence of peoples under colonial or foreign domination. The period has also witnessed other actions by States contrary to the Final Document. The consequent tensions and confrontations have retarded progress in disarmament and have in turn been aggravated by the failure to make significant progress towards disarmament.

It was stressed that in a world of finite resources there is an organic relationship between expenditures on armaments and economic and social development. The vastly increased military budgets since 1978 and the development, production and deployment, especially by the States possessing the largest military arsenals, of new types of weapon systems represent a huge and growing diversion of human and material resources. Apart from the significant capital costs that these military expenditures represent, they have also contributed to current economic problems in certain States. Existing and planned military programmes constitute a colossal waste of precious resources which might otherwise be used to elevate living standards of all peoples; furthermore, such waste greatly compounds the problems confronting developing countries in achieving economic and social development.

The General Assembly regrets that at its twelfth special session it has not been able to adopt a document on the Comprehensive Programme of Disarmament and on a number of other items on its agenda. However, on two agenda items, relating to the United Nations programme of fellowships on disarmament and the World Disarmament Campaign, there are agreed texts (see Annexes IV and V) for consideration and appropriate action by the General Assembly. The General Assembly was encouraged by the unanimous and categorical reaffirmation by all Member States of the validity of the Final Document of the Tenth Special Session as well as their solemn commitment to it and their pledge to respect the priorities in disarmament negotiations as agreed to in its Programme of Action. Taking into account the aggravation of the international situation and being gravely concerned about the continuing arms race, particularly in its nuclear aspect, the General Assembly expresses its profound preoccupation over the danger of war, in particular nuclear war, the prevention of which remains the most acute and urgent task of the present day. The General Assembly urges all Member States to consider as soon as possible relevant proposals designed to secure the avoidance of war, in particular nuclear war, thus ensuring that the survival of mankind is not endangered. The General Assembly also stresses the need for strengthening the central role of the United Nations in the field of disarmament and the implementation of the security system provided for in the Charter of the United Nations in accordance with the Final Document and to enhance the effectiveness of the Committee on Disarmament as the single multilateral negotiating body. In this regard the Committee on Disarmament is requested to report to the General Assembly at its thirty-seventh session on its consideration of an expansion of its membership, consistent with the need to enhance its effectiveness.

Member States have affirmed their determination to continue to work for the urgent conclusion of negotiations on and the adoption of the Comprehensive Programme of Disarmament, which shall encompass all measures thought to be advisable in order to ensure that the goal of general and complete disarmament under effective international control becomes a reality in a world in which international peace and security prevail, and in which a new international economic order is strengthened and consolidated. To this end, the draft Comprehensive Programme of Disarmament is hereby referred back to the Committee on Disarmament, together with the views expressed and the progress achieved on the subject at the special session. The Committee on Disarmament is requested to submit a revised draft Comprehensive Programme of Disarmament to the General Assembly at its thirty-eighth session.

The other items on the agenda on which the special session has not reached decisions should be taken up at the thirty-seventh session of the General Assembly for further consideration.

The General Assembly is convinced that the discussion of disarmament problems, which it has undertaken at the special session and in which representatives of Member States – among them some heads of State or Government and many Foreign Ministers – have participated, and the active interest shown by peoples all over the world will provide a powerful impetus to Member States to redouble their efforts in the cause of disarmament. The General Assembly hopes that the World Disarmament Campaign, which it solemnly launched at the opening meeting of the special session, will further contribute to the mobilization of public opinion to the cause of disarmament and the strengthening of international peace and security. In this regard the campaign should provide an opportunity for discussion and debate in all countries on all points of view relating to disarmament issues, objectives and conditions.

The third special session of the General Assembly devoted to disarmament should be held at a date to be decided by the General Assembly at its thirty-eighth session.'

Impact of the Session for NAC

The importance of SSD II for the success of NAC cannot be estimated exclusively with reference to the decisions reached by the General Assembly. Although they failed to gain acceptance by consensus, several important initiatives were taken and some significant unilateral commitments were made, as reproduced in the text or listed in Annexes II & III of the Report.[9]

The publicity generated by the Session itself had an educational value, as well as providing organisational benefits for those wishing to express concern, groups intent on arranging seminars, issuing publications and so forth. Among these collateral movements the one most likely to remain influential in the longer term is the 'nuclear freeze' movement, calling for immediate cessation of the production, deployment and use of all nuclear weapons pending agreement to decrease stockpiles. The objectives of the movement were incorporated into a draft resolution jointly sponsored by Mexico and Sweden[10] which, in operative paragraphs 1 to 3 –

1. *Urges* the Union of Soviet Socialist Republics and the United States of America, as the two major nuclear-weapon States, to proclaim, either through simultaneous unilateral declarations or through a joint declaration, an immediate nuclear-arms freeze which would be a first step towards the Comprehensive Programme of Disarmament and whose structure and scope would be the following:
   (a) it would embrace:
      (i) A comprehensive test ban of nuclear weapons and of their delivery vehicles;
      (ii) The complete cessation of the manufacture of nuclear weapons and of their delivery vehicles;

(iii) A ban on all further deployment of nuclear weapons and of their delivery vehicles;

(iv) The complete cessation of the production of fissionable material for weapons purposes;

(b) it would be subject to all relevant measures and procedures of verification which have already been agreed by the parties in the cases of the SALT I and SALT II treaties, as well as those accepted in principle by them during the preparatory trilateral negotiations on the comprehensive test ban held at Geneva;

2. *Requests* the above-mentioned two major nuclear-weapon States to submit a report to the General Assembly, prior to the opening of its thirty-seventh session, on the implementation of the present resolution;

3. *Decides* to include in the provisional agenda of its thirty-seventh session an item entitled 'Implementation of resolution S-12/– on a nuclear arms freeze.'

Stimulation of interest in NAC continues to induce initiatives even in States where low priority has been customarily accorded to those issues. For example in Australia, where the Opposition has assiduously avoided nuclear weapons related subjects in recent election campaigns, a call for a nuclear-weapon-free Southern Hemisphere was launched by the shadow Foreign Minister in the context of a pre-election marshalling of positions,[11] shortly after the Session ended in New York.

The most direct influence on NAC exerted by SSD II, was the acceptance by the Soviet Union of the principle of systematic on-site inspections as a verification method for arms control.[12] This was in addition to on-site inspection on challenge, a principle that had been accepted already on several previous occasions. While systematic on-site verification was accepted by the Soviet Union only in relation to the dismantling of chemical weapons – and was later explained to be subject to a *quota* on the number of inspections – such verification would be an invaluable, maybe indispensable aid for supervising the dismantling of some nuclear weapons. Also, for the first time, IAEA safeguards on nuclear facilities for peaceful purposes were accepted by the Soviet Union during the course of the Session.[13]

An undertaking not to be the first to use nuclear weapons, also by the Soviet Union,[14] along the lines of the long-standing Chinese undertaking to that effect, was perhaps of greatest significance to the latter country. It has been rightly pointed out that the promise of non-use is an undertaking that cannot be specifically enforced. However, that is a characteristic which it has in common with all NAC obligations undertaken and, like those other undertakings, what is achieved is that the State's credibility is put at stake.

A noteworthy Western initiative at SSD II was an outline of principles and processes to be utilised for the prevention of nuclear war.[15] Several suggestions also emerged for summoning the help of individuals, 'wise men' of high international reputation, with the mandate to intercede between antagonists and to offer solutions in their individual capacities, in times of crisis.

A trend that casts a shadow over SSD II and its aftermath has been the hardening attitude of the United States, pointedly and consistently indicating a disinterest, occasionally even definite opposition, to NAC.[16]

While it has been repeatedly alleged by that Government that its reason for so doing is a defensive one, arising from a fear of being militarily superseded, post-SSD II developments reveal unmistakeable aggressive measures taken with a view to achieving military pre-eminence. The implications of attempting to gain an outright advantage by any State on the basis of nuclear-weapons superiority have already been explored above. Although no unequivocal statement has been made on behalf of the United States, during SSD II or since, acknowledging an overall waning interest in NAC, the following postures adopted during and immediately after SSD II speak for themselves –

1. The United States did not initiate or take part in any noteworthy step during SSD II to promote NAC.[17]

2. At the concurrent Strategic Arms Reduction Talks (START), the proposals advanced by the United States were so heavily weighted towards a United States advantage as to greatly surpass what could be considered a legitimate bargaining edge.[18]

3. At the concurrent negotiations on Intermediate-range nuclear forces (INF), the United States has persisted with the 'zero option' proposal which is founded, *inter alia*, on excluding from consideration the nuclear forces of France and the United Kingdom in the assessment of the balance of nuclear forces in Europe.[19]

4. The United States has terminated and has refused to resume the trilateral negotiations with the United Kingdom and the Soviet Union on a CTB. Participation in a Working Group on a CTB was accepted only on the understanding that a CTB was seen as an 'ultimate' goal. In that context it was declared that the United States intended to continue nuclear-weapons testing not only to supervise existing stockpiles but also for the improvement of weapons.[20]

5. The United States took an uncompromisingly unco-operative stand on a number of issues of vital concern to other States, including those relating to the prevention of nuclear war. For example, previously accepted terms of a draft Treaty on the Law of the Sea have been repudiated; there is continuing refusal to ratify the Threshold Test-Ban Treaty and the Peaceful Nuclear Explosions Treaty, while unsubstantiated accusations are being made that the Soviet Union has breached the terms of those Treaties, coupled with a threat to abandon the Treaties;[21] there has been a refusal to resume bilateral negotiations or to participate in a proposed multilateral Working Group on Outer Space; refusal to participate in the European Economic Commission on energy and related issues, and so forth.

6. An invitation by the United States to President Brezhnev to attend a Superpower Summit Conference was foreclosed by the United States for no stated or apparent reason.[22]

7. The policy option contained in Presidential Directive 59 has been further extended, replacing a deterrent stance with an attempt to acquire a nuclear war fighting capability, in the apparent belief that nuclear war is, or could become winnable.[23]

8. The United States has relaxed its commitment to the prevention of horizontal proliferation.[24]

205

9. A 'nuclear freeze', namely a halt to vertical proliferation pending agreements to impose reductions of nuclear weapons, was refused by the United States.[25]

NAC in Jeopardy

There are two predictable consequences of the position adopted by the United States, during and subsequent to SSD II, with special relevance to NAC. One consequence will be to retard the process of NAC, a factor that could in itself prevent ultimate success, as noted previously. However, another emerging attitude could lead to a more direct and rapid destruction of NAC by the disruption of international law. This could occur as the result of an outright refusal to be bound by international agreements, whether or not the refusal was disguised as retaliation for unproven or unrelated wrongs, namely wrongs pertaining to matters gratuitously and subsequently 'linked' to the original agreement.

It is too soon to say that NAC has failed. There are signs that the allies of the United States may increasingly take action in a bid to reassert the influence of international law in general and of NAC agreements in particular.[26] Equally significant is the dissatisfaction of some of the most influential sections of United States decision-makers with that State's present stance on NAC issues.[27] While the outcome of those contests still hangs in the balance, there can be no doubt that the destruction of international law, with the abandonment of the obligation to observe NAC agreements, would be the precursor of inevitable nuclear war.

In previous Chapters it was claimed that strategic superiority cannot be attained surreptitiously. That assertion was made in reference to a deception of the other Superpower. It does not exclude the possibility of deception by the military of public opinion, including some politicians, allied Governments, and other powerful and responsible groups of people.

Viewed in retrospect, it seems that the apparent ambivalence of the United States to NAC since the mid-seventies was, at least in the calculations of some influential strategists, to be converted into an unambiguous quest for military pre-eminence during the period of change of leadership in the Soviet Union. The change took place later than expected and the period of instability, which was anticipated to occur with the passing of Mr Brezhnev, did not enventuate when the new leader, Yuri Andropov, took office. Consequently, the retreat from NAC by the United States in recent times has been more difficult to disguise than it might have been.

Despite persistent allegations by United States officials that the Soviet Union has broken NAC agreements, and that the United States has been militarily superseded, no credible facts have been adduced to support those claims. On the other hand, persons with long experience and demonstrated integrity who have served in previous Administrations, such as Paul Warnke, former head of the Arms Control and Disarmament Agency, have repeatedly asserted the falsity of those claims on the basis of Government records.[28]

The genuine mainspring of United States policy to emerge since SSD II has been spelled out by unofficial but knowledgeable commentators, for example in publications of the United States Department of the Air Force.[29] These expositions have credibility because they coincide at every point with declared and unconcealable war preparations by the United States. Plans to deploy the Pershing II missiles, as well as commitment to the MX missile and proposals for its basing in contravention of the spirit, if not the letter of the SALT II Treaty, are only the tip of the iceberg.

The real race for meaningful superiority, in the form of a first strike capability, is evident from the vast new allocations to the arms race in space, including DEW research, together with an unwillingness to seriously consider negotiating arms control agreements in those areas. A new propaganda mythology has been invented to make the accelerated space race acceptable, stressing the non-nuclear nature of space weapons while endeavouring to overlook their direct and crucial relationship to nuclear weapons systems. United States Air Force (USAF) terminology refers to 'defensive' weapons in a so called 'post-nuclear era' when it will be possible to attain superiority in space without incurring the risk of nuclear war, despite the existence of nuclear arsenals.

Assertions that a build-up of armaments in outer space would avert a nuclear war, or that space wars could be fought in lieu of a third world war on earth, are the zenith of sophistry. The exact opposite is the case. An arms race in outer space is bound to disrupt both crisis stability and strategic stability between the United States and the Soviet Union, to the point where world nuclear war would become almost unavoidable. Furthermore, although strategic destabilization may not occur for another decade or more, crisis stability is already being undermined with the continuing militarization of outer space. *The growing instability is in anticipation of the possibility that a pre-emptive strike to space systems may become the only defence against the emergence of a disarming first strike capability by one of the Superpowers.*

The most dismaying aspect of the 'space wars instead of earth wars' deception is that it is not only directed against potential enemies, or even against political opponents and professional rivals at home. Recent statements on the subject reveal that the deception is partly in the nature of self-delusion, practised by those who find the concept of the strategic stalemate psychologically intolerable.

A need to accept the impossibility of achieving meaningful coercive superiority, in a battle against the chief selected rival, is entirely novel in human history. It runs counter to patterns of both individual and collective motivation and conduct. Due to the novelty of the situation, social institutions – notably the various organs of the United Nations – are still not adequately adapted to cope with international rivalry in which a coercive outlet is entirely blocked. It is only this condition of overwhelming frustration that could give rise to a divorce from realism on the massive scale that has occurred in strategic planning during the past few months.

Soviet acquiescence to space-related strategic superiority by the United States is assumed with touching confidence in that country's exemplary restraint and reasonableness. For instance, Major Steven E. Cady of USAF states:

The possibility must also be entertained that the Soviet Union might launch a ballistic missile attack against the United States in desperation before the new American weapon system made its missiles useless.

However, he adds the following reassuring thoughts:

... the record of the Soviet Union in its foreign and military policy has never been one of rashness; it has avoided or drawn back from confrontations with the United States, as in Cuba and Vietnam, to prevent igniting a nuclear holocaust. It is reasonable to assume that the Soviets would act with similar prudence if the United States opted for directed-energy weapons.[30]

Dr Barry J. Smernoff, also writing in the USAF publication, has similarly consoling words for:

Analysts who believe that first-generation space based lasers could be so provocative that adversaries may be sorely tempted to preemptively attack a partial constellation during its deployment in space (before adequate levels of self-defense are possible) . . .

He assures his readers that:

Early space based laser systems will not constitute such total defenses as to threaten block obsolescence of the opposing strategic triad and a revolutionary shift in the strategic balance and arms competition.[31]

Presumably Dr Smernoff believes that the other Superpower will refrain from action until later-generation systems *do* 'threaten block obsolescence of the opposing strategic triad'.

One can only hope that the era shortly preceding and subsequent to SSD II was an aberration in United States policy, and that the will to continue the NAC process will reassert itself while there is still time.

Notes

1 A/S-12/10; see also Recommendations of the Preparatory Committee in 1982, A/S-12/1 (VIII), p. 15.
2 Dahlitz, J., 'The Second Special Session of the General Assembly Devoted to Disarmament', *Disarmament: A Periodic Review by the United Nations*, 1982, Vol. V No. 2.
3 A/S-12/2.
4 See Chapter III E.
5 A/S-12/1, Annex I.
6 A/S-12/32 and Annexes I to VI.
7 Ibid, Annex V.
8 Id. paras. 57-66.
9 Id. Annex II.
10 Id. p. 11.
11 Knez, T., 'ALP Plan to Ban Nuclear Weapons', *The Australian*, 27 July 1982.
12 '. . . on site inspection on an agreed basis.' A/S-12/AC.1/11.
13 Ibid.
14 A/S-12/AC.1/10.
15 Proposal by the Federal Republic of Germany, Netherlands and Japan on *Prevention of War, in Particular Nuclear War*, A/S-12/32, Annex III pp. 3-5.

16 Infra, points 1 to 9.

17 See A/S-12/AC.1/51, 52 and 53.

18 E.g. see *Daily Bulletin* (United States Mission, Geneva) 29 June 1982, p. 1.

19 Id., 27 June 1982, p. 4; also see 'Kremlin is Willing to Cut Missiles, Bombers: In Return, US is Asked to Forgo Deployment in Europe', *International Herald Tribune*, 2 August 1982, p. 1.

20 'US Said to Decide Against New Talks to Ban All A-Tests', *New York Times*, 20 July 1982, pp. A1 and A4.

21 Miller, Judith, 'Nuclear Arms Control: Is There Any Hope Left?', *International Herald Tribune*, 9 August 1982, p.4; see also supra Table II.

22 'Reagan, in New Approach, Offers Little Hope for Brezhnev Summit', Id. 2 August 1982, p.3.

23 Scheer, Robert, 'Pentagon Plan Specifies Methods of Winning Protracted Nuclear War', Id. 16 August 1982, p. 1.

24 E.g. 'US Plutonium Plant Test Opposed', Id. 28 July 1982, p. 2; 'Nuclear Power: Approval Linked With Peace Pledge', Id. 9 August 1982, pp. 8S and 11S.

25 'Reagan Calls on House to Defeat Resolution for a Nuclear Freeze', Id. 28 July 1982, p. 3; 'Democrats Exploiting Nuclear Freeze Defeat', Id. 10 August 1982, p. 3.

26 Cook, Don, 'Europe's Growing Fears of "California Gaullism" ', Id. 13 August 1982, p. 4.

27 E.g. 'US House Votes to Bar Spending on Nuclear Arms Banned by SALT', Id. 30 July 1982, p. 1; 'US Lawyers' Unit Urges Negotiations Over A-Arms Race', Id. 12 August 1982, p. 5; '6 Former Negotiators, 21 Senators Criticize Reagan on Arms Curbs', Id. 13 August 1982, p. 3.

28 Wood, David, 'MX Scheme Sparks Hot Debate', *The Age*, 25 November 1982, p. 7. (Reprinted from *Los Angeles Times*).

29 Smernoff, Barry, 'The Strategic Value of Space Based Laser Weapons', *Air University Review*, 1982, Vol. XXXIII No. 3 p. 2; Cady, Maj. Steven E., 'Beam Weapons in Space A Reality We Must Confront', Id. No. 4 p. 33; Humble, Ronald D., 'Space Warfare in Perspective', Id. No. 5 p. 81.

30 Cady, Maj. Steven E., op. cit. p. 38.

31 Smernoff, Barry, op. cit. pp. 15 and 16.

Conclusion

At present there are five States heavily armed with nuclear weapons, including the two Superpowers which are at the start of a further spiral in the nuclear arms race. Detonation of those weapons could exterminate humankind. A survey of NAC negotiations since World War II, reveals that the overall situation today is the outcome of many lost opportunities by the international community to outlaw nuclear weapons.

However, in the course of concluding various agreements to partially control the spread and use of nuclear weapons, a vast reservoir of experience has been gained and efficient administrative machinery has been established. As a result, the nations of the world have acquired a much greater capacity than hitherto to accomplish NAC tasks, although the immense quantitative and qualitative increase in nuclear arsenals has made the undertaking more formidable.

In the early post-war period, when it would have been physically possible to do so, the opportunity to forestall the nuclear arms race was not grasped. It would seem that this was partly due to misconceptions about the limits of acceptable encroachment on national sovereignty, and an inability to devise NAC measures consistent with those limits.

Despite the growing nuclear menace during the 1960s and 1970s, or perhaps because of it, many multilateral and bilateral NAC agreements were concluded during that period. While some of those agreements are only of marginal relevance, a number are of fundamental importance in the avoidance of nuclear war, both in the short term and by inhibiting the nuclear arms race in the longer term. Apart from a few ambiguities concerning interpretation, all of the NAC agreements in the form of treaties have been satisfactorily observed by all parties. When assessing the possibility of successful application of international law to NAC, the significance of this factor cannot be overemphasised.

There is ample evidence that during the 1980s, the problems associated with NAC are going to be of a different order than they were previously, due to vast technological advances taking place. Developments are constantly made by improving and diversifying the performance of nuclear weapons, and by introducing perfected delivery and targeting mechanisms for their projection. Simultaneously, defensive systems are planned in attempts to counteract the improved weapons, such as anti-ballistic missiles and anti-satellite weapons. When statesmen are unclear about the military utility of these weapons, it is doubly difficult to determine what agreed restraints in their manufacture and deployment may be consistent with national objectives.

Conclusion

Complexities arising from the uncertain nature of benefits to be derived from nuclear-weapons systems, as well as the technical expertise required to devise methods for their limitation, are exacerbated by the importance attached to the perception of power which nuclear weapons are said to impart. Hence, the currently proposed NAC agreements are seen not merely as mutual restraints on weapons, but as offsetting one perception against another. In this morass of complexity, the clear aims for NAC remain the avoidance of nuclear war, the prevention of nuclear blackmail, and minimising the human and material resources devoted to the nuclear arms industry.

While nuclear war has been avoided so far, and progress has been made in the attainment of the other major NAC objectives, the momentum of progress in NAC is not sufficient to keep ahead of regression occasioned by the increased number of nuclear weapons and the technical improvements in their performance. In particular, reluctance to conclude a Comprehensive Test-Ban Treaty can be read as a signal of impending failure of the NAC process.

It has been universally accepted that NAC can best be achieved by the conclusion of appropriate treaties recognised by international law. The methods for doing this, established over the years and perfected in 1978 during the course of SSD I are, broadly speaking, adequate for the task. Only relatively simple organisational improvements in the treaty-creating process for NAC are required, chiefly in the sphere of greater backup and administrative facilities, both at the United Nations and within Member States. Endowed with resources more commensurate to the task, the Committee on Disarmament could successfully grapple with crucial issues, instead of habitually evading them. Many of these issues have a legal character, requiring greater input by officials who specialize in international law.

Similarly, norm creation for NAC in the deliberative bodies of the United Nations charged with that responsibility, being the Disarmament Commission, the First Committee, and the General Assembly, is not hampered by any significant methodological problem. In particular, it was demonstrated in the General Assembly during SSD I, that a heavy volume of exceedingly controversial material relating to NAC and other arms control issues could be processed at some speed, leading to consensus on many substantive matters.

Notwithstanding the relatively satisfactory machinery available, the NAC process is often thwarted by a pervading scepticism regarding the significance of NAC related norms, including those created by treaty as well as those resulting from United Nations deliberations. The reason could be that, although the importance of the so called *generally accepted principles of international law* applicable to NAC are often alluded to in United Nations debates and resolutions, it is well known that those principles and rules are vague, contradictory and anachronistic. Likewise, procedures for the settlement of disputes concerning NAC and other matters crucial to the security interests of States, are unsatisfactory. The above considerations greatly reduce the significance attached to the conclusion of the relevant treaties and the endorsement of United Nations resolutions.

Especially inappropriate for contemporary requirements are the imprecise tenets of international customary law, and the consequently wide personal discretion that must fall to judges of the International Court of Justice, or to any other adjudicators who may be called upon to apply that body of law. As a result, very few cases are referred to the Court. On the one occasion when an NAC case was brought to the International Court of Justice, the majority of judges avoided handing down an Opinion on the merits because they evidently deemed that it would be unacceptable to the international community for them to do so.

The deficiencies of the Court, and the law it is presently required to administer, have not been sufficiently compensated for by other organs of the United Nations system, notably the Security Council and the General Assembly. This hiatus has a directly inhibiting effect on the NAC process. It also gravely hinders the peaceful settlement of international disputes on a wide range of subjects involving the security interests of States – a situation that encourages resort to armed might, both for the maintenance of security and for gaining advantages.

No simple procedure is available for solving the abovementioned difficulties. Constant repetition of stereotyped phrases in resolutions on the need for the peaceful settlement of international disputes, whether in the form of Declarations or Conventions, appears to have little impact. It is opportune, therefore, to re-examine the general principles of international law, with a view to creating a fundamental change in outlook consonant with contemporary requirements. Several initiatives are under examination in this regard. The proposed draft Code of General Principles of International Law, elaborated in Chapter 7, is an additional attempt to aid those endeavours.

The nuclear arms race has a horizontal and a vertical dimension. A propensity to the horizontal spread of weapons, involving more and more States, is related to the impetus for vertical proliferation of nuclear weapons by the nuclear-weapon States, especially the Superpowers. It will require increasingly stronger anti-proliferation commitment, and the further improvement of the IAEA safeguards system, to counteract proliferation tendencies generated by the availability in additional countries of the requisite technology for the construction and delivery of nuclear weapons. An increase in the number of nuclear-weapon States would put immense strains on the international legal system. There are no sound reasons to suggest that restraint on the use of the weapons would be easier to enforce than the prevention of their acquisition.

The most serious impediment to the prevention of horizontal pro-liferation, as well as the greatest danger of nuclear devastation, is occasioned by the continuation of vertical proliferation and the consequent growing instability of the strategic nuclear balance. The resolution of conflict between the Superpowers is not amenable to traditional remedies – either by confrontation or by third party adjudication. Even international opinion can only have an indirect role.

An unprecedented relationship that exists between the Superpowers, founded on their vast nuclear arsenals aimed at each other, has been managed during the past decade by the application of a quasi-judicial process. That process consists of the elaboration of NAC treaties on the basis of agreed general principles of justice and practicality, together with the auto-interpretation of the treaties and auto-adjudication of the required standards of performance. The continuing effective implementation of these uniquely difficult tasks is bound to be rendered impossible if extraneous considerations are permitted to intrude.

Rapid conclusion and strict observance of treaties to neutralise areas of most acute and imminent conflict are needed for minimising the immediate dangers occasioned by the stockpiles of nuclear weapons. At the same time, far-sighted innovations must be made for the long term management of nuclear weapons systems, with a view to their eventual elimination.

Presumably, if extraneous conflicts were to become uncontainable for example leading to the threatened disintegration of one of the Superpowers due to apprehension of physical assault with non-nuclear weapons, or occasioned by economic chaos or social upheaval, then those extraneous considerations could not be divorced from the process of NAC. However, any step leading to interference with the bilateral NAC process would have to be taken on the understanding that it would almost certainly be the prelude to universal disaster.

Nevertheless, if a determined effort were made to keep the process of NAC isolated from other conflict areas, and if those extraneous antagonisms could be contained within supportable limits, the groundwork has been laid which would facilitate the rapid expansion of the principles and rules of international law so as to make NAC effective in the foreseeable future.

The second Special Session of the General Assembly devoted to disarmament had only a minor inhibiting effect on the nuclear arms race, due to increasingly clear signals given by the United States Government, both during and after the Session, that an attempt would be made by that country to gain strategic superiority. However, as the attainment of a meaningful superiority, on the basis of a disarming first strike capability, could not be achieved for about another decade, it is still possible for that country's contemporary stance to be reversed. Yet it cannot be overlooked that the continued quest for superiority, which would soon necessitate the abandonment of NAC agreements, would make a return to the stabilizing policies of former Administrations extremely difficult.

In the event that NAC agreements were abandoned, the incentive to resort to nuclear war could develop quite rapidly. Under those circumstances the *rate* of deterioration in stability would depend on the ability of the Soviet Union to keep abreast of technological advances in the nuclear arms race on earth and in outer space. If this became no longer possible, the only choice open to the Soviet Union would be to surrender to the omnipotence of the United States over all nations, or to destroy those facilities which contribute to ultimate superiority prior to its attainment. Any suggestion that, at the critical point, the attention of Soviet leaders could somehow be diverted from this dilemma is entirely absurd. The law of the jungle and a disarming first strike capability are incompatible. They cannot exist together in the world.

Acronyms, Abbreviations and Specialist Terms

ABM* – Anti-Ballistic Missile

ARMS CONTROL – Any measure limiting or reducing forces, regulating armaments, and/or restricting the deployment of troops or weapons which is intended to induce responsive behaviour or which is taken pursuant to an understanding with another State or States.

ASAT – Anti-Satellite (weapon)

ASBM* – Air-to-Surface Ballistic Missile

ATOM BOMB – A bomb whose energy comes from the fission of heavy elements, such as uranium or plutonium.

BMD – Ballistic Missile Defence

BREEDER – A nuclear reactor that produces more fissile nuclei than it consumes. The fissile nuclei are produced by the capture of neutrons in fertile material. The resource constraint for breeder reactors is thus fertile material, which is far more abundant in nature than fissile material.

C^3 – Command, Control and Communications

CCD – Conference of the Committee on Disarmament

CD – Committee on Disarmament

CM* – Cruise Missile

CTB – Comprehensive Test-Ban

DEW – Directed Energy Weapon

DISARMAMENT – The reduction of a military establishment to some level set by international agreement.

ENDC – Eighteen Nation Disarmament Committee

ENRICHED MATERIAL – Material in which the percentage of a given isotope present in a material has been artificially increased, so that it is higher than the percentage of that isotope naturally found in the material. Enriched uranium contains more of the fissionable isotope uranium-235 than the naturally occuring percentage (0.7 per cent).

ER – Enhanced Radiation (Weapon), also known as the Neutron Bomb

FISSION – The splitting of a heavy nucleus into two approximtely equal parts (which are nuclei of lighter elements), accompanied by the release of a relatively large amount of energy and generally one or more neutrons. Fission can occur spontaneously, but usually is caused by nuclear absorption of neutrons or other particles.

---

*Used for singular and plural

FROD* – Functionally Related Observable Difference

FUEL CYCLE – The set of chemical and physical operations needed to prepare nuclear material for use in reactors and to dispose of or recycle the material after its removal from the reactor. Existing fuel cycles begin with uranium as the natural resource and create plutonium as a byproduct. Some future fuel cycles may rely on thorium and produce the fissile isotope uranium-233.

FULL SCOPE SAFEGUARDS – IAEA supervision of all nuclear facilities in a State to ensure that fissionable material is not utilised for weapons manufacture.

FUSION – The formation of a heavier nucleus from two lighter ones (such as hydrogen isotopes), with the attendant release of energy (as in a hydrogen bomb).

GATT – General Agreement on Tariffs and Trade

GREY AREA WEAPONS – Medium-Range Nuclear Missiles stationed within range of a Superpower in a manner that could affect the strategic balance.

GROUP OF 21 – A caucus of Non-aligned States in the CD of varying membership, with a majority of members also belonging to the Group of 77.

GROUP OF 77 – A caucus of more than a hundred developing nations in the UN with a varying membership, largely overlapping with the Group of 21.

HEL – High Energy Laser

HYDROGEN BOMB – A nuclear weapon that derives its energy largely from fusion (thermonuclear bomb).

IAEA – International Atomic Energy Agency

ICAO – International Civil Aviation Organisation

ICBM* – Intercontinental Ballistic Missile

ILO – International Labour Organisation

IMF – International Monetary Fund

INFCIRC – Information Circular of the IAEA

ISMA – International Satellite Monitoring Agency

MARV* – Manoeuvring Re-entry Vehicle

MIRV* – Multiple Independently Targetable Re-entry Vehicle

NAC – Nuclear Arms Control

NTM – National Technical Means (of verification)

NUCLEAR WEAPON – A collective term for atomic bombs and hydrogen bombs. Any weapon based on a nuclear explosive.

NWMD – New Weapons of Mass Destruction

ODF* – Observable Design Feature

OPANAL – Agency for the Prohibition of Nuclear Weapons in Latin America

PBW – Particle Beam Weapon

REPROCESSING – Chemical treatment of spent reactor fuel to separate the plutonium and uranium.

R & D – Research and Development

SALT – Strategic Arms Limitation Treaty (Talks)

---

*Used for singular and plural

SCC – Standing Consultative Commission

SIPRI – Stockholm International Peace Research Institute

SLBM* – Sea Launched Ballistic Missile

SSAC – State System of Accountancy

SSD I – First Special Session of the General Assembly devoted to Disarmament

SSD II – Second Special Session of the General Assembly devoted to Disarmament

SUPERPOWERS – The United States and the Soviet Union

THRESHOLD STATE – (Also known as Nth Country) – A nation judged to have high
potential of becoming a nuclear-weapon State because of its technical and
economic ability and/or its political motivations.

USAF – United States Air Force.

---

*Used for singular and plural

Bibiliography

Books and Monographs

Akehurst, Michael B., *A Modern Introduction to International Law*, Allen & Unwin, London, 2nd Ed. 1971.

Arangio-Ruiz, Gaetano, *The United Nations Declaration on Friendly Relations and the System of the Sources of International Law*, Sijthoff and Nordhoff, Maryland 1979.

Austin, John, *The Philosophy of Positive Law*, J. Murray, London 1885, 5th Ed. by R. Campbell.

Baker, David, *The Shape of Wars to Come*, Patrick Stephens, Cambridge 1981.

Bhupendra, Jasani, (Ed.) *Outer Space – A New Dimension of the Arms Race*, SIPRI, Taylor & Francis, London 1982.

Bokor-Szego, Hanna, *The Role of the United Nations in International Legislation*, Amsterdam 1978.

Brownlie, Ian, *International Law and the Use of Force by States*, Oxford 1963.

Chayes, Abram, and Bennett, Lewis W., (Eds.) *International Arrangements for Nuclear Fuel Cycle Facilities*, Ballinger, Cambridge, Mass. 1976.

D'Amato, Anthony A., *The Concept of Custom in International Law*, Cornell University Press, Ithaca, New York 1971.

D'Amato, A.A., Falk, R.A., and Weston, B.H., *International Law and World Order*, St Paul, Minn. West 1980.

David, A.E., *The Strategy of Treaty Termination: Lawful Breaches and Retaliations*, Yale University Press, New Haven, Conn. 1975.

Dean, Arthur, *The Importance of International Law in the Maintenance of Peace*, Oceana, Dobbs Ferry, New York 1963.

Doxey, Margaret P., *Economic Sanctions and International Enforcement*, Published for the Royal Institute of International Affairs, London 1980.

Dunn, Lewis A., and Kahn, Herman, *Trends in Nuclear Proliferation, 1975-1995*, Hudson Institute, Croton-on-Hudson, New York 1976.

Engels, Frederick, *Anti-Dühring*, Lawrence & Wishart, London 1942.

Epstein, William, *The Last Chance: Nuclear Proliferation and Arms Control*, The Free Press, New York 1976.

Epstein, William, *New Directions in Disarmament*, Praeger, New York 1981.

European Security and Co-operation: Premises, Problems, Prospects, Progress Publishers, Moscow, Eng. Translation 1978.

Falk, Richard A., *Human Rights and State Sovereignty*, Holmes and Meier, New York 1981.

Falk, Richard A., *The Status of Law in International Society*, Princeton University Press, New Jersey 1970.

Fischer, D.A.V., *Nuclear Issues: International Control and International Co-operation*, Australian National University, Canberra 1981.

Frei, Daniel, *Risks of Unintentional Nuclear War*, UNIDIR, Geneva 1982.

Friedmann, Wolfgang, *Law in a Changing Society*, Stevens, London, 2nd Ed. 1972.

Galtung, Johan, *The True Worlds: A Transnational Perspective*, The Free Press, New York 1980.

Goldblat, Jozef, *Arms Control: A Survey and Appraisal of Multilateral Agreements*, SIPRI, Taylor & Francis, London 1978.

Goldblat, Jozef, *The Arms Race and Arms Control*, SIPRI, Taylor & Francis, London 1982.

Gompert, D.C., Mandelbaum, M., Garwin, R.L., and Barton, J.H., *Nuclear Weapons and World Politics*, McGraw-Hill, New York 1977.

Greig, D.W., *International Law*, Butterworths, London, 2nd Ed. 1976.

Gross, Leo, *The Future of the International Court of Justice*, Oceana, Dobbs Ferry, New York 1976.

Haraszti, György, *Some Fundamental Problems of the Law of Treaties*, Budapest 1973.

Henkin, Louis, *How Nations Behave: Law and Foreign Policy*, Frederick A. Praeger for the Council of Foreign Relations, Columbia University, New York 1968.

Higgins, Rosalyn, *The Development of International Law Through the Political Organs of the United Nations*, Oxford University Press, London 1963.

Holsti, K.J., *International Politics: A Framework for Analysis*, Prentice-Hall, New Jersey 1967.

Howe, Russell Warren, *Weapons*, Sphere Books, London 1980.

Ikle, F.C., *How Nations Negotiate*, Harper and Row, New York 1964.

Internationalization to Prevent the Spread of Nuclear Weapons, Stockholm International Peace Research Institute, Taylor & Francis, London 1980.

Jenks, C.W., *International Law in a Changing World*, Oceana, Dobbs Ferry, New York 1963.

Kissinger, Henry, *The White House Years*, Wiedenfeld and Nicholson, London 1979.

Bibliography

Lall, A., *Modern International Negotiation: Principles and Practice*, Columbia University Press, New York 1966.

Lipsky, Mortimer, *Never Again War: the Case for World Government*, Barnes, South Brunswick, New Jersey 1971.

Mally, Gerhard, *Interdependence: The European-American Connection in the Global Context*, D.C. Heath, Lexington, Mass. 1976.

McWhinney, Edward, *The International Law of Detente*, Sijthoff and Nordhoff International Publishers, 1978.

Millar, T.B., *Political-Military Relationship in Australia*, Working Paper No. 6, Australian National University, Canberra 1979.

Nicol, Davidson, *The United Nations Security Council: Towards Greater Effectiveness*, UNITAR, 1982.

Outer Space – Battlefield of the Future? Stockholm International Peace Research Institute, Taylor & Francis, London 1978.

Panofsky, W.K., *Arms Control and SALT II*, University of Washington Press, Seattle and London 1979.

Pisar, Samuel, *Coexistence and Commerce: Guidelines for Transactions Between East and West*, McGraw-Hill, New York 1970.

Politzer, George, *An Elementary Course in Philosophy*, Current Book Distributors, Sydney 1950.

Quester, George, *The Politics of Nuclear Proliferation*, The John Hopkins University Press, Baltimore 1973.

Rechid, Ahmed, *Islam and Jus Gentium*, The Hague Academy of International Law 1973.

Répertoire de la Recherche sur le Désarmement, UNIDIR, Geneva 1982.

Röling, B.V.A., *International Law in an Expanded World*, Amsterdam 1960.

Rosas, Allan, *International Law and the Use of Nuclear Weapons*, Essays in Honour of Erik Castren, Helsinki 1979.

World Armaments and Disarmament, SIPRI Yearbooks, 1972-1982, Taylor & Francis, London 1980.

Schachter, Oscar, 'Towards a Theory of International Obligation', *The Effectiveness of International Decisions: Proceedings of the Conference of The American Society of International Law*, Oceana, Dobbs Ferry, New York 1971.

Schwarzenberger, Georg, *International Law as Applied by International Courts and Tribunals*, Stevens, London 1976.

Short History of the CPSU (Bolsheviks), Corbett Publishing House, London 1943.

Shubik, M., *Game Theory and Related Approaches to Social Behaviour*, John Wiley, New York 1964.

Stockholm International Peace Research Institute, *The Second NPT Review Conference*, Reprinted from SIPRI Yearbook 1981.

Stone, Julius, *Of Law and Nations: Between Power Politics and Human Hopes*, William S. Hein, Buffalo, New York 1974.

Szasz, P., *The Law and Practices of the International Atomic Energy Agency* (1970) Legal Series No. 7 of the IAEA.

The United Nations and Disarmament 1945–70, United Nations, New York, Department of Political and Security Council Affairs.

The United Nations and Disarmament 1970–75, United Nations, New York, Department of Political and Security Council Affairs.

The United Nations Disarmament Yearbook, United Nations, New York, Department of Political and Security Council Affairs, Vols. I–V 1976–80.

Trofimenko, Henry, 'The "Theology" of Strategy', *Arms and Control and Security: Current Issues*, Ed. Hanrieder, Wolfram F., Westview Press, Boulder, Colorado 1979.

Tunkin, G.I., *Theory of International Law*, Harvard University Press, Cambridge, Mass. 1974.

Twitchett, Kenneth J., *International Security: Reflections on Survival and Stability*, Published under the auspices of the Royal Institute of International Affairs, Oxford University Press, London 1971.

Venhata, Raman K., *Toward a General Theory of International Customary Law; Toward World Order and Human Dignity*, Essays in Honor of Myers S. McDougal, New York 1976.

Willrich, Mason (Ed.), *International Safeguards and Nuclear Industry*, The John Hopkins University Press, Baltimore 1973.

Willrich, Mason, and Taylor, Theodore B., *Nuclear Theft: Risks and Safeguards*, Ballinger Publishing, Cambridge, Mass. 1974.

Wohlstetter, Albert, et. al., *Moving Toward Life in a Nuclear Armed Crowd?*, Pan Heuristics, Los Angeles 1976.

Wolfke, K., *Custom in Present International Law*, Wroclaw 1964.

World Federation of United Nations Associations, *The Legal Principles Governing Friendly Relations and Co-Operation Among States*, WFUNA Seminar, A.W. Sijthoff, Leyden 1966.

Periodicals and Papers

Ahmed, M., 'Laser and Charged Particle Beam Technology', *Islamic Defence Review*, 1981, Vol. 6 No. 4.

Bibliography

Andelman, David A., 'Space Wars', *Foreign Policy*, Fall 1981, No. 44.

Anderson, J.E., 'First Strike: Myth or Reality', *The Bulletin of the Atomic Scientists*, November 1981, Vol. 37.

Andrews, Walter, 'Soviet Military Space Threat Bared', *Army Times*, 8 March 1982.

Arbatov, Georgi, 'The Soviets on SALT', *Newsweek*, 28 May 1979.

Ashbeck, Frank, 'The Militarisation of Space', *Armament and Disarmament Information Unit Report*, April/May 1980, Vol. 2 No. 2.

Aspin, L., 'The Verification of the SALT II Agreement', *Scientific American*, February 1979, Vol. 24 No. 2.

Baldwin, David A., 'Inter–Nation Influence Revisited', *Journal of Conflict Resolution*, December 1971.

Basmanov, V., 'For a Weapon Free Space', *International Affairs* (Moscow), November 1981.

Beres, Louis Rene, 'Steps Toward a New Planetary Identity: the 1980 Rabinowitch Essay', *The Bulletin of the Atomic Scientists*, February 1981, Vol. 37 No. 2.

Bessonov, Anatoly, 'Triple Link-up in Orbit', *New Times* (Moscow), January 1978, No. 4.

Betts, K.R., 'Hedging Against Suprise Attack', *Survival*, July–August 1981, Vol. 23.

Blechman, Barry M., 'Do Negotiated Arms Limitations Have a Future?', *Foreign Affairs*, Fall 1980, Vol. 59 No. 1.

Bogdanov, R.G., 'Strategic Arms Limitation and Reduction – an Urgent Problem', *Disarmament*, May 1981, Vol. IV No. 1.

Bos, M., 'Theory and Practice of Treaty Interpretation', *Netherlands International Law Review*, 1980, Vol. 27.

Brzezinski, Z., 'How the Cold War was Played', *Foreign Affairs*, October 1972, Vol. 51 No. 1.

Bhupendra, Jasani, 'Outer Space: A New Dimension to Warfare?', *Disarmament*, October 1981, Vol. IV No. 2.

Cady, Steven E., 'Beam Weapons in Space – A Reality We Must Confront', *Air University Review*, May–June 1982, Vol. XXXIII No. 4.

Carnesale, A., 'Reviving the ABM Debate', *Arms Control Today*, April 1981, Vol. 11.

221

Carrington, P.A.R., 'Arms Control and International Security: Some Practical Problems', *Vital Speeches of the Day*, 1 December 1980, Vol. 47.

'Cause for Concern', *New Times*, June 1981, No. 24.

'China and Nuclear Non-Proliferation Issues', *Institute of Defence Studies and Analyses*, July–September 1980, Vol. 13.

Christol, C.A., 'International Space Law and the Use of Natural Resources: Solar Energy', *Revue Belge de Droit International*, 1980–81, Vol. XV.

Clarke, D.L., 'Arms Control and Foreign Policy Under Reagan', *The Bulletin of the Atomic Scientists*, November 1981, Vol. 37.

Coleman, J.P., 'International Safeguards Against Non–Government Nuclear Theft: a Study of Legal Inadequacies', *The International Lawyer*, Summer 1976, Vol. 10.

Corrat, Hugh, 'NAVSTAR', *NATO's Fifteen Nations*, March 1980, Vol. 25 No. 1.

Dahlitz, J., 'Arms Control in Outer Space', *The World Today*, April 1982, Vol. 38 No. 4.

Dahlitz, J., 'Co–existence, Reciprocity and the Principle of Marginal Restraint', *Australian Outlook*, April 1981, Vol. 35 No. 1.

Dahlitz, J., 'Proliferation and Confrontation', *Australian Outlook*, April 1979, Vol. 33 No. 1.

Dahlitz, J., 'The Second Special Session of the General Assembly Devoted to Disarmament', *Disarmament: A Periodic Review by the United Nations,* 1982, Vol. V No. 2.

Deleon, P., 'Nuclear Power and Nuclear Weapons: the Tenuous Link', *Comparative Strategy*, 1981, Vol. 3 No. 1.

Dobra, P.M., 'The Role of Technological Evolution in the International Law of Arms Control: Scylla or Charybdis?', *Jurimetrics Journal*, 1980, Vol. 21.

Doubb, William O., and Fidell, Eugene R., 'International Relations and Nuclear Commerce: Developments in United States Policy', *Law and Policy in International Business,* 1976, Vol. 8.

Drell, S. and Wisner, K., 'Formula for Nuclear Arms Control', *International Security*, 1980/81, Vol. 5 No. 3.

Dunkel, Winifred M., 'Nuclear Proliferation – a German View', *Military Review*, November 1977, Vol. 57.

Einborn, Robert J., 'Treaty Compliance', *Foreign Policy*, Winter 1981–2, No. 45.

Ellsberg, Daniel, 'Will We Use Them?', *Current*, June 1981, No. 233.

Bibliography

Epstein, William, 'A Ban on the Production of Fissionable Material for Weapons', *Scientific American*, July 1980, Vol. 243 No. 1.

Epstein, William, 'The Proliferation of Nuclear Weapons', *Scientific American*, April 1975.

Falk, R.A., 'The Quasi–Legislative Competence of the General Assembly', *American Journal of International Law*, 1966, Vol. 60.

Feldman, S., 'Nuclear Middle East', *Survival*, May–June 1981, Vol. 23.

Fischer, D.A.V., *Preventing the Spread of Nuclear Weapons*, Unpublished Paper, Department of International Relations, Australian National University, Canberra, April 1981.

Fischer, D.A.V., 'Safeguards Under the Non–Proliferation Treaty', *Disarmament: A Periodic Review by the United Nations*, July 1980, Vol. III No. 2.

Fitzgerald, E.M., 'The Command of Space', *RUSI – Journal of The Royal United Services Institute for Defence Studies*, March 1981, Vol. 126 No. 1.

Franck, Thomas M., 'Growth of the International Community and Qualitative Shift in International Legal Relations', *The Spirit of Uppsala* (JUS 81) Manuscript No. 54.

Fried, J.H.E., 'First Use of Nuclear Weapons: Existing Prohibitions in International Law', *Bulletin of Peace Proposals*, Vol. 12.

Fuchs, Georg, 'The Neutron Peril', *New Times* (Moscow) January 1978, No. 1.

Gangl, Walter T., 'The *Jus Cogens* Dimensions of Nuclear Technology', *Cornell International Law Journal*, Winter 1980, Vol. 13 No. 1.

Garn, J., 'The SALT II Verification Myths', *Strategic Review*, Summer 1979, Vol. VII, No. 3.

Garthoff, R.L., 'Banning the Bomb in Outer Space', *International Security*, 1980/81, Vol. 5 No. 3.

Ghosh, S.K., 'China's Space Programme' *IDSA Journal*, April–June 1980, Vol. XII No. 4.

Grahl-Madsen, Atle, 'International Law for Our Times', *The Spirit of Uppsala* (JUS 81) Manuscript No. 41.

Gray, Colin S., 'New Debate on Ballistic Missile Defence', *Aviation Week and Space Technology*, 11 May 1981.

Greig, D.W., 'The Interpretation of Treaties and Article IV.2 of the Nuclear Non–Proliferation Treaty', *Australian Yearbook of International Law*, Faculty of Law, Australian National University, 1978, Vol. 6.

Haig, A.M., 'Strategic American Foreign Policy', *NATO Review*, 1–7 December 1981, Vol. 29.

Handel, M., 'Numbers Do Count: the Question of Quality Versus Quantity', *The Journal of Strategic Studies*, September 1981, Vol. 4.

Higgins, Rosalyn, 'The United Nations and Law–Making: The Political Organs', *American Society of International Law – Proceedings*, 1970.

Howard, M.E., 'On Fighting a Nuclear War', *International Security*, Spring 1981, Vol. 5.

Humble, Ronald D., 'Space Warfare in Perspective', *Air University Review*, July–August 1982, Vol. XXXIII No.5.

Huisken, Ron, *The Cruise Missile and Arms Control*, The Strategic and Defence Studies Centre, Australian National University, Canberra 1980.

'India Rockets Ahead with Observation Satellites', *New Scientist*, 11 June 1981, Vol. 90 No. 1257.

'International Reports and Comments', *Beijing Review*, 9 November 1981, No. 45.

Jack, Homer A., 'Progress Towards a Comprehensive Program of Disarmament', *WCRP Report*, 1982, SSD II/7.

Johnson, Bo, 'Changes in the Norms Guiding the International Legal System – History and Contemporary Trends', *The Spirit of Uppsala* (JUS 81) Manuscript No. 44.

Kapur, Ashok, 'Nuclear Proliferation in the 1980s', *International Journal*, Vol. 36.

Karas, Thomas H., 'Implications of Space Technology for Strategic Nuclear Competition', *Occasional Paper 25*, Periodical of the Stanley Foundation (Iowa USA) July 1981.

Kassar, N.T., 'The Legal Limits to the Use of International Force Through the United Nations Practice', *Revue Egyptienne de Droit International*, 1979, Vol. 35.

Keegan, J., 'The Human Face of Deterrence', *International Security*, Summer 1981, Vol. 6.

Kincade, W.H., 'Missile Vulnerability Reconsidered', *Arms Control Today*, May 1981, Vol. 11.

Kiselyak, C., 'Round the Prickly Pear: SALT and Survival', *Orbis*, 1979, Vol. 22.

Kratzer, Myron, 'Nuclear cooperation and Nonproliferation', *Atomic Energy Law Journal*, Winter 1976.

Kronman, Anthony, 'Aristotle's Idea of Political Fraternity', *The American Journal of Jurisprudence*, 1979, Vol. 24.

Bibliography

Krugmann, Hartmut, 'The German–Brazilian Nuclear Deal', *The Bulletin of the Atomic Scientists*, February 1981, Vol. 37 No. 2.

Lee, J.M., 'Opening Windows for Arms Control', *Foreign Affairs*, Vol. 58, 1979.

Lider, J., 'Towards a Modern Concept of Strategy', *Cooperation and Conflict*, 1981, Vol. 16 No. 4.

Liu, Leo, 'The Nuclear Policies of China and India', *Internal Problems* (Tel Aviv), Fall 1977, Vol. 16.

Mani, V.S., 'The 1970 Declaration on Friendly Relations: a Case Study in Law Creation by the UN General Assembly', *International Studies*, July–September 1979, Vol. 18.

Mazing, Valery, 'Dialogue, Not Missile Build–up', *New Times*, 1981, Vol. 18.

McCgwire, M., 'Soviet Military Doctrine: Contingency Planning and the Reality of World War', *Survival*, May–June 1980, Vol. 22.

Metcalf, A.G.B., 'Editorial', *Strategic Review*, U.S. Strategic Institute, Summer 1981, Vol. IX No. 3.

Meyer, S.M., 'Anti–Satellite Weapons and Arms Control: Incentives and Disincentives from the Soviet and American Perspectives', *International Journal*, Summer 1981, Vol. 36.

Mitic, Miodrat, 'Convention on Physical Protection of Nuclear Materials', *Review of International Affairs* (Belgrade), March 1980, Vol. XXXI.

Mohan, C.R., 'Nuclear Arms and Latin America', *Institute for Defence Studies and Analyses Journal*, July–September 1980, Vol. 12.

Molinev, Harold, 'The Impact of Strategic and Technological Innovations on Nuclear Deterrence', *Miliary Review*, January 1978, Vol. 58.

Nascimento e Silva, G.E., 'New Ways for Treaty–Making and International Legislation', *The Spirit of Uppsala*, (JUS 81) Manuscript No. 71.

Nathason, Eugene, 'International Management of Radioactive Wastes', *Environmental Affairs*, Spring 1976, Vol. 5.

'News', *Military Review*, December 1980, Vol. LX No. 12.

Nitze, Paul H., 'Is SALT II a Fair Deal for the United States?', (1979) reproduced in *SALT Hand Book: Key Documents and Issues 1972–1979*, (Ed.) Labrie, Roger P., American Enterprise Institute for Public Policy Research, Washington.

Nogee, Joseph L., 'Soviet Nuclear Proliferation Policy: Dilemmas and Contradictions', *Orbis*, Winter 1981, Vol. 24.

Nye, Joseph, 'Non–Proliferation: a Long Term Strategy', *Foreign Affairs*, April 1978.

Nye, Joseph, 'Prospects for Non–Proliferation', *Survival*, May–June 1981, Vol. XXIII No. 3.

Ogunbanwo, Ogunsola O., 'International Law and Outer Space Activities', *Journal of Legal Education*, 1977.

Ohlin, Göran, 'Can World Order be Negotiated?', *The Spirit of Uppsala* (JUS 81) Manuscript No. 42.

Ovinnikov, R., 'How the USA Orchestrated the Attack on Detente', *International Affairs*, August 1980, No. 8.

Perera, Judith, 'Was Iraq Really Developing a Bomb?' *New Scientist*, 11 June 1981, Vol. 90 No. 1257.

Pfaltzgraff, R.L., Jr., 'Verification of the SALT II Treaty', *International Security Review*, Summer 1979, Vol. 4 No. 2.

Quirt, J. 'Washington's New Push for Anti–Missiles', *Fortune*, 19 October 1981, Vol. 104.

Richter, R., 'Testimony From a Former Safeguards Inspector', *The Bulletin of the Atomic Scientists*, October 1981, Vol. 37.

Roberts, E.V., 'China and Nuclear Arms Limitation Agreements 1949–1980', *Institute for Defence Studies and Analyses Journal*, July–September 1980, Vol. 12.

Rogoff, M.A., 'The International Legal Obligations of Signatories to an Unratified Treaty', *Main Law Review*, 1980.

Roots, A., 'Settlement of the Iranian Hostage Crisis: an Exercise of Constitutional and Statutory Executive Prerogative in Foreign Affairs', *New York University Journal of International Law and Politics*, Spring 1981, Vol. 13.

Rosas, Allan, 'Customary Law: from "Universal" in a European System to "Regional" in a World System', *The Spirit of Uppsala* (JUS 81) Manuscript No. 56.

Rubin, Alfred P., 'The International Legal Effects of Unilateral Declarations', *American Journal of International Law*, January 1977, Vol. 71 No. 1.

Rumble, Wilfrid E., 'Divine Law, Utilitarian Ethics, and Positivist Jurisprudence: A Study of the Legal Philosophy of John Austin', *The American Journal of Jurisprudence*, 1979, Vol. 24.

Sahovic, Milan, 'The Nonaligned and International Law', *Review of International Affairs*, May 1981.

Schachter, Oscar, 'Towards a Theory of International Obligation', *The Effectiveness of International Decisions: Proceedings of the Conference of the American Society of International Law*, Oceana, Dobbs Ferry, New York 1971.

Bibliography

Scott, A., 'Strategic Reconnaissance and the Verification of the SALT II Agreement', *Armed Forces Journal*, June 1979.

Shea, G.P., 'The Study of Bargaining and Conflict Behaviour', *Journal of Conflict Resolution*, Vol. 24, 1980.

Sieghart, Paul, 'Nuclear Power and Human Rights', *International Commission of Jurists*, June 1977, No. 18.

Smernoff, Barry, 'The Strategic Value of Space Based Laser Weapons', *Air University Review*, March–April 1982, Vol. XXXIII No. 3.

Sommereyns, Raymond, 'United Nations Peace–Keeping Forces in the Middle East', *Brooklyn Journal of International Law*, Spring 1980, Vol. VI No. 1.

Soviet Aerospace, 2 August 1979, Vol. 25 No. 9.

Soviet Aerospace, 22 January 1979, Vol. 24 No. 3.

Spence, Jack, 'South Africa's "Bomb in the Basement" ', *Armament and Disarmament Information Unit*, October/November 1980, Vol. 2 No. 4.

Steinbruner, John D., 'Nuclear Decapitation', *Foreign Policy*, Winter 1981–82, Vol. 45.

Strategic Survey 1980–1981, Published by the International Institute of Strategic Studies, London 1981.

Suy, Erik, 'A New International Law for a New World Order', *The Spirit of Uppsala* (JUS 81) Manuscript No. 43.

Szulc, T., 'How Kissinger Did It', *Foreign Policy*, 1974, Vol. 15.

Toon, [U.S.] Ambassador Malcolm, 'Signs of Change in Russia', *U.S. News*, 9 January 1978, Vol. 84.

Torrey, Lee, 'America's New Missiles Fail to Impress', *New Scientist*, 4 June 1981.

Turner, R.F., 'Legal Implications of Deferring Ratification of SALT II', *Virginia Journal of International Law*, Summer 1981, Vol. 21.

'US Strategic Weapons Modernization: Reagan Leaves the Window Open', *International Defense Review*, Vol. 14 No. 11.

Vlasic, Ivan A., 'Disarmament Decade, Outer Space and International Law', *McGill Law Journal* 1981, Vol. 26 No. 2.

Walden, Raphael M., 'Subjective Element in the Formation of Customary International Law', *Israel Law Review*, 1977.

Wickham, S., 'Transfer of Western Technology to the USSR: Conditions for the 1980s', *NATO Review*, December 1981, No. 29.

Wohlstetter, Albert 'Spreading the Bomb Without Quite Breaking the Rules', *Foreign Policy*, Winter 1976–77, No. 25.

Worner, Manfred, 'NATO Defenses and Tactical Nuclear Weapons', *Strategic Review*, Fall 1977, Vol. 5.

Wyer, R., 'Prediction of Behaviour in Two-Person Games', *Journal of Personality and Social Psychology*, 1969, Vol. 13.

Cases

Aegean Sea Continental Shelf case (Greece v. Turkey) I.C.J. Rep. 1978.

Anglo-Norwegian Fisheries case (United Kingdom v. Norway), I.C.J. Rep. 1951.

Asylum case (Colombia/Peru) I.C.J. Rep. 1950.

Barcelona Traction, Light and Power Company Limited case, Second Phase, I.C.J. Rep. 1970.

Case Concerning United States Diplomatic and Consular Staff in Tehran (United States of America v. Iran) I.C.J. Reps. 1979, 1980.

Expenses case, I.C.J. Rep. 1962.

Fisheries Jurisdiction case, I.C.J. Rep. 1974.

North Sea Continental Shelf cases (Federal Republic of Germany/Denmark; Federal Republic of Germany/Netherlands) I.C.J. Rep. 1969.

Nuclear Tests case, I.C.J. Rep. 1974.

South West Africa case (Ethiopia v. South Africa; Liberia v. South Africa), I.C.J. Rep. 1966.

The *Lotus* case (the Case of the S.S. 'Lotus'), P.C.I.J. Ser. A. Judgment No. 9, 1927.

Document Series

Official Records of the -
Security Council
General Assembly
Committee on Disarmament
Eighteen Nation Committee on Disarmament
Conference of the Committee on Disarmament
Disarmament Commission
First Committee
Sixth Committee
International Atomic Energy Agency

Bibliography

Second Review Conference of the Treaty on the Non-Proliferation of Nuclear
  Weapons
United Nations Treaty Series
Preparatory Committee for SSD I
SSD I (A/S – 10/-)
Preparatory Committee for SSD II
SSD II (A/S – 12/-)

United States Government Publications

Arms Control, US Arms Control and Disarmament Agency, May 1978, Publication 96.

Brown, Harold, *SALT II: An Interim Assessment*, Report of the Panel of the Committee on Armed Services, House of Representatives, Second Session, 23 December 1978, United States Government Printing Office, Washington, 1978.

'Compliance With the SALT I Agreements', *Department of State Bulletin*, United States Government Printing Office, Washington, April 1978, Vol. 78 No. 2013.

Compliance With SALT I Agreements, Special Report No. 55, United States Department of State, Bureau of Public Affairs, July 1979.

Dean, Arthur H., 'Soviet Diplomatic Style and Tactics', reprinted from *Test Ban and Disarmament: The Path of Negotiation*, in *The Soviet Approach to Negotiation*, compiled by the Subcommittee on National Security and International Operations of the Senate Committee on Government Operations, United States Government Printing Office, Washington, 1969.

Harriman, Averell, *The SALT II Treaty*, Hearings Before the Committee on Foreign Relations, United States Senate, July 1979, United States Government Printing Office, Washington, 1979.

King, John K., (Ed.) *International Political Effects of the Spread of Nuclear Weapons*, United States Government Printing Office, Washington, 1979.

Kissinger, Henry, *The SALT II Treaty*, Hearings before the Committee on Foreign Relations, United States Senate, July 1979, United States Government Printing Office, Washington, 1979.

McGovern, George, *The SALT II Treaty*, Hearings before the Committee on Foreign Relations, United States Senate, July 1979, United States Government Printing Office, Washington, 1979.

Muir, Hugh, *Keeping a Check on Compliance With SALT I*, United States Information Service, 2 March 1978.

Nuclear Reduction, Testing, and Non-Proliferation, 94th Congress, 2nd Session, United States Government Printing Office, Washington, 1976.

Panel on the Strategic Arms Limitation Talks and the Comprehensive Test Ban Treaty, Committee on Armed Services, House of Representatives, United States Government Printing Office, Washington, December 1978.

Presidential Statement on Non-Proliferation, United States, 16 July 1981, reproduced in *Survival*, September-October 1981, Vol. XXIII No. 5.

Progress in United States and International Non-proliferation Efforts, United States Government Printing Office, Washington, 12 March 1979.

Report of the Panel on SALT and the Comprehensive Test-Ban Treaty, Intelligence and Military Application Subcommittee of the Committee on Armed Services, House of Representatives, 28 December 1978, United States Government Printing Office, Washington, 1978.

SALT II Agreement, Vienna, 18 June 1979, Selected Documents No. 12A, United States Department of State, Bureau of Public Affairs, Washington.

SALT II: An Interim Assessment, Report of the Panel of the Committee on Armed Services, House of Representatives, United States Government Printing Office, Washington, 1978.

SALT II: Some Foreign Policy Considerations, Congressional Research Service, United States Government Printing Office, Washington, June 1979.

Soviet Military Power, United States Government Printing Office, Washington, undated, approx. December 1981-January 1982.

The Department of State: Selected Documents, Bureau of Public Affairs, Office of Public Communication, February 1978, No. 7.

United States Department of State, *Current Policy*, No. 339 of 4 November, Bureau of Public Affairs, Washington, 1981.

Verification: the Critical Element of Arms Control, United States Arms Control and Disarmament Agency, Publication 85, Washington, March 1976.

United Nations Studies Relating to NAC

All the Aspects of Regional Disarmament, A/35/416.

Comprehensive Nuclear Test-Ban, A/35/257.

Comprehensive Study on Confidence Building Measures, A/36/474.

Comprehensive Study on Nuclear Weapons, A/35/392.

Implications of Establishing an International Satellite Monitoring Agency, A/AC. 206/14.

Institutional Arrangements Relating to the Process of Disarmament, A/36/392.

Bibliography

Israeli Nuclear Armament, A/36/431.

Reduction of Military Budgets: International Reporting of Military Expenditures, A/35/479.

Relationship Between Disarmament and Development, A/36/356.

Relationship Between Disarmament and International Security, A/36/597.

South Africa's Plan and Capability in the Nuclear Field, A/35/402.

Miscellaneous

Compendium of Arms Control Verification Proposals, Department of National Defence, Ottawa, June 1980.

Daily Bulletin, United States Mission, Geneva, 29 June 1982.

Disarmament Times, New York, 1982.

'Elements of a Comprehensive Programme of Disarmament', reproduced in *Disarmament: A Periodic Review by the United Nations,* May 1980, Vol. III No. 1.

Final Document SSD I, A/RES/S-10/2 (OPI/618-78-35909-July 1978-10M).

Final Document of the Second Review Conference of the Parties to the Treaty on the Non-Proliferation of Nuclear Weapons, NPT/CONF. II/22 of 7 September 1980.

International Herald Tribune, 1981, October 22, 24-25; 1982, July 28, 30; August, 2, 9, 10, 12, 13, 14-15, 16.

Larson, K.H., *Internationalizing the Nuclear Fuel Cycle: the Potential Role of International Organizations,* Occasional Paper prepared for the SIPRI Symposium on Internationalization of the Nuclear Fuel Cycle, Sweden, October-November 1979.

New York Times, 26 April 1981; 20 July 1982.

Records of the International Commission on Radiological Protection.

Records of the UN Scientific Committee on the Effects of Atomic Radiation.

Records of the UN World Conference on the Human Environment, Stockholm, June 1972

Report of the 38th Conference of the International Law Association, Budapest 1934.

Report SSD II, A/RES/S-12/32.

'How Israel Got the Bomb', *Time,* 12 April 1976.

Report of the International Law Commission covering its First Session, 12 April – 9 June 1949.

Report of the International Law Commission on the work of its Thirty-third Session, 4 May – 24 July 1981.

Report of the International Nuclear Fuel Cycle Evaluation INFCE/PC/2/1-9 of 29 February 1980, reproduced in IAEA publication STI/PUB/534.

Report of the Special Committee on the Charter of the United Nations and on the Strengthening of the Role of the Organization, A/36/33 Supp. No. 33.

Report of the Working Group on the Peaceful Settlement of Disputes, A/C.6/36/L.19.

Review of the Multilateral Treaty-Making Process, A/35/312/Add. 2 of 28 August 1980.

The Age, newspaper, Melbourne, 14 January 1982; 25 November 1982.

The Australian, newspaper, Sydney, 5 April 1982; 2 July 1982.

'Theory and Methodology of International Law', Report of the Working Group, *Fifty-eighth Conference of the International Law Association,* 1980.

Whence the Threat to Peace, Military Publishing House, USSR Ministry of Defense, Moscow, 1982.

Index

Themes that recur constantly throughout the book are not listed, in order not to overload the index. For the same reason, items of merely passing relevance are omitted, while only occasional reference is made to material contained in the notes.

For listing and summary of provisions of the major NAC agreements see Tables I and II on pages 24 to 31.

GREEDY LITTLE EYES

BILLIE
LIVINGSTON

Greedy Little Eyes

VINTAGE
CANADA

VINTAGE CANADA EDITION, 2010

Published in Canada by Vintage Canada, a division of Random House
of Canada Limited, Toronto, in 2010. Distributed by Random House of
Canada Limited, Toronto.

Vintage Canada with colophon is a registered trademark.

www.randomhouse.ca

Library and Archives Canada Cataloguing in Publication

Livingston, Billie, 1965–
Greedy little eyes / Billie Livingston.

ISBN 978-0-679-31324-3

I. Title.

PS8573.I916G74 2010   C813'.54   C2009-906707-2

Text design by Paul Dotey

Printed and bound in the United States of America

2 4 6 8 9 7 5 3 1

For Sweet Timothy

CONTENTS

Before I Would Ever Hurt You

GORD CAME BACK FROM THE BATHROOM and sat in the booth again. "I'm turning myself in." His smile was lopsided. He scratched the back of his neck, and blinked rapidly as if trying to clear his head. "What's the difference between locusts and grasshoppers?"

Rain fell hard behind me, battering the café's front window. The place was more diner than café, one of East Vancouver's kitschy attempts to recapture the '50s.

A waitress fishtailed by, raising her coffee pot. I pushed my cup toward her and then waited until she moved on. When no words came, I shook my head.

"The brown ones. They're locusts if they have the short antennas? Antenn-*ae*? It was bad. They were all over the kitchen, some jumped onto the stove and burned up right there. All over the curtains—in the dirty dishes even, floating in the water."

I had been finding patterns in the table's Formica, wondering again if I should have called someone. I looked him in the eyes now. "Am I the first person you phoned?"

"Everybody's hiding, but you."

"Nobody's hiding."

"You've got your own apartment now." He gave me that crooked grin again. "First Bernam in the phone book: *A* for Amy." He reached for my fingers.

I slipped my hands under the table.

Wincing, he flicked grey eyes at the ceiling fan and then back. "I know I haven't been really *there,* um, lately. But you and me are pals, aren't we? You understand even when I'm an asshole, taking off like that into the woods. No phone, no toilets, no nothin'."

Looking at his face some more, I tried to picture his girlfriend, Ruth, in that wooden kitchen of theirs. *No phone, no toilets, no nothin'.* I wondered at my lack of fear.

In the space between my big and second toe, I have a tiny brown dot. Not a freckle, it's too dark, almost black. Had it ever since I was born.

My father pointed it out. "Jesus, look at that, Peg, she's got Gord's dot. Same place and everything. If you two didn't hold each other in such low regard, I'd wonder."

Mom shook her head. "If she got his brains, we're in for it."

That dot though, it bonded Gord and me. My father said that for Gord, it was love at first sight on account of our shared peculiarity. When Gord saw the dot, he told my father that he would understand me when no one else could. And vice versa. He called us Dotters.

My mother talked to me about Gord once. It was a rare night in Vancouver, one too hot to lie in bed, and the two of us were at the kitchen table, drunk with sleeplessness.

Gord was *not right*, she told me. *In the head.* She and Gord had had another one of their verbal slap-fights earlier that night, over dinner. "It's none of your business," she had railed. "You sit there shovelling in my food and— and then shitting your opinions all over the house."

My father choked on his laughter. "Christ, nearly lost that beer out my nose."

Gord thumped his brother's back, laughing along.

Later, sitting at the kitchen table with me, each of us clutching our glass of iced tea as if hoarding it, her tone was almost pleading. "Everyone laughs it off. But it's not funny. He has his *own* family. He keeps shoving his nose into ours while his own wife and sons languish on the other side of town."

"He was a year ahead of you in school, right? Did he ever hit on you?"

"Oh for god's sake." She looked away and sighed. "He liked me. He was—I mean I liked him too but he was needy—pathetically so. Your dad told him to bloody well get on with things, make his own fun."

"So he was hitting on you."

"I was always in love with your father. I'm just trying to explain to you that I don't have the same sort of camaraderie with Gord that you do. He's an irresponsible idiot."

The first time I ever heard the phrase *if he had a brain he'd be dangerous,* it was my mother talking about Gord.

I was ten years old when the principal of the school called my mother in and laid out his concern before the both of us: "She waited until he was alone and then slammed the boy face-first into the schoolyard gravel. I would call that abnormally aggressive."

My mother looked at me. "Is that what happened?"

"Sort of. But he asked for it."

"Irregardless, young lady," the principal said, "you don't bloody another child because of words. Sticks and stones may break your bones but names will never hurt you."

My mother turned to him. Her expression soured slightly. "Well, he must have done something for her to have *bloodied* him, as you put it." She looked back at me.

"I was on the swing," I explained, "like, a few days ago. I had on a skirt and that kid, Brian, was standing there watching me go back and forth. *Then,* all of a sudden, when I swung up, like, with my legs out, he put his hand up my skirt. Right on my underpants."

"He touched your underpants?" My mother jabbed a look at the principal. "So you pushed him."

"No, cuz he took off. So I waited. Then yesterday, I was late from recess and that Brian kid was still outside too, and so I ran up behind. And I got him."

A brief satisfaction showed in my mother's eyes. She faced the principal. "I think that shed some light on things."

"I'm sorry, Mrs. Bernam," he said, shaking his head, "but you don't actually believe that. Children, in my experience, do not wait to retaliate. They are simple creatures."

"My child isn't *simple*."

"Irregardless, Mrs.—"

"There is no such word as *irregardless*." She picked up her purse. "Looks like you've got a sexual harassment charge on your hands."

When we got home Dad was at the kitchen table with his brother, having a beer. My mother scowled.

"Hello, fellow Dotter." Gord noogied my head.

I giggled and squirmed and jumped in his lap, took a sip from his bottle.

Mom plucked the beer from my hands. "For god's sake," she said, glaring at Gord.

"Oh, Peg, calm down; she had a sip of beer—not like it's Scotch." My father grabbed her around the waist and winked at me. "Wait'll we get you into the Scotch, Amy, then you can start coming to poker night."

"Not funny," my mother said and removed his hand. "This is exactly the problem, this lackadaisical—*this!*" She told me to go change out of my school clothes.

Soon as I'd rounded the corner, she started in. It never seemed to occur to them how close my room was, that I might as well have been sitting under the kitchen table. Truth be told, though, I was only half listening until Gord hollered, "She did it cuz I told her to do it that way. No little sonofabitch sticks his hand up my kid's skirt."

"*She is not your kid!*" my mother roared.

"She's my godchild. She's my niece, for chrissake."

She told him that part of my problem was him and his idiocy, his need to gratify every stupid urge that came upon him, and that he encouraged the same in me.

Gord bellowed, "Chrissake, she's defending herself against a would-be *rapist*. What would you—?"

"You couldn't suggest she tell a teacher. Or her *parents!*" she fumed. I could imagine her eyes bugging. "He needed stitches! He's ten!"

"I'm teaching her to stand up for herself." Gord's chair legs rubbed the floor as he pushed his seat back and stood. "A man wrongs a woman—she should have his goddamn head on a platter."

There was silence.

My mother whispered something.

"That's enough," my father said evenly.

"Why are you here? Why are you *always* here?" She sounded as though she might cry.

"Okay," Dad said, his voice low and sturdy. "Take it easy."

I heard Gord's approaching footfalls over my mother's strained whisper. "*Me* take it easy?"

My father's voice lowered more, his tone easing into that hopeful lovey voice he used just before he wrapped his arms around her shoulders to keep her body from thrashing.

A moment later Gord was in my doorway. "Dotter." He saluted.

I stared sombrely from my bed, threw a half-assed wave his way.

He pulled at the toe of my sock. "Is it true you beat a man within an inch of his life?"

My eyes rolled. "What a friggin' baby that kid is."

Gord sat and hoisted his back against the wall beside me. "Your mother's just jealous. She wishes she had the guts you do."

We each looked at our feet.

"Damn right," he said. "Little bastard'll think twice before he comes near you again."

"You should try not to piss her off so much."

Gord nodded.

Shortly before I graduated high school, my parents went to San Francisco for the long weekend. A second honeymoon, my father said. I drove them to the airport and my father attempted to get us all singing "I Left My Heart in San Francisco" in rounds. Too early in the morning for that, I was glad to dump them at Departures.

That night, I woke at 2:03 a.m., according to the neon of my clock, and saw dim light under the door. A little dazed, I wandered into the hall.

The house felt like its same old self, no strange breath in the air. I knew before I named it exactly who would be sitting in the kitchen.

He turned when he heard my shuffle, his eyes a little red and puffy. "Hey, Dotter, up already?" he slurred, and then shook his head, looking embarrassed. "Did I wake you, Amy? Sorry. I let myself in with the key outside there."

I headed to the stove and put the kettle on. "So?"

He sipped his beer, stared into his hands. "Ah, you don't want to hear this, all my shit."

I leaned against the stove. "Your shit's my shit."

Smiling softly to his bottle, he wiped his forehead. He held his breath and let it go. "Lydia says she's not happy."

I took two mugs out, put tea bags into them. I couldn't imagine what it might be like to be my aunt. He rarely spoke of her. He rarely spoke of my cousins either. It was as if he wanted to keep them separate from this part of his family. As if they were his job and he didn't want to talk shop.

"And then this morn—well, yesterday morning—the company asked me if I wanted to transfer to Calgary. Promotion and another fifteen grand a year."

Gord looked down, his head wobbling a little with each breath. "Lydia thinks it might be a new start. We might get to be a better . . . couple. I wouldn't be distracted and my boys and me would *bond*. Christ, another couple years and those boys'll be gone faster than you can . . ." His voice drifted off. "Swing a dead cat. Your dad says if I don't give it my all, I'll regret it." He looked over at me for a few drawn-out seconds. "He would, wouldn't he? I bet he wants me gone."

"Don't be stupid."

"Stupid. They're both pussies. He's afraid . . . and she's afraid to do anything about it."

I looked at him. "You're kinda looped there, Dotter."

"*You* know. Damn well. Elephant in the room, eh? You know."

I smirked as though I did know.

"Hey." He shrugged, ducked his chin into his neck like a blasé Frenchman. "Peg's beautiful. He knows it most of all. It's old hat. She knows it. She should've kicked him in the balls like I taught you, but here she is. That's who's *stupid*."

Heat rushed into my neck. I watched him another second. "Kicked him in the balls?"

"Lack of dedication. He forfeits. And she kicked *me* in the balls instead. I'm not impotent. This whole thing—" He raised his hands to his surroundings. "Mine. In a different plane: that's mine, this is mine, you're mine."

Suddenly the room felt tight and heavy. As though, even in Calgary, Gord would be too loud and too close.

We still saw him two or three times a year but he seemed more distant each time, as though less and less of him were actually in the room. Then two years almost to the day that he had moved, Gord up and left Aunt Lydia and my cousins in Calgary. He was at work, in the middle of a board meeting with all the mucky-mucks of Gibraltar Insurance, when the feeling hit him. Apparently they were discussing different strategies to increase profit margins, batting around ideas of how they might feasibly make cuts to existing coverage without alienating the clientele. Someone had raised the issue of prescriptions: if PharmaCare could refuse to cover certain prescriptions, then why couldn't they, as a secondary insurance provider, do likewise? In fact they should only cover what the government agencies would cover.

Gord's rebuttal shot down the length of the table. "If we're only going to cover what's already covered then we're providing fuck-all!"

When Gord told the story later, it took on biblical proportions. The men around him leaned in as they haggled, their gold rings and watches grazing the surface, teeth sharp, eyes craving. Gord slammed a fist down in the middle of the argument, and then rose from his chair and said, "From the days of John the Baptist until now, every time there's something good or true or right, assholes like you gotta take it away." Then he turned and left the building. He walked into the street, flagged a cab and headed to the airport.

He called my father once from Toronto and then there wasn't another word until six months later, when he showed up for Sunday dinner with a girl named Ruth on his arm. She wasn't much older than me; her hair was the same colour and texture as mine but it was centre-parted and hung down to her bum. She was an

artist—an *artisan*, she corrected me from where she sat
on the floor in our living room, leaning against the
couch and Gord's legs. Reaching into a tasselled suede
purse, she pulled out two small white boxes, and passed
one to Mom and one to me. Each contained a pair of
earrings that she had made.

Sitting rigidly in her wingback chair, my mother held
up a teardrop of silver wire threaded through three blue
wood beads. Her eyes, though, were on Ruth's smooth
blank face. No eyeliner, no lipstick. Ruth's thick hair
draped to her lap.

"These are *awesome*," I said. Seated on the ottoman
near my father's chair, I suddenly scooted onto the floor
too, as though Ruth might look like less of an interloper
if I were down there with her. "I *love* these." Holding it
by the shepherd's hook, I dangled a slim slice of smooth
wood, shark's fin shaped and caged in silver wire.

"Right on," she said. "They're guitar picks. My old boyfriend loved wood picks. Most of them are plastic, eh."

Earring still in hand, my mother appraised Ruth as if
a one-way mirror separated them.

My father cleared his throat. "So how long are you
two in town?"

"Just tonight and tomorrow," Gord told him.

Mom put the earring back into its box but she didn't
take her gaze from Gord's girlfriend. "You just look so
much like my daughter. If your hair wasn't so . . ."

"So damn long?" Ruth loosed a horse laugh on the
room. "Me and my crazy-ass hair. Actually you and Amy,
man, *you* two could be sisters."

A rueful gurgle in my mother's throat, then she looked down finally and set the box on the arm of her chair. "But for a few *decades* . . . Thank you, Ruth. I'll enjoy these."

"We're heading to the wilds of Vancouver Island," Gord interjected. "We've had it with *stuff*. No more *stuff*. We want to live the good life: all natural, no artificial preservatives."

Ruth smiled as she hugged her knees.

I looked at Gord but he didn't look back. He had hardly addressed a word to me all evening. Itchy and restless, I chewed at the inside of my lip.

"People," he announced later at the dinner table, "are getting brain cancer from telephones, you know." He paused with the last of his pork chop on the end of his fork.

"You mean cellphones?" I asked him.

"Cellphones, cordless phones, all of it. And Christ knows what havoc the computers are wreaking on us."

"Come on, babe," Ruth coaxed him and then winked as she chewed.

Gord winked back and shut up.

My father's eyebrows flicked from Gord to Ruth. He glanced at his empty plate, and then at my mother. He took a long drink of water, his Adam's apple cranking up and down. As he set down his glass, I searched his eyes for signs of envy.

☀

Three or four months later, Gord phoned us from a gas station about a forty-minute walk from his new place, wondering if the three of us could join him and Ruth for dinner.

My mother would not go. "He deserted his family and he's running around with some underage hippie. He's a pervert and jackass and I won't support it."

My father cajoled her. "You might have a point, *but* he left her the house, two cars . . . and all the phones and computers she could ever want."

She peered at him. "Is that funny to you?"

Dad and I took the ferry to Nanaimo and, from there, drove an hour through the rain into the middle of nowhere. A muddy dirt road with a skunk stripe of green down the middle took us the last fifteen minutes to Gord and Ruth's place.

It was quaint, I guess: a beat-up log cabin right in the thick of old-growth forest. Smoke floated out of the chimney through the drizzle.

The front door opened and Ruth flounced onto the porch in a heavy, ankle-length skirt. She wore a woolly cardigan and her arms were folded against the cold. "Right on! You made it!"

"You weren't kiddin' about moving to the wilds," my father said to her as he got out of the car.

She beamed. "It's a hump, huh?"

Banging out the screen door, Gord bellowed, "Come in, you're out!"

My father and I skittered up the wet steps, ditched our muddy shoes at the door.

A fire burned in the stove—an actual wood-burning stove—and the place smelled warm and savoury. I turned around and took it all in, feeling as if I were in an ad for country living though with a bit of a Haight-Ashbury feel: there were paisley curtains, dozens of candles, lighted oil lamps, God's-eyes in the windows and, in the centre of the room, a multicoloured rag rug.

"Nice job, Ruth. You did this all yourself?"

She smiled. "My old man chipped in a little."

"Chipped shmipped!" He squeezed her from behind. "Such a little bugger you are." He glanced at me and then kissed Ruth's cheek before blowing a raspberry into her neck.

I looked away.

"See those cupboards?" Gord said, releasing Ruth. "These babies are all mine!"

My father went to inspect Gord's carpentry while Ruth walked me up the wood ladder to the loft that was their feathered nest of a bedroom.

No bathroom, no running water. They used an outhouse and well water.

Dinner was wild rabbit. Gord had shot it and Ruth had cleaned and cooked it.

"No hormones or dye or preservatives, just good food," Gord reported from over his plate. He said there was no electricity out here to screw up your brains. He lectured us on the ill effects of power lines.

"Babe," Ruth cut him off. "Mellow."

"No. I won't *mellow*." His voice was sharp. "This is a

dangerous world and when you know something you got to talk about it."

"There goes Gordie, spreadin' the gospel," Dad teased. "How're you living these days?"

"Look around! I'm living *great!*"

Ruth winked at me. The tight smile I gave her reminded me of my mother's and so I mentioned again how good the rabbit tasted.

My father kept at him. "Gordie! What are you living *on?*"

"Don't worry about us, brother. We got it covered. Ruth makes her jewellery; she takes in sewing once in a while—these are *her* curtains, you know. I do a little carpentry, that sort of thing. See this, *this*"—he waved his fork around—"is what the government does not want. They don't want people living off the *grid*: killing and cooking their own food. They don't like this one bit—no phone lines to tap, no cookies in the computer."

"*Cookies* now, Gordie?" Coming from me, *Gordie* had a snide sound to it. The tines of my fork mewled against the plate.

"That's right, Dotter."

He hadn't called me that in a while. Ruth glanced at my father.

"A little cookie attaches itself to your browser with every stop you make on the Web. Same goes for your television. Don't kid yourself, that's how they getcha. Here in the woods, the infrared is screwed. Can't track you any more because of the warmth of the trees; the energy keeps the boys from being able to tell what's tree, what's deer, what's man."

My father stared.

I looked at my uncle. "What do they care what *you're* doing?"

Gord looked at me with a kind of pained disgust, as though the shared dot between our toes surely must be fading.

Ruth glanced from me to Gord. "Speaking of cookies, guess what's for dessert." She added, "The way this is going I should've put a little weed into them."

We didn't hear from them again for another few months. Between starting a new job and moving into my first apartment, I didn't have time to give Gord and Ruth much thought. My name was in the phone book for the first time.

Staring at my number on the grey-white page, I was in the midst of noting whose names sandwiched my own when the phone rang. It was Ruth. Calling from the gas station. She had tried calling me at my parents' and they'd given her my number.

"I'm in the book now," I told her.

The phone line rustled and crackled. It sounded as if she spat. "Sorry, the wind's going nuts here. My hair keeps blowing into my mouth. Amy, listen man, I hate to lay this shit on you but you're Gord's niece and it seems like you guys have a connection and, you know, I got no one here. Except for Irene at The Store, but I hardly know her except for selling jewellery."

Gord hadn't had a real conversation with me since he had left Lydia, and Lydia never would have talked to me about their marital problems. Ruth had not really made any friendship overtures before now. I felt caught in the crosshairs of her effrontery and my own greedy curiosity.

"What's going on?"

"He's wiggin' out. I thought he'd calm down out of the city, but he's worse. He's out hunting now and I'm supposed to be peddling my wares in town, whatever the hell that means. Anyone who wears jewellery's already bought all they want and everyone else grows their own anyway . . ." She sighed.

"Grows their own what?"

"Weed."

"Weed? What does Gord know about growing *weed*?"

"I used to grow it in Nelson. Nelson's a real town though, man. Not like *this*. I can't handle being cut off from people. There's no socializing. I couldn't get a job if I wanted and he's nowhere with the carpentry thing either cuz he got rid of the car. He's on this trip about how a car can be traced."

"What have you been living on?"

"His severance package, I guess. I don't usually even talk about money, but this whole year has been so trippy and fucked up. We paid seventy grand to buy the cabin. He totally *demanded* it be in my name, which is cool. But it's weird too. I don't think this is my scene."

She paused. I pictured her long mane whipping in the wind, round the phone cord, and her neck.

"And he keeps catching these goddamn grasshoppers—it's like he's relieved every time he gets another one. Keeps saying, 'And his meat was locusts and wild honey.'"

I told my father about Ruth's call.

"He never got a severance package. I thought they were renting. Are you sure that's what she said?"

"Why would he put new cupboards up in a place he doesn't even own?" I asked.

"Christ. The bugger must have looted Gibraltar. Sonofabitch. When they find out, they'll have his ass. Or they'll go after Lydia and the house . . . How'd you leave it with her?"

"By the end, she was talking about inviting some chick named Irene over for dinner. She said they'd get through it, that he was just having an attack of middle-age crazies."

"You buy a Corvette when you catch that disease, you don't collect grasshoppers." My father sighed. "When we were kids, right after my father took off, your grandmother sent Gord and me to Sunday school. I guess she wanted us to fly right. Or maybe she just wanted Sunday mornings to herself. Anyways, Gord was fascinated when we learned the story of John the Baptist. He liked how this guy lived in the wilderness and his meat was

locusts and honey—sounded full of principle or something, ascetic. And he liked all that King Herod stuff
too: John denounced Herod for ditching his wife and
taking up with his brother's wife. You know, our dad
had run off with his buddy's wife. Struck a chord." He
breathed into the phone. "I used to think he was in love
with your mother when we were in college. He never
wanted to go out with his own girl unless it was a
double date with us, and then he'd spend the whole
night talking to Peg. Here we go round the mulberry
bush, I thought."

In the end we did nothing. Nobody told Aunt Lydia—
if Gibraltar Insurance still hadn't caught the loss, maybe
they never would. Dad decided to let his brother and
Ruth sort themselves out. He asked me not to discuss it
with Mom. I did not need to be told.

A couple of weeks later, we got another phone call. I
was at my parents' doing laundry. It was Irene, Ruth's
friend from The Store, and she was in such a state that
Mom couldn't make out half her words.

Gord had shot Ruth.

Apparently, unable to take the mania any longer, Ruth
had taken the fish tank filled with Gord's grasshoppers
from the closet. Tank on the table, she threatened to let
them all go if things didn't change. Without a word,
Gord grabbed his hunting rifle and shot her in the leg.
Irene was there. She saw it all, the fish tank hitting the

floor, grasshoppers shooting around the room, lighting on the stove and landing on Ruth.

Irene held Ruth on the smooth wood floor of the kitchen, screaming at Gord to get an ambulance. Gord wouldn't let anyone out the door. Irene begged, telling him that Ruth would bleed to death. It wasn't that serious yet; they could get a doctor.

Instead Gord scrambled for his grasshoppers, zigzagging through the kitchen, slipping in Ruth's blood. He told Irene he would cut both their heads off if she dared open the front door. There they lay, Ruth whispering, "Call your brother, Gord," over and over, Irene begging, and all the while Gord tried to get the bugs into a paper bag, hollering for the door to stay closed.

Soon Ruth didn't make a sound. Tears but no noise, just waiting. Eventually Gord's frenzy ebbed. Shortly after Ruth stopped breathing, he told Irene to get out. So she ran, grasshoppers fleeing out the door behind her.

By the time police arrived, Gord was gone, the door was wide open and Ruth lay dead.

"Do you hate me, Amy?" The two of us in the diner. "I know how it seems, but I swear to God, I'm not crazy. Ruth was—I'd kill myself before I'd ever hurt you."

"I know, Uncle Gord." Felt strange to say *Uncle*. It had always been just plain Gord.

"You're not afraid of me, are you?"

No. Not afraid. I couldn't get a feeling sitting there

with him, couldn't get a vein. I listened as a new patron came into the café and remarked loudly about the downpour. I heard the wet soles of his shoes complain against the linoleum as he found a seat.

"I called the police," Gord said, "when I went to the washroom. I couldn't bear it if you were afraid of me. Just let me give you these things. Then you can take off before they get here. You're the only one who's really part of me." His eyes were watery. He took out a narrow tin box and slid it across the table. It was the sort of tin that housed miniature whisky bottles. I pulled at the lid.

"No." He stopped my fingers. "They'll be here soon. It's for you. You'll understand." Reaching under the table he wrenched a gym bag up onto the seat beside him and looked past me. "Oh, shit. No-no-no. I don't want them here yet."

I looked behind me and saw two squad cars out front. All lights, no sirens. Four cops started toward the door.

"I'm not ready," Gord cried as the front door jangled open. Clutching the gym bag, he unzipped it and pulled out something long and brown and alive. A rumpled paper sack fell onto the table. Tiny bodies flitted up Gord's arms, spitting from the rifle in his hands, from the gym bag, the paper bag, grasshoppers filling the room.

He stood and hollered toward the door. "Stay outside. I am not ready!"

Someone yelled, "Police!"

"Jesus Christ!" I looked for a way to disappear.

"Get out! Or I'll do it," Gord sobbed. He wrestled the barrel toward himself, trying to get hold of the trigger.

Screams careened, everything waving, dancing with kicking legs and flapping arms.

Gord's name came out of me and then, "Stop it. Please stop it!" As I slid under the table I cracked my head against the edge, feeling the crunch of insects under my knees.

Drop your weapon! Place your hands behind your head!

I could see the barrel of his rifle now; he had let it fall forward away from himself.

Then an explosion, the smell of firecrackers.

He dropped, flat on his rump the way a toddler might. His face was big-eyed shocked before it crumpled and a long howl poured out.

Heavy leather shoes rushed his way.

From under the table I watched as he reached for his foot, blood oozing from the sole of his shoe, rifle abandoned beside him.

The cops slammed him down onto his back and Gord's head smacked the floor before they turned him onto his belly. His howl was a wail now as they yanked his wrists behind his back, jammed cuffs into place.

I felt it running down my side, warm and sticky, and opened my eyes to Gord's whisky tin, lid off, lodged between my shoulder and the red vinyl seat, honey lolling thick from my arm and onto a crippled grasshopper on the floor. A muscle twitched in my wet cheek as I gauged the length of the bug's antennae, his legs pumping in the gold ooze. Shuddering, I picked him up, set him there on my shoe, about where my big and second toe would be, and rocked him with my heel.

Make Yourself Feel Better

I WANT TO STEAL SOMETHING SO BAD. I am standing in a music store, ogling new shrink-wrapped CDs and thinking of the rush I would feel waltzing past their anti-theft devices with my pockets full.

I just came from an annual checkup with my doctor, who believes I don't drink, don't smoke and jog three kilometres, three times a week. Really, I love gin, smoke Matinees and don't own a pair of running shoes. The clean version of me makes my doctor happy though. And that is healthy for me. Normally, as I walk into her office, my pulse races and I get knots in my stomach—nothing good can come of the whole exercise. The lies I tell her calm my pulse.

This time though, I wanted a prescription for some Ativan or maybe some Zopiclone. Insomnia comes and goes for me and I prefer to nip it in the bud. True to form, if I tell the truth, she wants me to see a shrink. She thinks

I have abandonment issues. My mother didn't abandon me. She died. When I was a baby, for chrissake. Try arguing with a doctor though. They all think they're gods. My father did not abandon me either, but she starts in with the ancient history: child services and how my dad was a pothead and a dealer and lacked judgment. That's not entirely accurate. Whenever I leave my doctor's office, I feel the need to do something terrible and immediate. I want to key expensive cars and break new china.

I pick a CD off the shelf and stare at Janis Joplin's sad grinning face and then over at the security guard by the door. Chewing my inner cheek, I remember it's two o'clock. I've got to be somewhere in fifteen minutes and I use up six of them, standing in line, paying for Janis.

Outside on Seymour Street, the sun has come out. A few feet down the sidewalk from me, a feral-looking street guy is pacing in small circles, shouting into the air and smacking one hand with the other as though he's trying to make a point to an invisible listener. I can't help but watch him as he looks up at the sky and hollers, "It's just a whole lotta *How come* around here. Isn't it? *Isn't it?*" Then he lowers his chin and stares right at me. He's stocky and dirty, and his hair is matted into dreads with a dried leaf or blade of grass stuck here and there. Above his beard, he's got lonesome brown eyes that remind me of my dad's. I smile a little. He doesn't smile back and I feel guilty. As if I've been eavesdropping.

I check my watch and get going, walk at a good clip and consider how many words per minute I'll claim to type when I get there. I rehearse lines like "Where I excel is problem solving" and "I am a team player at heart," then decide this pace is only making me nervous. Better to be a little late than a lot nervous. I slow just enough to sponge up the smiles of vaguely desperate-looking stockbroker types; they've got their hunting faces on. They've either won or lost big but either way they'd like to get laid on their lunch break.

Two minutes left now to get there and up to the thirteenth floor, talk them into believing what a good receptionist/file-clerk/data-inputter I would make. I can't believe they've got a thirteenth floor. What's the big deal about thirteen anyway? Oh yes, Christ and His Last Supper. You'd think the Lamb of God would be good luck; thirteen should be a rabbit's foot. Then again, "touch wood" is good luck and that refers to touching the crucifix, the wood that killed the poor bastard. I'm stuck on this thought—dead Jesus things deemed arbitrarily bad or good luck—when a slamming pain in the centre of my back sends me flying forward onto the sidewalk. I land on one knee.

Shock is lodged in my throat; a half-scream has stuffed me speechless. People stop to stare and I am ready to cry. Imprinted by cement, I stand and turn to face the wild man from Seymour Street. His fist still raised, his face triumphant.

I flinch as a man in a suit grabs the wild man's arm. Another, in jeans, gets him in a stranglehold from behind and they wrestle him to the ground.

The suit asks if I'm okay. "You don't know him, do you?"

"I . . . no." I look up at 1550 Pender, the building in which they will ascertain whether I am a worthy office temp.

The man on the ground struggles with the vagueness of a nature-show cheetah just shot with tranquilizer. The guy in jeans barks, "Call the police!" and he and the suit each pull a phone from their pocket.

My watch says 2:02. "I just . . . I have a job interview." I cup a palm over my knee. There is only one spot of blood, but as I straighten a run zippers my thigh.

I leave the three of them dogpiled on the sidewalk and rush through the doors and onto the elevator. I punch thirteen, pushing a smile at the woman already inside. She looks away.

"Some crazy person just punched me," I say.

She raises her eyebrows. "Never know who'll run into you downtown."

We stare up at the floor numbers lighting one after another.

Seconds later, I limp through the doors of Lowen Temporary Placement. "I have an appointment with Evelyn," I say to the receptionist.

She tells me to take a seat.

I wait with both hands over my roughed knee. When my name is called, I stand and shake a smiling woman's hand.

"I'm Evelyn, come on in."

She has the kind of cigarette voice that gives me hope as she leads me to her office and gestures toward a chair.

Sitting on the other side of Evelyn's desk I set my purse and CD bag on the floor and keep hold of my resumé. "Some crazy guy on the street just punched me in the back," I say.

"Just out here?" She waves behind at her window.

"I think the police are coming for him."

"Golly, I hope so!" Her eyes settle on the run in my hose. "You're all right?"

The word *golly* has deflated my hope. "Just a little shook up. Crazy. Street guy."

She sits forward in her chair and there's a pained-but-curious expression on her face. Seems an unending moment that she looks at me that way. I hear the papers on her desk settling, the clock on her wall ticking. But that can't be, the clock is electric.

Finally she speaks. "I've got an interesting letter here." She pauses to harvest a bit of mascara from the corner of her eye. "It was faxed to me by Harriet Almond."

Harriet?

She squints at me. "Harriet Almond. From Jasper Personnel?"

Right: Harriet, from my other temp agency. My eyes are stinging. Must be this dim office after that bright sun.

Evelyn gives me a kind of smiling grimace. "I know Harriet well. We had lunch today. She told me about a young woman they had to release from their roster."

My fingernails flick against one another, loud and conspicuous. I fist my hands to shut them up.

"I guess you know where I'm going with this." She picks up a page from her desk, begins to read a letter to

Jasper Personnel from a firm where I temped two weeks earlier. I hear phrases: *Hours surfing the Internet on company time . . . when confronted by supervisor, the employee responded with a tantrum . . . used profanity . . . threw files and paperwork to the floor, broke a desk organizer . . .*

"That's not entirely accurate. It didn't break. I was researching—My mother had an artificial heart valve and a piece of it broke off. She had a stroke, massive stroke . . . My father says I'm just like her. In my heart." I uncross my legs and hold my knees together, feeling the wet ache of that one bloody spot. "She was rude. That woman. Very rude. She didn't have to—"

Evelyn lays the letter on her desk. She looks sympathetic. I am pathetic to her.

I feel an unfitting giggle in my chest and let it escape just as I glance at the clock. It's not quite 2:20 yet. Feels like 4:00.

"Do you find this situation amusing?" she asks me, with an overly kind expression.

"A little," I tell her. "Normally, I'd say I feel like I've been punched, but this doesn't feel anything like that." I jerk my purse up off the floor, along with the CD bag. I drop the resumé, and pick it back up.

"Would you like to talk about this?"

I shake my head and, just before I turn to leave, make what feels like the same sort of kindly face Evelyn just gave me.

Out front of the building, there's a different commotion now. The two heroes who held my assailant are gone and in their place is a police cruiser and two cops.

They have driven their car right up onto the broad side-walk. The red roof light turns in a slow hot wink. I hesi-tate, then move slowly their way and see the wild man lying stomach-down on the ground, his hands cuffed behind his back, his head wedged directly behind the front wheel of the car.

One cop is squatting beside his captive's head, telling him something. I stop a few feet away. Something about me must be giving off a glow of involvement because the second cop turns and approaches.

"Are you the girl he hit?"

"Yes."

He juts his chin toward the car's front tire. "Hear that, buddy?" he calls. "Here's the lady you hit! Gonna tell her you're sorry?"

I look at the woolly man on the ground; he is quiet, with just a light shuffle of his legs.

The cop, the one nearest him, speaks loudly as if to a deaf person or a foreigner. "You don't deserve to be on this earth, do you, hitting this nice girl. I should back this tire right over your head. What do you think of that?"

The matted head mumbles. His legs shuffle again.

The cop chuckles, straightens up and meanders to where I am standing by his partner. "So you're the one?"

"I'm sorry I left, I had a job interview."

He grins. "Don't *you* be sorry for god's sake. He's the one that needs to be sorry. He would be too if he had a goddamn brain in his head. You want to press charges?"

"Uh . . ." I'm wondering if the wrong answer will get

me in trouble. I can't shake the feeling that I'm in it already. "I don't think I'll do that."

"No point really," Second Cop says. "As it is they'll just ship him back to the nuthouse and he'll be out tomorrow."

First Cop nods. "Want to know why he hit you?"

I look to the car and then back at First Cop.

"He says he saw you steal that CD and he had to stop you."

I look down at my music store bag in one hand and my purse and resumé in the other and wish I had a free hand to gnaw at. "Want to see my receipt?" I smile again, wishing I could stop.

The cop looks back at Wildman. "Did you get the job?" he asks me.

"Maybe. No, actually, no."

"Wanna see if you can hit him hard enough to make yourself feel better?" he suggests.

I laugh nervously.

He doesn't. "You're not gonna see any justice out of this. Go on, go hit him."

My jaw aches from clenching and I am afraid I'll scream, so I laugh again. Second Cop laughs too.

First Cop calls toward his patrol car. "Hear that, you sorry bastard, this lady is too nice to hit you. Now I got no *choice* but to run over your head."

Wildman's cuffed hands scratch at the small of his back, trying to get to the itch just inside his old-man trousers. It's the first time I realize how young he is; he couldn't be more than twenty-five or so.

"Yeah. Yup," he says.

"'Yeah, yup'? You're ready to die, then? You'd deserve it." First Cop's voice is friendly, as though he's passing out candy to kids.

Second Cop smiles at me. "So, what'll you do for the rest of the day? Go to the beach?"

I look back at the head behind the front wheel. I am struck with the urge to cover him with my body, cling to him and confess my sins. I shrug, screaming grin still plastered on my face.

Second Cop asks, "You got a bikini in that bag of yours?" He winks.

"Dave here's a flirt. He wants to see you in a bathing suit."

I try to think of something sharp, something that would poke a hole, let the air out of the bubble we're in. I wish I were across the road for a moment to see if it looks the same from over there. No one is stopping. Nobody notices.

Second Cop glances down Pender Street. "Here comes the paddy wagon. Sure you don't want to hit him?"

The wagon pulls up onto the sidewalk too.

Biting dry skin off my lips, I say, "Okay, well, bye," in an undone voice that I despise. I back away.

The cops wave bye-bye, and tell me to take care. More men get out of the wagon.

I keep backing, drop my resumé and pick it up again. I turn and start to jog, high heels clacking like teeth up Burrard Street, past the steps of a cathedral. Stopping, I look back and up at the God-sized doors, two flights of cement steps from where I stand.

On the landing is a shaggy-haired woman in Jell-O green polyester track pants and a linty wool sweater.

"Hey," she yells, and ambles down, stopping a couple of steps above me. "Got a smoke? Gimme a smoke?" She wiggles her fingers, crooked and bony like bird's feet, as she comes a step closer. I dig in my purse.

As far as valuable objects go, there are a few dimes, some pennies and a credit card, cigarettes and a bottle of red nail polish. I step up and cram my pack of Matinees in her hand.

"Miserable," she says, and stuffs the package in her pants pocket. "Miserable, miserable."

I grab the polish next and offer it up. She snatches the bottle and twists off the top, sniffs and winces. "Miserable."

"I stole it," I blurt.

"Miserable." She clamps her teeth on the tip of her tongue, concentrating, and reaches out with the dripping crimson brush.

I know what she's going to do, so I close my eyes. A moment later, the reek of liquid enamel cuts up my nostrils as she slops the brush, cool and wet, across my lips, and calmly paints on a Cheshire cat grin.

As the brush moves away, I breathe the acrid scent into my brain as if I might get clarity.

When I open my eyes, hair is sticking to my lips, and Miserable is gone, up the block, attempting to pawn my cigarettes.

Traffic seems suddenly shrill, more shrill than my painted-on grin or the ache in my blood-pocked knee. A double-long city bus lurches to a standstill behind me and I turn as it brays over a stalled car. The bus driver flails his arms in the air, an insect at the helm of a water buffalo. He drops his hands on the wheel and something about the bus's benign huff and grunt as it waits for the car's motor to turn over is vaguely calming.

Candy From a Stranger's Mouth

I FIRST MET PETRA WHILE STANDING in the rain at the scene of a serial murder. The notorious Pickton pig farm. Though it might be described more accurately as a sheep farm, the revulsion that reporters could instill in the public with an account of women's bodies apparently hacked to pieces among *pigs* was infinitely more ghastly.

It was 2002 and I had been commissioned to cover the Pickton story by a women's magazine whose readership was considered to be more educated than that of the magazines I usually wrote for, and I was eager to take on a topic of significance. Police had descended on the farm a month before, looking for a break in the case of sixty missing prostitutes from Vancouver's Downtown Eastside, and now the Port Coquitlam farm was being bulldozed, its earth sifted painstakingly for DNA evidence.

Swampy and littered with dilapidated barns and rusted-out cars, the farm was barricaded by a tall mesh fence. Mud-splattered yellow crime scene tape encircled the place. A sign on the fence, presumably placed there by the Picktons, said: THIS PROPERTY PROTECTED BY A PIT BULL WITH AIDS. Robert "Willy" Pickton denied any knowledge of the missing women.

The neighbours, loose-lipped in the first couple of days, were now mum. Police refused to speak with any media and presumably had told locals and family members of the missing to keep quiet or risk harming the case.

Standing in the gravelly muck, hunkered under my umbrella in the February drizzle, I watched other reporters pad up and down the fence like coyotes. A woman wearing a canary yellow rain slicker trudged my way, her pants tucked into gumboots. She stopped beside me and peered out from under her hood at the bulldozers.

"Why," she wondered aloud, "would those womens come so far out to this ugly place?" Her accent was German.

"I guess he promised them a party." Glancing at what I could see of her short chic hair, I assumed she was a tourist. Germans, I have heard, are fascinated by death. Death and shit. The Pickton farm reeked of both. "They were all from the same scuzzy part of downtown."

"Scuzzy," she repeated, staring across the sludge-covered ground to the nearest barn.

Mutually flattened by the rain and misery, we would meet later that day in Vancouver's glass-encrusted, genteel downtown core to have a drink at Petra's hotel.

Sitting by the fireplace in the Bacchus lounge, with its cherry wood panelling and plush burgundy velvet, she said, "Tourist brochures don't say 'Dead prostitutes are fed to pigs,'" by way of explaining her presence in Vancouver. "I cover dark travel."

Petra had a monthly column in a German publication that sounded like a cross between true crime and a travel magazine. Her job was to expose the underbelly of popular vacation spots. Petra's aim for next month's issue was to bring her readers the unspeakable darkness that lay in Vancouver too.

"Port Coquitlam is not Vancouver though," I said.

"The missing womens are from Vancouver. Nobody cared about these ones. And now the world is watching."

I looked off to the bar where lawyers and finance sorts loitered, laughing animatedly as they shmoozed.

"I don't think I can stand this." I stared into my glass. "I'm starting to think I'm better suited to write about what it means if your lipstick and shoes match."

She laughed: a staccato chortle full of deep throaty Ks and bits of tinsel.

Old enough to have given birth at thirty-two and have a grown son to show for it, she did not take herself too seriously. Her laughter knocked away my embarrassment. Petra's skin was smooth and elastic and that, along with hands that looked as though they belonged to an eighteen-year-old, a bobbed nose and starry brown eyes, gave her a childlike quality. But it was clear there was nothing naive about her. Her mother had been in and out of mental institutions and had killed herself when

Petra was twenty. The suicide note stated that having a daughter had been her mother's worst mistake. She demanded that all personal effects go to Petra's brother. Petra never married, and she raised her son on her own.

She had recently taken a married lover who spoiled her with adoration and appeared interested in her every word—why would she want a full-time man?

"Listen," Petra said suddenly, after a third round of drinks and far too much confession on both our parts. "I don't want to make this horrible pig man story either. I think I am tired of always these cynical worlds around me. Someone else can write it." She sipped a quick breath.

"Just like that. You're chucking your column?"

"Ya." She looked at me, her mouth upturned but set. "I don't feel happy to make it."

I must have looked incredulous.

"This is how I do things. I make up my mind and I do it—But listen, we can't be cruel to the editors, so I propose we make this last story together." She raised her glass. "Do you say yes to this?"

Petra felt deeply familiar to me, as I suppose a person does when she fears or loves in a way that is similar to the way you do.

I picked up my drink. "Yes."

Years later, when Petra called me in Vancouver, all I had in front of me was a deadline for a puff piece in a fashion magazine. It was summer and yet the drizzle outside continued unabated. From the pap of my employment to the sog of the city, I was beginning to question the consequence of my existence.

"I'm coming to your side of the Atlantic," Petra said. "My lover and I, we are going to stay in this suite at the Waldorf for two weeks. Why don't you get out of that rain and come see me?"

This article I'd agreed to write was a companion piece to a recent sex survey the magazine was publishing. The editor had just faxed me the survey questions, suggesting I might use one as a jumping-off point. I had been considering: *Under what circumstances would you be most likely to have an affair?*

When Petra first told me of her affair years ago, I thought I saw a brimming affection in her. Though she had never used the word *love* and said she had no desire for Andrew to leave his wife. The European affair, I inferred, was likely based more on pragmatism than on romance.

"You're still with him, huh?"

"Ya. We've been together longer than most people's marriages."

Listening to Petra on the phone now, I felt a longing to escape from my own world. I checked online as we spoke and found a cheap, last-minute flight. "You talked me into it," I said.

"Really? This is wonderful!" she exclaimed. Feeling wanted made me positively effervescent.

When I hung up, I called Felicia, a friend who lived in Greenwich Village, to see if her couch was available.

I met up with Andrew and Petra on Lafayette Street in the East Village, not far from where I was staying. They had reservations in a pricey restaurant that had seen its day a couple of decades ago and was now a bit of a kitschy hangout for twenty-somethings. Full of deep, thudding beats, horns and synthesizers, the music was turned up to a level that made it impossible to hear others speak unless you were all bent far into the centre of your table.

Two young women at the next table, Hepburn thin in their sleek dark dresses, bobbed their elegantly made-up heads as they glanced mutely around the room. Their men leaned in to each other, mouths open wide to get their big loud words into each other's ears, oblivious to the women in their company. I resented them for it.

My gaze turned back to Petra and Andrew, but because it was so hard to hear any conversation we tried to make, I did more observing than normal. Though perhaps that's a lie. I have been accused, in the past, of sitting back, busily thinking up pithy descriptors that I might later use in an article. To some people this is the behaviour of a scavenger. Others like to have a witness on hand—it gives them a feeling of importance and security. Besides, in a way I *was* working.

I searched her face that night, looking for joy, an irrepressible spark of glee that she was in New York City with a man who was married to someone else.

But her smiles conveyed more diplomacy than pleasure. I scanned the lover too, hoping to catch sight of—I don't know what—some keening sense of inevitability? Some suggestion of a trapped man who, though dutifully maintaining his role back home as husband and father, was tormented by the fact that his one great love was actually here, hiding out with him in the extreme public of Manhattan.

They did not hold hands; I saw no surreptitious brushing of fingers or feet. I saw no sign of their sultry need for each other. He seemed merely cordial.

Andrew had what was, to my ear, an unusual accent for a German. "My mother was a Londoner, you see. I spoke English at home first, and then, of course, German," he explained. "I consider English my mother tongue."

He seemed proud of that fact. His father spoke Swiss German, which, he said, had no formal grammatical rules and was not even a written language. "Only standard German is written," he said.

My eyes drifted down his starched shirt to his manicured fingernails.

"And you are from Vancouver," he confirmed. "What a coincidence." It turned out his wife had Canadian citizenship as well as German—her mother lived in Vancouver. "My wife is also perfectly bilingual."

I didn't know where to look for a moment. *My wife.*

Then he mentioned that his wife had just taken their two children to Vancouver. "They are there right now."

My gaze moved to Petra, who casually sipped a martini, her expression inscrutable in the dim light.

I ordered another drink, deciding that I too would be impervious.

"Lila, my honey," she said suddenly, "I have a proposal for you. Andrew and I, we will be making a trip the day after tomorrow and I am thinking it would be very nice for you to stay in our suite while we are gone."

I stared and leaned in trying to hear better. "Did you just say that you're leaving town?"

"Ya. It's unexpected. And the suite will be empty for two days. Do you like to?"

I was disappointed and a little stunned. On the other hand, when would I ever get a chance to stay at the Waldorf again?

After dinner, the three of us went to The Campbell Apartment, a bar off the west balcony of Grand Central Station. The big room, once a financier's private office, apparently looked just as it had in the '30s and '40s, like a room in a palace, furnished with Italian tables and chairs, a Persian rug on the floor, others on the walls, flowered vases, and a massive Florentine desk on which financier John Campbell once conducted his affairs.

When we arrived at the entrance, Ella Fitzgerald's "I Got It Bad (and That Ain't Good)" smoothed into our ears. The hostess gave us a blandly welcoming smile, her caramel-coloured mosquito-arms poking out of the capped sleeves of a blue jersey dress that advertised small hollows beside each hip and the pointy nubs of her shoulder bones. Her hair slicked back into the tight chignon of a ballet dancer, she breezily told Andrew his footwear would not be allowed into the establishment.

"These are Armani," he said, lifting one sporty leather shoe as though the fine craftsmanship might change her mind.

"We don't allow running shoes of any kind."

"Let's go," Petra said. "We don't need to be here."

"No." Andrew adjusted his shoulders. "You ladies get a table. I shall go back to the hotel and change. I won't be long, it's close."

A career problem-solver, Andrew would not engage in any further debate, and he left.

"He likes rules," Petra said after we had sat quietly a few moments. She gazed around the room, at the ceiling and eventually at me. "I am tiring of New York. It closes in and makes me suffocated."

Andrew reappeared in only a few minutes, so few that I was startled. He sat down with a hearty hello as though to make clear that an insect in blue jersey could not possibly dampen his mood.

"Do you live in the centre of Vancouver?" he asked as another round of drinks hit the table. "My children love Stanley Park. My wife took them in a horse-drawn carriage through the park. Have you done that?"

"No." I glanced down at the gloss of the brown oxfords on his feet now.

"*I* was in a horse carriage once. For New Year's Eve," Petra announced, her grin suddenly broad. "In Zurich! I was with Heinrich Vanderhoven. He's—he's a bit crazy." Her tone was slightly malignant, but her pronunciation of *kwazy* mitigated my sense of peril.

"We came very late to a nightclub and he was wearing

blue jeans and a tuxedo jacket. At this club it is very chic and you cannot ever wear blue jeans. But he was *Heinrich Vanderhoven!*"

Andrew nodded, expressionless.

Repetition of the man's full name seemed to be an important feature of the story. "Who's Heinrich Vanderhoven?" I asked.

"He owned half the magazines in Europe. He once owned the magazine I write for now, but he sold everything and went to make a meditation by the sea in California." Her shoulders bounced with laughter as she tilted forward. I wasn't sure if the memory of Heinrich Vanderhoven's denim-clad self was what tickled her so much or if it was the thought of him sitting hours on end, cross-legged, *ohm*-ing in the sand.

I tried to understand the nuance of the picture she painted. "He was your boss?"

"No." Her eyes glittered. "He was my *lover.*"

The word *sultry* kept ringing in my ears the next day as I tramped up Park Avenue, pulling my suitcase. July in New York can be so oppressively hot and damp that the word *sultry* should never be used to describe it. *Sultry* implies a sensuality, an underlying lust that one can barely contain, when in reality the stifling mug of it renders the thought of another body lying sticky against one's own nauseating. Or at least that's what occurred to me as I caught sight of a billboard featuring some oversexed nymphet hawking brassieres. Breathing the soupy air into my lungs, I wondered if I might be coming down with something or if I was fumbling toward an early menopause.

I negotiated my suitcase through the hotel's revolving doors. At the top of the marble stairs, I looked from a crystal chandelier the size of a Volkswagon to the art deco floor mosaic, plucked my shirt away from my sticky flesh and felt immediately gauche for sweating. This was, after all, the Waldorf. As I wheeled my luggage down the expansive corridor, my eyes darted wall to wall, from paintings and sculptures to glass-encased dresses.

In the main lobby, I sighed the relief of the air-conditioned. I had been sleeping on Felicia's sofa the last two nights and imagined now that those around me could tell how my last forty-eight hours had been just by looking, as though my skin were dented with the pattern of couch upholstery and the feet of the Holstein-coloured cat who had meandered up and down the length of me from midnight till dawn, enjoying the breeze of the nearby fan that seemed to hit my own skin only if I sat up.

I brushed the ghost of a cat hair from my nose and took in the other patrons: T-shirts, ball caps and designer jeans with deliberate and calculated fading. It appeared the wealthy had become an uncouth lot.

A long bank of black and gold marble reception desks was set into what I figured was a mahogany wall. Was I meant to feel pampered or intimidated as I looked up past the two-ton gold clock to the gold tiles overhead?

My entire immediate family, both parents, my brother and me, could be stacked and still not reach the ceiling. If any of us still spoke to one another.

Glancing at my luggage, I wondered if it looked cheap to the educated eye. An editor once complimented the skirt I wore, remarking that I had expensive taste. I was compelled to tell her that my skirt had cost twelve dollars at a chain store. Her mouth spread into open-mouthed delight, but the pleasure in her eyes dimmed and I regretted having set her straight.

I lifted the receiver of the house phone and asked to be put through to Andrew Kinderhaus.

Andrew answered with his very British "Yes, hello." He sounded calmer. I had called earlier, just before I left Felicia's place, and he had been breathless when he picked up the phone. I imagined him taking calls compulsively, listening to his wife tell him all about Vancouver while he was in the midst of a New York sex act. One that would leave a free hand.

"It's Lila," I said now. "I'm in the lobby." Anxiety started to rise in my chest like heartburn. I felt complicit in a way I hadn't expected.

A couple days after Petra had arrived in New York, she left me a playfully frustrated message. "Ya, Lila, this is Petra and I would like for you to call me at the Waldorf, but my lover is out and I cannot answer because I am in here with a married man. Shit." Her delivery tickled me— her *V*s in place of *W*s, her *zis*'s and *zat*'s—and the way she said what she'd said all in one breath: *Marriedmanshit*.

I turned to see them coming through the lobby

toward me. Walking past a tall urn that held a massive bouquet of fresh flowers, Petra looked perfectly at home amidst the grandeur.

I hugged her. Andrew shook my hand.

"So!" He clapped his hands. "Shall we register you?"

Petra held my suitcase while her lover and I went to the front desk.

The magazine's sex survey wondered if a woman might need an excuse to cheat in a way a man would not. Down the list was: *Who do you think is more faithful by nature?*

"So the two of you will be going to Maine?"

"Connecticut for me," he corrected. "And New Jersey for Petra."

"Right." I nodded as though I'd known all along that Petra and her lover were taking separate vacations from their vacation. "Where in Connecticut?"

He glanced at the desk clerk. "Near Massachusetts."

The clerk excused herself to program a key.

"Can I receive calls?"

"Yes," he said firmly. "No one will call me here this weekend."

The clerk handed me the new plastic key. We rejoined Petra and headed to the elevator bank.

"This is really so kind of you," I said, as Andrew pressed the call button. The words clanged falsely in my mouth even though I meant them.

Petra smiled.

"No," he responded, "we thank *you*. For looking after our suite."

Inside the elevator, I glanced at the beige plastic card in my hand, *The Waldorf-Astoria* stamped in cursive script on one side. "I would have thought the Waldorf would have nice old-fashioned keys," I mused aloud as we rose up the shaft.

Andrew's smile was patient. "The hotel would have to change the locks each time a person left."

"I guess that's true."

"It *is* true," he stated. "This clientele needs to have computerized locks."

Petra grinned as if this were all part of the Waldorf's never-ending capacity to delight.

Standing at the door of room 2320, she dipped the slice of plastic into the lock's slot, igniting a green light and setting off a soft click as the door unlocked. I watched her carefully as though the task were complicated and mystical.

Andrew suggested that Petra give me a tour of the suite while he finished packing.

She strolled with me past Andrew's walk-in closet to his bathroom—"He only has a shower; I like a bathtub"—and then into a living area. There was a plump sofa and coffee table, which faced an armoire that held a large television and stereo. Beside the armoire was an oddly suburban choice: a push-button fireplace.

An office centre with each of their laptops sat against the far wall. A Waldorf catalogue lay on an end table. Petra picked it up. "Look in here." She fanned it open. "You can order the Waldorf sheets and the Waldorf bed and take them home with you."

"But I won't have the Waldorf room service."

"Ya." She slapped it down. "That's a problem."

Off the bedroom was Petra's walk-in closet and her bathroom with what she pointed out was her very deep marble tub. "I could drown in that bath," she said, and then laughed her throaty, *K*-smattered laugh.

A king-sized bed stood with two of its four posts against the bedroom's cream and moss striped wallpaper. The mattress was topped with a similarly striped duvet cover.

"You're going to New Jersey." I gazed out the window at the monstrosity of New York City. Directly across from us was a dismal-grey building, big enough to house a town full of people.

"Ya." She sat on the bed. "Princeton. A friend of mine, she's teaching there now, and since Andrew has decided to go . . ."

I turned and she looked up from her lap.

"Andrew has friends in Connecticut, I have a friend in Princeton, and so we go separate for the weekend."

Andrew stepped into the room. I sat down on the bed near Petra. The two of us glanced at him, then at each other and we both laughed for some reason.

He looked at us, something close to worry in the tug of his brows. "What is so funny?"

Petra shrugged. "We are pleased with ourselves."

She laughed again and I wished she weren't about to leave town. There was something in the air now that relaxed us. Perhaps the sight of Andrew's vulnerability.

He took one thorough breath through his nose and smiled back at us. "Petra likes to order breakfast in bed and I think you would like that too. So go ahead and sign it to the room."

"Ya, you should!" Petra exclaimed. "Yesterday I felt sick and I lied in the bed all day long and had service. I love it."

She'd been sick. Perhaps hungover. It was a small relief to know that. I had been a little worried when I didn't hear from her the day after we'd all gone for dinner, concerned that perhaps I'd annoyed her somehow.

"Are you going to the train station together?" I asked them.

"No." Andrew flipped his wrist for the time. "I have to get to Grand Central and Petra must get to Penn Station."

"I thought we could have lunch before I leave," Petra said, looking at me.

Andrew grabbed his jacket off the nearby chair. "If you like Japanese, you should go downstairs. It is said to be one of the finest restaurants in the city. Sign it to the room."

"Wonderful!" Petra said and stood. "It's too bad you cannot join us." She walked to him, put her hands flat against his lapels and gazed up into his eyes.

He gave her a polite peck. "I will see you Sunday."

Downstairs we stepped into the sudden cool of the over-air-conditioned restaurant and followed the stiff kimono of the hostess, her feet mincing on wooden shoes.

"It's *fun* to be spoiled," I burbled, deciding to stop the analysis for once.

"Sometimes." Petra paused until the hostess was gone. "Other times I feel like a prostitute." She looked at me for a response. "I'm sorry. Does this sound terrible of me?"

I shook my head.

"He's an educated man," she continued. "He knows how to behave. But these things . . . these manners are only manners. They are not tenderness and they are not love."

We paused again as the waitress shuffled close, placed menus in front of us and then poured green tea before she bowed and disappeared.

Petra set her fingertips on the teacup and repeated, "They are not love."

"No."

"He's wonderful in bed, but this is not tenderness either. His shoes are always shined and I am like his shoes."

I told her that Felicia had asked me what Petra's man was like. Was he handsome? Kind? "Does he take her hand?" Felicia had asked longingly. "Does he look at her adoringly?" Felicia hungers after the romance of others. She wants to believe.

Did he look at her adoringly? Andrew opened doors, he stood when a woman approached the table, walked on the outside of the sidewalk and always picked up the cheque. Andrew took care. I didn't know if he was kind. And I hadn't known how to describe his looks either. Pleasant enough. He was tall-ish, grey-ish, stoic. I doubted I would recognize him in the street were we to pass each other.

"He doesn't seem to let his emotions get out of control," I told Petra finally.

Petra set her elbows on the table. "You noticed this too. He does not act like a lover. Not any more. Something has changed."

My gaze flicked to the Japanese screens nearby. Red-crowned cranes stood on fragile legs, their long dark throats bared to the world. I looked back at Petra.

"I thought maybe I am being critical, but it's true," she said. "You have seen it."

"I figured it was his doctor side. Clinical."

She rolled her eyes. "You asked him about his medicine at the restaurant. He said to me later that I should be careful in lying to my friends or I would get myself in trouble. 'It is not my trouble,' I said to him. 'It is you who gets in trouble.'"

The other night, when Petra had been away from the table I'd tried to make small talk with Andrew. "What sort of medicine do you practise?"

Confusion crossed his eyes. Then he said, "I don't actually have a degree in medicine. You could say I am a corporate therapist."

"He is a lawyer," Petra told me now. "I wanted to protect him. He is very famous in Germany because he represents many magazines. American businesses sometimes threatened to sue over my dark travel articles. This is how we met."

She didn't apologize for her dishonesty and I was slightly impressed by that.

"Andrew represented Heinrich Vanderhoven's business. Of course Heinrich Vanderhoven sold everything and he does not know that Andrew and I are now together in this way. Nobody in Germany knows this. I can be honest with you. You're not in that world."

After Petra had gone, I sat on the bed and stared into space. Even twenty-three floors up, you could still hear the impatient ranting of the city. It was only three in the afternoon and I wondered what I would do with myself now.

I gazed at the crown moulding, at the draperies and the armoire, and tried to feel decadent and special. Lying back, I kicked the mules off my feet, wiggled my toes at the ceiling and noticed the city's dirt dusted over them in broad stripes.

I had suggested to Felicia that we might go swimming, so I riffled through the guest services menu before phoning the front desk.

"No, Mrs. Kinderhaus. There is no swimming pool, but we do have a large fitness centre with spa facilities on the nineteenth floor."

I called Felicia's apartment, got her voice mail, and left a message lamenting the lack of a pool. The fact there was no pool made me oddly forlorn. I stood at the window and watched life moving so far below.

I took the subway down to Broadway and Astor Place, wandered along the baking concrete through the sweating crowds and choked traffic, hoping the heat might cook the blue feeling from my guts.

Petra's voice tripped around in my head. "Clinical," she had said. "This is a good word for him. He is not a doctor, but he is clinical. He does not look at me the way he once did. I asked him if he had another mistress, and he said, 'I don't have time for that. Between my work and my family and you, I don't have time for myself any more.'"

Along the sidewalks of New York that summer, women flip-flopped around with Chinese net slippers on their feet. Women of all shapes and sizes wore them with skirts, shorts or jeans. The slippers came in peacock, canary, silver—any shade you could think of—and were adorned with coloured beads and tinselly flowers. I ducked into a shop where stacks of them were displayed in the windows, and picked gold ones for myself. Since they were only $2.99 a shot, I grabbed a few pairs for the friends who had questioned why I would take off on a four-day trip to New York when I had debt and a pending deadline. People forgive you your foibles, I reasoned, when you can prove you were thinking of them all the while.

On the way back to the hotel, I picked up a deli sandwich and a couple of bottles of wine, one for myself and one a little more impressive.

Dinner in hand, I stood on the street outside the liquor store, turning one way and then the other. Finally

I put down my purchases to consult the map again.

"Are you lost?" A man stood near, his head tipped to peer at my face.

"I need the 6 train."

Attractive in a lived-in, well-fed sort of way, he looked at my map and never quite in my eyes and it hit me how much I longed for eye contact. From anyone. I couldn't help but look for his ring finger. *Who do you think is more faithful by nature?*

"You walked right in the wrong direction. Here, I'll show you."

I followed, glancing at the silver hairs woven into his temples as he walked me back in the direction from which I'd come. He asked where I was from.

"A Canadian! My sister-in-law is from Toronto," he said.

"Canadians are the new Golden retriever."

"Ha ha," he said, "that's funny."

His laughter sent a soft flutter through my lungs. Then he stopped and pointed out the direction of the station. I stared at his back as he walked away.

"Before I came here, I was writing an article about a vineyard, a nice place in the Italian countryside. I invited Andrew and he said he does not like the countryside. He cannot *stand* it and he prefers to see me when I come to New York City after. Now where does he go? The country. Rural Connecticut. For *two days*."

I thought of Petra's words, back at the Waldorf, up to my nose in bathwater.

I could drown in that bath.

Petra spoke of a text message Andrew had received from the former nanny of his children. The babysitter, as Petra had called her, now lived in Massachusetts. He messaged her for longer than usual and, according to Petra, he was nervous. He announced that he would get together with the girl for lunch one day. Petra suggested she might join them, but Andrew changed the subject.

"Perhaps he sees the babysitter in Connecticut," Petra mused.

I had envisioned the babysitter as a seventeen-year-old. But this one was thirty.

"And why must he always talk about his wife? Why do I need to know about these things, what he buys his children at FAO Schwartz. I don't *care.*"

As I listened to Petra, a large dollop of wasabi charged my sinuses, piercing my brain with euphoric pain. I wondered briefly if there was a masochistic element to all great food and sex. I asked her if she had ever seen the film *The Ice Storm*, the scene with Sigourney Weaver and Kevin Kline in bed after some extramarital rummaging. Klein launches into a monologue about work and golf. "You're boring me," Weaver interrupts. "I *have* a husband."

"Tell him," I suggested to Petra, *"you're boring me. I'm not interested in your little Weiner rats."*

Her face lit up and she hooted. "Weiner rats! Ya!"

Cringing later at how like the smell of blood Petra's

laughter had been, how it had sharpened my teeth, I slipped under the water of the Waldorf tub. I emptied my lungs, shook the water through my hair, and sank until my head tapped the bottom of an old memory.

My mother had just hollered again for me to get out of the bathtub. She had gone back to work part time and, I guess, as low man on the totem at her job she must have felt there was no reprieve. Lately every time she wiped a counter or picked clothing up off the floor, she sounded more exasperated. "Here she comes again, Queen of the *Shit* Jobs," she'd say.

The phone rang. I could hear it through the bottom of the tub, imagining it to be whale song. Like Jacques Cousteau I swam, inspecting the floor of the ocean, wagging my head and watching my hair wave like seaweed in the water, listening to my mother's garbled voice. Seconds later she stood over the bathtub, calling down through the fathoms. I shot up, gasping.

"Lila. Out. Now. Your father's idiot battery is dead again. I have to go pick him up and I want you ready for bed."

"Is Clay my babysitter?" I was six years old. Clay was in grade four.

"I'll be back as fast as I can." She scrubbed a towel over my head and body, then wrapped it around, secured it with a tucked corner under my armpit, and scooted me into the hall. "Clayton, turn that down."

Clay was in my parents' room watching TV.

"Clayton! How many times do I have to say it?" she yelled over the din. "I have to get your father. Make sure she goes to bed."

The TV held his gaze.

"Put your *pyjamas* on!" she called over her shoulder as she rushed away.

I stood, looking in at Clay who sprawled like a prince on the big bed.

"Clayton!"

The volume lowered.

"I'll be back as soon as I can." She stalked downstairs.

I trotted into the bedroom and climbed up on the bed with Clay, rested my head on his chest while he watched men squeal their cars around the corners of grey city streets, punch and shoot one another.

The dishwasher's hiss began downstairs. We heard the sound of my mother's shoes rushing in the hall, followed by the groan of the clothes dryer, metal bits clacking inside its steel belly, and then, finally, the back door slammed.

Clay turned the TV up to where appliance noise was drowned to nothing. I recall closing my eyes a while, the shooting and screech of tires against asphalt blaring through the room, and then suddenly nothing but the mild plink of piano keys. I opened my eyes to a screen full of lips. One of the shooters from earlier was now with a pretty woman and they were sucking on each other's mouths with altogether too much spit. It seemed to go on forever.

"Dad's got a magazine on his side. In the cupboard thingy," Clay said suddenly.

I was silent a moment trying to ascertain his point. Sometimes there was little left for me to do but use world-weary sarcasm. "So? Big whoop."

"So, you should see where they kiss each other in there."

I gawped up at him.

"There's girls kissing each other's kitties."

"Shut up. They are not."

"I'm not showing you, you'll just blab and we'll both get it. Me worse."

"I'm not a blabber, stupid. Show me."

Soon a glossy magazine with the words *Urban Swinger* across the cover came out of my father's bedside cabinet. Clay turned the pages between thumb and finger with an anxious delicacy that made it seem all the more exotic and mysterious. These were *pictorials*, pictures with a sentence under each that told a larger story: *Jack and Amy meet Nadia.*

I gasped. "Ew! That's where they pee out of!"

Amy and Jack taste Nadia. Nadia pleasures Amy, my brother read. The word *pleasure* used as a verb was almost as strange as what they were doing: Amy's tongue between Nadia's legs; Jack's tongue between Amy's legs.

The skin of Amy was cake-white, the tongue poking toward her licorice red.

I sat cross-legged in my drooping towel, astonished. "It's like ice cream," I said. I meant the way the tongues reached, trying to get a lick of someone else's treat. "Why are they doing that?"

Clay shrugged.

In the last picture, Amy appeared to be in some sort of polite anguish, her back arched.

"Ow—no! Does it hurt?"

Clay said that if he were to do to me what Nadia did to Amy it wouldn't hurt, which brought on a spasm of giggles.

This is how I remember it: my concern about pain, Clay's insistence that it could not possibly hurt. The pictures in the magazine, the two of us debating, and the nervous laughter—they were, after all, showing the bits we were supposed to cover up. Downstairs on our refrigerator door was an old picture of us in the bath together, me a toddler, Clay in first grade, bunches of thick bubbles bearding our faces. It had been made quite clear to us that we were too old to have baths together now. Too old.

I don't know how much time had passed, but on television the men were shooting each other again. Clay put his head between my legs and kissed me square on the kitty. He stuck out his tongue and I laughed and wriggled, hands over my eyes—until we heard our mother scream.

All in a rush, there were hands and arms and smacking, Clay's hair in my father's veined hand, my brother dragged off the bed crying, my own squeals, and my mother's screeching: "What is *wrong* with you?" The volume was of the sort that generally only happened if one of us had done something so life-threateningly stupid that neither parent could think what to do but introduce a bigger, louder, more immediate threat. The cacophonic pitch of this, though, was beyond the most desperate we'd ever heard.

My mother yanked me to my feet, screaming over the TV as it railed and fired and honked and roared. "I told you to put your pyjamas on."

"Clay did it," I sobbed, though I didn't know what he had done exactly, if we could get sick from it, end up in the hospital.

She slapped the towel back around me and then rushed to Clay's rising cries. I followed her into the hall and watched as my father batted Clay with both hands. I said nothing in his defence. I caught a last look at my brother's tear-streaked face, his red eyes and the hatred in them, before both our bedroom doors were closed behind us.

When it was finally quiet that night—the television squelched, voices silent—the air ached with its own bruising. We two were never left alone in the house again. They sent Clay to a psychiatrist.

I hugged a towel and stared in the bathroom mirror. Pulling on the hotel robe, I wandered into the bedroom and sat down on the bed to flip through the Waldorf catalogue. I was wearing the "Plush White Terry Robe" pictured. I straightened my spine, raised my chin, attempting the genteel bearing the copy mentioned. This hotel was one big commercial for itself. How could we feel the occasion was rare or exceptional when everything was so haveable?

I unwrapped my sandwich and flipped to a description of the bedding on which I reclined: *100% Egyptian cotton. These heirloom-quality linens . . .* A chunk of turkey and mustard hit the duvet. I rushed for a wet face cloth.

After the last bite, I called Vancouver. His voice mail answered.

Once the *beep* had sounded, I was suddenly tongue-tied. Mashing the receiver to my head, I said, "Hey, Clay. You'll never guess where I am: The Waldorf! In New York!" A nervous titter escaped and I wondered what had possessed me to call my brother. Clay took a special pleasure in his disgust for each member of his family. In his first year of graphic design school he began referring to us all as *hidebound plebs*.

"So . . . I haven't talked to you in a while. Thought maybe it'd be good to, uh, catch up." My eyes began to sting. "I miss you." Out the lips before it could be caught.

I put the phone down and turned to the muted TV. On screen was a contortionist, her back bent, legs crooked up and over her head, through her arms. Though she was twisted into a position that appeared more like affliction than skill, her face was serene.

The next morning a man who looked as though he'd been working here since the hotel opened its doors in

1931 wheeled in my breakfast. His hands all vein and bone, he set the cart at the foot of the bed and handed me the bill.

He offered it, you should take it, Petra had said over lunch when I asked if she thought Andrew had meant his breakfast invitation. I tugged my bathrobe tighter and looked into the faded blue eyes of the waiter. His mouth twitched and he stared at the floor. Tucking hair behind my ear, I stared at the figures, the cost of the eggs, the juice; I wondered what to tip a man who had probably seen so much he'd rather pluck out his eyes than see any more.

I scribbled down what a guilty man might tip and signed my name.

All the dishes were covered in silver domes, the grapefruit juice set in a silver decanter filled with crushed ice. Before opening the serviette, I rooted for my camera, put it on the windowsill and set the timer. A couple of flashes later I had proof that I once had breakfast in bed at the Waldorf. I examined the digital display, myself in the Plush White Terry Robe, holding up a slice of bacon, perched behind a table that glistened silver. I looked happy.

I decided my day should be spent in the presence of beauty. Setting off in my new gold slippers, I headed over to the Metropolitan Museum and slipped into the middle of a small tour as it snaked its way into the Tiffany section. I hung back as the docent lectured her group on the intent of Tiffany, the way he had weaseled his way around the secular use of stained glass and the potential outrage of the Church. As we trailed her to the Temple of Dendur in the Egyptian section, the docent spoke of the generous patronage of Jacqueline Kennedy Onassis. I recalled a story of Jackie finding a woman's pink panties in her pillowcase when married to John Kennedy. She is purported to have turned to her husband and said, "Would you find out who these belong to, because they are not my size." Infidels and infidelity.

My mother stepped up her hours and went to work full time the day I started junior high. Hospital Administration was what she did but I never knew exactly what that entailed. People answered to her though. I imagined that would be a relief: someone else could do the shit jobs around our place. But there was the unspoken issue of Clay and me being left alone that had to be addressed.

My mother found our new sitter at the hospital doing volunteer work. Clarita showed up at the house one Saturday morning toward the end of summer vacation. My mother toured her around, explaining what her duties would be.

I sat at the table eating cereal as my brother staggered into the kitchen on cue, barefoot in his pyjama bottoms and a T-shirt, bleary-eyed.

"Say hello to Clarita," my mother directed him. "Clarita, you're unlikely to see Clayton, he has so many extracurriculars on the go."

He grunted into the fridge and then tipped the open carton of orange juice toward his mouth. As he lowered it, he turned and stared blank-faced at Clarita.

Coming from a long line of tall thin WASPs, my mother may not have considered that a short, plump Mexican girl might be an object of desire. I could almost hear my brother's erection as he gazed into the new maid/babysitter's vulpine eyes. Her dark hair hung like heavy curtains opening to the main attraction: a caramel-skinned, full-lipped, Latina matinee. He left the room immediately.

Clay started coming home after school. He loitered around the kitchen, putting things in the dishwater, wiping counters. Meanwhile Clarita and I talked over grilled cheese sandwiches and I became smitten with the fact that someone in the house met my gaze as we spoke. She'd gone to a private American school in Mexico City. I loved the way she said "film," never "movie," "literature," instead of "books." Clarita was ferociously sophisticated.

Eventually Clay sat down and joined in the kitchen talk, staring like a snake at a flute when she spoke.

"English, Spanish, French *and* German," he repeated, astounded, one afternoon. "Man, I can barely speak English."

"Knowing it's half the battle." I didn't so much as glance his way.

"You're a smart guy." Clarita's fingertips tapped Clay's. "We learn best when we're young. Look at Lila, she's only twelve, her mind is gymnastic." She fanned her thick eyelashes toward me. "You are a watcher too," she told me. "You find the clues in body language. You would be a good detective."

A far cry from what I'd heard in the past. "You were born with your eyes closed and they stayed that way," my mother said once. She claimed that I would not open my eyes or hands for days after my birth.

Clay snickered. Clarita did not. He suddenly stared at me in a way that shut my mouth. It seemed as if he hadn't seen me in years, and I felt a strange panic that he would look away. The front door slammed and we all turned to see my father come into the kitchen.

He was home early for the first time in months. It was the first he set eyes on Clarita. He insisted she stay for dinner; we would order in.

That night Dad lobbed questions at Clarita and we discovered that her father had been a politician in Mexico. A scandal of the sort she didn't want to discuss over pizza had driven them north to Vancouver two years earlier. Her parents would go back when things calmed down. She wasn't sure she would go with them.

The room was tense with my father in it. Clay was tense.

My father's eyes followed Clay's glance to Clarita's fidgeting hands. I could see it plainly, as though the future were driving in fast down a long flat road, but I did not want to be a witness. I did not want my brother's gaze to slip away, to take on that old battered look again, the look of a boy who knew he was alone in this world.

The air had become lighter this past year. We could abide each other again. Every movie is the same though: eventually, the kissing stops and the men start shooting. I laugh and wriggle until somebody screams.

I came back to the hotel suite agitated by crowds, the constant sense of a different stranger dogging my heels. The message light on the phone flashed. I hesitated, then picked up the receiver. One new message: Felicia. She was sick, she said. I was welcome to come over, but she'd be lousy company.

"Lousy, lousy, we're all lousy," I muttered, and erased the message. The next one was in a woman's German tongue and I listened a few seconds as though I understood and then set the receiver down. Fidgety sparks scattered through my lungs and belly. I poured from last night's wine, got up and wandered around the suite.

Opening the door to Andrew's walk-in, I looked at the suits, the shirts, all hung neatly. I stared, hunting for a flash of truth. Reaching into the nearest jacket pocket, I felt a slippery square sleeve of plastic, condom-sized—but it was only an empty vitamin packet. I backed out and shut the door.

Television on, I crawled into bed just as some news from home came on screen. "Canada's most notorious murder investigation has yielded seven additional charges against alleged serial killer Robert William Pickton, bringing the total number to twenty-nine." In Vancouver the story would have been milked far longer; the screen would have filled with what looked like mug shots of lonesome-eyed, rough-skinned women. The anchor would have reminded us that most of the victims were drug-addicted prostitutes. But in America, he just moved on.

My mind flashed to Petra sipping sake yesterday afternoon. "You know how I make up my mind: fast. I will call and tell Andrew I am done. And this way it ruins his weekend with the babysitter."

I woke to the ringing phone. On the television, sitcom actors gesticulated wildly to the tune of canned laughter. I reached for the receiver.

Groggy, at first I thought it was my father on the line. It wouldn't be him though. It wasn't his resentment that I kept trying to appease. It wasn't his fury that tarred my dreams.

"Clay? What time is it?"

"Noon. What do you want?"

It was 3 a.m. in New York: midnight in Vancouver. I guessed that was "noon" bourbon time. The contempt in his voice made my chest pound.

"Why are you at the Waldorf?"

I burrowed into my pillow as I struggled for the words to extricate myself. Perhaps I had called him as one would a priest: I wanted absolution. "My friend and her, uh—*her lovah*—have a suite here for two weeks. They went away for the weekend."

"Lover? Is he *married?*" His voice had a wandering acid quality, nasty and sloppy at once. "Sure he is. You have no boundaries. This whole—This sleeping with someone else's husband, it's like eating candy from a stranger's mouth." His voice trailed. "The Pickton thing is on the news again. More of 'em. More and more. They just couldn't stay home, could they."

Two years ago, we had sat over a strained Christmas dinner in our mother's house. Dad was living in an apartment in West Vancouver and he preferred to spend holidays with his girlfriend. Over turkey that night, Clayton maintained that he had dated one of the women whose body parts had been found.

My mother shut her eyes. My jaw slackened in disbelief that he might actually try to shove *this* under our nails now.

It was Clayton, of course, who had caught our father with Clarita. His rage was explosive: full of thrown punches and screeching tires. Never mind the hell-fury of a woman scorned, it was Clay who smashed out the windows of our father's car and it was Clay who struck Clarita. There was talk of charges; money passed hands. In the end, my mother was left to be Queen of the Shit Jobs once again.

Clay had never dated a down-and-out drug addict. I was sure of it. My brother's taste tended toward the daughters of diplomats and CEOs. He had often referred to his girlfriends as *high-stepping show ponies*, and the more they loved him, the worse he treated them. He seemed to feel that love made each of those girls complicit in her own undoing and therefore deserving of his disdain. Perhaps he imagined those women out at Pickton's pig farm to have been the ultimate colluders.

"No surprise she became a hooker. Did she ever like to fuck!" he had hooted over Christmas dinner, and then shovelled more turkey into his mouth.

"Listen—" I said to him now.

"You listen. You *collude* . . ." He was too drunk to humiliate me with skill, to make my skin crawl the way he usually could.

"When's the last time you were at a meeting?"

"Don't you know *everything*? Live and let live," he said. The line went dead.

I looked to the television and thought of the Chinese contortionist.

Soon light began to seep around the drapes. I got out of bed, turned off the TV and repacked my bag.

On the nightstand I figured to be Petra's I set the bottle of unopened wine. On a bit of hotel stationery I thanked them for spoiling me, for breakfast and beautiful sheets.

Before leaving for Penn station, Petra had decided not to phone Andrew but to wait until they could talk face to face. "Besides," she said, "he turns off his mobile when he rides the train. I don't want to leave a message. It's not very dramatic."

2 : 19
000047

$22.00

-6.60
$15.40
$0.77
$ 1 6 . 1 7

ne would help facilitate a good
had once suggested (after thera-
ırn the room to a maudlin soup.
:e of drama either.

k around the suite, the hotel's
:over beckoned, its bronze art
ıg carelessly across *The Waldorf*
t want to bring any of this home
witn me.   �.yself out, I imagined the maids
coming, making things comfortable, each transgression
soon wiped away.

By the end of the following week, I had turned in my article on the state of romantic unions. I tossed in facts and
figures that illustrated the connection between ovulation
and infidelity, orgasms and offspring, adding tidbits of personal anecdote. Felicia enjoyed it when my fact-checkers
called her. To bolster my stories, she has been a lesbian
with a shoe fetish, a co-ed who strips to pay tuition and
now a travel agent who is sleeping with a wealthy, married
doctor. An American travel agent who is not called Petra.

The next time I heard from Petra, she and Andrew
had hashed things out. He had confessed his jealousies,
his fear that she would leave him. "I'm in a struggle,"
she wrote. "Can't stay and can't leave. I miss him when
he is away and don't want to go on when he is here."

In my article I quoted C.S. Lewis: *"We read to know
we are not alone."* We sleep with the married to know the

same thing. I can hear my brother rant that I have prof-
ited from the grief of others. *But people crave witnesses*, I
want to tell him. I am sure of it now. We crave the eyes
of others to know we are not alone.

You're Taking All the Fun Out of It

HE USED TO WEAR SUITS. These snappy looking slacks-and-blazer combos in rich chocolate browns and blacks so black they were blue. He was a snappy talker too, always had a clever comeback for the neighbours or cashiers at the supermarket. Not too clever though. I guess that's one thing I picked up watching him in those days, wondering what made him different from other witty guys in suits: a person hates to feel as though what comes out of his or her mouth is merely a set-up for what comes out of yours. When my father spoke, it was as if he were pleased you spoke first because he'd been waiting all day to hear you. And he'd say something double-ended, something that made your opening remark seem as funny and clever as his reply. I noticed the voice he used too, soft so you had to listen closely, a little conspiratorial. Nothing like an implied secret to make a person feel special.

Except for her. My mother never seemed to feel so special around him, that I recall anyway. Although she must have at some point. She was snappy in her own right, or perhaps *snappy*'s not the right word. She was effervéscent. That is, before she got so agitated.

It seemed, when I was about nine or ten, that a switch flipped and her playfulness became a humming energy that she could barely contain. She tried four or five different jobs, mostly clerical—light typing, filing, answering phones, that sort of thing—but her mind wandered. There just wasn't enough going on at a reception desk to hold her thoughts. As I recall, she quit, officially, once, was fired twice, and once she left for lunch and never came back.

At first the only thing that seemed to soothe her was driving, or rather, being driven; she didn't have a licence. But she loved moving fast down the highways; it seemed to give her a sense of peace that nothing else did. So on weekends, Dad would drive us out to the country and, each time, as the speedometer passed the sixty miles per hour mark, my mother would sigh as though she had just lowered herself into a warm bath. She would begin to smile and say things like, "Look, honey, sheepies," into the back seat at me. Playful and relaxed again, sheep were *sheepies*, eggs became *eggies*.

Problem was, my mother never seemed to see logistics in quite the same way he did and often the country drives would have the two of them very much in their own seats staring out the windows shaking their heads. My mother might see a small herd of horses along the highway. She would say something like, "Oh, look at them . . . sweet old things. Alan, stop the car, pull over." Trucks could be roaring by in the other lane, cars in front of us and behind. I would get excited, flinging myself half over the front seat, seconding the request, yelping for him to stop.

He'd zoom right past, though, and she would look back out the rear window with her mouth open and say, "Alan! Why didn't you stop? They're back *there*. Stop!"

Calmly, he'd reply, "Honey, they're on the other side of the road. There's nowhere to stop."

Then she would say something like, "Of course there is. Don't be silly. Come on, go back. You're taking all the fun out of it!"

He would chuckle as though she had to be goofing with him. He'd try to explain that he couldn't just pull over in all this traffic. There wasn't a turnoff. He needed a spot to pull off the highway.

She'd begin to sputter, "A *spot*? That *was* a spot. For god's sake, Alan, why can't you just pull over instead of making a big production out of everything?"

My father would grip the steering wheel with one hand, and start fiddling with the radio or something, or maybe just rub at his forehead as if he were trying to get a stain off. But usually he'd take a deep breath and sigh. After all, part of my mother's effervescence was her spontaneity. She liked to just *do*, rather than to "make a big song and dance out of it." It was about here that he would try to jolly her up again, laugh, and put a hand on her leg. She would most likely *tisk* and swat him away, and keep looking out the window, her elbow balanced on the bottom of the open window frame, touching the top with her fingertips. She might sigh again and drop her hand into the wind so she could swim her fingers through the air. This is where he would get her—reach over again and squeeze her leg, say something like, "You better watch your hand out there; you're going to accidentally punch a cow and make some farmer awful mad."

In those days, my mother would still tuck her chin and laugh in spite of herself, call him an idiot through giggles.

She'd been working as a sort of Girl Friday at a used car lot for two weeks the afternoon she showed up at school. I was in grade six. She walked into the classroom in her office clothes, informing the teacher that she had to take me for the rest of the day, smiling brightly and chucking my chin as she explained that I had a dentist appointment.

"What dentist appointment?" I asked.

"I don't like to get her upset by telling her ahead of time," she told Mrs. MacConnel. "It's easier to do it this way."

My teacher nodded, *Of course.*

I stared, wondering at my mother as she beamed, stuffing my arms into coat sleeves and pushing me along out of the classroom as if I were a toddler.

"Nice to meet you," she called as we left. "Thanks very much."

Outside the school, I wanted to know what dentist appointment.

"Oh, there's no appointment. I made it up. I was just tired of today and I felt like seeing you."

I stared over my shoulder at the school and back at her.

"Don't you ever just feel like tap dancing?" she asked me.

I waited for some sort of punch line, but she put her arm across my shoulders and we started walking.

She'd been at the car lot, she said, calling people all morning from a list they'd given her. She was supposed to call each number and ask how they were making out with the used car they'd purchased at Bobby Gordon's.

"Now the object of the game," she told me, "was not to find out if they really liked their car, it was just to make sure they still lived at the same address so fat old Bobby Gordon'll have a place to mail his flyers. He's starting up a carpet cleaning business. I had people on the phone screaming in my ear all morning, telling me what a horrible heap he'd sold them, how it was a piece of junk and fixing it cost more than the car did in the first place. All I could think about was tap dancing. I used to be a tap dancer, you know."

I knew. In a scrapbook she'd shown me once, there were black and white photographs of her when she was a kid, and two newspaper clippings, one at eleven years old, the other when she was a teenager, blonde hair in a swinging ponytail, trophy in her hand. She won the district tap finals when she was eighteen years old. She met my father right about then, though, and they were married soon after she'd graduated high school.

Tap dancing became sort of silly at that point, a stunt performed by fools and people who delivered singing telegrams. So she dropped it.

My mother and I made our way over to Broadway, where she took me into The Dance Shop and had me try on four or five pairs of tap shoes until she declared, "Yes, that looks like it." She stepped back and took me in from another angle, head to toe, corners of her eyes crinkling with pleasure. "What do you think? Are they yours?"

I tried to clack around the floor a little, dance the way I'd seen kids do on a talent show I watched Saturday mornings, but I had a nervous stomach all of a sudden, what with all this delinquency, hers and mine. In her case though, she wouldn't have an excuse; if she didn't quit Bobby Gordon's car lot, she'd get fired again. But still, at that moment I couldn't help feeling like a brand new car myself, she was so pleased with my feet.

When we got home, she had me put on some play clothes and she did the same. She got me to help her move each piece of furniture out of the spare room, which as of last year had become her sewing room. She'd seen some celebrity on television boasting that she made all her own clothes and my mother decided she could easily make all our clothes and save us hundreds of dollars—not to mention make us into one stylish family

with her knock-offs of designer outfits spotted in magazines. She made an apron.

Once the room was clear of furniture and sewing
paraphernalia, she went and grabbed any tools she could
find in the garage and we set to work ripping up the
carpet.

"You can't dance with no floor," she said.

Freeing up a corner of the carpet, she had a look at
the hardwood underneath and declared it to be in not-
too-bad-a-shape. But she wanted it to glint. We'd get it
resurfaced, she said.

I helped her rip free the rest and roll it up while she
muttered about its colour.

"*Beige*. Why did I ever let him talk me into a beige
carpet anyway? It's enough to bore me into a coma . . ."

Dad drove up just as we dragged it the last foot or
two into the garage. His face dropped when he saw the
long tube of short shag being pushed against the wall.
He asked what was going on.

"We're making ourselves a dance studio," she told
him and her voice had a choppy, defiant quality. As if she
were a brat and she knew it.

He looked from her to the rolled rug, took a breath
and closed his eyes a moment. As he composed himself,
he appeared odd to me, suddenly out of place. Opening
his eyes, he gave me a stiff sort of smile and asked if
I could go make us all some tea, which is when I noticed
the tail of his shirt coming out, spitting up over his
belt. I was so used to the button-down quality he normally possessed, the assured crispness, that this minor

dishevelment made him look to me as if he'd lost a battle he hadn't begun to fight.

He took my mother's arm and led her into the house and up the stairs. I followed quietly, hanging back a little, waiting until their bedroom door closed before I made my way nearer.

Their voices were low—his growling, exasperated, hers hissing and quick.

I heard: "Marion, that carpet's . . . six months! . . . What are you trying to prove?"

"Oh for god's sake . . . woman's prerogative . . . Would it kill you . . . ?"

"Woman's what? Just because . . . and why are you home from work?"

" . . . shysters anyway. I want to teach Mitzi to tap dance . . . *my own money!*"

" . . . you work, it's your money, but when I work, it's ours . . . you think it's boring just because it's not about you!"

His voice was getting closer. I snuck back down the stairs as the door opened, her words suddenly clear and sharp.

"Hardly! But I sure as hell think it's boring when it's about *you*."

After school the next day, I brought home Nancy Donner. She was in my class and wanted in on these tap lessons.

My mother was tickled to have a second pupil. Not only that but "Donner? Is that your last name? Isn't that a riot, my last name used to be Donner! Wouldn't that be funny if we were related!"

She told Nancy to call her Marion; she'd never liked "Mrs. Adler." Was never really her. I hadn't heard her say that before. I knew Donner was her family's name but it had never occurred to me that she might miss it.

She had bought two black leotards for me the day before and suddenly she was in my room, rummaging for the second so she could give it to Nancy. "You'll match," she said, a thrill on her face. "It'll be adorable."

As we changed into our outfits, Nancy whispered about how pretty my mother was, that she was beautiful like a movie star. I yanked at my underpants, trying to tuck them back under the leotard, and stared at my bedroom door as though I could examine my mother on the other side.

"How old is Marion anyway? She looks more like your big sister."

I could feel my face screwing up at the sound of "Marion." Seemed like Nancy was just showing off now. Both of them were.

"Old," I told her and glared at the door again. "She must be thirty."

When we came into the spare room, *Marion* had set up an old record player from the basement. She had scrubbed the floor and it wasn't looking too bad, not shiny exactly, but not bad.

She put us in the centre of the room and stood before

us, trim in her own woman-size black leotard and tap shoes. Nancy apologized for not having proper taps.

My mother told her it wasn't too important right now. Maybe we could get her some later. In the old days, they just slapped some coins on the soles of street shoes anyway, to get the sound.

"The sound's what makes it come to life!" She grinned at Nancy and began her instruction with *heel-toe heel-toe heel-toe*.

I picked up the move right away, but Nancy's feet insisted on toe-heel toe-heel.

My mother came and stood next to her, demonstrating slowly. Once Nancy'd caught on, Marion stepped up the pace with a shuffle demonstration, then a double shuffle, then the grapevine. By now, Nancy was getting it all down fast and she and my mother laughed at their feet as they shuffled and snapped the floor. My feet weren't in on the joke. Marion went to the record player and set the needle down on a 45 of Sammy Davis Jr. singing "The Candy Man."

"Wait, Mom, wait for a sec, I don't get it."

I could swear she sighed when she came over and showed me again, a little more slowly, the shuffle and the grapevine. Meanwhile, Nancy appeared to be ad libbing on her own, new little grooves in the standard steps, and my mother gave her a small ovation. I rolled my eyes.

"The Candy Man" played and reset itself over and over, and by what had to be the forty-seventh time that Sammy Davis asked us who could wrap a rainbow in a sigh and make a groovy lemon pie, Nancy and Marion

were side by side, dancing up a storm, my mother inter-
jecting "Good girl" and "Nancy, look at you go!"

I was beginning to feel like a six-month-old beige
carpet.

I slipped out of the room, telling them I needed a
drink of water.

A few days later, I came home to find my mother in
the kitchen, laughing and red-headed. Her hair was still
long but it looked thick now, wavy, and Ann-Margret
flaming, high at the crown with a few long bangs brushed
off to the side.

Nancy Donner was already there, as if she'd cut class.
She and I hadn't talked much the last few days. I was sick
of looking at her; everywhere I turned, there she was.

They were laughing, as usual, Nancy at the kitchen
table, my mother at the counter making sandwiches. My
mother grinned when she saw me and spun around.
"Ta-dah!"

I looked at her.

"Well! What do you think? Do I look like Ann-Margret
or what?"

So, it was intentional. I didn't know if I wanted some
big-haired Kitten with a Whip for a mother. Nancy's face
split wide in a grin. They were waiting. Some sort of
uplifting and generous response was in order.

"Kind of. Why would you dye your hair that colour?
I thought you said you wanted to keep it blonde and cut
it to look like Grace Kelly."

"What would I want to do that for? The chick can't
dance." She smirked and snapped her fingers like Sammy

Davis. The two of them cackled. My mother made a face at me, mimicking the one I wore. "What are you so sour about?"

"Nothing."

She glanced at the ceiling and sighed, then said, "Oh, and guess *what*! I'm taking driving lessons. Took my first one this morning. My instructor thinks I have a natural instinct for traffic."

I looked from her to Nancy and back. "Aren't you a little old to be learning to drive? Aren't you s'posed to do that when you're a teenager or something?"

"Oh, piffle on that—where do you get these stodgy old man ideas, Mitzi? You're as bad as your father." She sounded a little clipped. At least she'd knocked off the gushing though.

She walked over to the table and set sandwiches down for Nancy and herself. "There's another one on the counter if you want it, but I'm sure you'll turn your nose up at that too."

Nancy bit into her ham-and-cheese and grabbed a magazine lying on the table. She set her sandwich down and folded the magazine open, then turned around in her seat to show me an old picture of Ann-Margret. She swallowed as much as she could and said, "Your mom's gonna get an outfit like this and run away with Elvis Presley!" and laughed. She wore on her feet the tap shoes my mother'd bought me.

I was in the living room watching a program about a guy who swallowed an entire Volkswagon Bug piece by piece, when my mother pulled up alongside the curb in the Shining Star Driver's Ed car. Watching over the back of the couch, I could see her smiling wide and holding up a pink sheet of paper, then laughing and shaking her head, smoothing the page down against her steering wheel.

A man sat in the passenger seat, his hands resting on his own steering wheel; he was too shadowed for me to make out any expression. I assumed the way she was laughing and prattling on, though, that he must be doing the same. After two or three minutes she got out of the car, and he got out of his side and came around the front end to hers. She left her door open, stepping out from behind it as he came close, and threw open her arms. He walked into her embrace and squeezed her back, his bald head smothered in her long red hair. She took a couple of gleeful hops as she held him. He stood back from her, smoothing his shirt front, fingers of one hand dancing to his breast pocket, touching his pens and then fluttering down to his sides. He folded his arms and unfolded them.

My mother kissed the pink paper in her hands, blew him a kiss and walked back to the house, waving over her shoulder. He watched after her with a moony sort of smile, started back to the passenger's side and then stopped, shook his head, and came back toward the driver's.

I turned from the window as the front door flew open and my mother breezed into the living room with

another one of her *ta-dah*'s and screamed, "I passed!"
Then she put her arms in the air and danced a Broadway
musical to the tune of "I passed I passed I passed!"

"You don't have to tell the whole world, already."

She froze in mid-flounce, dropped her arms and
looked at me, face blank. Her head wobbled a little, her
eyes growing watery, fixing on mine. She made a tiny
sound as though she were about to speak, then walked
out of the room.

That night and the next, I lay awake listening to the rise
and fall of my mother's and father's murmur in their bedroom. I couldn't catch much as far as actual conversation
went. It sounded as if he were holding back, never quite
raising his voice. As if he were afraid that a harsh tone
or sudden movement might cause her to evaporate.

I think now that maybe he was seeing something I
wasn't; he understood that the peace she got from car
rides had nothing to do with speed.

Come Saturday morning, I woke up to his rap on the
door. He poked his head in. "Oh, I thought your mother
might be in here."

"What time is it?"

It was ten. I felt as if I could sleep into the afternoon.
My father looked of the same mind. He'd slept the sleep

of the dead, he said. He had a vague memory of my mother kissing his cheek and saying something about coffee, but that was ages ago, seemed like it was the middle of the night. Maybe she went to the farmers' market for fruit or something, he said.

Then the phone rang. He ran off to get it.

A minute later he was back in my room. "You don't know where Nancy is, do you?"

I squinted and sat up, shaking my head. He went back to the phone.

Soon he was leaning in my doorway again. "That was Nancy's mother. Their car is missing. The old one. Nancy's not there either."

"Nancy can't drive."

"No kidding," he said. "They don't know what to think. Their daughter's not home and the car is missing."

We had given it a day before calling the police; maybe the two of them had gone off for a drive in the country. The Donners' car was a convertible, a fun summer drive, a joyride. But luggage was missing and clothes, Nancy's and my mother's. The adults argued amongst themselves as to whether these things were all related: the car, Nancy, Marion. We shouldn't assume, we shouldn't jump to conclusions.

The police directed their questions more toward me than to my father: Nancy was my friend. Marion, on the other hand, didn't seem to have any friends.

My father looked away.

I explained that Nancy and I hadn't talked much in the last few weeks; she and my mother hung out more, they tap danced. I shrugged. Nancy wanted to dye her hair red too.

The police took notes, leaning back as I spoke. They asked me what I thought my mother's interest in Nancy was. If I'd noticed anything peculiar in the way she behaved toward her, anything inappropriate.

My father glanced at me and then stared at the cop who'd posed the question with the same sort of expression my mother had worn that afternoon I burst her bubble in the living room, somewhere between pain and mystification.

I looked at my father's arms poking out from the sleeves of his T-shirt and I thought how peculiar they looked, white and rubbery. It was rare I ever saw his bare arms. To my father, a T-shirt had always been more of an undershirt, the first of two layers.

Finally one of the officers turned to my father and inquired whether he thought my mother might have a friend somewhere. Dad repeated the question as though he were trying to translate from a language he hadn't heard spoken in years.

The cop looked uncomfortably at me, then back at him.

"Normally," the cop explained, "that would be the first question, but this"—he cleared his throat—"this situation is a little less usual."

My father shook his head no and began to cry, head

rocking side to side in his hands, fingers buried in his hair, his chest jerking quietly. My gaze blurred down over his pale arms again. They were bent at the elbows. Like flippers. Fins.

Nancy's mother called twice after the police left, wanting to know if we'd heard anything.

She called again that night. I watched Dad's back as he stood at the wall, the receiver not quite at his ear. Nancy's mother wailed through the phone. I could hear her from my chair.

"What kind of man can't control his wife?" she demanded to know.

It was less than a week before someone turned my mother in. She and Nancy had taken a leisurely drive to Vegas. When they arrived in town they went to the Tropicana so that Marion could apply for a job as a dancer in one of their shows. She and Nancy, mother and daughter, sat in a lounge talking with the manager, who couldn't make Marion understand that he wasn't the entertainment director, he didn't hire showgirls. That was a whole 'nother department, he told her. The lounge television was tuned to the news, sound off. Marion pulled out her scrapbook, explaining she really could dance if she could just get an audition. He let her go on, jabbering like her freakin' life depended on it, he said later. He looked away, thinking that maybe he'd offer her a cocktail job, on account of the fact that this was Vegas and she was too old to start dancing. That's when he glanced up at the TV screen and saw pictures of my mother with her straight blonde hair and Nancy with hers, bold print stating: *Marion Adler, age 30, grand theft auto and kidnapping of Nancy Donner, age eleven.*

Though they were both redheads now, the manager recognized them instantly, aided by the fact that my mother had given Donner as their family name. Apparently she didn't see the television, or if she did, she didn't absorb the content. Nancy didn't notice either. Head down, she was too busy counting the nickels she'd won at slots.

The manager excused himself a moment and called Security and the police. Turned out his own wife had run off with his son the year before, and as much as this Donner broad was a looker, he told police, he didn't have any kind of sympathy for what she'd done.

Back home, Nancy and the car were handed over to the Donners. The Nevada State Police delivered my mother to the local authorities, who charged her and put her behind bars to await trial. I saw her only on the news; no one would post her bail, they said.

We turned off the TV altogether and didn't leave the house unless we ran out of food. Not for school or work, not until the trial was over and my mother had been convicted. My father stayed away from work so long they eventually had to let him go. I stayed away from school so long my father agreed to let me switch, to take the bus to another to avoid the looks and whispers. We lived on unemployment insurance. My father mortgaged the house.

I saw Nancy twice before the Donners moved: once on the news, the back of her head bobbing as she walked down the courthouse steps, her parents ducking away from the press and into their cars. The second time was at the corner store. I had just picked up some milk and bread and canned stuff that my father'd written down on a list.

On her way in, Nancy stopped and faced me with an uncertain "Hi." She appeared shaken, as though I were a car accident she'd witnessed.

"Hi."

Then she just stood there, staring, blocking my way out. When I tried to go around her, she reached for my arm, and I flinched like I'd been burned.

"Wanna go play or something?" she asked me. "Like maybe go with my brother and his friends to the waterslides?"

"Go to hell." I shoved past her out of the store, the bell jingling summer-clear behind me.

It was two years before my father came out of his stupor. My mother was released on parole about the same time. There must have been a correlation. He started to leave the house more regularly again, never walking anywhere, only driving. He would disappear all day, just driving, he said. I don't think it calmed him exactly. I think it woke him up, or maybe it would be more accurate to say that it got him breathing. As if continuous motion kept him alive. Soon he applied for a job as a courier, driving packages all over town.

My mother showed up after school one afternoon, a couple of weeks after she was released. She waited outside, scanning the crowd of kids until she caught sight of me. I saw her first and felt a bit sick, as if the school bully were waiting. She took several nervous steps and stopped. Her hair was back to blonde and her skin was thinner, drier, as though she'd aged suddenly.

I walked in the other direction toward the swings and monkey bars and she followed.

Sitting down on a swing, I watched her come closer, her feet delicate in heels, crunching and wobbling on the pebbles, her trench coat flapping in the breeze. She eyed the swing beside me but kept her distance, hands worrying over a gnarled up Kleenex. I wished she would turn and vanish. I sat in the swing, turning myself instead.

"Mitzi?" Her voice cracked. She sounded fragile, uncertain.

I closed my eyes, spinning the chains overhead to knots.

"Will you let me talk to you just for a minute?"

She stuffed the Kleenex into her pocket, then rubbed her fingertips at her forehead the way my father used to when they fought.

Finally she said, "I must've started a hundred different letters but I didn't know what to say. I just—"

I let the swing unspin from its tangle and then caught the earth with my feet, dizzy, the ground breathing under me.

"Hey, I, uh, I enrolled in university while I was away, you know. Through correspondence. I'll have a Bachelor of Fine Arts degree soon."

I didn't speak.

"Are you okay? Is everything okay for you?"

I opened my eyes at the ground.

"How about Nancy? Do you still see her?"

"Nancy can go to hell," I said matter-of-factly, the way you might give someone a weather forecast.

She was quiet a moment. "You've gotten so old in two years." She looked away. "A day hasn't gone by where I didn't—I just thought I should tell you that I'm going to be in the phone book. Under 'Donner.' For when you're ready. I thought you should know."

Tipping my head back to look at the sky, I took in all the air I could swallow and still felt as if I might suffocate. I saw the hem of her coat out of the corner of my eye. I turned my head and got off the swing, walked across the football field and through the opening in the chain-link fence.

I walked across town instead of taking the bus, walked up and down the streets in our neighbourhood, until long past dark. It was after eleven when I wandered up our driveway.

My father sat in his car staring straight ahead with the windows down, no motor running. His elbow balanced on the bottom of the window frame, fingertips touching the top as though a Sunday breeze were playing at them. A street light shone through the rear window, illuminating a dry cleaning bag, its wispy plastic glistening over pairs of dark boxy shoulders.

I headed for the house, slowing to touch his shirt sleeve as I passed.

Clown Lessons

THE BANK HAD CALLED EACH DAY to find out when I'd be in again, offering up "casual Friday" as some sort of carrot—as though the lure of staying in my sweats might just bring my fever down. The third time the assistant manager phoned I clung to my blanket and apologized for the spot I'd put him in, promising I'd let him know if I was well enough to come in the next morning.

James yanked a suspender back onto his shoulder and pulled off his spongy red nose. Grabbing the receiver out of my hand, he said, "Who's this? Gerald? Listen, Gerald, you try and get my sister out of her sickbed before she's ready and I swear to Christ, I'll come down there, rip your head off and stuff it back up your ass!" He slammed the phone back in its cradle.

Sitting forward on the couch, I rested my head in my hands. "Thanks, James. Now I have to apologize for you, too." I could feel flu tears swell with heat and pain and inflated emotion. I reached for the receiver.

"No. Clarisse, just relax. It's about time they figured out how valuable you are. They pay you dog shit. They're using you. You're not going back unless you get a raise. You can help me instead."

I raised my knees and dropped my forehead against them. It felt like it might sway and roll off under the couch, given a chance.

"Come on," he said, "help me with my makeup. I can't get the lines straight, my hands are shaking."

I shut my eyelids tight. "I can hardly sit up, never mind do your makeup. It's not my fault you got pissed out of your tree last night—go take that hangover remedy you claim is so brilliant."

"We don't have any eggs."

He sat down on the couch beside me, took the black felt pen from the bib pocket of his polka-dotted overalls.

"James. Don't make me do this."

"Come on, it'll only take a sec." He picked up his template mask from the coffee table.

"All right. But you're doing the greasepaint yourself."

He kissed my hot cheek and, with hangover-hands, held the mask firmly against his features. I leaned in and carefully traced black around the outside, setting his face in relief. The symmetrical cut-outs allowed me to outline what would soon be rosy round cheeks, enormous eyes of cartoon blue and a giant red mouth: The face of Bulbous the Clown.

Oh, and the tear. Mustn't forget the tear.

By dinnertime, my fever was down and I was starting to feel as if I might live. I had called Gerald back to say it would likely be best for the other employees if I stayed home until Monday and to apologize on my brother's behalf, explaining that James wasn't feeling well himself.

"Yes," Gerald said, with the smug courage afforded him by my brother's absence, "the twenty-six-ounce flu, I'm sure."

Gerald and James did not get on well. They had had one or two classes together before James decided university was for sheep and shmucks and dropped out. He now referred to Gerald as a pencil-pushing little yutz. Gerald, having seen James tossed out of bars more than once (including an occasion when James had taken hold of Gerald's wife's breast, much to her surprise but seemingly not to her displeasure), had all the ammunition he needed. My brother embarrassed me and everybody knew it.

A little after six, James stormed in, cussing and slamming the door, dropping his hockey bags, flailing at balloons, both flaccid and blown up, as he kicked his giant yellow clown shoes off his feet and down the hall.

I blew my nose. "You don't drive in those things, do you?"

"No, I don't drive in them for chrissake. How the hell could I drive in them? I couldn't carry them from the car so I wore them into the house, that's all." He was tangled up in gloves and balloons and suspender straps. He yanked off his blue fuzzy wig and flopped to the floor, rolling and kicking, dragging himself free of his costume like some pale and terrible sea creature extricating itself from the shell. "Fuck!" he bellowed. "This city is such bullshit!"

"Can you not yell at me."

"You have no idea what it's like out there in the real world, outside of that pastel palace you work in where they steal people's money and it's all perfectly legal. I make people happy! But that's *illegal*." He stalked into the living room in his boxers and T-shirt and dropped into the armchair.

I looked at him.

"What?" he snapped.

I blew my nose and faced the TV. The news was on. Turning the channel, I searched for something with a laugh track.

James shoved his back into the chair. "All right, I'm sorry. But all you had to do today was be sick and watch *Oprah* while I was out trying to make a living, trying to be fun and playful, and the bastards told me today my permit was turned down. The type of permit I need doesn't even *exist* any more. Bulbous the Clown is no longer *welcome* in Stanley Park."

"How come?"

"They say I'm not a busker because I'm not really an entertainer. I don't have a show; making balloon animals is not entertaining, it's *vending*."

"Well, that's sort of true, isn't it? You sell balloons."

"Screw you, Clarisse. This is so typical—I've never gotten any support from you in *any* of my endeavours."

"Except for financial," I croaked through phlegm, "and emotional, and—"

"Well, stop sounding like a goddamn bureaucrat."

I went back to flipping channels. "I thought they told you ages ago they wouldn't renew your permit."

"I assumed it was just a formality. I've been at that zoo for five years. The guy from the parks board or the aquarium or whatever the hell told me today I was supposed to be out of there last week, to pack my shit and go. Can you believe that? Those goddamn kids love me!"

"Couldn't you get a vending permit?"

"No! They only want parks board *popcorn* vendors. What's left for those kids? They got rid of the pony rides, they got rid of Squirrelman, the jugglers. It's nothin' but a whale jail now."

"What about the kids' parties? You make better money at those anyway, don't you?"

He glared at the bright yellow socks bagging around his ankles. "I hate those parties. Always some shit-assed brat sitting on my shoes, yankin' on my balls. The mothers are always bitches. Except for that one." He laughed. "And one of her friends."

That one was a pretty young weather girl from a local station who had hired James for her son's fifth birthday. Midway through the celebration, James pulled her into a closet. Apparently she nearly had herself into his big clown pants when one of the kids found some matches and started a fire; her husband came home early and the closet door jammed. Despite a big song and dance about a balloon surprise that needed a two-person set-up, James got punted down the steps. He did get gigs from three of the weather girl's friends though.

"Anyways," James said, "I got a plan. I called up a bunch of newspapers and TV stations and this buddy of mine who works Queen Elizabeth Park as GoGo the Clown. We're gonna go out tonight, toss back a couple and iron out the details, but man I got somethin' good cooked up. They can't kill me off when *they* say. *I'll* say when I die, and tomorrow's my goddamn funeral in the park. There'll be an outpouring of emotion like y'never *seen!*" He jumped up and headed for the stairs.

"Hey, can you take your junk with you, please?"

He paused over his hockey bags and clown suit heaped at the front door, then started toward the stairs again, until I added, "And the hydro bill—I need your half today."

"Can't do it. They really hooped me this afternoon." He came back and heaved the hockey bags over his shoulders, wincing dramatically under the weight.

"James, I can't carry you this month. We just got our third warning and they're going to cut us off. I need a hundred and fifty."

"I told you, you should get a raise. Or a different job."

I glared at him.

"Okay, I'll pay it. Give me the address and I'll drop it off."

"Sure. You give me the cash or we'll be eating cold spaghetti from a can tomorrow."

"Jeez, you can be a tight-ass. They're not going to cut off our hydro." He groaned, dropped his bags and rummaged in his overalls, scooping a handful of two-dollar coins before he tossed me a cloth sack with the rest. "There should be around a hundred-fifty bucks there. A hundred anyway."

The next morning, Gerald called to see how I was. Part of me felt guilty. I was about ready to get out of my pyjamas, and well enough that I could imagine being back at work. But I was still a little dizzy and I sneezed onto the mouthpiece. Gerald said he'd better let me go. Once he'd hung up, I searched under the kitchen sink for the Lysol spray, misting the receiver and wiping it down.

An alarm clock went off upstairs. I tried to remember the last time James had set his alarm—for a morning wake-up, that is. He'd happily set it for midnight so he wouldn't miss a party, but 10 a.m.? It was against everything he stood for.

Half an hour later, I heard him crashing down the stairs, hockey bags banging into the walls. His face wasn't made up and he wasn't in his gear yet. "I'm going over to my buddy's to get ready. Watch the news today! Bulbous the Clown's gonna rock this town, baby!"

As he left he slammed the door behind him.

July had been cool and rainy, but the day warmed up and in the afternoon I sat on the back porch reading.

It was the first I'd been out in three days, other than to mail a cheque for the hydro bill, which wasn't actually due until the following week. There had been a hundred and seven dollars in James's pouch, which, after the hydro, left just enough to cover his share of the phone bill.

Shortly after four, I heard the doorbell and leaned around the back of my lawn lounger to look through the house. The bell rang again. Likely a Jehovah's Witness. Or kids. Or someone wanting a donation—maybe for cancer, I thought. With a twinge of guilt, I hoisted myself up, grabbing my wallet on the way. By the time I got to the front door, the porch was empty. I wandered through the kitchen back to the porch and noticed someone in the yard: an old man, small and curved, in a rumpled suit. I stood at the top of the stairs and watched him move around the yard, bending to look at small purple flowers whose names I'd never learned, running his hand across the heads of the tallest snapdragons.

I started down the steps, paused, and then took them as quick as I could. "Daddy?"

He kept moving around the edge of the lawn, touching the flowers.

"Daddy!"

He turned finally and smiled. "Hello. Are you here to see me?"

"What are you doing here?" I asked softly as I came near and draped my arm across his back.

"Suzette. Oh, look at you, you've grown your hair again. A woman with long hair is—"

"Daddy, it's me. Clarisse." I steered him toward the house.

"Who?"

We walked up the steps. "Clarisse. I'm your daughter."

He giggled and told me he didn't have a daughter.

"Yes, you do, you big silly. This is your house and I'm Clarisse, your little girl, except I'm big now, remember?"

"Where's Suzette?"

I brought him through the door. "Suzette passed away."

"What?"

I sat him at the kitchen table.

"Suzette died, Daddy."

"No, that's not true." His eyes pleaded with me until they shone.

I felt sick. For him she was still alive and I had killed her in three words. Why hadn't I said she was at the movies, or she'd gone on a cruise? I touched his sleeve. "I'm sorry. I shouldn't have told you that."

"Who would want to kill Suzette?" He began to sob.

This was something else again now, a reference to an aunt I'd never met who had been murdered back in Quebec when she was a teenager—a memory from before I was born.

"Nobody hurt Suzette. Remember? She got breast cancer. She didn't hurt; we got her good drugs and we told her jokes and she was happy right up till the end." Then I started to cry, too.

Old enough to be our grandmother, my father's sister, Suzette, had moved into the house after my mother died and raised us herself. According to Suzette, my father was numb the first two or three years of our lives, mumbling day after day to his sister about his wife's youth, how he'd had twenty-five years' more time on this earth than she did, how he should have called an ambulance right away.

I came first, Suzette told me, at seven o'clock in the evening, slipping toward the birth canal as my mother's cervix dilated in an unexpected yawn. No time to get a doctor, no time for much of anything. She'd been arguing for a natural birth all along and now her babies were coming and there was nothing anyone could do to thwart her plans.

My mother had been lying on the couch listening as Aunt Suzette read aloud from an old Nora Ephron essay about Ayn Rand. Suzette hollered down the hall to my father, "See, I told you, Marcel, it's Ayn Rand, pronounced *ine* not *anne*—Ayn rhymes with *pine*! It says so right here." She shook her head at my mother. "He never listens to me. He's always so sure he's right."

My mother screamed. Suzette laughed until her eyes bugged in realization. She called out to my father, who bellowed, "All right, I get it, I'm wrong!" But Mother continued to scream as the ocean in which my brother and I had been floating for eight months and two weeks chopped and heaved around us, then drained in a rush, leaving us heaped on each other, clammy and agitated in her belly.

Finally my father rushed in and, seeing his young wife, the flooded couch, he picked up the phone. My mother cried and laughed at once and told him to put it down, said she could feel us wrestling with each other, trying to wriggle free—we would be out any minute. My father announced that he was going to call an ambulance anyway, but before he could do much of anything my soft head began to nose from her body.

Suzette says I hesitated as though making sure it was the best move, then came all at once in a slippery rush. When they saw what was coming after me it became clear from whom I was rushing. What they feared might be a deformity was actually James's hand; his red fingers had an iron grip on my ankle. The fingers could not be pried loose and it was thought, at first, that we were conjoined. Suzette shouted for my father to cut the cord, to make sure I was breathing, while she worked to free James, fearing for my brother's neck—with an arm and shoulder coming first, his head might snap sideways.

There was no laughter now; my mother's screams grew to a cataclysmic pitch. My father called the ambulance while Aunt Suzette tried to pry James's fingers from my ankle, to no avail. She then reached her small hand inside and manipulated his head and shoulders, tried to make them slide out together. Squealing, she pulled her hand from my mother, claiming something had bitten her. Till the day she died she would not be persuaded that my brother had no teeth.

My father hung up the phone, picked it up again, put it down. He knelt by my mother and looked up at the ceiling, praying for help, his atheist leanings set aside for the moment. His wife's pelvis began to buck, guttural howls wailing from her body, as James's head emerged in a tide of blood, his body lurching out, dragging the walls of his former home with him.

Our mother died before the ambulance arrived, James still holding fast to my ankle and the uterus he refused to leave behind.

My father blamed himself and he blamed James, who he believed embodied everything terrible he'd had to carve from his own soul before he was good enough to meet someone like our mother. For the first few years he wanted nothing to do with his son for fear he might try to beat his own demons out of the boy.

On our sixth birthday, Aunt Suzette hired a clown named Cheeno for the party. Cheeno was clever and silly and made a dizzying array of balloon creations. Our friends all told us it was the best party ever as they traipsed down the sidewalk after it was over, balloon bracelets on their wrists, balloon swords in their hands. Cheeno stayed behind, and James and I were stunned to discover that it was our own mumbling, sad father under all that greasepaint.

It was something of a turning point, this sort of whimsy. Prior to the birthday party, our father had been a ghost to us, a nine-to-five, depressed, alcoholic ghost who avoided us at all costs. Now we begged circuitously through Suzette for clown lessons, and suddenly James and I had something in common with this man we hardly knew.

Daddy earnestly taught us how to twist and squeeze the long airy tubes into puppies and dragons and daisies. He showed us how a clown applies makeup using a template made especially for his or her face, how to trace each feature so that the clown-face was the same every time. We were enthralled. Nothing could break our focus from these magic secrets, secrets we kept from other children as though their release could mean the end of the world.

Still, our clown lessons were about the only times we got near our father. Outside clowning, his sorrow never lifted. And if it's true that depression is only anger turned inward, James grew into a more extroverted version of our father. There were no moody silences in James, just broken windows, schoolyard fights, stealing and cursing and yelling.

The final blow-up came when we were twelve. James and I had been arguing all the way home from school, James yelling that I thought I was better than him, me saying I didn't think any such thing. I did explain, however, that if he would just act more like me in the first place, he wouldn't get into the trouble he was always in.

"Like getting suspended today, for example," I threw at him as we came into the house. "What you did to that boy was extortion. You're an extortionist."

Livid that I'd nailed him with an insult he'd never heard of, James told me to shut my trap and gave me a good shove. I turned and slapped him the way any decent movie heroine would. He tried to retaliate with a swing, but missed and called me a bitch.

I replied with, "Asswipe!"

He took another lunge but I knew his moves better than he did. His knuckles slammed into the wall and the look on his face sent me into paroxysms of laughter. Tears started to come as I cackled "Asswipe" again for its pleasing sibilance. James's face shone like a blister. Seeing him lose control—the rage, the seething fury— always gave me a greater sense of accomplishment than anything else in my world.

His eyes flicked sideways and filled with hope. I saw the baseball bat leaning against the wall and took off down the hall. He grabbed it and tore after me through the kitchen and back into the front room.

His first swing took out a lamp. It was old with a faded shade and only worked now and then, but it had belonged to our mother. The shock of its body exploding against the bat, falling to the floor in pieces, stunned us into temporary paralysis, our mouths stuck in an O, our arms frozen mid-air.

Aunt Suzette called down from upstairs. Our father called from the back porch.

James moved first, his eyes darting up from the shattered lamp as he hissed, "It's your fault—you're *dead!*"

I backed up. They were going to get him for this and he was going to get me first. He moved slowly, matching me step for step. We could hear my aunt coming down the stairs and our father coming through the kitchen, and we both leapt into motion, me rushing toward the bay window, James hurtling after me just as Suzette and Daddy's shock pierced the room. Their voices worked like a cattle prod on James and he swung the bat, missing my head and smashing the window.

Daddy had hold of him before he could even drop the bat. He grabbed him by the throat and slammed him against the wall three times, cracking a picture frame's glass with my brother's head before tossing him down on the floor. The baseball bat lay near him. Our father picked it up and held it in both hands over James as though he were about to batter his son to a pulp.

"Marcel!" Aunt Suzette screamed.

He glared down at my brother. "You've been rotten from the start. You've always been rotten! I should have drowned you like a rat the first time I saw you!"

"Enough!" Suzette yanked the baseball bat away from our father and ordered him out like a dog. Stone-faced, he turned and left the room.

Suzette pulled James up off the floor, took his head in her hands and looked into his eyes, feeling around for injury, asking if he was all right. He solemnly nodded. She started to cry, to beg him, "Why? Why?"

She tossed me a look. I was still cowering by the broken window.

When she turned back to James, he shouted, "Why can't I be like Clarisse? Clarisse is a fucking saint!"

She grabbed him by the muzzle. "If you ever speak to me that way again, you're on your own. Whoever wants you can have at you!"

If she was talking about our father, she needn't have worried. It was the first time we'd ever seen his temper and it would be the last. So shocked was he with himself, so afraid of the reflection he saw when he looked into James's face that day, that he went away to France, to the resort town where he'd met his vacationing bride-to-be back when he was still clowning.

It would be eight years before we saw him again.

I set a cup of tea in front of him. "Daddy, maybe I should call Mountainview. I bet they're worried."

He sipped from his cup. "You're a very nice girl. Are you French?"

"French Canadian." I smiled. "On my father's side." I got up to get the phone just as the front door opened and James came ploughing through.

"Goddamn pigs!" He dropped everything in the usual heap. "Pigs!"

I grabbed the cordless and ran to simmer him down. His face was painted blue with demon flames shooting red from his eyes and mouth. He raged on: "They came on *horseback*! I'm there, staging a funeral and—look at me!" His fingers jabbed at his face. "I'm Diablob, Bulbous's evil twin. I sold balloon flowers at my own funeral! The Mounties came and cited me for public mischief, vending without a permit, and for uttering *threats*! Since when is it a crime to tell someone you'll kick his ass? If they're gonna ticket me anyway, I may as well kick an ass and get my money's worth!" He stormed past me, sputtering, "And did the media show up? No one gives a—"

"James."

"What the hell is *he* doing here?"

Our father watched us from the kitchen. Seeing James in full clownalia, he clapped his hands, saying, "Oh-ho!" and doffed an imaginary hat.

James glared. "Why did you let him in?"

I hauled him back into the living room. "For chrissake," I whispered. "He hasn't been here in three years. It's his house!"

"What are you whispering for?" he barked. "Crazy bastard doesn't know his own name. You're just making it harder on him because he sure as hell ain't stayin'. I got enough to deal with."

"It always comes down to you, doesn't it."

"What did he ever do for me? Or you, for that matter? Just because he conveniently lost his mind doesn't mean I have to take care of him now. The only time he ever really spoke to me was the time he tried to kill me. Before he abandoned us."

"Where'd you learn to do *this*, then?" I waved at his face, his bags on the floor. "He left so he *wouldn't* kill you. He probably thought you didn't have a hope in hell with him around."

"Gimme the phone. He's gone."

"Fuck you, James." I went back to the kitchen, phone in hand. "How you doin', Daddy? Want some more tea?"

James tromped behind me into the kitchen. "Gimme the phone!"

I set the kettle on the stove, and asked my father if he'd like something to eat.

James yanked the phone from under my arm, jabbing the air between us with his finger. "I'm calling them, so fuck you too."

Voice cold and flat, I told him, "If you don't give me back the phone, I will walk out that door and you'll never set eyes on me again."

He looked startled and his nostrils flared. We watched each other until a sob broke the air and we turned to see our father crying.

Tears streamed down his cheeks as his head moved back and forth. He looked up and held out his hands to James, pleading, "Non, je m'excuse, s'il vous plait, Papa, je m'excuse."

We stared. Neither of us had ever heard him speak French. Suzette never did, and we knew our mother had never learned a word.

I covered my mouth. James set the phone down on the counter and swallowed, running his fingers through his hair, then stuffing his hands into his pockets. He took a couple of steps, pulled a hand free and moved a chair closer to our father. Looking to me first, he sat and awkwardly patted Daddy's forearm.

"It's okay. It's no big deal, man. Let's just have a beer. All right?"

Daddy nodded solemnly at James.

I grabbed the Kleenex box and set it between them, yanking one for myself. Our father looked at the box. I pulled one free for him but he blinked up at me, lost, until I held it to his nose and told him to blow. He honked, I wiped.

James laughed nervously. "Nice one, buddy."

He went to the fridge, grabbed two beers and the phone off the counter. He twisted off the bottle caps and set one in front of Daddy and one in front of himself before he dialed Mountainview Nursing Home. He told them our father was here and demanded to know why they had never called to tell us he was missing. Furthermore, he asked, in the three years his father had been in that home, why had James never received any reports? If the nurse had anything to say, if she tried to mention that perhaps James didn't know anything about his father because he had never been to see him, I couldn't tell. James wasn't letting her get a word in edgewise.

We made supper together that night. Showered and clad in jeans and a T-shirt, James sat at the kitchen table with a cutting board and showed his father how to slice an onion, the way one would teach a small child: how to peel it, how not to cut your fingers, the difference between mincing and chopping.

"Where'd you learn that?" I asked him.

He told us about a chef he had dated and loved, how she had dumped him. James had begged to stay with her, but she told him to be gone by the time she returned. After she left, James wandered her apartment, the air clammy from a wet spring. All he wanted to do was hang on. Finally he stole her apron, he said, so he wouldn't feel so alone. I thought of Suzette's story, the way James came into the world holding fast to our mother's womb.

After dinner, I pulled out James's mask—our father's mask, which had always fit James's face perfectly. I put it in Daddy's lap and let him hold it, watching the flicker of memory in his eyes as he ran a finger over the contours of the cheeks, the forehead, and the nose that he and his son shared. James and I both watched him.

Then I took the mask carefully from his hands and raised it to his eyes, pressing it close till the tip of his nose poked through. I handed my brother the black felt tip. Daddy grinned like a birthday boy as James began tracing him a new face.

Did You Grow Up With Money?

OUTSIDERS NEVER SAW HIM, but we did. Money'd sit up late with my father, drinking, smoking a joint—Dad liked him there cuz he could roll. All night they'd be up playing Johnny Cash over and over: *I fell in to a burning ring of fire. I fell down, down, down, and the flames went higher.* In the morning they'd be gone but it was obvious he'd been at it again—showing Dad how to mark cards, mark time, make a mark out of a sucker.

Oftentimes he'd ditch Dad and hang out with my mother; he was a big drinker so he got along with everyone in the family. He'd sit with her, run his fingertips lightly over her throat, bite her gently, and they'd laugh a laugh that came straight from their groins. I'd have to leave the room.

Nobody ever said anything about Money. One day we were happy—as happy as a family can be, trying to get through it—and the next, Money was a part of our lives.

We guessed that Dad had brought him home from a game, since that's what they seemed to do all day: play cards, practise cheating at cards. We didn't know anything about him, didn't know his real name or who he was outside our house. He seemed like a war vet: tattooed numbers here, a dramatic slogan there. But he never talked about war, not the regular kind anyway. Dad adored Money, though, and always had an arm for his shoulder, a loving slap for his jaw. He didn't notice the way Money had the same for Mom and Mom's behind. He didn't notice or didn't care.

My sister was six years older than I was and I adored her. She was the most perfect creature on earth, with her long chocolate hair and willow-thin limbs. The night Money hid in her closet to watch her undress, things'd gone too far, but still we didn't say anything. Beth found him nestled in her shoes, skirts and blouses dripping down his face. She was standing in her bra and jeans when she opened her closet and she carefully shooed him out as if he were a strange dog playing with her child.

She told me this later, so matter-of-factly that I could find no reaction in myself. It was as though we couldn't react. Money just was.

It wasn't long after that he came roaming around upstairs as I got ready for bed, came into the bathroom as I brushed my teeth. I turned to see him but I didn't say anything. Just kept brushing and he watched, his eyes following the brush as I moved it back and forth, in and out of my mouth. Too self-conscious to spit in front of him, I was considering swallowing the foam when Money spoke. He asked my age. Toothbrush in one hand I held up five fingers of the other and blinked them twice like an eye before stuffing my head deep in the sink, covering my face with an arm as I turned on the cold water. Rinsing and spitting. I felt his eyes move down the length of me. My nightie was old and threadbare and I wondered if age had made it see-through. Money remarked that I would probably look like Beth in a few years, that it was nice looking at me now, knowing it was just the beginning.

I rolled that around a moment, confused by my nerves. I thought Money was nothing to be afraid of. He moved from the door frame and came round behind me, looking over my head into the mirror. His arms fell down on either side of me, hands resting on the counter. I still held my wet toothbrush and I started to fidget, elbows close at my sides, avoiding the insides of his arms. A sinewy hand came back and landed on my hip.

"You've already got an ass like your sister's." He moved his hand around, sandwiching it between his crotch and my backside.

I couldn't speak and I didn't want to cry in front of him.

"You like this, don't you—you're just like your sister." He watched me in the mirror while his fingers gathered material, easing up my nightgown. I gripped the toothbrush at my chest like the cross. The cold water was still running.

"You fuck!" howled off the bathroom walls, and something long and wild tackled us.

Beth hurled herself on Money and suddenly we were all sprawled on the floor, screaming. I clambered out of the thrashing arms and legs and crawled between the toilet and the wall to cry. Beth was still on Money, banshee-screaming, smashing her fists into his neck, his face, her dark hair snaking in all directions.

"You fuckin' touch my sister, I'll fuckin' kill you—I'll kill you, you cocksucker."

I held onto the side of the toilet. This wasn't Beth. Beth didn't know those words and Money wasn't real and Beth didn't talk to Money and I was ten and men don't touch ten and nobody said Money's name and no one else could hear so none of us were here. I crawled farther in behind the toilet.

Money got hold of Beth's wrists. He slammed her over onto the bathroom tiles and scrambled on top of her, holding her arms over her head, against the floor. He forced her knees apart and pushed his hips against her. Beth's wrists were now in one of Money's hands and she was pinned. He moved his face close to hers, stared in her eyes, and said, "Don't fuckin' tempt me."

Beth spat. Money used his free hand to wipe the saliva off his cheek and back onto hers. He slammed her wrists against the floor once, like an exclamation point, and let her go before he stood. He ran a hand through his greasy hair. Beth lay still. Money smiled and gave a two-fingered salute from the crown of his head, then turned and left the room, closing the door behind him.

My sister had me sleep with her that night and her door stayed locked once we were behind it. All doors stayed locked if we were behind them.

The next morning, I woke up to Beth's breathing. She was still sleeping hard and the air smelled stale and used from dreaming. I climbed out of bed and went downstairs to the kitchen toward my father's voice. His words were bent by corners and by the time they reached me I could make out only their garbled sides. Just enough to know that Dad was making a point, the kind where he used a lot of table thumps to underline the important bits.

As I moved nearer, the words were clearer, something about *kids* and *value.* Coming through the doorway, I didn't see my mother. I saw my father, cards and chips and Money sitting across from him. The breath stopped moving so well in my chest. I didn't look into any eyes.

Money turned to watch as I opened the fridge and my father interrupted his speech to tell me, "Milk's sour," before he went on. I took the juice, put it on the counter and picked the least dirty glass in the sink to wash.

"These freakin' kids don't know the score—they couldn't tell ya the value of a goddamn buck to save their souls. Half of 'em take off and jump on the freakin' welfare gravy train. Ya can't tell 'em nothin'—and you sure as hell can't give 'em nothin', cuz I'll tell ya, you take one of these little buggers today—"

I chewed on the inside of my mouth, trying to be small, unnoticeable, just pour juice and not have to answer a trick question—not have to say the thing that would bring on a table thump and a *See, what'd I tell ya!*

Money was chuckling, waving off Dad's theory, saying there were good kids around who knew what was what. I heard chair legs groan against floor as he pushed himself away from the table, and I rushed to get the orange juice back in the fridge. I got back to my glass just as Money did.

He pushed the juice out of my reach and put himself between me and it. Stuffing a hand into his pocket, he looked at me. "This little one here knows what's what, don'tcha darlin'?"

I watched the crack of the open silverware drawer, thought about falling through the little line of space and lying with my head in the hollow of a spoon.

Money pulled his hand out of his jeans along with a crisp, folded ten-dollar bill. Opened it flat and smoothed a yellow thumb and forefinger along its clean perfect crease. Then put it on the counter and slid it toward me.

"Tell Money whatcha'd do with a ten-spot."

I looked at it. Said nothing. Beth was coming down the stairs now. I could hear her slippers scuffing toward the kitchen.

Money watched me. "Go head, sweetheart, pick it up."

Didn't want to look him in the eyes. I looked at the bill some more. Then picked it up off the counter and held it, running a nail along the sharp edge. Beth's slippers were sliding across the kitchen floor now. Money looked away from my hands and smiled at Beth as she came up beside me.

I looked at Money smirking at Beth.

He said, "How 'bout you, Angel, what would you do with ten bucks right about now?"

Beth smirked back and gently took the bill out of my hand. She only had it a second before she tore it in two and handed half back to me. "I always share," she said and rested her hand on the back of my neck.

Dad had already started up again as we left the kitchen: "What'd I tell ya. In a nutshell. In a goddamn nutshell!"

Beth's face kept a hard look after that. We stayed in her room mostly and mostly she'd sit in silence, nodding all the while as if someone were giving her instructions. We didn't talk much about Money, said almost nothing about what had happened, probably because it was still happening.

About a week later, she sat me down. For the next couple of days, she said, I was to be nice to Money; we were both going to be very nice to Money.

And it was two nights later that she asked me in the hallway upstairs if I'd like to go down to the river. The toilet flushed and Money came out the bathroom door, face to face with Beth's queer smile.

At ten o'clock that night we were standing upriver in the shallows, Beth peeled to her underwear and me in the smallest of her old dresses. It was July but nights were still a little cold to be standing half naked with water rushing over our legs. We knew he'd show up, though, weasel out of whatever drunk fest our father had planned and look into the friendly reception he'd been getting from us lately. So we stood and shivered a while and, sure enough, about fifteen minutes later we saw him, lead-foot-drunk, tripping his way along the rocks, wearing the same dirty buckskin coat he wore all year round, a bottle in one hand, his Johnny Cash tape in the other—he seemed to think there'd be a cassette player everywhere he went.

My sister waded a little farther out, up to her knees, her long body icy in the moonlight; she was the irresistible decoy, "Money, you bad boy, did you follow us out here?"

He cackled and splashed out into the water, throwing his arms wide as if they were old army buddies. I smiled, scared, trying to look like sex, like Beth. My sister walked to meet him and I followed, taking care not to slip on the smooth rocks, straight legs sticking out under the faded wet flowers on my dress.

"It's a party," he said, and belched wolf calls in the air, drowning them in another swig of Scotch. He reached Beth, ran his hands down her neck and brushed the strap of her bra down her shoulder. "You waitin' fer me, beautiful?" and he took another drink and left the bottle in his mouth, holding it between his teeth while he stooped to roll up his drenched pant legs, showing off the serial number tattooed on his left ankle as if he were a sailor showing us the panther on his chest. He showed that number a lot, had showed it to my father a few times, said it was the number on the first fifty he ever won at cards.

He straightened and took the bottle from his mouth, ran his tongue over a chipped side tooth (he'd been showing my father how to uncap a beer without an opener the day before when my mother walked in and distracted him).

My sister moved out of his reach and he turned to her. "Where ya goin'? Show me those pretty tits of yours, Beth."

She giggled. "You gotta give a little to get a little."

Money gave a snort as he tried to undress. He jammed the bottle between his knees and stuffed Johnny Cash in his back pocket, freeing himself to yank off his coat, pulling the sleeves inside out in his impatience. He threw it to the nearest tree overhanging the river. He missed.

"Turn around and let us look at you," my sister told him.

He was giggly and flattered and he staggered himself around, showing off his rangy old arms. My sister motioned me closer with her head. I winced. Couldn't bear the thought of him touching me.

She said, "Doesn't Sarah look pretty tonight? This used to be my dress." She paused to finger the tiny pink bow at my neckline. "She's never seen a man, you know—naked, I mean."

"Is that so! Shit you girls are hot tonight." Money looked at the thin straps on my shoulders and worked his eyes down to the wet hem hanging not much below my behind.

I stayed close to Beth as he yanked off his dirty T-shirt and threw his arms wide. I tried to giggle and look happy the way my sister did, and he chuckled, going for his belt.

Soon he stood there naked, smiling like he'd just shot himself a deer. Looking down, he stoked himself, and I looked away, scared. But Beth laughed like I'd never heard her, the way our mother did, and splashed at Money with her foot. He splashed back and gave her a smile.

"Beth, can I have a piggyback?" I asked.

"No, sweetie, my ankle's still sore. Get Money to give you one, he looks strong."

Money glowed. "Sure, I'll give ya a goddamn piggy-back. Com'ere, darlin'."

He bent low for me. I climbed aboard and tried to hold straight as he romped around the river like an old nag.

My sister laughed as if this were the night to end all nights. Money galloped me in circles, yelping and bark-ing, whinnying, slipping now and then, until finally he tired and Beth splashed through the water toward us. She stopped where he had, the two of them gulping summer air. She licked her lips and reached for his hand. He panted chuckles and she swung his arm between them like a skipping rope before cupping his palm to her breast. From over Money's shoulder, I stared at the hand glued to Beth's bra until he ducked his head and the sight was lost.

Beth pulled his head up and pushed her tongue into his mouth. Her fingers tangled in his hair as she pulled his head back and tilted his mouth away, licking down his chin, his neck. I stared, sick. Couldn't tell if she winked or if I just wanted her to. Then her left eye splashed wide, ordering me.

I shook myself smart again, still hanging off Money's neck, and swallowed the sour sound of their mouths together, concentrating, feeling for the metal in the pocket of my dress. Money's moans strained from his throat as his head fell back and he gazed past my ear.

I pushed myself up higher on his hips, pulled the blade from its slot in the handle and did what my dad took pains not to do every morning—dragged the edge hard into his throat.

Quiet. Like the quiet in a room after a joke nobody gets. Money's arms jerked from my legs and I slid down his back into the water. He caught hold of my wrist with one hand, the other on his throat. "What the hell are you tryin' a—?" His words cut off in a choke and he let go. My sister's mouth fell open a little while she watched him stagger backwards—she almost looked hurt.

Money was confused, too drunk to know what was happening, and his head fell forward, blood pouring through his stiff fingers. His face caught the light as tears trickled out to join the red.

I got a stillness in my ears as if I were holding my breath under water. Looking down the river, I saw everything blue and swaying, the trees, the rushes across the way, the water swirling over rocks and broken branches. I could feel the air against my skin moving little hairs on my arms and legs and giving me goosebumps. It seemed like someone should fall in love right now. I turned back to Beth's face and it had taken on a sweet sort of calm too. She was watching a child taking his first steps. Coughing. Gurgling.

She looked at me finally. "Well. What should we do? Would you like to bring him down the river?"

I said I would and looked down at the straight razor still in my hand, ran my finger over its round tip. Dark and light drizzles sparked against the moonlight. I knelt and folded the blade under water, let the river wash it clean, before dropping it back into one of my drooping pockets. When I stood back up, Beth and I took Money by the arms like a doddering old man. I held his hand, Beth asked me if I was cold, if I'd like her to wash my hair when we got home, and he let us lead him downriver as if we were taking him to safety.

Do Not Touch

You are never as lonely as when you are lonely in the company of your lover. I know I'm not the first to say that. Thomas used to say, "Another duckbilled platitude from my funny valentine." On the other hand, Thomas said I could synthesize information quicker than anyone he'd ever encountered. They made me assistant manager at the music store where I work when Thomas told them that. Thomas has clout in the music world.

The first time we met was when he walked into the store one week before a big interview he had to do. He asked me for everything we had from Diana Krall. He was chewing a stir stick. His hands dashed around, pushing his glasses up with one hand while he yanked on that stir stick with the other.

I walked up and down the jazz section, pulling from here and there and the next thing Thomas knew he was standing in the aisle with an armload of Diana Krall solos, duets, and the miscellaneous liner notes of other artists who had worked with her.

"God, you're, uh, you know your stuff." As he spoke, the stir stick fell out of his mouth and hit the floor. Staring down at it between his feet, he looked devastated.

I wanted to pet the scant hair on his oddly round head. The thing with me is nervousness—other people's nervousness, that is—I find it very calming. A stutterer slows my pulse down to about thirty, I swear to god. Perhaps it's a maternal instinct of some sort.

I wrote him a list of other related notables we didn't have. He could download them from iTunes, I suggested. Thomas shook his head. Like a smoker, he said, he enjoyed the ritual: it was like unwrapping a little gift—the sight of that fresh, shining CD.

I printed my name on one of the store's business cards. "Call me if I can help." And I gave him a new stir stick from our coffee station.

He came back looking for me the next day.

Thomas interviewed highfalutin people for the arts section of the biggest magazine in the country. I was so impressed in the beginning—a big-brained guy like Thomas taking a shine to nobody-me. I had just cut off all my hair to about an inch from my skull. I used to have crazy curly long hair. For years I had been the girl with the hair, and I decided that that was getting me nowhere. I wanted to be wanted for something harder to come by and harder to lose. Be careful what you wish for.

I should have known something was wrong when Thomas sucked back the better part of a twenty-sixer of Glenlivet before he could kiss me the first time.

I met the watchmaker when my Timex broke; I was embarrassed to take it in because it was just a cheap old drugstore thing. But the watchmaker took it all very seriously, opening up the back, turning its face to his own, his hands brushing its. Seeing him touch my watch there on the glass display counter lulled me, as though he were brushing my hair or whispering fingertips along the inside of my elbow. Eyelids thickening, jawbone slack, I thought I might fall across the glass into his arms.

When he was done, I smiled, relaxed and dreamy. It was just a simple thing, he told me. Handing him ten dollars, I felt slightly desolate, anxious about there being no coins in the transaction, nothing that might bring our hands closer.

I went home and knocked on Thomas's office door.

"Working," he grunted.

Thomas had asked me to move into his house three months after we first touched. *Yes!* I said. I thought he was crazy about me, that I was turning him into a mad, impetuous lover.

"I'm thinking of having a bath," I told him now. "Do you want to join me? I could add some bubble bath and make us a couple of mojitos."

"Working!" It wasn't quite a shout, more like a cry from between gritted teeth.

I put my hand on the door, let my fingertips trace the grain.

In the bathroom I turned on the hot water in the tub. I fingered my hair in the mirror and wondered if I should let it grow wild and tangled again.

I opened the cupboard over the sink. Picking up Thomas's prescription, I rattled the few little blue pills on the bottom. They had worked at first. Perked him right up down there. At first. Then nothing worked. I added in some sexy showers and lingerie, hot oil massages.

He was embarrassed, apologetic. "It's just stress," he said.

I tried to talk to him about it. He doesn't like to discuss sex. "It's prurient," he said.

"Is that bad?" I asked and laughed.

He threw me a look of distaste, sucked back the rest of his seventh can of Coke that day and chewed on what was left of his plastic straw.

They say there are ways to tell if a situation like ours is emotional or physiological. I woke in the night once and reached for him, ran my fingertips along his hip, the inside of his thigh. It was only a few moments before he was raring to go. He woke to find himself in my hands, my mouth, to see me sliding back up the length of him, and as his mind cleared, he shrunk back and pushed me away.

"What if I did that to you?" he asked, as though I had crossed some obvious line. It was a violation, he said, a kind of rape.

It wasn't until Thomas stopped touching me that I looked up the lyrics to "My Funny Valentine." They aren't kind.

I closed the cupboard door now, opened a drawer and rummaged for more dead watches. I found two.

After waiting three days, I brought in another. "Maybe it's time I resuscitated this poor orphan too," I told the watchmaker, "while I have the money."

He asked if I could leave it with him and pick it up in the morning. I glanced around at the other people in the store, told him I could wait, that I'd really like—and I lowered my voice—to watch. His cheeks pinkened a little and he set my watch behind him on the shelf.

I offered to go and get him a coffee while he took care of his other customers. He nodded and did this thing where he averted his eyes, lowered them and then cast his dark pupils straight into mine for a full-on eye-lock. It just killed me.

Slinking into his shop with the last of my watches, I explained that I'd found this one last summer at the park; I had put ads in the paper but no one had claimed it. With this third broken body, I had become obvious.

He read the engraving, jeweller's loupe cuddled by his eye socket. "*Madge from Jim 1940*. Wow. That's a lot of time." He shook his head, the tarnished strap looped across the fingers of his right hand, while my eye hooked on the polished gold band on a single digit of his left.

"Do you think it's worth hanging on to? Fixing, I mean?"

"Well"—he peered more closely—"it's gold fill. If it were karat, I'd say definitely. On the other hand, it is a good solid Swiss watch."

He looked up at me and set his mouth a moment as though he had something serious to say. "I cannot fix it today."

I nodded, looked down at the glass counter and imagined the closed door of Thomas's office.

The watchmaker called me a couple of days later to tell me that Madge and Jim's lost watch was breathing again: fixed. His voice sounded funny. He said he would be in for another hour and then he would be nipping out for a coffee.

"I'll come by," I said and hung up.

I stared at the phone. My skin felt ticklish for a few seconds, itchy with guilt bugs, and I scratched my arms hard before I walked past Thomas's office. He was out but his door was open. Thomas isn't fussy about privacy so long as he isn't working.

I paused and looked in. Walking to the middle of his room I stared at the walls, his framed National Magazine Awards, his signed Chet Baker album cover, his signed

Blossom Dearie. I breathed in the air, wishing for some answer to come out of its thinness.

I sat in his chair. His laptop yawned open. Tracing my finger over the keys, the monitor woke from sleep mode and displayed Thomas's Facebook page. He'd been in the middle of a conversation with someone before he left. The last message displayed was his: "Don't tempt me, you little fox. The things I could do to you, twist you into a slick pretzel and taste every part."

Heat rushed up and down my neck. My guts shifted. I glanced over my shoulder, and back at the screen and then clicked the previous message. Her picture was there. She was young and wore a pink camisole with a black bra underneath, hoisting her little breasts up as far as they'd go. Her bangs hung in her eyes like something from the cover of *Barely Legal Magazine.* Her message said: "You're not bringing the Excess Baggage, are you? Tell me you're going to come here alone and make me scream."

Thomas was supposed to fly to Toronto next week.

My hands shook as I clicked back over the thread of messages. There were nineteen.

Before the last I went to the bathroom to throw up. When nothing came, I put a finger down my throat.

I sat down across from the watchmaker at the café next door to the watch repair shop. His face fell into a strange look of pleased fear. He said hello as though he were choking on it and told me he hadn't brought the watch with him. That it was back at the shop.

My hands had not stopped shaking. My voice quavered when I said, "I don't know why I'm here."

"We could go back to the shop. I mean I could—Are you okay?"

I nodded, eyes aching. "Allergies."

"Maybe, you should have coffee."

He glanced at the clock on the wall and then at his wrist and finally at the table. He ordered something milky with coffee and chocolate from the barista for me.

I stared at the froth when it arrived, my palms up on the table.

He peered at me and then down at one palm. "You have a tremendously deep heart line."

I sucked a breath as he reached over, tentatively pushing the tips of my middle and index fingers down against the table and thereby stretching out my palm. He swallowed and his brows flicked up a smidge. I could feel him like a fork in the toaster. And yet the pain of him was a gentle, easy one, his fingertips jolting something warm and jittery up and through and down into my pelvis and down some more—the way I feel liquor on an empty stomach.

Thomas was back in his office by the time I returned. His door was open. When I came in he swivelled in his chair and came to rest, staring at me. He took a heavy breath.

We stayed that way a few seconds until I said, "Are you sleeping with her?"

He shook his head.

"You've never said those words to me. You said it was *prurient*," I shouted.

His body seized at the sound of my raised voice. He nodded. He put one hand across his eyes. "I met her once two years ago and she friended me on Facebook last month. It's just talk."

"Excess Baggage?"

"It's just a game. She wants to intern at the magazine." He clasped his hands and began to crack his knuckles one by one. "I have a problem. You don't know"—he shook his head—"the half of it."

We talked until two in the morning. "Didn't you ever notice the phone bills?" he asked me.

I shook my head. "Calls to that little twink?"

He shook his head. "1-900 numbers are blocked."

When Thomas had first moved to Vancouver from Winnipeg, he was alone. He called 1-900 numbers. Each night, for hours, he was on the phone with a new voice, a new orgy of raunchy debauchery.

The telephone company contacted him after his first bill came through. He owed over three thousand dollars. "We've seen this before," they said. They offered to block 1-900 calls from his use. Block temptation.

In the beginning, he paid to look at websites with bodies and sex, and then as the Internet opened up there was so much for free, he no longer needed to. He didn't have to pay and nobody would ever have to know.

"It's not like—" He paused. "I never touched anyone."

"And can you, I mean, do you get hard like that? When you see girls 'twisted into slick pretzels'?"

He winced. "Don't talk like that." He looked at the floor. "I used to."

For the next four days, the watchmaker and I met after work, at 6:15 exactly, for half an hour. We'd meet and swallow creamy, sweet espresso drinks and say very little. Neither of us told our secrets. Instead I would lay my palms out for him, letting him touch them, trace a course down my lifeline, a fingernail across fate. I let him bend my hands up, buckling the flesh on the insides of my wrists, counting the creases there and at the sides of my pinkies, pricks of sweat rising from the pads of my fingers—everything thickening, liquefying, nosing closer under my clothes, swelling to be touched.

Yesterday, he held one of my hands and it hurt, the fleshy part beside my thumb. It felt bruised and sore, deep inside like an overworked muscle. I said nothing; he felt it.

"Do you have a headache?" he asked me, and I said I did though I didn't. I just wanted the easy hiss of *yes* off my tongue right then. He said something about adrenal glands and pressure points, things I couldn't quite make out through the fog of his pale smooth hands cradling the backs of mine, his thumbs kneading the ache in the bellies of my palms. His wedding band glinted. A moan nestled in my throat waiting for release, and it was then I could feel my soul lifting. Not in any joyous sense; it was as though I were losing myself, as if my soul were seeping away, and I started to cry. I didn't know the watchmaker's name.

Last night, Thomas said that he couldn't go to a therapist. It would get out, he said, and spread like wildfire: *Thomas Gary is a porn addict.* He'd be a laughingstock.

I fingered my watch. *Madge from Jim 1940.*

Thomas slept in his office again. He left for Toronto first thing this morning.

After work today, I got into the car and drove past the café without stopping. If the watchmaker could really read palms, he'd have seen this coming, he would understand. I drove past the watch repair and the café and past the turnoff toward home. Wading into the thick traffic on Highway One, I headed east until I was lost—nothing but farmland and the odd strip mall.

I passed a sign that said VANCOUVER ZOO AND AQUARIUM, made a U-turn and parked.

I am at the zoo now and the sun is setting. It won't be open much longer but I feel as if I am prowling, groping for something. I wish I had a child on my hand right now. Something in a size small with messy curls and a precocious mouth, a child who has just learned to talk a blue streak but doesn't know yet how to censor herself.

I pass by the reptile pavilion, stopping only briefly before I realize I'm not interested in snakes. The cat cages don't work for me either; their restless paws make my heart race. The penguins look too fishy and the fish too hungry. Instead, I am drawn to the monkeys, which normally I am not, but I don't question. This morning I made a decision to have what I crave.

The first cage has the orangutans. I stop and watch them: frantically hairy, they stretch arms out to each other, to food, to the chain-link fence, to outside bodies. It's a slow day at the monkey cage and only two other people are there: a woman and her bored boy-child who is whining, "Ma-a-wm. The *sharks*." He needs to get to them before their official feeding time, he insists. His mother *yes*-es him, absently, but she is busy: she is engrossed. She's leaning across the thin moat that's supposed to discourage patrons from getting too close to the cages. It's only about a foot wide, though, not all that discouraging. A young orangutan, barely her son's age, has attached himself to the fence near her, one hand and both feet entwined in the chain link, the other hand reaching through, reaching for her. She ignores the DO NOT TOUCH sign and takes his hand. They stare at each other. He sighs a little, wraps his fingers loosely in hers and closes his eyes, then opens them on her, tilting his head. She kisses the fingertips of her free hand and touches them to his, and her son says, "Mom,

I'm going. I'm serious, I'm going." But she is transfixed. The orangutan's mouth turns up and he looks grateful and loving and resigned in a way that he can't find words for. The boy huffs and stalks away, toward the big-fish house.

Ten minutes later, the woman is still holding that dark hand, running her light thumb over the fur at his knuckles. He's resting his lips on his own wrist, on his side of the cage. He looks as if he would squeeze himself through one of those two-inch diamonds in the chain link, as if he would gladly let her tear his hide through, limbs scraped off in the process, if it meant he could curl against her breast on the other side. Her eyes are welling and her son is long gone, watching big-toothed fish swallow chunks of flesh the size of dachshunds.

I am mesmerized. And watching them—her and the monkey—gives me a peculiar twinge: sympathy and jealousy all mixed up. And hunger: the real kind and the figurative kind. I suddenly want to swallow everything I come in contact with, and I wonder if I should have gone along with that boy of hers to commune with the sharks.

I am only four or five feet from the woman and the orangutan, when the zoo guy comes between us.

"Excuse me," he says. "Ma'am! Can't you read the sign there? Do not touch the animals and do not feed them; don't touch 'em, don't feed 'em. Understand?"

She turns her head, eyes red and brimming. "I'm not feeding him."

The orangutan doesn't look at the zoo guy, just squeezes his other hand through and takes hold of the woman's forearm, pulling her closer.

The zoo guy scowls. "Now, look what you did. These animals are very unpredictable and you riled him. It's almost closing and now we've got to extricate your damn arm outta there."

The woman gives the furry face a closed-mouth smile and smoothes the fingers on her arm. The orangutan takes sharp breaths and holds tight. She turns her head just a little, snuffles quietly, and says, "Please go away. We just need a couple of minutes. I promise I'll be gone by the time you get back."

"I'm gonna go get the primate guy. And Security. Bet your ass you'll be gone," he mutters. And he heads off in the zebras direction.

The woman looks back into the monkey's eyes, tears sliding toward her jaw, and starts to sing, her voice cracking, *"Lullaby and good night . . ."*

The orangutan lets go of her forearm and reaches farther, straining his hand to her face. She leans her wet cheeks closer and lets him touch her jaw as though she is beautiful; as though she is the most wondrous thing he has ever seen, until they let each other go.

According to Madge and Jim's watch, it's nearly seven o'clock. An announcement comes over the loudspeaker: the zoo is closing in ten minutes.

I'm not ready to leave and I don't know where I'll go when I do. I feel as if there is just too much blank space around me suddenly. I need to sit a minute and collect myself.

Walking toward the duck pond, I move fast to wake up, get some adrenalin going, some fight-or-flight. I ball up two fists and dig my nails in and take a lot of sharp breaths and shake my head hard when the wrong thoughts come in, and I don't care what kind of lunatic I look like.

My calves ache a little by the time I sit down on a bench—it looks brand new, wood stain, no slats, and sanded smooth as a pup's ear. Sun hits the pond and droops lower in the sky, falling into an orangutan-coloured haze, and I take off the watch, set it beside me, whisper to it to go back home, where it belongs.

Greedy Little Eyes

SHE RIDES SHOTGUN IN SOME EARLY-SEVENTIES *convertible, candy apple red and the top's down. Playing her boyfriend is a twenty-something guy sporting a great white Dentyne smile. He shifts gears and regards her with a whole and perfect love. She glances at the map and grins back; her smile is Pepsodent. They are so beautiful and clear-eyed and strong; together they could win best of breed.*

Eventually, they spot it, the cabin; in the midst of a wheat field, not another building in sight, not a person, not a thing, nothing but this cabin and endless waving grain. The cabin sits on stilts as though it were near water and built for flooding. Seeing her uncle outside the door, plump in a suit, smoking a cigar, a fat black moustache behind the smoke, she and the boyfriend climb out of the car and run up the stairs. The uncle smiles and holds his arms open, gestures them inside to a small, single room. Her heart sinks. There is nothing inside but a bed and a dresser. On the dresser is a pile of flawless white eggs and a heat lamp. They have been duped.

It is clear now that she and the boyfriend have been lured by this uncle of hers to procreate and leave the egg behind, where it will be hatched, the baby sold through the black market. The door closes.

Knowing they will be held until they comply, they do what needs to be done and add their egg to those warming on the dresser.

They break past the uncle before he can change his mind, rush back to the red convertible and speed off. Until her furious boyfriend stops the car only minutes from the cabin.

She panics. "Drive!"

"I'm not leaving it."

"Forget it! They can't be alive with just a heat lamp. They're dead. Drive!"

"I've not leaving without it."

"You're on your own." She gets out.

The boyfriend turns the car around and leaves her in the dust.

She's scared that he'll be killed, that they'll come after her or she'll die there alone in the long yellow grass. But he returns in seconds with an egg-filled sheet, its four corners twisted together, transforming it into a sack. She leaps back into the car. Suddenly another vehicle gives chase.

The boyfriend is fierce now, driving for his life. She holds the sheet of eggs in her lap until the prairie grass ends and they are suddenly in Vancouver, rolling right onto the beach. The car stops and she jumps out, eggs in hand, rushes down the hot sand. The sun is falling; the horizon in front of her is

turning pink and orange as her feet hit the ocean. She has a
stranglehold on the sheet, swings with both hands like a batter,
sending the eggs into the setting sun until they splash, bobbing
light on the water. Peach rays shine through the eggs, illumi-
nating the babies inside, their hands held up to the warmth
and bright. "They're alive. They'll die now and it's my fault."

Fern jolts from sleep and stares at the ceiling.

She is giving out Lindt balls in a department store, handing each shopper a Swiss-made blob of sugar, cocoa and
hydrogenated fat, wrapped in one layer of red foil and
another of clear crunchy plastic, twisted at either end,
giving them the look of legless flying bugs in gaudy
formal wear. Fern has an agent who rents her out at sixteen bucks an hour—three for the agent, thirteen for
Fern—to hand out food and drink samples in supermar-
kets, liquor stores, wherever they want a shiny-faced girl
with a quick smile and a miniskirt.

Prior to this job, like, say, when she was working as an
office temp in glassy high-rises downtown, Fern could not
have imagined anything so staggeringly dull as six hours
spent lurking in department store aisles, lips opening and
closing like those of a dying guppy, the same words falling out over and over, *Would you like to try a Lindt Swiss*
Milk Chocolate Truffle? Not that one really need ask when
holding a wicker basket full of eyeball-sized gobs of chocolate. All day long, hands open under her nose and lips
demand more—for their children, husbands and mothers,

visible and not. During the lunch rush today, they lined up all the way out of Candy and into Gourmet Foods.

It's not even three o'clock yet. Fern breathes and stretches to keep from trying out the Kick Boxercize she's learned from infomercials and booting down six-foot displays of Mon Chéri and Ferrero Rocher. She prays for one of those lonely old mall-women to come and talk preserves with her, talk about her sons, her hip replacement. The air prickles her nose as though something might just haul off and happen any minute now. She breathes slow and deep, tries to think serene thoughts as she turns around into a breathless shopper's face.

Fern laughs softly and steps back. The woman *oopses* and *ohs* and touches Fern's arm, setting her purse at her feet, gasping, her heavy bosom heaving. "Oh Jeez." Her hand flits off Fern's arm, then lands again. "You got any idea what's going on in the mall, hon? There's a bloody jewellery heist upstairs!"

Fern smiles and waits for the "highway robbery" punchline. "No," she says. "I haven't heard a thing."

"Yes! I'm tellin' you, right upstairs. The cops are there and the two guys got those, uh, those black toques that go right over your face. They have a hostage! A girl your age, they're using her like a *human shield*."

She says *human shield* like it's something rich and exquisite, the way she might say *movie star* or *diamond tiara*. Or perhaps that's just the way Fern hears it.

"Upstairs? Now?"

The woman nods, quivering from her cheeks to her arms.

"They have a *hostage*?"

More nods. The woman lets go of Fern's arm and takes a chocolate from Fern's basket. "Oh Lord," she says, still catching her breath, pulling the wrapper's ends, letting it spin itself open, then popping the brown ball in her mouth and sighing as though it were a sedative. She pats Fern's hand in thanks and walks away.

Fern scans the floor for the supervisor from the food distributor's office who just might have picked today to come in to check that her smile is in order, and that she insist the customer eat the candy there on the spot thereby upping the chances that they might buy buy buy.

No supervisor in sight. She drops off her basket behind the candy counter, mumbling to the clerk— whom the store dresses in a white doctor's coat, as though he really is doling out sedatives—that she's going to the bathroom.

Police have blocked off the escalators and stairs to the second floor of the mall. Fern gazes up longingly past pissed-off teenagers who demand to know why they can't go upstairs. The officers don't seem to be parting with any information and Fern swallows the lump of desire in her throat. She imagines the hostage in the thief's arm, his free hand holding the gun out in front of them. Fern can feel his arm there across her own chest, can feel herself being pulled backwards along the glossy mall floor. He'd bring her to the getaway car and they would tear out of town, him, her and the driver, diamonds falling in her lap, biting into her thighs with their sweet toothy ridges. She looks at her watch. One more hour of candy-flogging.

The problem with voyeurs is they think it's all about them and their greedy little eyes. They never stop to think about the exhibitionist. Ask any old exhibitionist you like, and they'll tell you: exhibitionism is *by* the exhibitor *for* the exhibitor. Fern sits on her couch, watching the six o'clock news, and bites into another cracker with cheddar as she carves out this new theory of demonstration and spectacle as though it were a letter to the editor.

A performance artist named Martin Flash is the second lead story tonight, the pink underside of his cape snapping in the wind as he calls out over the small crowd in front of the Vancouver Art Gallery: "In exactly one week, I will perform living art, here, at the bottom of these very steps which were once the steps of the Vancouver Courthouse, the steps to so-called justice, the steps on which we are left to scramble in despair like so many rats." With a flourish of his long bony hands, he presents a fat black rodent encased in a clear container the size and shape of a five-pin bowling ball. Flash goes on to say that seven days from now at exactly 4 p.m., he will drive a steamroller over this rat between two art canvases. Fern titters at the screen but feels queasy. The crowd is beginning to heckle as Flash picks up his ball of rat, bows to the cameras and strides off. She pictures herself in that steamroller beside him, the crowd screaming as the two of them make history and the six o'clock news together.

The segment cuts to some reaction sound bites. Owen Almond from the Life Is All Right movement announces that Martin Flash is a sick individual and that, as long as he is chairman of LIAR, not a single hair on that rat's head will be harmed. Almond goes on to say that the mandate of LIAR is to expose abortionists and murderers and these sorts of so-called artists for the liars that they are. Looking straight into camera, he says, "Freedom to kill is a lie."

Fern reaches beside her for another cracker to go with the last slice of cheese, her eyes on the screen as a girl with pink dreadlocks and a pierced eyebrow shrugs into the reporter's microphone and says, "He's just some loser trying to get attention."

"It's not the rat, it's the message!" Fern shouts at the pink-haired girl. She thinks for a moment. "A decent exhibition is the only thing that brings the obscure from darkness into light."

She is sitting on a rock, has given up—the sand is liquid and soupy and can't be walked on. She's tried and her feet sink. She slipped in up to her knees the last time, like she was in quicksand, the type that swallows you up to your neck and then holds you there, lets you hover until some passerby reaches out with a stick and drags you to safety. At least that's how it used to work on Gilligan's Island, *but perhaps in real life there would be no hovering.*

Sand and rocks and ocean—she is stranded there and the only living things she sees are green pokes of grass sticking up

through the wet sand. Until he appears. Just like that, he comes
toward her, but he's not wearing his cape. He's a regular guy
in jeans and a T-shirt and he's walking just fine. His nose is
a real beak—it's large and hooked and she wants to touch the
bump and slope of it with the tip of her tongue. He walks
across the soup to her without a care; he walks on quicksand
like Jesus on water. He asks her if she would like a hand and
she says yes, yes please. He bends and picks her up, cradles her
in his arms. Each step he takes, each time a foot dips into the
silt, it becomes a bird foot, clawed with short webbing, and
each time he pulls one out, toes again, human. She looks into
his eyes. "Where did you learn to do that?"

"I saw it in a movie," he tells her. And she is in love.

At the supermarket the next day, Fern is giving out mini-
paper-cups of non-alcoholic cider and she's cold and
frustrated. Too much bloody air conditioning, she thinks,
who needs to be this cold? Her mind strays nervously
to Martin Flash and how he appeared to her as a bird-
man in her dream. She's never dreamed about a person
having bird-like qualities before. Never. Only herself
with the whole egg-laying business.

Fern has always assumed she is a bit nuts with these
egg dreams. She remembers the very first one, when she
was a teenager. She'd always had the feeling she was
waiting to perform some big, important task, that even
though she didn't know what it was, she was late—she
was missing it. The sense of it niggled at her, constantly

there in the back of her mind while walking home from school, having a bath, doing sit-ups in the middle of P.E. class—she *had* to get going, now. *Hurry the hell up* was the general gist of the feeling. It drove her to distraction and confusion and then, wham, the first dream: birds. Dream birds were creating something monumental and they sent for Fern, because they desperately needed her help. She had to make a journey and on that journey she would learn her purpose; she would know what she was meant to do. She walked along, cutting through the backyards of strangers, giddy with anticipation.

Then—Grab. Shake. "What are you doing? Fern? What's wrong?"

Oh for god's sake, I've got to go, she'd wanted to say, but there she was in the kitchen all of a sudden, her mother touching her shoulder and demanding answers to foolish questions when anyone could see that Fern was almost *there*, it was just around the corner.

She tried to push past her mother, brush her off with "The thing—I gotta . . . *Thing!*"

Fern's mother grabbed hold of her with both hands then, voice rising, "What's wrong with you? Are you *on* something? Fern look at me! Are you on drugs?"

She never forgave her mother. How could she? But now this Martin Flash with his rat. Him turning into a bird the way he did, it had to be a sign. A premonition of some kind.

She filled the cups with raspberry and apple-lime cider, and thought of Flash standing before those screaming people, hating him, threatening him. She saw his webbed feet again, carrying her away. She thinks of that Jesus poster, the one with the single set of footprints. Something was gelling in her mind but she couldn't quite make it out yet. Maybe if she could just talk to Martin Flash, find the missing link, it could all make sense.

"Are these on sale?"

Fern squinted up. "Huh?"

"Performance artist, Martin Flash, or The Flash as he's known in some creative circles, announced three days ago that in one week's time, that's the tenth of July, he will act out what he calls the ultimate human experience when he drives a steamroller over a rat. Here to comment on this increasingly controversial stunt are animal rights activist Ryan Turner as well as . . ."

Fern is reading the newspaper while she listens to the six o'clock news, dropping cracker crumbs on a picture of Martin Flash.

The Province quotes him as saying, "Art is the ultimate question, it is the provocateur, and it is life itself. Protesting art is tantamount to embracing a totalitarian state. It is death. These are the same people who get exterminators in their homes to kill pigeons, mice, squirrels, roaches, whatever they can snuff out. These rats, at the pet shop—the majority are purchased to feed snakes." His face in the paper is a black and white portrait of lonesome courage, Fern thinks.

When another news item comes on, Fern changes the channel. She catches the tail end of the Flash story on another channel. When it ends she continues to flip stations until she hears Middle Eastern music and a voice saying, "And just as in his dream Peter Bailey woke that night to a house in flames."

A small bald man appears in an armchair and says, "If it weren't for my dream I would not have gotten out alive."

Fern checks the TV guide: *Dreams, Visions and Intuition.*

The bald man continues. "Khalil Gibran said, 'Trust in dreams for in them is the hidden gate to eternity.'"

Fern gawks at the screen and rubs her stomach, trying to calm the flutter.

The two birds chirp in her ears, breathless, but she understands them. Exhausted, their breasts heave. They have been building all day, laying eggs, one each.

Fern knows they are far too tired, there is barely anything left of them. They beg her to help, lay the third egg. She cries for them. She understands now. Three. Three is the magic number.

She is at Costco giving out samples of Melba toast with a new kind of peanut butter and she's thinking to herself how she's becoming like that girl in the Margaret Atwood book, *The Edible Woman*, the one who found herself so repulsed by life she could eat nothing but bread and peanut butter. Except with her it's crackers and cheese.

She can't stand food or people or anything. She can't even remember the last time she returned a friend's call. Does this mean I don't have friends any more? she wonders. The idea isn't terribly troubling, and just as her eyebrows raise in curiosity at her own indifference, Molly MacRae walks right up to Fern's peanut butter stand and pops a piece of Melba in her mouth.

"Long time no see, stranger," she says to Fern, sputtering a few crumbs.

Fern wipes away the one crumb that's landed on the back of her hand. "Yeah," she says for lack of witty repartee.

Molly MacRae's baby is parked in a stroller beside her and Molly absently jiggles her baby, who drools a small smile at anyone who will look. "Where the hell have you been, Ferny? Haven't heard a peep out of you since Christ was a kid."

Molly's from Cape Breton and *Christ* and *hell* figure a lot in her conversation. Fern finds this particularly irksome right now for reasons she can't quite place. Perhaps it's the use of Jesus' last name like that, as though he were prime minister. Or a serial killer. Fern tries to smile but thinks that for a bunch of Catholics, Cape Bretoners wouldn't know something sacred if it bit them in the ass.

"So?" Molly stares wide-eyed at Fern. "What's up?"

"I'm"—Fern looks away for two or three moments as though she might be going into a trance, then looks back at Molly—"going to have a baby."

Molly gasps. "Jesus, Mary and Joseph, Fern! I didn't even know you were seeing anybody. Wow! That's great! Isn't it?"

Fern smiles sheepishly, then beams. "Yeah, it's pretty great. It's what I'm meant to do. This baby is—This baby will complete the world."

Molly lets go of the stroller and comes round to hug Fern. "Oh god, that's terrific! That you're happy and all, and, and who's the proud pappy?" Then she whispers, "You didn't run off and get married already, did you?" Fern shakes her head. "But you're going to, right?"

"We haven't decided yet." Fern's smile becomes smug.

Molly holds her at arm's length. "Chrissake, Fern, you're bringin' a baby into the world. Get yourself married."

"Why? Mary and Joseph weren't married."'

"What? Of course they were married! Jesus had brothers and sisters for god's sake."

"You're just assuming that. And Jesus wasn't married either."

Molly lets her go, puts one hand on her hip, the other over her mouth and shakes her head as though wherever they just let this girl out of, there is no choice now but to take her right back.

After a moment she says, "Fern, Jesus never got married because He's God. You know? He was a *virgin*. The man never so much as looked at a woman."

Fern looks at her with pity. "Oh sure, he and Mary Magdalene were just *platonic.*"

The heat is on now and not just for Martin Flash—the whole town is suffocating in record temperatures. But it must be especially bad for him, Fern thinks, being on the lam and all with his rat. She thinks of the rat's impending doom and feels a momentary sadness. But it is only through death that life can come.

Her eyes well at the thought as she rubs her hand in circles over her belly, round and full now with crackers and cheddar and jasmine tea. At least there's only one more day to wait. Tomorrow Flash will show the masses a thing or two about a thing or two and Fern will be there. She's already turned down two jobs for tomorrow and one of them would've paid double her usual salary. It involved dressing up like a bumblebee and giving out samples of tuna salad downtown. No matter: tomorrow she will be dressed in a manner befitting a mother-to-be and she will find him and take his hand and instantly he will know, live on camera, that she is *the one.* No one will ever forget Martin and Fern Flash.

At 3:30 p.m. the next day, Fern is making her way downtown. She is frustrated with herself because she'd meant to be there by now. She wanted to be standing right

beside the steamroller where she could smile into Martin
Flash's eyes as he turned the ignition. He would know
her instantly and bring her into his light.

But instead, she's stuck on the Burrard Bridge and
traffic is at a standstill. A sunny Friday summer afternoon in this city and the whole place goes mad; they
don't know what else to do but run to their hopeful little
Miatas that have been sitting with their miserable tops
up for a month of soggy Fridays, jump in and peel off
to somewhere blue and glinting, anywhere just to be
seen in the sun by the water, looking breezy and blessed.

Fern smoothes her new dress and glances at herself
in the rear-view mirror, noticing her eyes are a little
baggy. She could hardly sleep last night, and as soon as
the stores opened, she spent hours changing in and out
of dresses. She wanted something gauzy and flowing and
visited ten or twelve different shops in Kitsilano trying
to find *it*. She would know *it* when she saw it, just the
way she knew Martin when she saw him and the way he
would know her. And she'd finally found it all right—this
was the dress. She felt radiant just having it against her
body. She looked down, patting her belly. "We'll get
there. We'll get there because we'll get there, that's all."

Robson Street is so packed with traffic, Fern is on the
verge of abandoning her car smack in the middle of the
road and walking the last couple blocks. She searches
for an all-news radio station. Toward the end of the

dial, a female reporter quacks about an angry mob gathering in front of the art gallery. Martin Flash has yet to be seen.

Fern's heart jumps through her new dress. She looks at her watch and screams out the window, "It's five to four, you bastards. Move it!"

She manoeuvres and darts ahead, ignoring the honks and curses of surrounding drivers. If she has to, she will pull up onto the sidewalk and park, tow trucks be damned.

Coming up on Georgia Street, she can hear the crowd. She turns up the radio. The reporter's voice bites through the airwaves. " . . . and pockets of schoolchildren are chanting in unison, 'Free Shnooky, Free Shnooky.' As you may know, the black rat that Martin Flash will crush has been dubbed Shnooky by children across the city. They've climbed onto the steamroller parked here in front of the gallery, and the children vow they will put a stop to the rodent's murder—Here he is! Martin Flash is coming down the steps of the gallery in a black and pink cape. Flash is smiling but he does not appear to have Shnooky the Rat on his person and—Oh no—Martin Flash has been hit! Someone from the crowd has struck Flash and he is on the ground—Police are moving in . . ."

Fern churns round the corner now, laying on the horn, screaming at the top of her lungs. About thirty metres ahead, men and women heave together as one contorted mass, spewing rocks and obscenities. The caped figure of Flash wrenches himself free, and tears across the grass, the sidewalk and through parked cars. Hypnotized by the sight of his cape snapping toward her, Fern's foot continues to shove the gas until something large flies out from the crowd. Martin Flash is slapped across her windshield like a scrap of paper before he flutters down and off the hood of her skidding car.

Fern is paralyzed, her foot jammed into the brake as police demand public order over bullhorns in the distance. Protestors stand in the street, mouths open, staring at Fern.

She stares back. The sun has shrunken her pupils to nothing, giving her pale eyes the look of the blind. Pushing the gear shift into park, she steps out of her car and around to the front.

Furious strangers glare from all sides as she hunches beside Martin Flash. A rat hangs dead from a pink lined pocket inside his cape.

Fern puts her cheek to his, says, "Forgive them, Lord, they know not what they do," and carefully lays her body down beside his.

"Shh." Flash slits one eye open just enough for her to catch it and whispers, "Lie still," as cameramen cut through, circle around and crouch for a clear shot.

You Sound Tiny

A PETULANT MOAN FILLED THE ROOM, the bawl of something small that would one day grow into its large paws. I could feel the vibration of whimpers through his hands as he clutched my hair, edged a blade harder against my neck—or maybe it was just the nails of the hand holding the knife that bit me.

"You can't let her go," Ed insisted. Then into my ear, "Tell them who you work for. Where is my *mouse* money!"

He was demanding cash again as if I were a bank teller, as if I had control over more than renewing overdue books.

A police officer inched forward, hands expansive, arms wide. He said, "Before I became a cop, you know what I was going to be? A marriage counsellor! Let's just sit down and talk, the three of us. This doesn't solve anything, does it."

Two more police officers stood outside the library doors. A walkie-talkie squawked from the hall and a hand rushed to silence it.

Ed stomped his foot.

Butterflies taste with their feet, I recalled. I have a tendency to recite trivia when I am nervous.

"She's *not* my wife," Ed said. To my ears the words had a liquid quality, as if they'd been left in the rain.

There was no one else but us in the library now: the cop, Ed and me. Everyone else had slipped out the emergency exit. He had let everyone else go.

Then suddenly Ed let me go, spread his arms wide and waved the knife in the air. It must have looked as though he was dancing, like in a Gene Kelly movie. It reminded me of how romantic he could be. With Ed to the side now, I could see into the policeman's sugary-brown eyes, the nearest one, who might have been a marriage counsellor. It seemed we were exchanging some kind of ocular smoke signals. My eyes dipped to see his holster undone, and just as I began to understand he might shoot Ed in the gut, Ed barked another obscenity and slammed his knife on the returns counter.

"What's the point?" He shoved me away. "You're in on it, *they're* in on it."

Suddenly the room was a thunderous flight of heavy shoes, uniforms and hands. Ed reached out to his knife again just as he was tackled backwards in a braying heap.

The blinds in my apartment are closed. The ringer on my telephone is off. I am wearing earplugs because without them it sounds as though war has broken out across the road. It's only condos going up but I cannot bear the rapid fire of their nail guns, the sound of saws chewing through what comes near.

I'm reading Dr. Seuss again—the first children's book I ever read, thanks to Ed. It was his gift to me and probably the reason I fell for him. Growing up, my parents, my father in particular, assured me that children's books encouraged a form of idiocy and discouraged rational, lucid thought. Ed, on the other hand, was a proponent of idiocy. Through the two menstrual cycles I knew him, during the worst period day, he would bring home helium-filled balloons, tie one to each of my big toes, then lie beside me, rubbing my cramping belly, and reading me the words of Seuss's Star-Belly Sneetches, the snootiest beasts on the beaches.

He was nicer during the first period than the second. Marriage changes everything.

The greatest economic loss from mice is not due to how much they eat, but what must be thrown out because of damage or contamination. I met Ed as a result of a curvaceous brown mouse who strolled brazenly from a hole in the baseboard of my kitchen cupboard. She would walk to centre-floor, stare at me with a bored cynicism, pick up a crumb, then swing her big behind round and saunter back from whence she came. Her attitude was what got me, the impudence. I let it go on for a week before I opened the phone book to Pest Control. I called Allsfair Pests. The man who answered said they couldn't get an exterminator out until the following Monday; it was infestation season.

"You're going to kill her?"

"What'dja think we were gonna do, put her in a home for wayward girls?"

I hung up, stared into the phone book and dialled Whoville Critter Control. Ed answered.

Of course I didn't know he was Ed then and I asked what steps he would take in a case like this—if he would be exterminating.

There was silence at the other end until finally he said, "What kind of crummy question is that?"

He showed up with a catch-and-release contraption. A dollop of peanut butter was placed well inside the trap, which was set in the middle of the kitchen floor. Then Ed joined me in the living room to wait and watch from a distance. I offered him tea. Or perhaps some juice. There might be wine in the fridge. He declined, said he needed his full faculties when on the job. Besides, it would mean re-entering the suspect zone.

I smoothed my dress, folded my hands in my lap, and there we sat, in silence. Waiting. I could smell his Juicy Fruit chewing gum. His lean back curved forward, slim shoulders coming around as if to cup his heart. And his lips, so red against pale skin, made him look Pre-Raphaelite.

Within twenty minutes, the mouse sashayed out of her hole to survey Ed's trap.

Watching her inspection, I whispered, "Do you think she's calculating the risk factor?"

Ed tilted his head toward mine, moved his mouth to my ear. His breath was warm and fruity as he let the sweetest *shhh* breeze from his lips. I would have been much more popular at the library if I knew how to shush people that way. My head nosed up against his mouth, my ear stealing a kiss just as the trap door slammed me back into my skin.

A week later, my father called while Ed was in the shower. Pretty winged things had fluttered inside me when I thought of my very own Ed down the hall, but my father's tone was something of a fly swatter.

"What's this bill here: Whoville Critter Control? One hundred and seven dollars. Says, 'mouse,' on the bill."

"I had a mouse and I called someone to take care of it."

"Nobody has mouse. They have *mice*. Why didn't you let *me* take care of it? Did you know that this Whoville Critter Control is just a one-man show? He works out of his home. *Edward Margolese*. Did you let *Edward Margolese* into the apartment while you were alone?"

My father collects apartments. He owns several in my building. Including mine. He calls it *the* apartment, never *your* apartment.

I listened to him shake his head before saying, "You should quit the library. It would make more sense if you worked for me. I could teach you how to budget."

Each time he suggested this I would think wistfully of those paper bodies all around me at work, sober and available, willing to open wide and present their knowledge, but only in the event that I should ask.

I held the receiver a moment and then told him, "When six hundred managers from a broad spectrum of Canadian industry were surveyed in 1992, about one-third of them reported that poor literacy caused serious difficulties with introducing new technology and productivity."

There is heavy machinery in my father's warehouse. The sounds careened under his office door, but still I could hear his sigh.

Three days after Ed was taken hog-tied from the library, tearing a screech through the world, after I have reread his copies of *Winnie-the-Pooh*, *Stuart Little* and *Alice in Wonderland*, I decide to turn the ringer on my phone back on. There are messages from the library, from a police therapist, two from my father and one from my mother expressing my father's concern. I hear the *beep* of an incoming call as I listen. It could be anyone and I don't wish to talk to just anyone. I hang up.

The ringing starts again. The number on call display is unfamiliar but it occurs to me I'd rather talk to a stranger than anyone I know.

It's Officer Mike, the voice says. Officer Mike is the policeman who tackled instead of shooting Ed. Ed had gotten hold of his knife and stabbed Officer Mike. Just in the arm. I don't believe he did it on purpose. Ed is afraid of blood. It makes him feel sick and scared.

I ask Officer Mike how his arm is. It's fine, he says, just a flesh wound. In a serious tone he tells me that Ed is undergoing psychiatric evaluation, but that I can rest assured he will remain in custody.

This does not make me feel safe. It makes me feel as though I've just seen blood. Nobody needs to be afraid of Ed. "Okay."

"You know, they have counsellors to help you through the aftermath of situations like these. Department therapists."

"I'm fine."

"You don't sound fine."

"How do I sound?"

"Tiny. Fragile. Do you have food there? Do you have anyone to help you?"

I'm quiet a moment. It comes to me that I have not eaten today. And maybe not the day before either. I can't remember. Maybe this is shock. Or mourning. Or maybe, just as violence begets violence, once a person forgets two or three meals, the brain becomes less likely to pick up hunger signals; forgetting two or three meals could lead to weeks of starvation.

Officer Mike, perhaps taking my silence for the embarrassment of the lonely, says, "Look, why don't I just bring you a few things—Do you like Chinese?"

After the first time Ed made love with me, he lay stroking the slope of my temple and said, "I thought you were a rumour."

It was our third date. The third date is, statistically, when most couples decide to have sex. No one will think any the worse of you for doing it then.

I didn't know what he meant, but it sounded romantic. Being with Ed made me feel as though I were a rare and resplendent species.

I had refused my father's attempts to get another exterminator to my apartment and he responded by having his secretary phone each of his seven units to discuss pest control. No one else had seen a mouse or evidence of such. They did not want fumigation. They did not want pest poison in their homes.

I maintained my position that the mouse was a loner, that she had no friends or family and there was nothing further to worry about as we had set her free in Stanley Park.

"Who's *we*?" he demanded.

By our third week (and twelfth date), Ed had an inkling that my father did not approve. Perhaps it was the return of Ed's Whoville Critter Control bill with *N/A* scrawled across the face of it and an attached letter reading, in part, "Conclude all transactions through this office. Do not contact site of infestation."

By the fourth week, Ed had moved in. I insisted. Out of both love and necessity. Two months before, he had seen a news story on television about an eighty-two-year-old woman robbed at knifepoint, her wheelchair stolen. Her family had no money and she would be on a lengthy wait list for a government-subsidized chair. The story made Ed cry. His grandmother had raised him from the age of twelve until she died when he was seventeen. Unable to bear the thought of the woman on television housebound, he called the news station and sent her his rent money as well as money for his electricity, phone and cable.

Ed was eating popcorn for dinner, staring at his eviction notice, when the lights went out. He called to ask if he could spend the night just before his line went dead.

That night, he came to me with a suitcase, games of Boggle and Whodunit, and all his DVDs including *A Charlie Brown Christmas, A Year Without a Santa Claus* and *Rudolph, the Red-Nosed Reindeer.* We spent the warmest night of the year watching yuletide specials. I loved Ed more than words.

Officer Mike opens all the Chinese takeout boxes. He spoons out servings of chow mein, egg foo young and chop suey onto our plates, then tops it off with an egg roll each. He hands me a napkin and offers me a choice of chopsticks or fork. I choose sticks; Chinese food tastes peculiar from a fork.

As we eat, flashes of Officer Mike in the library come to mind—arms open and extended, bent as though waiting for a small child. I know now why he struck me that way. Being such a large man, he stoops slightly when walking through door frames. He looks as though he feels guilty for taking up space.

When we finish eating, Officer Mike brings our plates to the kitchen and stops to look up at the burnt-out lights inches above his head. Two out of the three bulbs are dead. Dimness has offered a certain comfort lately.

He frowns and asks if I would like him to change them while he's here. I think of the Abominable Snowman in Ed's copy of *Rudolph, the Red-Nosed Reindeer*, monstrous and bumbling, but his incredible size makes him the perfect candidate to place shining gold stars atop Christmas trees. I go into my cupboard and find replacement bulbs, stand outside the kitchen and watch him make the changes. No chair necessary.

The phone rings. I keep my gaze on his hands as they twist and secure all they touch.

He glances. "You're not going to answer that?"

"I imagine it's my father."

The ringing stops for two or three moments and resumes.

"Would you like me to answer? No point making your family worry."

"I don't make them."

"Do they know what happened?"

"Did you tell them?" Something about the sheer bulk of Officer Mike, the bulbs, the phone, tilt up the corners of my mouth.

The ringing stops. Officer Mike and I look at each other and he says, "Is there anything else I can do for you? Could I take you for a walk? Many victims don't feel safe to go out alone after—" and he stops because I am very near him now.

Holding his wrist, I carefully unbutton his cuff, slowly push up the sleeve, and ask if I can see his wound.

He stands calm as a horse allowing his shoe to be checked. "It's nothing. Seemed like a reflex the way he stuck me with it. Doesn't hurt much."

I trace the surgical tape with my fingertip. "You're able to use it?" And I stare up into his brown-sugar eyes the way I did three days ago. I have the strangest urge to be lifted, raised to the ceiling. Officer Mike stares back then, nods and bends, picks me up. He stands with me that way a few moments. I'm high enough to feel the warmth of new bulbs on my face.

Carrying me down the hall, his head bowed, he murmurs, "Whatever I can do for you."

In the fifth week, Ed sat me on the couch and knelt at my feet. "I have no money and I know I have to do something about that." He took his cellphone from his pocket and placed it on the coffee table. He hadn't had another mouse call since we met. "But in the meantime, until we get some, I have a promise ring for you." From his jacket, he took a small yellow cube he'd fashioned from a Tim Hortons doughnut box. Inside the cube was a Timbit, a doughnut hole that had been tunnelled through. He held my hand, took the sugary ball from its box and pushed the doughnut onto my finger. "With this ring, I thee wed."

I grinned at him. "I thought you said it was a promise ring."

"It is. I'm wedded to the promise of marrying you. Now seal it." He held my ringed finger between us, until we each parted our jaws and took a bite.

In the sixth week: "Do you mean to tell me you've got that horse's ass living with you? In the apartment?"

"I'll thank you to refrain from calling Ed a horse's ass," I whispered into the phone. Ed was in the bedroom still sleeping. "And it is *my* apartment."

"*Your* apartment?" My father laughed a little too long, a little too loud. "You are living under my roof and you'll do so alone until such time as you marry and become someone else's problem."

"For your edification, *Father,* Ed just asked me to marry him."

Another of those horrible laughs. "Don't be ridiculous. Have him out by the end of the week." He hung up.

I lowered the receiver and turned to see Ed, not in the bedroom, but standing close by, looking rumpled and defeated.

"My dad used to call me a horse's ass too." He looked at the floor. "You're a horse's ass!" he hollered suddenly. He looked up but his eyes darted away. "I guess it's unanimous."

"No," I said, shaking my head. "No!" I explained to him that my father had never seen me in love, and suggested that perhaps he was jealous. I had read about that sort of thing.

Nevertheless, that is when Ed changed. It was as if something dark and tar-stiff filled his being and I didn't know how to shine light on him.

He fell asleep on the couch that night and didn't come to bed. He did the same the next night. On the third night, I thought I heard the bedroom door squeak and I turned over, hoping to see him. The room was dark and shadowy. He wasn't there, and yet I felt him. I sat up, still dozy and thick-headed. I wondered if I had been dreaming of Ed, craving him. Perhaps it was just the last bits of dream haunting me.

I wondered if he was awake too and I leaned forward to see around my dresser, see if he might be out in the hall. On the floor, on the other side of the dresser, a dark figure hunched. I strained to see through the darkness and then suddenly it moved—raised its head. I shrieked and scrambled back against the wall.

"It's me, it's just me!" Ed said as he jumped up. "I'm sorry!"

"What were you doing down there?"

"Listening to you breathe." He sat on the edge of the bed.

I dropped my head against his arm. "Why are you doing this? Please come to bed."

He set me back from him and said, "You don't know who I am. You don't know who you are."

I tried to touch his face.

Ed gently put my hand back on the blanket. "Do you know what a horse's ass is? A screw-up—useless, aimless—I'm a horse's ass." He got up and left the room, closing the door behind him.

That morning as I swallowed back tears and readied myself for work, Ed dressed himself too: black Levi's, black shirt, black tie, and an old black blazer. His face was stony. I asked if he'd be home for dinner and offered to make us piggies-in-blankets.

He walked out the door.

He wasn't there when I came home from the library and it felt bad in my apartment. It felt like *the* apartment. Turning every light on, I tried to feel warm. Curled up on the couch, I didn't move until I heard the sound of his key in the lock the next morning.

Ed came into the living room, long limbs looking skeletal. He stood over me. His tie hung like a noose and his chest jumped a little under his shirt.

I sat up. "I miss you," I said.

"You shouldn't." It looked as though he hadn't slept either.

I thought of an article I'd read once in *Mademoiselle* magazine. Among the tips for weeding out Mr. Wrong: "If a man says he's not good enough for you, believe him."

Ed sat on the coffee table. "My dad died."

"Oh god. Ed. When?"

"Five years ago. I never went to the funeral. I went to see my aunt yesterday and we had a little memorial service. Sometimes I think I wasn't weaned properly. You know? You must. You and I are so opposite, we're the same."

Ed told me that we weren't doing each other any good. He couldn't speak for me, he said, but he was going to have to grab his life by the ankles and shake it upside down. "I need a program."

The next day he showed up at the library. Who knows how long he'd been standing in the entrance when I saw him. I was busy with a lineup of checkouts, but I did look up and wave. He gave me a nervous smile and then poked a number into his cellphone. He talked for just a few seconds before sticking the phone back in his pocket and striding to the front of the line.

"Where is my mouse money?" He sounded sarcastic. I had just scanned someone's card and Ed snapped it from my fingers. "Jesus Christ," he barked at the card's owner. "Don't let her do that."

The young woman reached for her library card with a mixture of bemusement and fear.

I decided to laugh. I told her that Ed was being silly. That's when Ed pulled the knife, stabbed it into the counter and said, "How's this for silly?" He threw his arm against the woman in the manner of a driver protecting his passenger during a sudden stop. She jumped back and the rest of the line scattered and cried out. There were only women in the library and none wanted to play hero.

Ed squinted at me. "Think you're pretty smart? Tell them who you work for, bitch!"

After he was arrested, Ed used his one phone call to reach me. He whispered, "Sorry I called you a bitch, but I needed your reaction to be genuine. I sounded pretty nuts, huh? Mouse money?" He said he knew a guy who worked in a place for the criminally insane. They do therapy and job training, he said. Most guys spend a year there and then they're rehabilitated back into society. "It's a real program."

"This is crazy, Ed."

"Would you testify to that?"

Officer Mike lays me carefully on my bed. As he straightens, he is so giant-like that I find it difficult to take the whole of him in at once. Beside the bed, he lowers himself on one knee and says again, "Whatever I can do for you."

"Would you switch places?"

He doesn't question, only replaces my body with his own, lies calmly over the space I just occupied. As I stand, I marvel at what it must be like to come in and out of places so fearlessly. I move my feet to where he stood a moment before and try to let it fill me, that bigness.

The phone rings on my dresser. There is no call display on my bedroom phone and Officer Mike and I watch for three rings before I decide.

The voice at the other end says, "It's me."

My heart spasms.

"I'm here at the place. I had a counselling session already, baby."

Ed has never called me "baby" before. I don't like it.

Ed whispers, "I think they're still evaluating me."

I don't respond.

"My buddy," he says, "the guy I told you about. He let me use the phone."

Officer Mike's eyes are on the ceiling.

Silence from the receiver. Finally Ed whispers, "If they talk to you, make sure, you know—tell them I need help. I'm not a criminal." He laughs, a bit breathlessly.

I turn my free hand palm up and stare at it. "The fingerprints of koala bears are virtually indistinguishable from those of humans, so much so that they could be confused at a crime scene," I say and drop the receiver back in its cradle.

Turning my gaze back to Officer Mike, who is floating on my vast bed as if it were an ocean, I back up to the space where he stood earlier and position myself just so. Still staring down, my splayed fingers fade out of focus and then I see my feet. This time I feel it like Alice must have felt it in Wonderland and I am amazed.

Georgia, It's Me

"You're not as funny as my mummy," said Dusty's cake-y scrambled egg.

"Dusty, stop making egg-puppets and eat your breakfast," I told her.

Loose springs of blonde hair dangled above her plate, longer straighter bits stroking her bacon. "*Mummer is way funner*," she sang. The hand holding scrambled egg drooped at the wrist and Dusty did her impersonation of a wealthy Southern gentleman. "Lovey," she drawled, "this is not egg"—she jiggled the yellow mess toward me—"it's unborned chicken baby."

"Yup, I know it." I picked the plastic honey pack off the table and drizzled the rest into my tea. "Your mother tell you that?"

"Yepper depper, yes she did." Dusty pointed at the honey. "And *that*, my darlin', my honey-bunny, is bee barf."

"You're grossin' me out, kid."

This from the waiter who Dusty also thought was way funner than me. Jeans slumped around his hips, and a T-shirt hugged his reedy torso as he refilled my aluminum teapot with hot water and let the lid clank down. The smudgy transfer on the front of his T-shirt said *Supertramp* and was so old its black dye had faded to a sulky grey. His clothes were likely older than he was, and that irritated me. I could imagine him using the expression *back in the day* when talking about music from five years ago. I was not in the mood.

He picked up Dusty's crumpled napkin and waved it across her mouth before he took a fresh one from his back pocket, shook it with a flourish and laid it in her lap. "It's lucky you're so good-lookin' or I'da tossed you outta here by now."

Aren't you droll, I thought.

Dusty giggled ferociously as she wiggled in her seat, sounding like her mother—my sister. God, I could just see her in a few years, smiling so hard her eyes would well with tears, just exactly like my sister, my little skinless sister.

When our mother died, Dad said Alice lost her skin. Any little thing could penetrate her; a light breeze could set off a crying jag. We kept Alice away from the evening news, butcher shops and sad movies—none of those Disney things with the brutality-of-life lessons.

When I was nine years old, I took Alice to see a matinee. *Charlotte's Web* was playing and we couldn't wait to see it because Daddy said that Paul Lynde from *Hollywood Squares* would be playing the rat. He dropped us off in front of the Orpheum with three two-dollar bills and we stood under the marquee a few moments, making plans for buying up the entire refreshment stand.

Minutes later we were sitting in the grand old theatre, its red velvet curtains and gilded banisters far too sumptuous for its new role as a movie house, slurping our drinks and shoving more popcorn into our mouths than would fit. Gorging on licorice and Smarties and fizzy orange pop, Alice and I turned to each other and stuck out our tongues, each attempting to exhibit the more gruesome display of chew-goo possible before the lights went down.

We squealed as the curtains closed and reopened to signify that the feature was about to begin.

It went downhill from there.

Alice's face shone with tears from the point at which Wilbur the baby pig died and was resuscitated—basically, right from the start—until the end when Charlotte, the spider, died and was not. She shrieked as Charlotte sighed her last breath and fell away from the cartoon barn rafters. Then she wailed in a way that brought the ushers running. Her sobbing seven-year-old body had to be lifted from her seat and carried out of the theatre.

I wanted to call our father, but Alice fell into hysterics. She wouldn't let me out of her sight for even a minute and I had to tell the manager our phone number so he could make the call. My eyes and throat ached as she sobbed grief into my neck. I thought then that Alice's sorrow was heavier, more lush, a truer blue than any I could ever feel.

Dusty peered across at the guy who had just sat down one table over. He had a little more blue-collar appeal than the patrons who generally hung out in Caffe Barney, which was, despite its name, more bar than café. Windowless but for the sidewalk facade, and one or two skylights overhead, the front third of the room sported an aged wood bar. Farther back were heavy tables set close together and running deep into the café, which was easily five times as long as it was wide. At night the place jumped with alt-rock for the jeans-clad university crowd that bantered about their respective intellectual pursuits as they sucked up microbrewed beers and Australian shiraz thick as jam in a glass.

The new guy's hair was something like Dusty's own but a little less wild and cut to his jaw. My niece appeared to be trying to inspect him surreptitiously. Feeling around in the bib pocket of her overalls as though for something small and precious, she ogled him through her tangled mop. I could see her eyes dance up his thick arms, across his chest and down over a gently protruding belly that also matched her own.

Dusty cupped the side of her mouth, asking me in her little girl's whisper, "Do you think he's pretty?"

I guess he was attractive: pale eyes, brawny and solid. He looked like a landscaper or something. But I'd lost my eye lately. I felt drained and indifferent to sex.

I leaned toward her. "Don't whisper about strangers."

Dusty bent forward so that our foreheads were nearly touching and said, staring deep into my eyes, "You're like a crabby old gramma, you know."

When Alice turned fifteen she told me she liked girls as much as boys. I was startled, I suppose, but it wasn't as though it were out of character. I'm sure she thought being bisexual was fair. She had always brooded over justice, the equality of souls, but this idea exhausted me, as if it were yet another stray she wanted to bring home.

"What do you mean, 'as much'?"

Her laughter jangled around the room. "Am I freaking you out?"

She had climbed into my bed, the way she usually did on Friday nights, weaving her limbs through mine, rustling with gossip and whispering nonsense that sent us both into fits of laughter. When she was in her teens, her joy was as frenetic as her sadness was bleak.

"No," I said flatly. Frankly, I thought, she should come up with a better reason for trying sex with a girl— or sex with anybody. Life wasn't, after all, just one big chorus of "How Much Is that Doggy in the Window?" There were real people involved. Other people besides herself.

"Are you scared I'm going to squeak your boobies?" she teased and then grabbed one of my breasts like a squeeze-toy.

"Get out!" I smacked her hand away and giggled despite myself. "No. I'm just—I don't know. I never heard of anyone your age being into girls before."

"What's the difference? Why can't I fall in love with a girl same as a guy? If I was a French writer-chick, no one would give it a second thought."

"Anaïs Nin was a self-absorbed twat," I announced. Which made her squeal with pleasure.

"So, now what?" I pressed on. "Are you going to get yourself a girlfriend or something? If Dad finds out, I'm the one who's going to have to pick up the pieces, I'm the one who'll have to talk him down off the water tower."

She wrapped herself a little tighter around me. "If Dad's pissed off, it's my problem."

I sighed. "Fine. Your problem."

"Promise you'll still love me like stupid even if I turn out to be a lezzie?" Alice sang "*Lezzie girl, lezzie girl*" to the tune of the *Spider-Man* theme song. Soon she had the two of us bouncing with sleep-deprived laughter because the only thing that seemed to rhyme with *girl* was *squirrel*.

Our giggles eventually eased and as we caught our breath, Alice broke the spell. "Do you think she killed herself?"

A non sequitur, but the subject in question was clear. There was no other "she" at this time of night.

"It was a car accident. Why would you think she killed herself?"

"I don't know. Who knows."

Our mother was an overripe fruit, plump and succulent, and ready to burst out every which way. She was like Alice, emotionally. Or Alice was like her. Daddy was wrong about Alice becoming thin-skinned when Momma died. That's not what happened, I don't think. His memory has painted Momma as a perennially joy-filled Mother Earth. And she was that. But she could also be struck down by grief the same way Alice can. She could watch the news, hear of famine, rape and murder, and soak the sofa with her tears. Sometimes she would get up in the night, enveloped by fear.

I remember the first time I woke to the sound of frantic jabbering in the dark hallway outside my room. It was a woman's voice, sort of like Momma's—maybe a dark cousin of hers. I listened to the creak of hardwood as light footsteps passed from one end of the hall to the other, followed by the sound of Daddy's murmur, heavy feet hurrying after hers. Alice was in my bed, tiny snores wheezing from her, as I crept to the door.

I could hear whimpers and hoarse half-made words, but nothing intelligible. I could hear my father soothing—*there-there, come back to bed*. I cracked the door open, moon and street-light cutting a stark bright swathe against the long hall wall. My mother was nude, and the way the light hit her it looked as though she were two-toned, black and white, cream breasts and charcoal legs. Tossing her head like a spooked horse, she shifted from one foot to the other outside their bedroom door. Her nightclothes were strewn on the hall floor and her hands plucked as if at invisible garments, pulling them from herself as she shook her head. "No, no, h-h-huh, get out, too hot, no, go-go-go."

My father spread his arms, trying to corral her without embracing her.

"Georgia, Georgia, it's me, it's Arnie, Georgia, you're by the ocean where it's safe. You're safe, Georgia."

My mother's arms hung in the air and she stood still a moment. By now I was in the hall.

"Georgia?" My father moved slowly, brought one hand up to her face but got no reaction. As he brushed her hair from her eyes, my mother's spirit seemed to settle back into her body, and she began to sob, quietly.

"Arnie? Oh no, Arnie. Not again. Make it stop. Oh no."

Tall and bony, my father took hold of her then as if she were porcelain. "It's okay, you're okay," he said, and then, catching sight of me, "Sweetheart, you go back to bed now. Your mother's just had a bad dream."

The little pot-belly that swelled above his narrow hips somehow made him look even more vulnerable than she did at that moment. Shadows cut deep holes where his eyes should have been. He looked to me like a stretched and mournful ghost.

"I'm five-and-a-quarter," Dusty told the beefy landscaper at the next table—her current opening line.

"Really?" He smiled at her. "Well, you look fabulous. I wouldn't have guessed you were a day over four."

Dusty's smiled drooped. "No. I'm—What?"

He laughed and glanced at me. "She yours?"

"For the time being." I searched my purse for the right amount to pay our bill so I could avoid waiting again for our oozingly slow waiter.

"Do you have a girlfriend?" Dusty inquired.

He paused a moment, then asked, "Is she hitting on me?"

"Oh, definitely," I told him. "She's a regular Sadie Hawkins." Money on the table, I got up and came around to Dusty and pulled her sweater back on. "Come on, y'little tart, let's get out of here."

She smiled slyly at her quarry. "We're going to see my mummy in the loony bin."

I cupped a hand over her mouth and kissed the top of her head, trying to manage some sort of departing maternal grin as I whispered threats into her hair.

By sixteen, Alice was losing faith in just about everything. One Sunday, in a particularly indigo state of blue, she had gone into our basement to look at photos of us all together, wallow around in our once-upon-a-time story-book family perfection.

Rushing into the living room an hour later, she stopped and stood staring at me staring at the TV, dark wet shadows of mascara around her glittering pupils, a sheaf of papers under her arm, she demanded I turn off the TV and come with her up to my room, her safe place.

There she sat down on the bed, and I stood by the door, dread munching my insides as I watched her take short, panicked breaths.

"Why was she naked on the front lawn?" she asked.

My gaze dropped to the papers on her lap.

"No, look at me. I remember this, I remember police out front and her screaming and crying with no clothes on. And cops, there were cop lights and they had—What did he do to her? Why was she crying?"

On the night in question Alice would have been about Dusty's age today. Five sounded so blindly naive to my mind. *A five-year-old.*

Alice glared. "Why aren't you saying anything? Did he hit her? I swear to Christ, if he—"

"Of course he didn't *hit* her." Like a stone kicked up by the lawn mower, this sort of hard suspicion would pop from Alice when I was least expecting it.

"Children don't know everything their parents are capable of," she said.

"Alice. Daddy feels guilty beating an egg, for god's sake. It was her. She was crazy."

"Don't say that. She was *not* crazy."

Craving a solid surface, I sat down on the floor beside the bed. "Is this the first time you remembered that night?"

Alice pushed her lips out, looking scared and indignant. "Yes. I mean no. I've remembered flashes sometimes but I always thought it was a dream or a movie I'd seen, but then I saw this picture of her in one of the boxes downstairs, laughing, and at first it looked like she was screaming, like she was in pain. Then it just hit me— her on the lawn, her big—" she caught her breath a moment "—fleshy self and her arms covering her chest and then a blanket around her and police lights."

I leaned my head back against the bed and took hold of Alice's ankle, pulling her foot into my lap. "I think she just—She had some sort of disorder or something, these spells that were like night terrors where she'd think the house was on fire. I guess she thought she was on fire, because she'd start ripping off her clothes and tripping out. Like a panic attack but she was asleep. She'd get so freaked, I thought she might claw right through her skin to get it off her, the fire or clothes or whatever. Then that one time she ran out on the front lawn. Before that, Daddy'd always pulled her out of it. They were kind of tussling at the door, but he must have been scared he'd hurt her so he let go, and she went running down the road, banging on people's doors like someone was trying to kill her. One of the neighbours finally called the police. God knows what they thought."

"Where was I during all this?"

"In bed. You woke up and came outside. Daddy didn't

want you there so I took you to my room and I drew you some pictures."

"Fairies?"

"Mmm-hmm."

Sometime around then I had taken to copying the sweetest of the creatures from a book of fairies our mother had given me. Seeing them come out from the nothingness of my white page enraptured Alice.

"Easy to distract me," she said sombrely.

"I made up some story about how they were filming a movie and Momma was going to be a movie star."

"And I bought that."

"Why wouldn't you. And in the morning you put my fairies up on the fridge." I squeezed her toe, remembering Alice's susceptible little face. Alice, the child, was a luminous golden cherub, unsettlingly beautiful, just like her daughter was now. Few adults could pass without stopping to look.

"Oh," she said softly. A tiny smile flirted across her lips as she recalled something light and winged and sweet.

"What is that stuff anyway?"

She stared into her lap and those papers she'd found took hold of her brain once more. "Exactly. The accident report says her car had a gas can in the front seat. And matches."

"What accident report?" I snatched the papers from her. "Where did you find these?"

It was Alice who could spot the fairy dancing on the soft bare palm my mother would hold out. Our mother worked hard at teaching me to suspend my disbelief, to show me magic and glory, angels and other winged things. To me all that whimsy stuff was corny and embarrassing. Meanwhile, Alice could tell what colour skirt the invisible fairy wore, the shape of her ears, the length of her hair.

I attempted to argue once. "No, she's not. She's wearing overalls."

The two of them regarded me with mirthful pity, the same expression that so often met my father's remarks.

Given all this, you would think the fairy book would have gone to Alice. But, seeing the way I preferred to pass tools to my father and observe the arts of plumbing, carpentry and flat-tire repair, Momma must have felt I needed fairies much, much more than Alice did.

In the end though, the functional purpose was really all I ever saw in fairies. I started out by tracing them overtop of the book's pages, but the figures themselves didn't seem to be what engaged Alice. It was the magic: from a milky void, came shape and form. Something from nothing.

"It was love that made it come," my mother would say of my figures.

I would giggle. Lunk-headed and cripple-winged, they hardly resembled the nimble sprites I used as a template. It seemed utterly hare-brained to me, childish and fatuous, but at the same time I couldn't help but be struck by the purity of their response, the awe with which my mother and Alice held this ordinary activity. Unable to feel it myself, I did my best to generate it in them.

"Mummer!" Dusty spotted my sister outside her room at the end of the long medicinal-smelling hall and yanked free of my hand, charging down the shiny brown lino-leum. "Mummer, wummer, bummer!" she crowed and hurled herself headlong into Alice's belly.

As I followed I glanced around. This was the first time I'd ever been in a mental health facility. I had expected impassive-faced men in two-piece white cotton suits wandering the halls with electrodes, waiting to zap the unruly. It looked more like a youth hostel, with its easy-to-clean surfaces and plain, functional waiting area. Beige, brown and a sickly-pink were the dominant colours.

My sister *oof*ed and stared down a moment before letting her hands settle on Dusty's head. She looked nervous, as though she'd forgotten what to do. "Hey, Chum-bum," she said. On fawn legs, she unsteadily picked up her girl.

Dusty put a hand on her mother's cheek and stared into her eyes. Alice kissed her, and Dusty pecked back and then hugged her hard.

Alice watched me over Dusty's shoulder, her eyes dark and a little spooked. She glanced at the man coming up the corridor toward us. His attire was expensive-casual and I wondered if he was another inmate, but his spine looked too erect for that, his gaze too easy.

"Heyyy," Alice said softly as I came near, and she reached out to pull me close.

"Hello, Alice," the man said, passing slowly but not stopping. His smile verged on adoring. "You must be Dusty!" he exclaimed to my niece.

"This is my baby," Alice said, smiling finally.

"This is ma bebayy," Dusty repeated in her Southern shtick.

"My shrink," Alice whispered to me, nodding after the man.

"Do you want to kiss him?" Dusty asked her.

A startled laugh escaped Alice and she looked at her kid. "I missed you," she said, and like a Labrador retriever, my sister licked her baby's face.

Dusty shrieked and wiped, then licked back.

"Care to see my abode?" Alice walked us down the hall.

Passing the door next to hers, she jerked her head toward it. "Obsessive-compulsive," she whispered. "I walked in there by mistake a couple days ago and I think she's still disinfecting the place."

I glanced in and saw a young, thin woman, her hair pulled into a tight knot at the nape of her neck, on her hands and knees in the corner, rubbing at the linoleum.

"Seriously," she hissed. "She gets her husband to smuggle in rubbing alcohol and J Cloths and she wipes the whole floor and every inch of the walls until she's sure the room's sterile . . . Poor guy—he was crying in the hall last night. There's some new kind of lobotomy they want to do on her." Alice bared her teeth with nervous excitement. "They drill holes in your skull and stick hot wires in . . . *zzzt!*"

"Jesus."

She led me into her room, which was utilitarian, much like the waiting area. Against the wall sat a single bed with white sheets, a brown wool blanket, and one slim pillow. Beside it, a table with a reading lamp and a water glass. A writing desk faced the window. Eraser pink curtains with chocolate brown Venetian blinds.

"You look good," I told her. And she did too. Calmer than I'd seen her in months.

I hadn't seen Alice since we checked her in, eight days before, yowling like a wet cat. They told us to wait seventy-two hours before visiting, but my father stormed the reception desk after twelve. Scared he'd find a drugged-out vegetable rocking in a corner somewhere, he demanded to know what they were planning to do with her. The nurse told him he couldn't stay, that his daughter was not ready to see anyone. Dad got so frantic that eventually she caved and brought him to Alice's room to set his mind at rest.

I imagined him standing in the doorway as I was now. He told me that Alice had been huddled on her bed with paper cups of water all over her nightstand and the writing desk—there must have been a dozen. She was hugging herself, taking long deep breaths, slow-motion hyperventilation. When she saw him, it took her a moment to absorb who he was, and then she shook her head and looked past him to the nurse. She pointed at him and shook her head again.

The nurse gently led my father from the room. "She'd like you to leave. Until she's sure."

He felt awful, he said later. "I was furious with her. I feel foolish for it now." His chin quivered and then he set his jaw.

Sitting in the living room, lit only by the reading lamp, his broad round ears seemed even more pronounced, the tiny veins red in the frail flesh of them. He reminded me of one of those leggy male deer in the nature shows, the way they cock their big ears, waiting and listening as they will themselves to be strong, though ultimately they are no match for what is coming.

"The nurse was very professional. There's a reason for rules," he added at last, as though I might argue the point.

After Momma died, Alice took up drawing her own fairies. It struck me as odd that she didn't cry but she didn't seem to see our mother's departure as anything final. There were always euphemisms that I took to mean heaven: Momma went on to a sweeter place, yes, but Momma also "went through the keyhole," or she "rode a teardrop to the river."

Her sweeter place was inside Alice's sketchpad, where plump fairies with apple cheeks and soft dewy hands wrapped themselves in rose petals and danced to the tune of pixie kisses. Probably because she'd actually seen the little beasts first hand, Alice's creations went beyond anything in my fairy book. They seemed vital, frisky and mischievous. And they were the biggest of all the characters on her page. If some ugly gremlin did push its way into her picture it appeared shrunken and impotent, no match for the winged girls.

I had just graduated high school when Alice began her foray into equal-opportunity dating. She was sixteen and the girls she chose were generally older than she was by at least four or five years. I remember the first time I saw her on the street with a stranger who gave me pause.

The young woman by her side looked to be in her twenties. Their arms were linked as they came toward me but given Alice's affectionate disposition it was difficult to be certain of the nature of their relationship.

They were on their way to a Sunday matinee showing of *Peter Pan,* so we exchanged only a few words. *Peter Pan* was the last thing I wanted to see and, anyway, I was off to meet a date myself. Still I felt a twinge because I hadn't been invited along—or perhaps because Alice was so enthralled with her friend.

I turned to watch them go and was struck by the relatively slender waist this chubby friend of Alice's had, the way the slim band of her middle sloped down and out like an enormous inverted heart. I stood there, transfixed by the sight of Georgia's peach, as our father had always referred to Momma's bottom, swaying alongside my sister's slender figure, bouncing against her hip as they ran to escape the heavy rain that suddenly fell.

I didn't tell my father about any of Alice's lovers. Not that there was any sin in it, but I had a strong desire to look away, a sense that it was none of my business that these women resembled our mother. Besides, Alice didn't have a long attention span.

Alice's fairies had become so astonishing by the time she was in grade twelve that my father said he would pay for everything if only she would enroll at the Emily Carr College of Art and Design. Meanwhile I hadn't been able to figure out what I wanted when I graduated. Two years later and I was still in the job I'd taken while I considered my options.

Quills was a local shop that carried overpriced designer stationery and art paper—everything from fine Japanese rice paper to textured styles infused with rose petals, irises and tinsel. They also sold calligraphy pens, old-fashioned quills and ink, delicate sable brushes, moleskin notebooks, and Italian leather journals. Classes were held one night a week to teach calligraphy and simple Japanese characters for those who cared enough to write *I Love You* in a very foreign way. Seeing the paper for the first time, the bits of flora woven through the fibres, all I could think was, how?

My job interview consisted mainly of my expressions of awe over the process of papermaking. Glancing at a take-home papermaking kit on the shelf, my mind began to percolate. I told the Quills owner that she should expand her evening classes. Not only could I work there during the day but I could do a bang-up business for her if she would let me lead a papermaking class at night. The perfect hybrid of beauty and functionality danced in my head.

"Kits are fine," I said, "but imagine what you'd make selling a class."

She shrugged. "You realize this is minimum wage, right?"

"Minimum wage?" I bluffed. "To teach a class of ten or fifteen every week?"

I had no idea how to make paper but I'd buy one of those kits, I thought. I'd get books out of the library and learn.

"Whoa, whoa. I haven't even said yes to working a regular eleven-to-seven shift. Let's see how it goes. You really think that'd sell? A papermaking class?"

Alice had been increasingly moody lately. I wondered if her impending high school graduation had caused this, fear of committing to more school or work. During these dark withdrawals of hers she was not terribly verbal, but she often left her sketchbooks lying around for me to see.

Tarry-eyed sinister gremlins now loomed large and

menacing over her fairies. Meanwhile the fairies themselves had slimmed down, become bony and shrouded, their wings wrapped like a bat's around their shoulders. And Alice kept herself covered too; suddenly she avoided changing clothes in front of me. The one time I walked in on her, I saw a ladder of purple striations up the backs of her thighs.

"What happened to you?"

She jumped and pulled a sheet off the bed to hold in front of her.

Glancing over her shoulder at her legs, she said, "I sat out on my friend's fire escape for a cigarette and the steps left marks on me. Weird, eh? Guess I'm not getting enough vitamins."

It looked more like she'd been struck with wire or something. Repeatedly.

"You smoking these days?"

She rolled her eyes. "Once in a blue moon."

"What friend is this, anyway? Have I met her?"

"Do you *mind*?" she said with forced levity, indicating that she wanted to get dressed, and shoved me out her door.

Not long after, she didn't come home for five nights running. Calling only once during the hours when she knew no one would be around, she left a message that she was sleeping over at a friend's. The school phoned; she hadn't been showing up there either. Our father was incensed that she had not left a phone number, but all he could do was quietly fume and try to wheedle from me what I knew.

"I'm not her mother," I snapped, and immediately regretted it.

Alice reappeared as suddenly as she had vanished. I was at the store and had just gone in back to make myself coffee. When I came back out, a teenaged girl jerked her hand from the display case. I knew she had been feeling around in back of the fine art pens looking for a way in.

Straightening now, she gave me an exaggerated cocky grin like something out of *West Side Story*. Rock 'n' roll scrawny, she was older than I had first thought, though it was hard to tell with the way her papery skin clung to her mean little face bones and wiry arms. Her hair was dead-cat black, cut into punky layers. Sand-coloured roots showed here and there. She wore a studded belt on her slack black jeans and the sleeves to her denim jacket were rolled to show tattooed bands of thorn and vine on either wrist.

"Can I help you?" I asked her.

She looked to another girl who was stooping over the sample books, gazing down at the deckle-edged sheets of paper from the Bloom series.

Alice.

"Hey." My sister smiled wanly. "This paper is *beautiful*." Her finger traced the feathery edges.

I gravitated to clean precise lines myself and these pages with their wispy uncertain perimeters agitated me on some level every time I looked at them.

"Hey, stranger," I said as I took her in. "Where the hell have you been?"

I hadn't expected the heavy smudges of black eyeliner, incongruous with her gold curls, though her hair was dark with grease as if she hadn't bathed in days. Her lips were oddly pale. There was a yellowing olive patch on her jawbone, what looked like the tail end of a bruise.

She glanced sleepily at the self-styled Joan Jett, and with a start I realized they were together.

Alice's eyes wandered back to me. She was stoned. "This is my friend, Roni. Roni, this is Angela."

"Roni?" I repeated.

"Yeah" came her nasal reply. She gave a sharp nod. "What's up?"

She possessed what was, to my ear, the voice of a rat, and not one from *Charlotte's Web*. She glanced furtively at the hand-tooled Italian leather journals near her and then back at my sister.

Alice let the petal-infused page in her fingers drop, then drifted toward me and draped her arms around my neck. I watched Roni through Alice's lank, stale curls.

"I feel like I haven't seen you in forever," she said. "I miss you."

She smelled funny. Not like herself.

"You haven't been around much." I had the peculiar sensation that I should remain as still as possible, let her inhale, as though my familial essence were some kind of smelling salts.

She had done this with Momma when she was small. They had held each other tight and breathed in deeply whenever some particularly dark ghoul seized them.

Over Alice's shoulder, I caught Roni snapping up the smallest of the leather journals and slipping it into the front pocket of her jeans, then stuffing her hands deep to conceal the bulk of it.

The boldness of her move made me jump as though I'd stepped on something cold and raw. My sister eased away and looked back at Roni, then at me. It was the expression in Alice's eyes that confused me. Something like expectation. Or perhaps *need* was more apt; she looked as though she were pleading.

I stepped back, words tripping in my throat. I didn't know what Alice wanted.

My sister's pal had distanced herself from the journals and was now leisurely appraising the moleskin notebooks.

"Roni," I said evenly.

She turned her head as though I'd pulled her from deep thought. "Hey, what's up?"

I made my way toward her, ambling as casually as she had. "Thinking of picking up a leather journal?"

"Oh." She gave a snort of regretful hardship, glancing back at the display. "Na, too rich for my blood."

It took all my strength at that moment not to seek out Alice's gaze. "Maybe you were just distracted, then," I whispered, nodding to her pocket.

She gave a shrug and shook her head as though I weren't making much sense.

I am rarely as flabbergasted by anything as I am by unscrupulousness. I would go so far as to say I'm oddly impressed by it, the complete sense of entitlement that accompanies a person with no ethics.

The way Roni's hard little frame seemed to twitch made me glad I had my father's height. I reached out, and just then both her hands flew from her pockets to fend me off.

"Easy," I cautioned. "Your collar was flipped under."

She touched her denim lapel, and pulled it out. Smoothing it flat, she glanced down to see the small leather book now half exposed. In a hushed squawk, she said, "Fuck you."

"Excuse me?"

"*Fuck. You,*" she clarified, her voice level again.

She looked to Alice now and I did the same.

Without lifting her chin, Alice stared up at the ceiling. I wondered what she was hoping for at that moment, whether she wanted to be taken up bodily, or wanted help to come down.

"*What!*" Roni bawled. "I fuckin' did it for *you!*"

My sister's eyes dropped miserably.

"Fine." Roni glared and added, "Take it," as she threw the book to the floor. "I don't give a shit."

Alice didn't say anything. So I did.

"This isn't working out, Roni."

"Shut your face," she spat. She gave Alice an imploring look. "Are you just going to stand there?"

Alice remained mute.

"You are so pathetic." Roni set her jaw. "Come on, let's go."

My sister shook her head almost imperceptibly.

"Alice. Now."

Alice's foot inched forward.

I set my hands on my hips.

Roni eyed me. "Alice!" she mewled, this time with something akin to fear. "This is total bullshit." She made it to the door this time before she turned back. "You—" She jabbed a finger at my sister once. "Don't you dare come to my place again or I'll fuckin'—" Her voice cracked. She turned and, as she ran out the door, punched at the nearest window. The pane snapped, leaving a coin-shaped crack.

I was suddenly aware of the trembling in my limbs. "Nice thing to drag into my store, Alice."

She scrunched her eyes shut and then opened them on me.

I paced from one side of the room to the other. "Next time, do your own dirty work."

She nodded gloomily, walked to the window and spread her hands against the glass. The pane sighed under her fingers, and from the point of Roni's impact a crack veined its way up through the glass, splitting Alice's view.

Following the success of my papermaking classes I became manager of Quills, and now had my very own part-time underling to boss around. I had talked the owner into having "Quills'" red and white bottled at the local winemaking shop at a cost of three bucks a bottle. One glass per student could be incorporated into the price of a class at a 500-percent markup and still look like a deal.

Alice, meanwhile, had graduated high school and no longer showed interest in Emily Carr College. Fascinated by the rose petals, grass blades and glitter infused in our designer paper, she took up papermaking classes with my well-heeled wine drinkers, and, true to form, the concoctions she came up with were mesmerizing for both their visual splendour and tactile allure. Several of her classmates bought up whatever she created.

"I'm thinking I might buy the shop."

"What shop?" I asked, staring at our father over dinner.

"Quills," he said mildly, but his eyes were giddy.

He looked at Alice.

I looked at Alice.

"I've been thinking for some time about investing in my own business, a family business. I had considered picking up some kind of franchise, but why do that if the whole family is going to be working down there anyway. It'd make sense to just buy Quills."

He clearly expected a grateful reception.

"The whole family isn't working there," I said quietly. "Alice takes classes."

There was a moment of silence.

"Well"—he swallowed—"uh, she's making paper that's better than anything the store can order."

My father and sister watched me expectantly.

"Alice is good at whatever she does," I said.

"You really are, Alice," Daddy gushed. "Your mother was like that but she didn't throw herself into a thing the way you do. You know, we could expand and make a little gallery in the back. It'd be a great showcase for those fairies of yours."

My sister beamed. "Oh my god! Angie, what do you think? Wouldn't it be fun! And we could be together all the time and—"

"Quills isn't for sale." I forced as much calm matter-of-factness into my tone as I could muster, but my chest had tightened.

"I ran into your boss," my father explained. "She says you've really made this business into a decent little profit maker, Angela. She didn't think she'd ever be able to sell the place but now, after what *you've* done with it . . ."

Something in my expression caused Alice's face to fall. "Maybe Angie doesn't want to work in a paper shop forever, Dad. She might want to go back to school and learn to be a business tycoon."

My father glanced at me, surprised. "I don't know why you'd want to do that." He cut into his pork chop, forked a bite into his mouth and chewed as he looked at me.

I shifted my eyes to my plate, but I could feel him watching me.

"You've already got a flare for commerce, sweetheart. All they teach you at school is how to be a bean counter."

Soon after, my father put his savings together with a small loan against the house and bought the store I'd been managing for two years.

Alice promptly lost interest in papermaking.

Daddy commenced pilfering stock from Quills to bring home to her as encouragement. He drew up plans to expand the shop, build the small gallery where Alice could show her work; I would curate. We could bring in other local artists too. He called a family meeting to hammer out the details, but Alice couldn't make it.

She had gotten a job waiting tables in a Spanish restaurant over on South Cambie and had started dating Joaquin, a young Latin guitar player. A part-time waiter, Joaquin also played accompaniment for his sister, Emilia, who danced flamenco Tuesday and Thursday nights for the dinner crowd.

Alice bought a guitar and took lessons from Joaquin. She saw flamenco as her new true calling.

One night after dinner, she sat on the hearth and played us a piece. She was good, as usual.

Sitting in the living room by the fireplace, my father watched her slap a palm on the guitar's body between rhythmic strummings, the muscles around his eyes bunching. He seemed to be concentrating to the point of pain.

After the guitar had received Alice's last flamenco whack, there was silence in the room.

The fire snapped. Daddy cleared his throat.

"Well, that was something, sweetheart. You've been putting your heart into this. And it shows. You sure are terrific."

Alice's face looked cheerfully frail.

I slumped back into the armchair.

"What?" she said guardedly.

Had my sigh been audible?

"Well." He hunted in his hands for a way to begin. "Alice. I—We invested a significant amount of money and energy into a family business almost four months ago now and I don't think you've set foot in there since. You haven't been paying any attention to your artwork . . . and you've stopped making your beautiful paper. I thought this could be a real enterprise for you. A focal point."

"Why should I focus on one point?" She set the guitar down beside her.

"Why?" he repeated, his tone still gentle but equally baffled.

I had never heard my father raise his voice. There were articles written about people like him, about how they all seemed to end up with cancer or ALS. " . . . to be a success," Daddy was saying, "a person's got to discipline her mind and choose what she *wants*."

"Why do I have to give up what I love to make other people happy?" Without warning, tears rolled down her cheeks and she wrapped her arms around her ribs.

Daddy reached out a hand toward her.

"No." She flinched from his touch. Then she got up

and walked out of the room, head down, as if trekking through a blizzard.

My father drooped with helplessness, his expression the one he wore when no amount of corralling could contain the women in his life. Then he smiled sheepishly. "I guess it's hard for a couple fellas like us to know how creative types like Alice and your mother feel."

I smacked my palms against the chair arms and stood. "Guess I'll go see what gives."

Alice's reaction seemed extreme until I discovered that only hours before, her guitar-playing waiter had discovered that his lover was also seeing his sister. Alice's fireside concert, it turned out, had been a swan song. Sometime during my father's inquisition, it had hit home for Alice that Joaquin had walked out of her life for good and taken his sister with him.

At two the next morning, deep in sleep, my sister wandered into the hallway and began to wail, "Don't burn, no, Momma, please, I don't want to . . ."

She dreamed that our mother had come to life, climbed from the depths of a canyon, only to slip backward over the edge. Clutching the rocks and vines, she begged for Alice to come with her, crying that she was afraid to go down alone.

Alice went into such an awful funk after losing both Joaquin and Emilia at once that she was essentially bed-ridden through the Christmas season. Daddy and I bundled her down to the couch each morning as though she were a terminal patient and babied her as best we could, but she was pretty non-responsive until I started up with my old trick of drawing fairies—these ones adorned with Santa hats and sleigh bells. They rode the backs of antlered, red-nosed mice under toadstools that had been draped in coloured lights. The details were not readily apparent to my family until I explained them, but, bit by bit, my feeble renditions got a laugh. It was something of a heart-suck, though, to hear those lost old words from Alice: "It was love that made it come."

Soon Alice took the sketchbook back in her capable hands. Slowly her fairies grew plump again, like the voluptuous creatures from the past, only now they appeared to be more in the realm of heavenly angels, sweet cherubs watching over God's children.

Alice told me one night after our father had gone to bed that she'd been thinking maybe this wasn't right, this business of having multiple lovers. Forty, fifty? How many lovers would she have by the time she was done? She'd be so far into the triple digits, she'd need an abacus to keep track.

Peering into my eyes she added, "There's no joy in frivolous sex, Angie. I'm lonesome."

Suddenly self-conscious, I wondered if my envy was always this apparent.

"Maybe I never should have gone with girls at all," she said. "The Universe is about miracles, and creativity and life. Two girls can't create life. Two girls . . . must make no sense to God."

Days before Alice's eighteenth New Year's Eve, she made the resolution that she was going to become more spiritual. By which she apparently meant Christian. She started to read the Bible—off-putting for my father and me, but aside from the theological navel-gazing she seemed in much better spirits. I even managed to persuade her it was time to join the human race again, commune with God's other creatures and have a glass of Jesus-juice.

We went to a house party brimming with some artsy types I figured my sister would enjoy. There was enough male pulchritude to keep me and twenty Alices happy, but my sister was on a whole new kick and all night long she kept talking up the Father, the Son and the whole damn thing.

As we rang in the new year, one of the guys hollered, "Here's to getting laid!"

To which Alice responded: "The full soul loatheth an honeycomb; but to the hungry soul every bitter thing is sweet." From Proverbs, she informed me.

I moved to the other side of the room, slammed a shot of tequila and began necking with a stranger.

As the night wore on Alice became the object of relentless teasing.

"Alice, if you go for a walk with the Lord, can you pick me up some smokes on your way back?"

"Alice, did you know Jesus couldn't play hockey for shit—he always got nailed to the boards."

Letting them go at her that way, unchecked, bothered me some, but a larger part of me enjoyed it. My guilt was assuaged by the fact that the more they ribbed, the more beatific she looked.

The Sunday after, she headed down to a neighbourhood church, Good News Community, which had a parish of about two hundred youthful congregants. Afterward she easily found their new youth pastor. Or, more likely, he found her. The two of them had a chat in the foyer, which extended downstairs into the parish hall for after-service coffee and cookies.

Alice came home elated. "You can feel the love. You can see it in their eyes, hear it in their voices when they sing. They've really got the *Joy joy joy*," she sang, "*down in their hearts.*"

Soon Alice joined the choir, and over the next few weeks became the youth pastor's right-hand man. There was talk of her teaching Sunday school eventually, once she really got her bearings, once she'd been baptized.

After Alice started at the church office as a part-time secretary, Daddy gave up trying to entice her back into the family business. She worked mostly for Pastor Clint, her partner-in-Christ, and apparently her assistance was invaluable.

My mother and father had had some Sunday school in their childhoods but neither had seemed interested in their own kids attending. While growing up, Alice and I were both fairly ignorant of the Bible's contents. Now, Alice crashed headlong into the scriptures. Once she finished with Proverbs she took to reading and rereading the Book of Matthew, The Sermon on the Mount in particular, gobbling verse after verse, regurgitating bits here and there whenever she considered it warranted.

Hearing the words made me feel as if I had bugs in my clothes.

I was past the age of dressing to my father's specifications, but he was entitled to hope, I suppose. Sitting in his La-Z-Boy staring over his newspaper one night, he gave me the once-over as I walked into the living room. I had on a new dress, one that I considered an appetizing yet chic choice for the evening.

"Is that absolutely necessary?" he asked.

I looked down at myself and threw up my hands in mock exasperation.

Alice sat curled on the sofa, poring over some Clint work she'd brought home. She glanced up. "What do you want her to do, Daddy? Hide her light under a bushel?"

"I don't want her casting her pearls before swine, dear, that's all." He turned the page of his paper with exaggerated calm and tilted his head back as he perused the headlines.

Alice snickered.

A car honked out front.

"'Kay, gotta go." I took a couple of steps toward the door.

"You will not." My father set his paper down.

"What!" I said, closer to expressing genuine irritation.

"Angela." He switched to a cajoling tone. "Where's your self-respect? Your mother—"

"Oh Jesus." I rolled my eyes. I wasn't planning to marry the guy, for god's sake.

"Oh!" Alice looked from her paperwork again. "Before you go, I've been meaning to ask you . . ." She tapped her pen on the pages. "I'm working on something for Clint—"

"*Clint*," I repeated. "Nobody's really named *Clint*."

Alice grinned.

Another honk from out front. I dashed for the hall and grabbed my coat.

I heard my father thrash the newspaper against his legs. "Angela," he pleaded. "Please let this fool inquire at the door like a gentleman."

"He's just a friend, Dad." I poked my face back into the living room. "Later!"

"Ange, wait," my sister called. "Clint is starting up a sandwich project for homeless people. Could you volunteer for our first day? Either to make sandwiches or to give them out. And then you could meet Clint too!"

"Angela!" A distant bellow from outside.

My date. I suddenly felt a bit old to have a juvenile delinquent waiting out front in a souped-up car, with my father staring daggers through the walls. I came back into the room and flopped onto the couch beside Alice.

Daddy marched for the front door.

"Dad, just let it—"

He went out and the door closed carefully behind him.

"I gotta get my own place," I said.

"We start this Friday." Alice prattled on as though I hadn't said a word. "From 9 a.m. to 10 a.m. But if you can't make it—I don't know why that would be because the store doesn't open until eleven—but maybe you could make sandwiches the night before? Clint said in L.A. they liked meat loaf the best."

Clint had gone to Bible-thumping school in California. Whether he had been transferred by the Good News people or had relocated of his own volition wasn't clear, but he had headed north and immediately commenced a multimedia overhaul at the Vancouver location.

I turned my head to look at Alice—her corkscrew curls were sickeningly angelic and bouncy right now—then twisted around for another look at the door. "You ever hear any more from that Roni-chick?" I asked, irritated that she'd managed to have an affair with a complete thug without our father being any the wiser.

Her eyes dimmed, then brightened. "No. She was a good person . . . but misguided."

Christ, she was loving her enemies now. It was a relief that she was out of her fragile phase, but this patience-of-Job routine made me want to pound her with her own Gideon.

My father appeared in the door with a hand on the shoulder of my date. "Alice," he said, "I'd like you to meet Vincent. Vincent's going to join us for dinner tonight."

"Hey," said my date, previously known as Vince, as in *convince*. He slunk nervously into the glare of the front hall light, his legs suddenly scrawny, shoulders stooped, dwindling before my eyes, never to regain stature again.

At 7:45 a.m., Friday morning, Alice and I hauled the sandwiches we'd made over to Clint's apartment. She had neglected to mention the set-up entailed in this production and I was feeling chilled and resentful. This morning was the city's first fall frost, as far as I knew. I hadn't been awake this early in some time.

When he opened the door, even in my groggy state I could see what she saw in him. He looked like a Clint. Handsome but not pretty, with an unsettled coyote quality about him despite his earnest veneer.

"Look at you girls," he said with a lost-in-the-sheets hoarseness. "Up to the armpits in alms! You must be Angela." He extended his hand to me. "Wonderful to meet you."

We shook.

His face, like tanned-soft leather, was close shaven and his blue shirt ironed smooth. Something in him looked refurbished to me. Maybe it was the low rasp of his voice, as if he and Jack Daniel's had once sharked their way through pool halls and back alleys, hustling and lusting, bosom buddies—until he met Jesus.

His gaze held mine for a couple of moments. It's striking how rare that is. Most eyes flit and avoid extended contact at all costs. A steady gaze is almost suspect.

I dropped mine and felt as though I'd lost a game of chicken.

"I'm almost ready," he said, and we followed him to his kitchen where a box of sandwiches sat on the counter. "I'm just finishing up a cigarette on the balcony."

"Oh my gosh." My sister beamed, and peered inside the box. "You must've been up all night making those."

Clint smiled and winked at her, then headed for his smoke on the other side of the sliding glass doors. I followed a few steps into the front room. The sparse furniture was mostly pine. The walls were regulation rental-white. Framed on one was a poster from Cecil B. DeMille's *The Ten Commandments*. Clint's Special Collector's Edition displayed a white-bearded Charlton Heston lifting his golden tablet. A bolt of lightning cut through Technicolor clouds and struck the commandments in ferocious Heston's mitts.

The poster next to Moses featured a throng of men running across a sandy seashore: *They will sacrifice anything to achieve their goals . . . Except their honor. Chariots of Fire.*

I watched Clint as he stepped out onto his balcony. He looked toward the North Shore mountains bathed pink in the early morning light. He took a deep drag off his cigarette and folded his arms, his leather coat pulled tight across his shoulders.

I stepped closer but remained on the inside of the glass doors. I hadn't thought Born Againers smoked.

As though reading my mind, he glanced back and shrugged. "My last bad habit."

Alice braced herself against the metal balcony door frame and leaned into the cool air. "Man, it's so beautiful—like a spirit came and painted the sky with all its finest."

"One did," he said, grinning at her, his voice low and warm. He reached his empty hand to her cheek and gave it an adoring-but-paternal brush with the topside of his fingers. He ran his cigarette hand through his own tousled hair as he took in a last eyeful of the city and turned back, just in time to catch me staring.

I looked away.

"You a Christian, Angela?"

My head jerked as though I'd been caught stealing. "Excuse me?"

"Do you love Jesus?" Clint and his honey-and-sand voice.

"Just as a friend." I forced a smile and backed toward Moses.

On the Downtown Eastside, Pastor Clint had set up a coordinated effort with an outreach centre on Powell Street. Once the rollicking centre of town, the area was now one of the bleakest in all of Canada. Rundown Chinese produce stores nestled behind the barred windows of defunct businesses. Pawnshops and dilapidated beer parlours lined the streets while drug-jonesing hookers and boozehounds staggered down the sidewalks.

I stared out the window of Clint's van at the grizzled homeless, layered in filthy old clothes, some pushing carts, some sharing a bottle in the tiny park nearby. Most squinted as if a smash in the face were looming, their knuckles and scabby noses proof that one usually was. The morning didn't look so beautiful any more and I cursed Alice for it.

We unloaded the van at the outreach centre and a couple of staff came out to greet Clint and help us set up our tent next to the sidewalk. Clint laid out church leaflets on the fold-up table. The outreach workers thanked us again and went back inside.

I stood back as Clint and Alice stapled posters along the edges of the table. When they were done, *Taste and see the goodness of the Lord* and *Good News is Good Food* hung down like an evangelical hula skirt.

Alice attempted to plaster more along the sides of the tent, juggling paper and tape, dropping posters and catching sticky ribbons of plastic in her hair.

I grudgingly moved in to help, only to lose the end of the tape against the roll. I cursed under my breath and then snuck a look to see whether Clint had heard. His eyes met mine as if they'd been waiting, and I swung my gaze away as fast as I could.

A few neighbourhood men hung back, watching and asking questions.

"Is this real food or is this just Bible shit?"

"Gonna try and holy-roll our asses?"

Clint assured them in a booming voice that there would be real sustenance to fill their bellies. Jesus fed the multitudes and so would we.

"Jesus was a stand-up guy," someone muttered pensively.

"Fuckin' cocksucker," a female voice shrieked. "Jesus was a fuckin' cocksucker!"

My eyes searched to find the woman behind the voice. Gaunt and coltish, she wore her coat hanging open, exposing an orange-spandex–covered belly that popped like a blue-ribbon pumpkin. I couldn't take my eyes off that belly as she argued with the man now scolding her.

Clint's cell rang and broke the spell. I looked back as he confirmed for his caller that we were all ready.

Once our tables were set with sandwiches, the outreach workers brought out two coffee urns.

Soon it looked as if half the neighbourhood had lined up for breakfast. A news van pulled up and unloaded camera gear; a reporter hopped out of a cab and walked up to the front of the line. She flashed a press card as she juggled her purse and notepad.

Clint flashed a grin and nimbly stepped out to speak to her.

As I stuck a ham-and-cheese into a pair of outstretched hands I wondered what the media could possibly find so fascinating.

When I glanced around for Clint minutes later, he was in the middle of a mini media scrum. His voice verged on explosive and his hands gestured as he talked about his vision, the television ministry that, if he had estimated rightly—and he was sure he had—would solve this city's Downtown Eastside problem. He described the businesses soon to start up: Good News Goodies, a bakery that would employ former prison inmates and street people; Good News Gasoline, a service station with soul; Good News Florist, which would make the spirit grow.

"All of them employing the very people you see around you," he said.

It was my sister's voice—"Isn't he amazing!"—that made me notice that everyone around seemed to have been seduced by Clint. Or wanted to be.

A freckle-faced woman manoeuvred herself breathlessly into the tent beside me.

"Hi there, Alice." Then to me: "You must be Alice's sister. I'm Helen. Oh, look! I think those are mine," she said, grinning at my hands, which held the meat-loaf sandwiches that had been on Clint's kitchen counter this morning.

"This is the first time I ever made *meat loaf*," she said incredulously. "I was up half the night with it, but that Clint . . ." She looked at him, playfully reproachful. "He's very persuasive."

"You from Good News?" I asked. Her flannel gingham dress and grey sweater made her the very picture of a church mouse. She was much younger than her attire suggested.

"Mmm-hmm," she affirmed, her eyes still on the preacher. "Clint's the sort of man people follow."

"A regular Pied Piper."

I put a sandwich into another hand and then noticed its paltry filling, one side runty with the crusty heel of the loaf, and forced my eyes up past the orange swollen belly in front of me. It was the pregnant Christ-hater.

"This is nice of you, lady."

The shame was so instantaneous, my tongue fell dead in my mouth, until I managed to say, "There's ham and cheese too if you don't like—" Reaching behind me into the other box, I tried to meet the girl's gaze, which, now that she wasn't cursing a Tourette-ical blue streak, was fixed and piercing. "It has mayo and mustard."

I held out a second plastic-wrapped choice, and she snatched it away, knocked into the guy behind her and scurried off with both sandwiches.

On the news that night, it was reported that Pastor Clint Reynolds had distributed food to over two hundred homeless and that he planned to exceed that target on a daily basis. His was a practical ministry, the perky blonde reporter declared, one that sought to embrace the most vulnerable in our city by not only feeding them but enabling them to feed themselves. The camera panned across me and Alice, her complexion glowing, her pale locks ruffled softly by the wind.

"Who's that one, the homely little one in the plaid dress?" Daddy asked.

"Helen," I told him. "You think she's homely? I thought she was sort of . . . pleasant-looking. She said she wanted to give out sandwiches too but Clint didn't need her."

My father snorted. "I'm sure he didn't."

The night I dreamed of Clint, I woke up in a sweat, guilt beading behind my knees and elbows, dampening my hair. I turned on the light to wash away the sight of his slick chest, his terrible naked face. It was wet between my thighs, as though he truly had been inside me and had spent everything he had. I covered my face to keep from seeing Alice through the wall. There is nothing stronger than the grip of dreams in the small hours of the morning.

Somewhere in the house a door clicked softly and my chest seized. Then came the soft creak of stairs, the *wisp* of sneaking sock feet in the hall.

"Angela?" A light scratch of fingernails on the door accompanied Alice's whisper.

I opened up to the sight of her in her trench coat, bra hanging out of one pocket, mascara-streaked cheeks, a ghost of lipstick left on her mouth. I yanked her into my room.

Her words came out in slushy chunks. "Clint doesn't want me any more."

"You're sleeping with him? Fuck, Alice. How could you sleep with that jackass?"

"Don't," she whispered. She sat down on the bed. Her head drooped.

"You're not pregnant," I pleaded.

Both hands covered her face.

"Alice! Even that knocked-up meth addict knew he was a cocksucker."

She started to sob and I took a different tack. "Shh. I'm sorry. Let's calm down." I drew in a breath and sat down beside her. "Are you sure? Aren't you on the pill?"

She dropped her hands. "I went off it when I accepted Christ," she said. "And then when I fell in love, I loved him so much . . . I didn't want there to be anything between us. I imagined his baby in me, and I just wanted it."

I sank my teeth into my tongue to still the sickening sense that Clint had been in my own bed minutes before.

"He said God led him to me. And me to him."

"Does he know?"

She nodded. "Last night."

"Last night?" I was amazed that she could have hidden this big a secret from me for twenty-four hours. "When did you find out?"

"Three days ago. He says if I keep it I'm going to destroy the ministry. It's a . . . bad tooth." She put her hands back over her face.

"What?"

"I tried to explain to him tonight: it was God's love that made it come. We could have it together and minister too—but he got so mad."

Good old Pastor Clint. In his fit of pique he had told my sister that they had to nip this thing in the bud and move on. He reminded her that she was eighteen years old, she had her whole life in front of her and he, at thirty-two, didn't have time for a mess like this, not when he was on the cusp of making great change in the world.

"Listen to me, Alice," he told her. "Don't be a fool. For once in your life, use the sense God gave you and be practical. To have a child under these circumstances is cruel. It's like a bad tooth. Sometimes you've just got to yank it."

Alice began to sob and he tried to calm her the best way he knew: he made love to her. Alice being Alice, she thought he had come around.

Afterward, with her melted beside him, he must have thought he now had her in a malleable state of mind, because at that point Clint offered her money. Being American he assumed she would have to pay out of her own pocket for the abortion. He offered not only five hundred for the procedure but another five grand—his entire savings, he claimed—if she would join another church and never speak of their relationship.

"You're a beautiful soul, sweetheart. But part of being a Christian is learning to sacrifice. Let's put this flame out before it burns the house down."

I pictured her getting up from the bed, standing there in the shadows of his bedroom, turning to face him, naked, her curls gone Medusa, when she said, "You are no Christian—I won't put the flame out because I hope you burn."

"How could I say that to him?" she cried now and put her fingertips in her mouth, six years old again. She gazed at my bookshelf and said, "I left the fairies." She spun back toward me. "The book."

"*My* book?"

"I'm so stupid." She squeezed her eyes shut.

"What did you have *my* fairy book over at *his* place for anyway?"

"I'm sorry." She grabbed my hand and held it to her face. "I'll get it back."

I wanted to say that no one really forgets anything at her lover's house; it's the oldest subconscious trick in the book. I wanted to accuse her of being just what he had said, impractical and foolish—but a mountain of repudiation wasn't going to wipe away the feel of Clint lingering between my thighs.

Alice showed up at the store the next afternoon, a jittery mess. Still no book. Clint wasn't answering his phone. He wasn't answering his door. She went down to Good News and a new secretary intercepted her as she headed toward the pastor's study saying that Clint was busy with both a sermon and a proposal to Citytv for *The Rock That Never Rolls*, his idea for an urban youth music hour that would feature Christian bands, and himself, of course, as emcee. The stage show, the secretary said, would be filmed at Good News Hall to start with and then, as momentum grew, move downtown to the Commodore Ballroom.

The secretary herself was terribly excited—she sang in coffee houses, now and then, she told Alice. Clint thought he might be able to make room for her in the Up-and-Comers segment.

Every day for three days, Alice returned to both his apartment and his study but he was never there.

On Sunday morning we slipped into a row near the back of the sanctuary. Most of the crowd—and there didn't seem to be many of them over forty—were clad in tight jeans and T-shirts or some variation on the theme, and most remained on their feet, while on stage the worship band played earnest folk-rock tunes.

Clint stood near the stage chatting with an older man in a suit who I imagined to be the senior pastor.

There were no hymnals. The words of each song were projected onto a large screen that hung from the ceiling. Were it not for the capitalized *H* in *He*, the lyrics were indistinguishable from those of any other shmaltzy love song. I whispered questions to Alice, whose gaze had been glued on her lover since we'd come through the doors.

There were three or four worship bands that rotated each week, she said. In general they stuck to playing covers so that everyone could sing along.

"Covers of *what*?"

She didn't dignify that with a response. Apparently these were all monster hits on the Christian pop charts. Not only that but we could expect the band to play on for at least another hour before the preacher got the show started. I wished I had just bombed Clint's apartment and let it go at that.

All around us, people sang with hands cupped in front of them as if catching raindrops. A few chatted and laughed in small groups. Some embraced new arrivals, swaying together for several seconds before the newcomers went off to find space to spread out and sing.

Straight ahead, I spotted Helen from The Sandwich Project. In her prim blue dress and cream lace collar she was far from the norm at Good News.

I couldn't put my finger on what was peculiar about it all (besides the obvious) until a raven-haired gym rat, wearing a second-skin black Lycra cycling shirt, planted himself next to me. He smiled at me and sang a few bars, then leaned forward to tap the shoulder of someone in the row ahead. They shared some mutual laughter before he straightened and grinned at me again, this time offering his hand.

"My name's DW."

I shook it and glanced at Alice, whose eyes were welling as she watched Clint move around the front of the sanctuary.

"Aren't you going to tell me yours?" DW asked, his electric blues honing in.

I sighed and told him my name, then looked ahead to the big screen, attempting to worm those unctuous lyrics out of my mouth. "*'You are my light. Even late at night . . . '* Oh for god's sake," I muttered.

"You don't look familiar." DW smirked.

"First time."

Leave it to Alice to find the biggest Christian pickup joint in town.

Up at the stage Clint was fussing with sound equipment. A pretty band member knelt down to speak with him. Their smiles brought Alice's tears over the edge, her fingers twisting hard together. Afraid she might break a bone, I put my keys in her hands as distraction.

"You'll like it here. Everyone's young, always buzzin' upside. You got plans this afternoon?"

DW came on so strong, I was convinced he was a closet-case.

Suddenly there was Clint walking toward us down the centre aisle. My keys jangled in Alice's hand. As he passed, his eyes skimmed over the crowd, seemingly carefree, but the tension in his mouth was a giveaway.

Helen jumped up and caught hold of Clint as he went by. She gave him an airless hug until Clint patted her back and moved on.

Alice switched the keys from hand to hand.

"We're having a barbecue," DW continued in my ear. "You're invited."

"Clint!" I shouted. The strange pitch of my voice echoed in my head.

Clint's head didn't turn.

Alice had turned into a patchwork of red blotches, manifesting prickles of embarrassed adrenalin.

I pushed past her out to the aisle, trotted after Clint and caught hold of his sleeve.

He turned to me with a brittle smile. "Hey! How are you?" He waved at someone behind me and then, settling his arm across my shoulders, said, "Can I talk to you a sec?"

He couriered me through the swinging doors and out to the foyer. I wasn't prepared for the way he turned on me, the fury in his face, once the doors had closed behind us.

"What do you want?" he enunciated coolly. Pushing his face in close to mine, he gripped my elbow.

His quiet voice was far worse than if he'd screamed. Face hot, I found my hands trembling as I hunted for incisive words.

The doors to the sanctuary swung open again and without turning my head I could feel my sister.

Clint's eyes didn't waver. His fingers dug into my bone. He modulated his voice so that a few feet away Alice would be certain to hear each word. "Whatever crap you think you're going to pull here, think twice, little girl, because you will know what public humiliation is when I'm done with you."

"You have something of mine, *Clint*." My sister's voice was eerily bold.

He looked at Alice.

She was close now and she said it again. "You have something of mine and I want it back."

In one swift motion, Alice's fisted hand swung across his jaw. She seemed to miss, yet Clint gasped and clutched his face, then checked his own hand for blood. Two stripes ran along his jaw. The blanched scratches suddenly burbled pinpricks of red.

He glared and bit off his words. "God bless you, Alice."

Alice examined the keys that protruded through the fingers of her right hand and then took my wrist and pulled me out the front doors. I didn't see her face when she tossed back, "Likewise."

I let Alice drive.

Back home, she seemed renewed. It was the only time I remember feeling dwarfed and ineffectual next to her. She got up from my bed and shuffled through my junk drawer until she found matches.

Opening her beaded gypsy purse, she pulled out her Bible and sat down beside me on the edge of the bed, one thumb riffling the gilt-edged pages of Clint's gift.

"There's this story," she said, "in the Book of Revelation. God tells his angels not to kill the people, just to torment them with scorpions for five months. The tormented ones will want to die, it says, but God won't let them." Alice folded the covers back like wings until they met, and hung the Good Book sideways from her fingertips, pages waving loose and parched. "I didn't think angels would do that."

She asked me to strike a match.

It was Alice who explained the situation to our father. She did not say she was pregnant, she said she was going to have a baby. She spoke as though it were information she had gleaned from the papers, news of a significant but not earth-shattering event.

My father paid a visit to the pragmatic Pastor Clint that night. Daddy not only got into Clint's apartment, but he returned with my illustrated book of fairies. What was said or done was never spoken about, but our father did report that the pastor had decided he was homesick, besides which he had not been feeling his best—it seemed this relocation to the damp Vancouver climate had not suited his constitution.

Clint went back to California before the week's end.

Alice knew Dusty's name long before she was born. She developed cravings for music during her pregnancy like some women do for foods and the last trimester was night and day Dusty Springfield. She went so far as to request that I bring a boom box into the birthing room to ensure Springfield's voice would be the first one little Dusty would hear. Her glistening purple head popped out just as Big Dusty's husky drawl sounded "Son of a Preacher Man."

I moved out of my father's house shortly after the birth, getting an apartment close by that didn't feel quite so crowded with maternity. Alice stayed with Daddy and he seemed to thrive on it, going to work every day, coming home to mother and child.

Alice rarely left the house except for daily walks with the stroller. She loved her new role as mother. She and Dusty shunned television and, instead, baked intricate desserts, Dusty reclining quietly in her baby seat on the counter, watching, or sifting flour when her hands got big enough that Alice could wrap them round the sifter's handle and squeeze. Alice learned to sew, mastering complicated stitching on homemade jumpsuits and sleepers. Once Dusty could walk they learned to dance the cha-cha from instructional DVDs, Alice whisking Dusty in her arms around and round the living room.

For the first four years of Dusty's life the two of them "played house," as Alice put it. She talked about going back to school when Dusty started kindergarten. She kept a sketchbook, and as soon as Dusty could hold crayons, they would draw together for hours on end. Sometimes they'd go down Robson Street or to Stanley Park and draw strangers for money—caricatures or straight likenesses, Alice could get a face down either way. Dusty would draw her own version: blue hair on a potato head with trophy-handle ears and two teeth. The customer would shell over twenty-five bucks and leave clam-happy with both.

Then kindergarten happened. Dusty started school three months before her fifth birthday and suddenly, after a half-decade abstention, Alice turned on the television again and took to sitting and staring at the screen, eating junk food and phoning me at the store several times a day.

I tried to get her to come down to the shop again. I suggested she sketch women at the papermaking classes on her self-made paper. It would be both inspirational and a money-maker.

She should get out, I said, and meet people. She'd lost touch with all her friends.

She came once, had half a glass of Quills red, her foot tapping constantly, like a woodpecker's beak, at the floor. She couldn't concentrate enough to draw and didn't want to make paper. Why did the world need more paper?

She left halfway through the class and the paper pupils looked relieved to see the back of her.

She couldn't sleep at night either. My father worriedly told me that he often woke to her creaking up and down the hall, or going down to the basement. She couldn't seem to manage regular meals and her clothes hung loose and sloppy on her. Crying jags started up frequently. She was terrified of Dusty becoming infected by her sadness, and the idea of it drove her to the doctor.

She was diagnosed with Generalized Anxiety Disorder and armed with an anti-anxiety prescription as well as a benzodiazepine for emergencies.

Alice quieted down again, in a peculiar way.

It was summertime and as usual half of North America seemed to be ablaze. Forests everywhere were closed to hikers; planes whining overhead doused the flames. By this point, Alice was watching nothing but news: CNN, CBC, morning news, noon news, evening news. She'd phone me at work, telling me about the latest evacuations and deaths.

It must have been two o'clock one morning when I woke to the phone ringing. I picked up and heard her whispering in my ear.

"Spontaneous combustion," she said.

"Huh?"

"I know now. The gasoline, I know what it was for."

"What are you talking about?"

"Momma. She was using it to put out the fire."

I thought of that David Bowie song about putting out a fire with gasoline.

"She wasn't crazy," my sister said. "She was a genius."

Alice muffled the receiver and spoke to someone in the room—Dusty, presumably—then back into the phone. "I'll explain so you understand. You know how they put out forest fires? They start another fire. It's tricky: a second fire ahead of the first fire. There's nothing left to burn when the original flame gets there. It's like a person; it's alive and it knows when there's nothing left to eat so it tries to go back but it already ate that up too, you see? But it's tricky. You never know what fire might try. See, she *tried* to stop her fire. She almost got away but it's tricky. She got tricked."

After I hung up the phone that night and fell back asleep, I was in the back seat of my mother's car. She was driving. It was sunny and warm and my legs were bony and brown. Every now and then she would touch her rear-view mirror and smile at my reflection, her thick golden arms looking like dessert. I wished I could suckle them, climb underneath and curl up in the soft pits.

The sun was setting and my mother said we needed to get there before it did—that was the only way to put out the fire. I did up my seat belt.

"Not now, hon," she said. "You've got to be ready."

The seat belt was important. I was supposed to unbuckle it at the right moment, but how could we ever make it to the sun before it set?

Momma slapped the steering well. "No-no-no. Not yet, just wait," she called toward the glare, and whoever was controlling it.

So orange it was red, the looming glow took up the whole of the windshield. We were nearly there and

Momma reached into the passenger side for the gas can.

"Hurry and open this up for us, sweetheart."

I couldn't get myself unbuckled now and Momma was losing her temper. "For god's sake, drink it!" She twisted the cap with one hand while trying to steer with the other. The car was lit with neon sunlight. My mother bellowed at the rear-view mirror, "Drink it up! We're here, we're here!"

I woke up to more ringing beside my bed. It was Dusty calling.

When they found Georgia, she was in ribbons, punched halfway through the windshield. My mother's body lay on the hood of her car, the nose of which was crushed against a gas pump, cracked now and spraying. Emergency vehicles had closed off the streets for fear there would be an explosion. Hers, fortunately, was the only car at the now-closed service station.

When I imagined it later, I saw it as lovely somehow, romantic: her flung body serene like that of a child dozing, her flesh soft and luminescent. There was no blood in my picture, just the street's white lights radiating purity through the spritzing liquid as it fell gently over the scene.

At first it was thought that she had gone to fill up an emergency gasoline container for some future need, perhaps another driver stranded somewhere nearby, but as luck would have it, she had ended up at a station that was already closed for the night. Perhaps in her rush to be a good Samaritan, she had somehow lost control of her vehicle, careening headlong into the pumps. But an accident investigation unearthed no witnesses, no breakdowns in the vicinity. Her own car's tank almost full, the emergency gas can was now emptied all over the dashboard, thoroughly soaking the front and back seats.

There was a box of wooden matches sprayed across the passenger side, none used. The report would show the vehicle's steering was solid and tight; the brakes were fine. There were no skid marks. Her final destination, it appeared, had been planned and purposeful.

Dusty played at the foot of the grassy slope with a visiting cocker spaniel. Alice and I sat up top, on the brown wool blanket from her bed, holding hands and staring down over the lawn and trees out back of the hospital.

Alice fidgeted with a bare foot in the grass. "I remember it was getting to be suppertime and I was going to take a bath and the next thing I remember is Daddy standing in my doorway."

I waved down at Dusty, who grinned up at us now as she coaxed the dog to dance with her. "It was about four in the morning when she called," I said. "I told her to go wake up Granddad."

Alice closed her eyes, rested her chin on her knees. "I quit the happy pills. I was on so many, you know— there was, like, Buspar and Xanax and this one and that one till they found the right thing. But I couldn't stand it, not feeling anything. I'd've rather been miserable than nothing."

Air pushed through my nose in what sounded like derision before I could decide if it actually was.

She looked at me. She had pulled her hair back in a band and it gave her a clean, studious appearance. "Okay." She inhaled as if a confession were in the works. "It wasn't bad at first when they found the right cocktail. I felt pretty good." She rolled her neck a moment, getting out the kinks. "So I started taking extra. Then I got all jittery, like it was coke or something. And I liked that. Sort of. I liked having energy again. Then the heartburn started. Like hot coals through my chest, and by then I was taking, like, four times the dose and I thought, God, I'm always poisoning myself. Why can't I just be normal? And I flushed them all down the toilet. Man, the heartburn after that!" She laughed half-heartedly.

My jaws hurt and I realized how clenched they were. "There was water coming under Dad's door when Dusty woke him."

Alice took another big breath and released it in quick little bursts, nodding. She stared down toward her daughter. "I keep seeing her little feet in the water on the bathroom floor, and I just want to—" She squeezed her eyes shut.

"You said you weren't going to die like her and you weren't going to get tricked, they were trying to trick you into swallowing fire."

"Nice." She turned to me and held my hand in her

lap like a prayer book. I could feel a prepared statement coming on.

"I'm going to do better, Angie. I have to. They said I could leave here, you know—but I'm scared if I don't get straightened out, you'll all get sick of my shit and ditch me. And Dusty will go with you."

I opened my mouth wide and the crack of my lower jaw seemed extraordinarily loud. I wanted to crush her hand in mine. Break all the tiny bones apart.

"It's okay." I pulled away. "Dad and I have Dusty covered."

I clasped my hands in my lap. Alice looked down at them, her expression wounded.

It was silent for a good minute or so.

"You can't stand me."

"I don't want to stand," I croaked. "I mean—" I scratched hard at my scalp for a second. "I'm sick of being the dependable one, guaranteed to stand up straight. I don't get to just fall apart whenever the mood strikes."

"I know," she whispered.

We looked to the bottom of the slope. Dusty and the spaniel danced the cha-cha around below until it occurred to them to run through the sprinklers, back and forth.

"Dusty, come on, don't do that," I called.

My sister watched her, a blissful look on her face.

The dog's people looked up just as Dusty and the spaniel loped toward them, wet to the skin now. The spaniel shook his dripping self all over the two on the blanket and they screamed in protest. Dusty put both hands over her face and doubled over. When she took her hands down, her face was contorted and red. Tears ran as she raced back up the slope toward us.

Acknowledgements

I would like to express my sincere gratitude for the support of the BC Arts Council, The Canada Council for the Arts, The MacDowell Colony, Ledig House International Writers' Residency and The Seaside Institute's Escape to Create Residency.

Perhaps most of all I would like to thank my editor Anne Collins and Random House for continuing to believe in the power of the story, both long and short.

Publication History

"Make Yourself Feel Better" first appeared in *THIS Magazine*, and was recorded by Rattling Books for *EarLit Shorts 6*, an audio short-fiction anthology.

"Clown Lessons" first appeared in *Toronto Life*.

"Greedy Little Eyes" first appeared as "Shiny as Film" in *Prism Magazine*.

"You're Taking All the Fun Out of It" first appeared in *THIS Magazine*, and reprinted in the *Journey Prize Anthology*.

"Georgia, It's Me" first appeared in a shorter form as "Thin-skinned" in *Fiddlehead*.

"Did You Grow Up With Money?" first appeared in *Other Voices Magazine*, and reprinted in *Sub-Terrain Magazine*.

"Before I Would Ever Hurt You" (as "Locusts & Honey") first appeared in *Prairie Fire Magazine*.

Stories in this collection have been awarded fiction prizes from *THIS Magazine*'s Great Canadian Literary Hunt, The Lawrence House Fiction Prize, *Prism Magazine*, The *Fiddlehead* and *Other Voices Magazine*. "You're Taking All the Fun Out of It" was shortlisted for the Journey Prize.

BILLIE LIVINGSTON published her critically acclaimed first novel, *Going Down Swinging*, in 2000. Her first book of poetry, *The Chick at the Back of the Church*, was a finalist for the Pat Lowther Award. Her second novel, *Cease to Blush*, was a *Globe and Mail* Best Book. Her award-winning short fiction has been published in Canada, the U.S., the U.K. and Australia. Born in Toronto, Livingston now lives in Vancouver.